ROSENNE'S

THE WORLD COURT
WHAT IT IS AND HOW IT WORKS

LEGAL ASPECTS OF INTERNATIONAL ORGANIZATION

VOLUME 41

Shabtai Rosenne

UNITAR

ROSENNE'S

THE WORLD COURT
WHAT IT IS AND HOW IT WORKS

Sixth Completely Revised Edition

Edited, Revised and Updated
by
Terry D. Gill

With the Assistance of
Harm Dotinga
Erik Jaap Molenaar
Alex Oude Elferink

MARTINUS NIJHOFF PUBLISHERS
LEIDEN / BOSTON

P.O. Box 9000, 2300 PA Leiden, The Netherlands
cs@brill.nl
http://www.brill.nl

Distributed in Canada, USA and Mexico by:
Brill Academic Publishers
P.O. Box 605
Herndon VA 20172
United States of America
Tel: +1 800 337-9255 (toll free, Canada & USA only)
+1 703 661-1500
Fax: + 703 661-1501
E-mai:l cs@brillusa.com

Distributed in all other countries by:
Turpin Distribution Services Ltd
Blackhorse Road
Letchworth
Hertfordshire SG6 1HN
United Kingdom
Tel: +44 (0)1462 687528
Fax: +44 (0)1462 480947
E-mail: brill@turpinltd.com

A C.I.P. Catalogue record for this book is available from the Library of Congress.

Printed on acid-free paper.

ISBN 90-04-13633-9

Brill Academic Publishers incorporates the imprint Martinus Nijhoff Publishers.

Printed and bound in The Netherlands.

CONTENTS

The Peace Palace (Photo: PE Fotostudio, Wassenaar)

Composition of the Court in 2002. *From left to right – front row:* Judge Ranjeva, Vice President Shi, President Guillaume, Judges Oda, Herczegh; *middle row:* Judges Higgins, Koroma, Fleischhauer, Vereshchetin, Parra-Aranguren; *top row:* Registrar Couvreur, Judges Buergenthal, Rezek, Kooijmans, Al-Khasawweh, Elaraby (Photo: PE Fotostudio, Wassenaar)

FOREWORD

It gives me great pleasure to write this foreword to a newly revised edition of "*The World Court: What It is and How It works*" as my tribute to its author, Professor Shabtai Rosenne. Over half a century from the very day of inception of the International Court of Justice, Rosenne has untiringly dedicated much of his career to the study of the Court's work. His contributions in this respect have gained full recognition within the international legal community. Of all his writings on the Court, this book has become, to use the words of a former President of the Court, Judge Bedjaoui, "*a classic in the literature of international law,*" along with his four volumes of the revised edition of "*The Law and Procedure of the International Court of Justice, 1920-1996*".

This sixth edition is completely revised by Professor Gill of Utrecht University at the request of Rosenne. The publication of this newly revised edition is indeed not only necessary but is also timely for at least two reasons:

First, since the publication of the fifth edition in 1995, the Court has delivered quite a large number of Judgments and other decisions, in which some of its statements and rulings deserve the attention of States Members of the United Nations and the international legal community at large. Thus, for example, in its Advisory Opinion on the *Legality of the Threat or Use of Nuclear Weapons,* the Court states: "There exists an obligation to pursue in good faith and bring to a conclusion negotiations leading to nuclear disarmament in all its aspects under strict and effective international control"(*I.C.J. Reports 1996,* p. 267). Again, in the *LaGrand* case, for the first time in its history the Court ruled in explicit terms that the provisional measures indicated by the Court are binding upon the litigant Parties.

Second, in view of the increasingly heavy caseload of the Court, and in order to cope with this new situation, the Court is in the process of revising a number of its Rules and is seeking to adopt a certain degree of flexibility in applying its internal judicial practice. The results of some of its efforts to improve efficiency in its judicial work are reflected in the latest amendments to its Rules and in its Practice directions, which are occasionally published by the Court.

I am glad that, in preparing this sixth edition of Rosenne's book, Professor Gill has carefully taken into account all these new developments in the work of the Court. The present edition of this book, like its previous editions, is designed for the consumption of "the politician, the diplomat, the Member of Parliament, the student of international law and international relations, and the enquiring members of the public at large." I sincerely hope that this new edition will contribute further to the dissemination of the Court's functions and operations and to the ideals of the rule of law and justice pursued by the International Court of Justice, as reflected in its Judgments, Advisory Opinions and other decisions.

SHI Jiuyong
President, International Court of Justice

FOREWORD

During its lifetime of over fifty years, the International Court of Justice has undergone a tremendous evolution. The Member States of the United Nations are *ispo facto* Parties to the Statute of the Court. The original members numbered 51; today they are 191. The decolonization process ended the restriction of access to the Court for many regions of the world. Moreover, the end of the Cold War greatly diminished the self-exclusion of former Socialist States from international jurisdiction.

In addition to the increase in the Parties, there has been an unprecedented rise in the number of cases submitted over the last decade or so. This heightened interest in the International Court has been accompanied by a wider range of issues being submitted to the Court's jurisdiction. Deviating from the direction of its predecessor, the Permanent Court of International Justice, mainly operative within the tradition of arbitration proper to the XIX the century, the International Court of Justice has greatly broadened the scope of subject matter considered appropriate for international regulation. In the vast majority of cases submitted, the decisions of the Court have been accepted by the States concerned and generally implemented without major difficulty. Records regarding compliance are indeed very positive.

Most noteworthy also, is the Court's contribution to the development of substantive International Law, both through its rulings and its advisory proceedings.

Sometimes considered as a shortcoming of the Court, the restrictions towards non-State entities is being progressively and partially addressed by the establishment in the recent past of new international courts and tribunals. Most of these grant access of international jurisdiction to institutions – sometimes individuals – not accepted by the Court Statute.

The International Court of Justice is one of the six principal organs of the United Nations, a *par inter pares.* It plays a fundamental role in dispute resolution. Of course, not all disputes can be resolved by law, many being deemed diplomatic and/or political. The Court is thus one of the major partners in the global international decision-making mechanism and contributes to the ideal of establishing peace and security through law, reason and justice – an objective which may be as ancient as the first attempts at collaboration of the community nations.

Shabtai Rosenne has been an eminent professor and a very distinguished diplomat for many years. He has followed the history of the various modern attempts towards international jurisdiction while tirelessly analyzing the evolution of the International Court of Justice. The unusual combination of his reputation for teaching international law and his experience in conducting inter-governmental negotiations explains why his work on the "World Court" is considered as a necessary reference to students, observers of international relations and the public at large. We are confident that this new revised edition will meet the expectations of the broadest range of readers.

Marcel A. Boisard
UN Assistant Secretary-General, Executive Director, UNITAR

PREFACE TO THE 6TH, REVISED EDITION

A book which has gone through five previous editions should need no lengthy introduction. This is especially true of a book bearing the name of an eminent author writing on a subject which he or she is uniquely qualified to deal with. Such is the case with Shabtai Rosenne and the International Court of Justice. The lifelong interest of Professor Rosenne in the Court has produced a very large number of scholarly books, articles and commentaries relating to the International Court and its practice and case law extending over nearly half a century. Virtually no aspect of the organization, functioning or impact of the Court upon international law and international relations has escaped his attention. Rosenne's work on the Court has achieved an authority matched by few and surpassed by none and can without exaggeration be qualified as the benchmark by which all other writings on the subject are measured.

That is why when asked by Professor Rosenne to carry on with his work in relation to one of his publications, *The World Court: What It is and How It works*, I was somewhat daunted, as well as honoured, to be asked to carry on with a work so near to his heart. In doing so I was well aware of my own limitations and I am under no illusion that I am his 'successor' in dealing with the Court.

Nevertheless, I readily agreed to his invitation and have endeavoured, to the best of my ability, to carry on with his tradition; preserving as much of the original text and approach as possible, while providing a thorough revision, update and as many new insights as I thought were strictly necessary to maintain the work's relevance and accessibility. That is the explanation behind the book's title, which gives just recognition to the original author, and the fact that this edition is a continuation of his work and is in every respect a sixth edition of the original. It also is the reason behind my own designation (at Professor Rosenne's insistence) as editor, revisor and author of this new edition. This was felt to be unavoidable in order to enable me to make the necessary abridgments, alterations and updates to keep the book within manageable proportions, while at the same time covering developments which have occurred since the publication of the last edition.

I have been fortunate to have the assistance of several of my colleagues at the International Law Department, including the Netherlands Institute for the Law of the Sea alongside the Institute of Public International Law of Utrecht University, in the preparation of a number of the case summaries appearing in Chapter 6. These include Mr. Harm Dotinga, Dr. Erik Jaap Molenaar and Dr. Alex Oude Elferink who prepared the summaries of the recent law of the sea and environmental law oriented cases.

I am extremely grateful to the secretary of the International Law Department, Ms. Hanneke van Denderen, for her invaluable assistance in the preparation of the manuscript. I would also like to thank Mr. Wybo Heere for preparing the index to the present edition.

Another debt of gratitude is owed to Mr. Arthur Witteveen and his assistants of the Court's Registry for their assistance with the Appendices and in providing the new photographs for the present edition. I am also thankful to Ms. Annebeth Rosenboom and the technical staff of Martinus Nijhoff for their support with the publication as well as to Mr. Alan Stephens as literary executor of Professor Rosenne's work.

Most of all, I owe an immense debt of gratitude to Professor Rosenne for his long lasting and continuing friendship and inspiration, as well as for the honour of carrying on with this noteworthy and useful publication.

As was true for the previous editions, the present edition is aimed towards the non-specialist reader: including the politician, the diplomat, the journalist, the student of international law, and the interested layman, who are interested in the functioning of the International Court of Justice and its place in international relations.

The present edition takes the latest amendment of the Court's Rules of Procedure of December 2000, as well as its new Practice Directions into account. All of the cases which have been initiated since the completion of the previous edition in 1994 through the end of 2002 are included in Chapter 6 below.

The present edition was completed on 28 February 2003.

Terry Gill

NOTE ON BIBLIOGRAPHY

The publications of the Permanent Court of International Justice (PCIJ) were organized in the following Series:

A. Judgments and Orders. Nos. 1-24 (1922-30)

B. Advisory opinions. Nos. 1-18 (1922-30).

These were amalgamated in 1931 to form

A/B. Judgments, orders and advisory opinions. Nos. 40-80 (1931-40).

C. Acts and Documents relating to judgments and advisory opinions (Pleadings). Nos. 1-19 (1922-30), 52-88 (1931-45).

D. Acts and Documents concerning the organization of the Court. Nos. 1-6 (1922-40).

E. Annual Reports. Nos. 1-16 (1925-45).

F. General Indexes. Nos. 1-4 (1922-36).

The publications of the International Court of Justice (INTERNATIONAL COURT OF JUSTICE) are now organized as follows:

Reports of Judgments, Advisory Opinions and Orders (Rep.). Annual since 1948.

Pleadings, Oral Arguments, Documents (Pleadings). One or more volumes, containing the Court record, for each case.

Acts and Documents concerning the Organization of the Court (Acts). The current (fifth) edition (1989) contains the basic texts, in

English and French, relating to the functioning of the Court.

Yearbook. Yearbook of the International Court of Justice, covering the period 16 July-15 July. Annual since 1946-47.

The Bibliography of the International Court of Justice. Nos. 1-18 formed Chapter IX of the *Yearbook* up to the 1963-64 edition. Beginning with No. 19 the *Bibliography* has been issued annually as a separate fascicle, arranged so as to facilitate the binding of several numbers together.

All the above are in bilingual editions except Series E and the Yearbook *(Annuaire),* which are published in separate English and French editions.

Since 1968 the annual *Report of the International Court of Justice,* covering the period 1 August-31 July, has been published as a Supplement to the *Official Records of the General Assembly.* It is available in the six official languages of the General Assembly (Arabic, Chinese, English, French, Russian, Spanish).

Other abbreviations

AJIL-American Journal of International Law

Documents-Documents on the International Court of Justice (1st bilingual edition, compiled and edited by Sh. Rosenne, 1991)

GAOR-United Nations General Assembly, *Official Records*

INTERNATIONAL COURT OF JUSTICE YB - *Yearbook of the International Court of Justice*

ILCYB-Yearbook of the International Law Commission (since 1949)

ILM-International Legal Materials (since 1962)

ILR-International Law Reports

Law and Practice Sh. Rosenne, *The Law and Practice of the International Court* (1965, reprinted 1985 and new edition 1996)

RADI-Académie de Droit International / Academy of International Law, *Receuil des Cours/Collected Courses*

RIAA-United Nations, *Reports of International Arbitral Awards*

UNTS-United Nations, *Treaty Series*

References to cases in the International Court of Justice are to the annual volumes and page alone. References to cases in the Permanent Court of International Justice are to the Series number and year. References to arbitral awards are to one or more of the current series as listed above.

NOTE ON CONTRIBUTORS TO CHAPTER 6

Mr. Harm Dotinga supplied the commentary on the *Gabčíkovo-Nagymaros* case, the *Maritime Delimitation between Nicaragua and Honduras* and the *Maritime Delimitation between Nicaragua and Colombia* cases.

Dr. Erik Jaap Molenaar supplied the commentary for *Fisheries Jurisdiction* (Estai) case, the *Kaskili/Sedudu Island* case and the *Pulau Litigan and Pulau Sipidan* case.

Dr. Alex Oude Elferink provided updates and revisions on the *Maritime Delimitation in the Area Between Greenland and Jan Mayen* and *Maritime Delimitation Between Guinea-Bissau and Senegal* and the commentary for the *Maritime Delimitation and Territorial Questions Between Qatar and Bahrain* case, as well as part of the commentary relating to the *Land and Maritime Boundary Between Cameroon and Nigeria* case.

What the Court is

In the last resort, recourse to international justice depends on the will of governments and on their readiness to submit for legal decision all of which can and should be preserved from the arbitrament of violence. As for the Court, it means to accomplish to the full the duties incumbent upon it; and it will not weaken in that resolve - Judge J. Gustavo Guerrero, President of the Permanent Court of International Justice (1936-45) and of the International Court of Justice (1946-49), on 4 December 1939.

The Court in Session during the Hearings on Provisional Measures in the *Armed Activities on the Territory of the Congo* case (*Dem. Republic Congo* v. *Uganda*) in June 2002 (Photo: PE Fotostudio, Wassenaar)

1

THE FORERUNNERS

The idea of resolving international disputes through disinterested third parties on the basis of law and justice, as an alternative to war and violence, is a deep-rooted human aspiration. Its origins can be found in religious sentiment which tends to recoil from the horrors of war and to seek other ways of eradicating violent conflicts of international interests. At times the idea was expressed in Messianic terms, as by the Prophets Isaiah and Micah: "And it shall come to pass in the end of days... And He shall judge between the nations, and shall decide for many peoples; and they shall beat their swords into plowshares and their spears into pruninghooks; Nation shall not lift up sword against nation, neither shall they learn war any more."[1] At others, it is cast in the language of political programme, as by Hugo Grotius, for many the father of modern international law: "Christian kings and states are bound to pursue this method [arbitration] of avoiding wars... for this and for other reasons it would be advantageous, indeed in a degree necessary, to hold certain conferences of Christian powers, where those who have no interest at stake may settle the disputes of others, and where, in fact, steps may be taken to compel parties to accept peace on fair terms."[2]

EARLY BEGINNINGS

As an ideal, this concept seems to have been widespread: in practice, however, its application was far from general. It was found, for instance, in the early periods of Middle Eastern history and in sacred codes of the Far East,[3] and it is encountered in the experience of Islam.[4] But it was in Europe that the concept most took root. Its attraction for the European mind was that it sought to transfer the absolute values of the discipline of the law, on which the well-being of the national society in Western Europe was thought to depend, to the problems of the international community. The Greek city--states, for instance possessed a well-developed system of third-party settlement of their disputes, within the framework of their own Hellenic culture, especially through the instrumentality of the Delphic Amphictyonies.[5] Here, indeed, there is something approaching true disinterested third-party judgment between nominally equal political units -the city-states -on the basis of a rudimentary system of law or custom by which the correct behaviour of those political units might be judged. With the growth of the big empires – Macedonia, Rome, Byzantium – this form of third-party settlement fell into disuse, partly, no doubt, because of the impossibility of finding any true disinterested third party, and partly because the general imperialist and expansionist tendencies of those super-Powers, and their centralized system of government, would not easily be reconciled to the idea of the settlement of *their* disputes by application of "law" (however rudimentary international law might have been a that time). On the other hand, the classical historical writings contain many circumstantial accounts of those Powers "deciding" disputes between their various clients and vassals through a procedure which resembles partly a system of arbitration, and partly a system of mediation and conciliation – and partly a mere concealment for force.

In medieval Europe, too, both types of "arbitration" are found.

For instance, in Switzerland, where peculiar geographical conditions impressed their stamp on the political organization in a manner reminiscent of that of ancient Hellas, several cases are known in which disputes between two or more cities were arbitrated by disinterested ecclesiastical and secular authorities, who tried to reach a settlement by a combination of methods of persuasion and of decision.[6] Something similar seems once to have existed for the city-states of Italy. On the other hand, the tradition of the Roman Empire was largely continued by the Popes and Emperors, whose system of government contained built-in machinery for resolving disputes between their vassals and subordinates. Here it has been said that the major premise was that the church knows what is right and wrong, and that the peace-maker, if he is the delegate of the church, must begin by judging, not by conciliating, the parties.[7] It was in this period too that the theologian-jurists began developing the theory that the existence of central institutions in the Papacy for the settlement of disputes implied that the princes were not entitled to take the law into their own hands – an idea closely connected with the theory of the just war and the unjust war or (as we would say today) the war of aggression.

THE NINETEENTH CENTURY

The origins of modern arbitration are usually traced to the so-called Jay Treaty of 19 November 1794, between the United States and Great Britain (which settled a number of lingering questions resulting from the American War of Independence). This provided for the setting up of three different commissions to resolve outstanding questions. Two of these commissions successfully completed their task. However, the third ran into difficulties which were only resolved later by direct diplomatic means. The commissions were composed of American and British nationals exclusively – a fact which negatives any idea of third-party settlement. The proceedings before the commissions were conducted on the model of court actions, and the commissioners tried to reach their decisions by applying rules of law.[8] This type of proceeding was in substance diplomatic more than judicial in character, since there was no impartial arbitrament between the two parties represented on the commissions. But the Jay Treaty and these processes led to a renewal of general interest in the possibilities of using legal and judicial techniques as a method of resolving certain types of international conflict, especially, though by no means exclusively, when the international dispute includes or embraces a large number of private and individual claims. Occasionally there are instances in the early part of the nineteenth century in which true third-party settlement of a dispute is invoked -the third party being nominally either the Head of a State or one of its organs, acceptable to the States in dispute. When this happened, the process began to lose its purely diplomatic character, and to assume that of true judicial arbitration.

A major development in the history of international adjudication occurred in the well-known *Alabama* case, arising out of the American Civil War. This, commonly regarded as the watershed of modern international litigation, was a spectacular affair. It implicated fundamental questions of the law of neutrality and of warfare at sea, and impinged upon serious political interests of Great Britain, the respondent. The dispute originated in the departure of the *Alabama* from the Merseyside shipyards on 29 July 1862 to join the Confederate Forces and prey upon U.S. shipping in the Atlantic. It caused great political bitterness on both sides. It was not until the Washington Treaty of

8 May 1871 that the two countries agreed to submit the dispute to arbitration. The significance of this act lies in the nature of the tribunal. This was composed of one national of each of the two parties, together with three neutral members -nationals of Brazil, Italy and Switzerland. The Treaty also contained another innovation. It specified some (though not all) of the basic legal rules concerning the duties of neutral States, which the Tribunal was to apply. After complicated proceedings held in the Hotel de Ville at Geneva the Tribunal handed down its award (reached by a majority of four to one) on 14 September 1872.[9] Despite the dissent of the British arbitrator, the British Government paid the damages to the tune of over $15,000,000 within the time stipulated. The spectacle of two important countries submitting a dispute of this character to impartial third-party settlement on the basis of law, and the loser complying with the terms of the award, naturally gave a great fillip to the development of the concept of international arbitration as an alternative to allowing political tension to smoulder indefinitely. The fact that the two countries were both English speaking, and shared the same basic legal culture of the common law, undoubtedly made it easier for them to reach and to carry out the political decision to settle the dispute in this way. For similar cultural reasons, the independent States of Latin America have also had frequent recourse to arbitration, especially for territorial disputes.

THE HAGUE CONFERENCES OF 1899 AND 1907

The experience of the *Alabama* Arbitration and other important instances of arbitration proceedings in its wake, taken together with the crushing financial burden of modernizing Russia's armed forces, induced the Tsar Nicolas II to convene the First Hague Peace Conference of 1899. Prompted by public opinion and the efforts of bodies such as the Institute of International Law, the Inter-Parliamentary Union and others, President Theodore Roosevelt of the United States, who had been instrumental in mediating an end to the Russo-Japanese War in 1905, took the initiative in convening the Second Hague Peace Conference, but relinquished the honour to the Tsar of Russia at the latter's request. The Tsar issued invitations for a Second Peace Conference which was held at The Hague in 1907.[10]

Among other things, these conferences attempted to find a way of repairing a number of obvious cracks in the system and practice of international arbitration, as it had been developing during the nineteenth century. The agreements to have recourse to arbitration had all been reached *ad hoc.* All the instances of international arbitration up to this time, even when successful in settling the political dispute, had been marked by acute political difficulties in reaching agreement on the composition and procedure of the arbitral tribunal and on fixing precisely the points on which it was to be asked to decide. This was because no standing arbitral machinery existed, and no clearly accepted concepts of international arbitral procedure, and it is rarely easy to reach agreement on these highly complicated and at times extremely technical matters in the heat of a political controversy which may leave little room for manoeuvre. This added to the difficulties of invoking disinterested third-party judgment and increased the psychological obstacles which, in the nature of things, always make it difficult for a government to empower outsiders to reach binding decisions on delicate matters of direct concern to it. This had the consequence that if political passions became too inflamed, the governments concerned might find it politically impossible to agree to settle the matter by arbitration even if they wanted to, or, what was worse, they could make illusory agreements, or frustrate their declared intentions by other means. For reasons such as these, enlightened persons, and governments, began looking for a method by which permanent arbitration machinery could always be at the disposal of States. Some went even further, and began thinking of the possibility of making it *compulsory* for States to have recourse to arbitration, if not for all then at least for certain types of international disputes, especially legal disputes.

At this point two almost insuperable problems made an appearance. They are mentioned here because they have dogged the whole history of international adjudication and their influence is felt in the International Court. The first was the composition of the tribunal. The second was how to define its jurisdiction *in advance.* Neither of these problems was fully solved by the Peace Conferences of 1899 and 1907.

On the question of composition, the experience of the diplomatic arbitrations of the nineteenth century showed that even if the balance in an arbitral commission should be held by neutral arbitrators or a neutral umpire, States, for reasons which are essentially emotional and psychological, could not normally be expected to agree to submit their disputes to a tribunal in which there was not a single national of their own. This aspect was the easier to resolve, basically on the principle that the balance in an arbitral tribunal, in which the parties too should be represented, should be in the hands of neutral members. More significant, however – and it was this which really made it impossible then to establish a permanent arbitration court – was the attitude of the European Great Powers of the time. Loosely organized in the Concert of Europe, these felt that their international interests and responsibilities (including their general responsibilities to preserve the peace between the Small Powers and to maintain the balance of power between themselves) were sufficiently heavy and universal to justify a demand that if any permanent international court were created, a national of each one of them should be a member of it. Experience showed – and this was no more than a matter of political reality – that it was one thing for Powers, even Great Powers, to agree to settle their existing disputes through arbitrators of their own choice. It was quite another thing to expect them to agree *in advance* to submit their future disputes, with parties and on matters unknown, to a permanent tribunal whose composition was already fixed and on which there might not be a member of their nationality.

The difficulty of setting down in advance and in general terms the jurisdiction of a tribunal had its roots no less in experience and political realism. It derives from the view which is firmly held and valid as a matter of political doctrine (however repugnant it may be to legal theory) that not every international dispute, especially when it is one involving a serious clash of interests or of aspirations, can be said generally and in advance to be suitable for settlement through disinterested judges applying legal techniques and criteria exclusively, and at any time. Before the international judicial process can be successfully invoked, the dispute has to be "ripe" for that process. Many of the most intractable and dangerous international disputes are born out of an aspiration to alter the legal position, for instance when it is embodied in an unpopular, but legally binding, treaty. This difficulty, which is a real one, has led to a long series of attempts to define the types of disputes which can be inherently regarded, in advance, as suitable for settlement by arbitrators or judges, to set down the tests for the "justiciability" and "non-justiciability" of disputes, to employ a common term (borrowed from the experience of the United States Supreme Court in dealing with certain constitutional matters). These attempts may be regarded as satisfactory technical advances: but it would be an illusion to think that they have solved the problem, as can indeed be seen by the frequency with which respondent States challenge the jurisdiction of the Court (see p. 81 below).

In 1907, no workable solution was found to either of these problems (partly because the German leadership thought that an effective system of arbitration would give their potential enemies a useful instrument for delaying political events, and in that way enable them to overtake the German superiority in armaments). As a result, a compromise was adopted. The idea of compulsory arbitration, even for limited categories of disputes, was for the time being dropped. It was replaced by a system of voluntary arbitration which for each instance required the consent of the States concerned, both to the composition of the tribunal and to its terms of reference. On the other hand, it was recognized that certain types of disputes were probably more suitable for arbitration than others. The value of the institution of arbitration had proved itself, and there was a widespread desire to transform it from an exclusively *ad hoc* diplomatic process into one having elements of permanency. The attempt was made to formulate the main lines of arbitration procedure (which, nevertheless, States were free to modify at will). This technical aspect was important as a step towards simplifying the drawing up of arbitration agreements and thus reducing the opportunities of frustrating a political decision to resort to arbitration.

THE PERMANENT COURT OF ARBITRATION

The element of permanency was created by the establishment of the Permanent Court of Arbitration. In fact this institution is misnamed, for it is neither a court nor permanent. It consists of a panel of arbitrators nominated by the contracting parties (they may each nominate not more than four persons, of known competency in questions of international law, of the highest moral reputation and disposed to accept the duties of arbitrator). From this panel the States may choose a tribunal to decide their particular case, the balance in the tribunal being confided to neutral arbitrators. The Permanent Court of Arbitration has an Administrative Council, consisting of the diplomatic representatives at The Hague of the contracting parties. It also has a small permanent Secretariat, the first international judicial organ to have a permanent secretariat. Its headquarters were established at The Hague (where they still are).

The First Hague Convention of 1907 for the Pacific Settlement of International Disputes (replacing the First Convention of 1899) therefore contains an elaborate code covering a number of processes for the settlement of international disputes, in the event of failure of diplomatic negotiations to produce satisfactory results, and arbitration is included among them. Others are the procedures of good offices, conciliation and mediation, and arrangements for international commissions of enquiry, essentially for the elucidation of disputed facts.[11] The Convention defines the object of international arbitration as "the settlement of disputes between States by judges of their own choice". It imposes no obligation on the Parties to have recourse to arbitration, but Article 38 states that: "In questions of a legal nature, and especially in the interpretation or application of international conventions [treaties], arbitration is recognized by the contracting Powers as the most effective and at the same time the most equitable means of settling disputes which diplomacy has failed to settle." Consequently, it was desirable to have recourse to it in that type of case. But it was never obligatory, even after arbitration had been decided upon, to have recourse to a panel of the Permanent Court of Arbitration: that was maintained primarily as machinery to facilitate recourse to arbitration. Since 1960, the Permanent Court has broadened the availability of this machinery to disputes in which one party is not a State, and it is now examining a further extension to disputes in which neither party is a State.

These difficulties, above all, made it impossible, in 1907, to establish any general obligation to have resort to arbitration. All that could be done was to create machinery and to lay down a series of general rules for the conduct of arbitration proceedings, leaving their application in a concrete case to the unfettered will of the States concerned. Therefore, in order to set arbitration proceedings in motion, there must be a special agreement for that purpose (sometimes called technically, even in English, a *compromis)* – whether an agreement, bilateral or multilateral, providing for the submission of certain types of disputes to arbitration, or one providing for the submission of a specific dispute to arbitration.

The codification of the rules of arbitral procedure which resulted from the Hague Conference has proved useful in practice, even for arbitration proceedings which were formally not conducted before a panel of the Permanent Court of Arbitration. These rules are often incorporated in international arbitration treaties. Attempts by the International Law Commission of the United Nations to bring this branch of the law up to date were only partially successful.[12]

Even before the 1899 Conference, two other developments in the practice of States started to appear. The first was the inclusion in general treaties of a "compromissory clause" – a stipulation to refer disputes arising out of the interpretation or application of that treaty to arbitration. The second was the conclusion between pairs of States of general treaties of arbitration, as distinct from special agreements, sometimes coupled with other machineries for the settlement of disputes. In these treaties too the problem of defining in advance the type of dispute which they were intended to cover was found to be extremely difficult. Usually they excluded from their scope disputes involving the vital interests, national sovereignty, independence or honour of the contracting parties, and in so far as this formula granted the State concerned a right of unilateral determination that a given dispute came within that category, the treaty was to that extent illusory.

Apart from the Permanent Court of Arbitration, mention must also be made, for the sake of completeness, of two other attempts to establish permanent international tribunals. Both were unsuccessful, although their failure may have contributed to the later success of the Permanent Court of International Justice. The first was the attempt, also made at The Hague in 1907, to establish an International Prize Court to deal with claims between neutrals and belligerents arising out of the exercise of the belligerent right of prize at sea. Apart from difficulties inherent in the nature of the subject-matter, the principal technical obstacle to the establishment of a permanent tribunal of this character lay in the inability to find a satisfactory procedure for electing the judges and guaranteeing their independence. The second was the Central American Court of Justice, established by the Treaty of Washington of 20 December 1907, between Costa Rica, El Salvador, Guatemala, Honduras and Nicaragua. This Court was in existence between 1908 and 1917, and dealt with several cases. It foundered because of serious faults in its organization, including inadequate measures to assure the independence of its members, and in the definition of its jurisdiction. But above all it collapsed on the rock of political difficulties, including some which originated outside Central America.

Its decision of 1917 in the *Gulf of Fonseca* case between El Salvador and Nicaragua was an element in the *Land, Island and Maritime Frontier Dispute* case before a Chamber of the International Court of Justice in 1992 (see p. 184 below).

Despite these weaknesses, the Hague Conferences gave a great impetus both to the process of concluding bilateral arbitration treaties, and to the invocation of arbitration proceedings. It has been estimated that between 1900 and 1914 more than 120 general arbitration treaties were concluded between pairs of States. Between 1902 and 1920, fourteen disputes were handled by panels of arbitrators chosen from the Permanent Court of Arbitration and more than fifty other disputes were arbitrated in some other manner.[13] Since the end of the First World War to 1993, over ninety cases of international arbitration are known.[14] Of these, twenty-five are claimed to have taken place before panels of the Permanent Court of Arbitration or with the co-operation of its Bureau, and the balance before *ad hoc* arbitration tribunals. In addition to these, both under the Peace Treaties of 1919, and under the 1947 Treaty of Peace with Italy and the 1951 Peace Treaty with Japan and the long series of corresponding arrangements with the Federal Republic of Germany, a number of Mixed Arbitral Tribunals, Conciliation Tribunals and the like were established, and these dealt with an extremely large number of cases. Since one of the parties was an individual, these cannot be regarded as international arbitrations proper: that term is rightly limited to litigation in which only States, or at the most an international organization composed of States (inter-governmental organization), are parties. In 1980 the Iran-United States Claims Tribunal was set up, and *is* still working. It has jurisdiction both over claims by nationals of either State against the other, and over claims by one Government against the other.

By the outbreak of the First World War (1914), the main lines of international arbitral procedure were firmly drawn. From the starting point of the voluntary character of the whole process, its principal features may be noted.

Firstly, it had become widely accepted that if in the course of the proceedings a dispute should arise concerning the Tribunal's jurisdiction, *that* matter should normally be settled by the Tribunal itself, and should not be referred back to the diplomatic channels, unless the arbitration agreement provided otherwise. Thus one way of frustrating the work of the arbitration tribunals was blocked.

Secondly, it was accepted that the arbitrators should all be persons of recognized competence, independent, and of the highest standards of integrity. Where the Head of a State was appointed arbitrator, as was frequently done, he could delegate the work to his own officials or other persons in whom he had confidence, but the award was promulgated personally and under his own authority. The mixed diplomatic and judicial quality of international arbitration was generally preserved by the appointment of national arbitrators (who in the tribunal tended to cancel each other out), leaving the real power of decision in the hands of a group of neutral arbitrators or even a single umpire.[15]

Thirdly, accepted elements of the normal judicial techniques (whether those of the common law systems or those of the continental civil law systems), including features such as the equality of the parties, the right of both parties to an equal hearing, and, of course, the independence of the arbitrators, were fully incorporated into international practice. International political thought began to appreciate the implications of the maxim that justice must not only be done but that it must be seen to be done.

Fourthly, the outlines of fairly regular patterns of procedure began to be settled. These included the exchange of written pleadings (briefs), usually simultaneously, followed by a hearing, the parties meeting face-to-face, closed deliberations of the tribunal, the promulgation of its award (unless for any reason the parties desired to keep the whole arbitration secret, which they were entitled to do), the duty of the tribunal to give reasons for its award, and the right of any member of the tribunal to express his dissent (this latter was not invariable: the custom of dissenting opinions is essentially of a "common law" origin, and is not familiar to continental jurists).

Finally, it became established as a rule of law, not requiring specific mention in an arbitration agreement, that the agreement to have recourse to arbitration automatically implied the obligation to abide by the tribunal's award, and (to carry it out in good faith. The award was "final" and "binding" as a settlement of the dispute, unless adequate grounds could be produced for it to be declared a nullity. It is this which distinguished arbitration from other diplomatic processes such as conciliation and mediation, in which the binding quality was not always present or was even deliberately excluded, the proceedings then terminating in some form of recommendation which the parties are free to accept, with or without modification, or to reject.

These essential features of international arbitration have been preserved to this day, and have exercised a formidable influence on the development of international adjudication proper, through the International Court.[16]

THE LEAGUE OF NATIONS

One of the reasons for the difficulties confronting all the earlier attempts to establish permanent international tribunals of general jurisdiction was the absence of any central political administration for the international community. Before the First World War, no regular international machinery existed, either on the political-diplomatic level or on the administrative level. The so-called Concert of Europe of the time was an informal system of consultation between the Great European Powers of the day. It lacked all the attributes of system and constitution, and its machinery was that of the traditional techniques of nineteenth century diplomacy.

The establishment of the League of Nations by the Peace Treaties of 1919 changed this. Especially significant was the differentiation between the Council and the Assembly. The League Council was conceived as a small executive body in which political responsibility – and power – were concentrated. It was composed of a number of permanent members, who were the surviving Great Powers which were members of the League, and elected (rotating) members. On the other hand, the League Assembly, which met once a year in regular session, was the general deliberative body of the total membership. The League was equipped with a permanent administrative organ, the Secretariat, and a regular budget. Obviously, the existence of such a pattern of international organization opened new perspectives for a permanent international judicial organ.

The relative success of the 1907 Conference – which only served to highlight the obstinate political difficulties in the way of true international adjudication – inspired a significant movement which was not satisfied with the partial solution and looked forward to the day when there would be a permanent international tribunal with compulsory jurisdiction over at least some types of international disputes. The Hague Conference had adopted a resolution admitting the principle of obligatory arbitration as well as a project for the creation of a court of arbitral justice, but nothing had come of it.

Important bodies, however, kept hammering away at the theme, including the Institute of International Law (resolution of 1911) and others. During the War, the neutral Scandinavian States prepared a joint plan for the organization of an international judicial organ, and this was followed by other plans prepared under the aegis of the Swiss (1918) and Netherlands (1919) Governments. The movement also had powerful backing in the United States, and among the Western Allies in general. It was a movement which could not be ignored by the peacemakers of 1919.

By the time the early drafts of the constituent instrument of the League of Nations were circulating at the beginning of 1919, the notion that permanent machinery for international adjudication must be included seems to have been accepted. It was perceived that the establishment of the League, in which the Principal Allied and Associated Powers would have a predominant position (they would be permanent members of the Council), opened the way to a solution of the problem of the composition of such a tribunal. It was also felt that the existence of a regularly established international organization might encourage a solution for the question of the extent to which the principle of compulsory arbitration could become feasible. Obviously, however, a great deal of work was required before these ideas could be translated into the language of reality. Article 12 of the Covenant contained a general obligation on the members of the League of Nations to submit to arbitration or settlement by the League Council any dispute likely to lead to a rupture, as well as provisions for the execution of decisions, and Article 13 contained a general declaration about the types of dispute which were regarded as generally suitable for submission to arbitration.[17] These included disputes as to: *(a)* the interpretation of a treaty; *(b)* any question of international law; (c) the existence of any fact which if established would constitute a breach of any international obligation; or *(d)* the extent and nature of the reparation to be made for any such breach. The first of these categories had appeared in Article 38 of the Hague Convention of 1907. The others, however, were new, and indicate the extent of the political and intellectual advances achieved since 1907. If the matter could be disposed of merely by means of definitions and classifications, the four categories together are broad enough to cover every international *dispute,* although not necessarily every type or instance of international tension which might occur. This formula has come to exercise a significant and on the whole fruitful influence on the work of the International Court.

Articles 12 and 13 of the Covenant contained general obligations binding on the members of the League. True, these obligations were vague and of indefinite scope, yet nonetheless they were obligations. That was as far as the Peace Conference could go in the time at its disposal. It could not establish the permanent judicial organ, and it therefore decided to leave future developments to the organs of the League. Article 14 of the Covenant consequently imposed on the Council the duty of formulating plans for the establishment of what was termed the Permanent Court of International Justice, which would be competent to hear and determine any dispute of an international character which the parties thereto submit to it. This Article also introduced a completely novel idea into international practice, by providing that the Court might give an advisory opinion upon any dispute or question referred to it by the Council or the Assembly. This is discussed on pp. 106 *et seq*. below.

The Council lost little time in getting down to work. At its second session in February 1920, it appointed a committee often eminent jurists (several of whom had participated at The Hague in 1907), from allied or neutral countries, to submit a report to the Council. The Committee's attention was called to the plans which had been drawn up in the meantime, and to certain assurances that had been given to the German and Austrian Governments during the Peace Conferences. By July the Committee adopted its draft scheme. That was based on the compulsory adjudication of legal disputes. The Council, however, was not prepared to go so far and introduced other revisions before forwarding the plan to the First Assembly of the League (1920). The Assembly, after further amendment, then adopted the Statute of the Permanent Court of International Justice, and its Protocol of Signature Was opened on 16 December 1920. The Assembly decided that the Statute would come into force as soon as it had been ratified by the majority of the members of the League. This process was completed by the beginning of September the next year, and the Statute then came into force. The first election of judges took place in 1921, and the Court was formally inaugurated in January 1922. The first case to come before the Court - an advisory opinion - was filed in May 1922, and the first contentious case was instituted a year later.[18]

In that way the concept of a permanent international judicial organ was translated into reality. On the other hand, the concept of compulsory jurisdiction of international legal disputes was not accepted into international practice. Submission to judicial settlement remained voluntary.

THE PERMANENT COURT OF INTERNATIONAL JUSTICE

Despite Article 14 of the Covenant, the Permanent Court, which was in existence from 1922 until the dissolution of the League on 18 April 1946, was formally not an organ of the League. The fact that a State was a Member of the League did not automatically make it a party to the Statute of the Court, although, as laid down in the Statute, it could participate in the elections of the Members of the Court, and it had to bear its share of the Court's expenses. This meant that what is sometimes known as the "international judicial community", i.e. the States which were parties to the Statute, was not identical with the international political community organized in the League. All members of the League were *qualified* to become parties to the Statute, but so too were other States if they met certain conditions. In addition, States which were not parties to the Statute could also bring their disputes with other States before the Court, whether as applicants or as respondents. The Court was created to serve the whole international community. Not for nothing was its seat established at The Hague, alongside the Permanent Court of Arbitration, and not at Geneva. The Court never became "tainted" with the "Geneva spirit".

Yet the Court was closely connected with the League -so close in fact that its fortunes were undoubtedly tied to those of the League. It could not survive the disappearance of the League. This meant that developments in the general international situation, which prevented effective political action by the League for the preservation of international peace, could not leave the Court unaffected, and that the progressive disintegration of the post-War political system had a direct impact on the Court. That was inevitable. On the other hand, that bond made it possible to find solutions for some of the problems which had prevented the earlier establishment of any permanent general international judicial organ. For instance, the difficulty over the composition of the Court was neatly solved by confiding the election of the Members of the Court to the two principal organs of the League, the Council and the Assembly. This ingenious device ensured not only the presence of nationals of the Great Powers on the Court, but also a balanced Court from the point of view of representation on it of the principal legal systems and the major political trends in the world as it then existed. This tie also overcame difficulties in meeting the Court's expenses. All this has now been taken over by the United Nations, and will be described more fully in the following chapters.

Although, as stated, the concept of the compulsory settlement of all, or certain types of, international disputes was not incorporated into either the League Covenant or the Statute, the general political climate of the early period of the League lent encouragement to the idea that States should voluntarily take upon themselves more precise obligations for submitting disputes to the Court. That objective was further facilitated by the Statute of the Court, and even more so by its practice. Nevertheless, the fundamental principle which had underpinned the international arbitrations of the nineteenth century, that the consent of the litigating States is the *only* basis for the exercise of jurisdiction, remained firmly enshrined as the *only* basis for the exercise of jurisdiction by the Permanent Court. The many and far-reaching changes which in the course of time international practice has absorbed have never departed from the fundamental principle.

After an experimental and tentative start the Permanent Court also made tremendous advances in international judicial procedure. This is above all thanks to the permanence of the institution and the accumulation of practice. Using as its point of departure international arbitration experience supplemented by the principles of procedure in the domestic courts (especially the highest courts), international judicial procedure is today a completely autonomous institution of international law and practice with only superficial resemblances to domestic legal procedure. The Permanent Court's procedure became crystallized by 1936 with the adoption of the last version of its Rules of Court. Together with the Statute those Rules were taken over, virtually unchanged, by the United Nations and the present Court until they were amended in 1972 and more thoroughly revised in 1978 (see Appendices I and II). How those procedures were developed and applied by the Permanent Court is today a matter of historical and professional interest. Naturally, there is a continuous process of development to meet the constantly changing requirements and patterns of international life and experience. In later chapters of this book the attempt will be made to describe their essential features as they are today, for only in 1972 did the present Court first promulgate a series of major amendments to the Rules of Court, preparatory to their complete revision in 1978.[19]

It is of greater importance to try and evaluate - or more accurately reevaluate - the work of the Permanent Court, because now, with the passage of time, its achievements can be looked at more dispassionately and from a distance. What can be learned from its experience that will be of value today in understanding the potentialities for, and the limitations on, the international judicial function?

The judicial statistics of the Court (see Appendix V) show that in the 18 years of its effective life, from 1922 to 1939, 66 cases were submitted to it. Thirty-eight were contentious cases and 28 advisory cases (all at the request of the Council of the League, five originating with the International Labour Office). Of those 66 cases, 1 advisory and 11 contentious cases were settled out of Court. In the 54 cases left for decision the Court delivered 27 advisory opinions and 32 judgments (two cases were pending when the Second World War silenced the Court). There were in addition a number of substantive pronouncements couched in the form of orders. This gives an average of nearly four cases filed per year, and a slightly smaller number of major judicial pronouncements – figures considerably in excess of anything experienced by international arbitration.

What were these cases about? What were the realities of the disputes with which the Permanent Court was called upon to deal? For as a matter of form by far the greater part of them superficially dealt with technical legal questions, indeed mostly the interpretation of treaties. But let us not confuse the form with the underlying causes of the disputes.

Their subject matter, as their political context and background, varied. But looking back on these affairs we may notice some interesting, and perhaps unsuspected, features. For example, much of the Court's business emerged from the tensions – which in time played a major role in the course of events leading to the outbreak of the Second World War – between Germany and Poland[20] and between Lithuania and Germany and Poland.[21] Other controversial aspects of the 1919 peace settlement also came before the Court,[22] as well as some arising out of the settlement with Turkey.[23] In 1931 the Council of the League was even not averse to referring to the Court for advisory opinion so explosive an issue as the proposed customs union between Austria and Germany – which the Court, some seven years before Hitler brought the *Anschluss* about by force, held to be incompatible with Peace Treaties of 1919, a fore-runner of Austrian neutrality after the Second World War. African affairs, too, occupied it – a harbinger of later events, although at the time prompted by European rivalries on that continent.[24] The Court, naturally, also had work in resolving other disputes, some of them quite serious, such as that between Denmark and Norway relating to the sovereignty over Eastern Greenland, and occasionally to give advice on the operations of the International Labour Organization. On the other hand, it was rare for disputes arising out of sudden, and perhaps unpremeditated, incidents unrelated to a more general political background to be brought before the Court.[25] It seems that this type of quarrel, often requiring quick treatment, may on the whole be more amenable to diplomatic settlement which will avoid raising the legal questions of principle and acute issues of national prestige which a reference to the Court is likely to encounter. Many people think that the mere existence of the Court makes it easier for States to settle this type of dispute without recourse to the Court. It forces them to consider the legal aspects dispassionately, and to plan their diplomatic steps accordingly.

We may also observe that both the United States of America and the Soviet Union displayed towards the Permanent Court attitudes very similar to those which they later showed during the first four decades of the United Nations towards the present Court. The United States, itself not a member of the League, signed the Statute of the Court, but the Senate twice withheld its advice and consent to its ratification.[26] On the other hand, there was always a Member of the Court of United States nationality. The United States was not involved, either directly or indirectly, in any litigation during that period. The Soviet Union did not go quite so far as the United States. It never signed the Statute of the Court. It never concerned itself that one Member of the Court should be of Soviet nationality. It rejected the competence and authority of the Court in an advisory case referring directly to its own affairs.[27]

This latter aspect changed after 1945. The formal reason for aloofness of this character is that these Powers (except the Soviet Union from 1934) were not members of the League of Nations. However, there is reason to believe that behind the formal attitude profounder considerations related to fundamental policies of the two great Powers which, after 1945, were to appear as the two most powerful nations on earth, the

Super-Powers, influenced their attitudes.

How, then, is the work of the Permanent Court to be assessed? One of the difficulties is to find the appropriate measuring rod. The real significance of the work of an international court cannot be based on mere statistics, or be determined merely by the formal consideration that its *ipse dixit* enjoys the formal status of being a final and binding settlement of the dispute before it. In fact very little of the final and binding settlements of the disputes brought before the Permanent Court survived the turmoil of the Second World War and its aftermath.

Let us take another look at the Court's judicial statistics, and relate them to the general developments of the political situation. We find that of the 66 cases brought before the Court, well over two thirds, 50 of them, were filed in the period 1922-32, in the heyday of the League. In the five-year period 1924-28 alone, when Franco-German *rapprochement* was at its closest after the Locarno agreements of 1925, 24 new cases were filed, an average of nearly five per year. That is considerably higher than the annual average over the whole period. No new cases were filed in 1929, the year of the major economic crisis, the Great Depression. This indicates the dependence of the idea of international litigation upon the existence of some modicum of general pacification and stability and relaxation of international tension. After the nazis came to power in Germany in 1933, 16 new cases were filed in the seven years 1933-39, a sharp falling *et seq*. This is not accidental, and some disputes of that period were litigated only after the Second World War.

Writing in 1944, a former judge of the Permanent Court, Manley Hudson, doubted if the Permanent Court had fulfilled a role as a "great bulwark of peace" (had the League of Nations?), though he recognized that some of the cases with which it dealt could have led to serious complications had they been allowed to fester. He thought that the Court's bolstering of the structure of peace had been accomplished more through the confidence it had inspired in its methods and the encouragement which it had given to the extension of the law of pacific settlement.[28] But placing the concrete, isolated, cases in the broader context of the general political situation may show that what the Court, as the organs of the League (and often in co-operation with them) really succeeded in doing, was for a time to keep a tense situation under some form of control. Given other political conditions, the League would have enjoyed greater long-term success, and the Court with it. As things were, the major disputes with which the Court dealt were connected with that very situation which sparked the Second World War. None of the skills of statesmanship and diplomacy available at the time succeeded in avoiding that cataclysm, and it is asking too much to expect more of the Court.

In addition to any purely political evaluation of the work of the Court within the context of the settlement of international disputes, it is generally recognized that it made a very significant contribution to the development of international law.[29] This is an indirect contribution to the maintenance of international peace, of no mean value, and may be set against the relative failure of the League of Nations (in contrast to the success of the United Nations)[30] in this field.

The real significance of the experience of the Permanent Court lies in a different direction. From its experimental beginnings it confirmed that a permanent international judicial organ is both feasible and necessary, even without going so far as to be accompanied by any true compulsory jurisdiction. The real measure of its worth is not to be found in the number of cases decided by it (though that is not to be belittled) or in its contribution to the development and clarification of the law (a by-product of the activity of all courts in all legal systems), but in the widely-held satisfaction at its performance. When the League disappeared and the United Nations took its place, it was never suggested that the Court had outlived its usefulness and could well be disbanded. On the contrary: the major concern was to increase its effectiveness and to strengthen its ties with the world political organization, and if too much could not be achieved in this direction, then at least to ensure that the judicial activities could be resumed where they had been broken off in 1939. It was never seriously proposed that the Court is unnecessary, or that it had failed in its primary mission, or that its organization was fundamentally faulty, even in quarters which for various reasons were critical of some of its decisions, or of the manner in which States sometimes invoke the judicial function.[31]

The experience of the Permanent Court, its dispassionate and unhurried consideration of the issues brought before it, the high standards of personal integrity, professional competence, and worldly wisdom, of its Members, the fact that the judicial pronouncements were endowed with strong moral authority in addition to their formal finality and the accumulation of experience in the Registry -all these constituted an intangible asset on the positive side of the balance-sheet. They provided the foundations for the reconstituted system of international adjudication after the dust of the Second World War had started to settle.

THE UNITED NATIONS AND THE COURT

Article 7 of the United Nations Charter establishes the principal organs of the United Nations. These are the General Assembly, the Security Council, the Economic and Social Council, the (now defunct) Trusteeship Council, the International Court of Justice, and the Secretariat. Article 92 states that the Court shall be the principal judicial organ of the United Nations, and that it shall function in accordance with the annexed Statute, which is based upon the Statute of the Permanent Court and forms an integral part of the Charter. Article 1 of the Statute repeats that the Court established by the Charter as the principal judicial organ of the United Nations shall function in accordance with the provisions of the Statute. These provisions contain – and emphasize – the general arrangement determining the position of the Court within the Organization. The Charter also deals with compliance with the Court's decisions, and the organs and organizations authorized to request an advisory opinion.

The ambiguity characteristic of the relations between the League of Nations and the Permanent Court of International Justice has now been replaced by clarity. The Statute of the Court is no longer a separate international treaty. It is an integral part of the Charter. Every member of the United Nations is thus *ipso facto* a party to the Statute of the Court. This emphasizes the quality and status of the Court as the principal judicial organ of the United Nations.

Let us see how this has come about, and what are its implications.

THE WAR AND THE SAN FRANCISCO CONFERENCE (1945)

Whatever may have been the original intentions of the founders, the Permanent Court, in the course of its existence and in the light of its accumulated experience, came to discharge three distinct functions. Two of these, envisaged in its Statute, were primary. The third, not originally contemplated, was secondary.

The Permanent Court's two primary tasks were, as mentioned in the previous chapter, to decide disputes between States, and to render advisory opinions in response to requests from the Council or the Assembly of the League (in fact the Assembly never made use of this power). The decisions were given independently of action by the League. The advisory opinions represented the Permanent Court's participation in the political activities of the League, and waxed and waned in sympathy with the political fortunes of the League.

The Court's third function, less known, was quite different. It was to appoint umpires, presidents of arbitral commissions and of other tribunals, and similar offices. Normally these appointments were made by the President of the Court at the request of a State, but occasionally the whole Court might be consulted. The Court gave its approval to this as far back as 1923. This has come to be known as the "extra-judicial activity" of the Court, since it is not mentioned in the Statute, and no firm rules have been promulgated to regulate its performance. It provides a simple way of overcoming difficulties in States' agreeing on the identity of a third arbitrator, which might lead to the frustration of an agreement for arbitration. It also forms the basis for a special arbitration procedure incorporated in certain types of agreements, especially agreements on important economic matters, in which one of the parties is not a State, and therefore cannot have access to the Court itself (which is only competent in disputes between States). International experience has shown that there is need for a form of arbitration in which the President of the Tribunal can be appointed by an independent and respected international official such as the President of the International Court.

This fills the gap between the area of public law and the area of private law, and makes it possible for governments and entities – including international intergovernmental organizations – which are not governments, to be placed on some sort of equal basis in the procedural sense. One of the best known transactions of this type was the Anglo-Iranian Oil Company's Concession Agreement of 1933 (which, in 1951, came up before the new Court in international litigation proper). This had been negotiated through the good offices of the Council of the League.

The outbreak of the Second World War in September 1939 put a stop to all these activities.

The question which arose during the Second World War was whether there was still need for an international judicial organ performing all or some of these functions and, if so, was an instrument fashioned on the lines of the Statute of the Permanent Court satisfactory for these purposes?

After thorough examination both on the technical and professional level and on the highest political level, an affirmative answer was given to those questions. There was little disposition, at least among the Western Allies, to doubt the necessity for an international organ resembling the Permanent Court. The real problem which faced them was one of method, but underlying the question of method were important political issues. The problem of method was posed as whether to continue the Permanent Court in existence with necessary changes in its Statute, or whether to re-organize the international judicial system and make it an integral part of the general international political organization which would be set up after the War was won. The political problems for which this was the procedural manifestation were of two kinds. The first, and the more important, related to the attitude towards the future international judicial organ of those members of the anti-nazi coalition, above all the Union of Soviet Socialist Republics and the United States of America. Both these Powers between the Wars had stood aloof from the League and the Permanent Court. The second, which, it seems in retrospect, may have been given undue prominence, related to the position of the enemy Axis Powers. They, on the contrary, had participated in the work of the Permanent Court and, as parties to its Statute, technically had a say in its future – this included *all* the Axis Powers. Both those problems were closely connected with the changes in the pattern of international relationships which began emerging during the War. Those changes were given their first formal recognition in the differences between the major political alignments of the United Nations in comparison with those of the League, the substitution of the Soviet Union and the United States of America for Great Britain and France as the dominant political factors in the Organization.

Interest in the future of the Court as a matter of immediate political concern began to revive about the middle of 1942. At that time both the British and the United States Governments on the one hand, and the Latin American Governments (through the Inter-American Juridical Committee) on the other, expressed approval in principle for the resumption of the machinery of international judicial activities after the War. In May, the British Government took its first concrete steps. It convened an Informal Inter-Allied Committee of twelve experienced international lawyers from among those who were available in London. They were asked to prepare an informal report which would not be binding on their governments, but which could be of use to the authorities in due course. The report which the Committee presented early in 1944 is the first comprehensive re-examination of the issues connected with the Court that had taken place since the outbreak of the War. In the history of international adjudication it is an important document. The Committee, which did not question the necessity for *a* Court, reached the conclusion that the Permanent Court had on the whole worked well, and that its Statute could be retained as the basis for the general structure of the future Court. It did not think that the Court should be reconstituted as an integral part of any future international organization. In the Committee's view, it was preferable to retain the Court as an independent international organism, but one always standing at the disposal of the Organization. It also found that the policy issues involved in the question whether to maintain the Permanent Court in existence as such, or whether to establish an entirely new Court, were outside its province.[1]

In the Moscow Declaration on General Security of 30 October 1943, the four Principal Allied Powers, China, the USSR, the United Kingdom and the United States of America, recognized the necessity of establishing a general international organization for the maintenance of international peace and security, though nothing was said publicly at that stage about the Court. In October 1944, matters were carried a stage further, when the same four Governments, now called the Sponsoring Powers, concretized their ideas on the future general political organization in the Dumbarton Oaks Proposals for the United Nations. These included express recognition that the International Court should be the principal judicial organ of the Organization, that all members of the United Nations should *ipso facto* be parties to the Statute of the Court which would form part of the Charter, and that non-members could become parties to the Statute on conditions to be laid down by the General Assembly upon the recommendation of the Security Council. On the vexed question of whether to keep the Permanent Court in existence or to create a new Court, and whether, in the latter event, the Statute of the Permanent Court could still serve as a basis, the Dumbarton Oaks Proposals were noncommittal, though preference was expressed for keeping the general lines of the old Statute.

By now it was clear that further work of a technical nature was required before the political conference, due to meet in San Francisco in April, 1945, and at which the Charter was to be finally completed, could profitably take the matter up. Both the Informal Inter-Allied Committee and the Dumbarton Oaks Proposals made it plain that comprehensive re-examination of the terms of the Statute was needed, despite their clear preference for making as few changes as possible. Accordingly, the four Sponsoring Powers decided to convene a Committee of Jurists in Washington to prepare a draft of the Statute, in preparation for the San Francisco Conference. All the members of the United Nations (that is, the members of the War-time coalition of States parties to the Treaty of Washington of 1942, and going under the name of the *United Nations*) would be invited. Forty-four States took part in the work of this Committee, at which the Permanent Court was also represented. In drafting the new Statute, the Committee was careful to respect the distribution of subject matter and numbering of articles as found in the Statute of the Permanent Court, which it adjusted. It felt that in doing so it would facilitate scientific work and the utilization of the precedents established by the

Permanent Court.

At the end of its labours it left three major questions open: *(a)* the form in which to state the Court's mission as the principal judicial organ of the new Organization; *(b)* how to conduct the election of the judges; and *(c)* to what extent should the jurisdiction of the Court be compulsory. Politically, that had now become the most significant issue. Behind it lay the more fundamental problem of whether recognition of the compulsory jurisdiction of the Court for all or certain disputes should be the condition *sine qua non* of membership in the United Nations. Such a question had not arisen, and could not arise, for the League of Nations so long as the Permanent Court was not one of its organs and the members of the League not *ipso facto* parties to its Statute.

In this form the question came before the United Nations Conference on International Organization, the San Francisco Conference. The draft Statute was examined in detail in Committee IV/1, where the Permanent Court was represented by two of its members. It became clear that while a majority of the smaller and medium Powers were in favour of making some acceptance of the compulsory jurisdiction of the Court a condition for membership in the United Nations, the major Powers, on which the prime responsibility for maintaining the Organization would rest, and especially the Soviet Union and the United States, were not prepared to accept so far-reaching an innovation in international practice. Therefore the underlying basis on which the Permanent Court had worked, that its jurisdiction to determine a case rests on the consent of the States concerned, was retained.[2]

With this out of the way there was little difficulty in establishing the Court as a principal organ and the principal judicial organ of the United Nations, or in deciding to create a new Court for this purpose. However, the relevant provisions of the Statute were drafted in such a way as to convey that this decision would not break the chain of continuity with the past and not undo the achievements attained in the field of international justice. Therefore, in some respects the new Court, called the International Court of Justice, may be regarded as the successor of the Permanent Court, although the United Nations as a whole is not the successor of the League of Nations. The Statute emerged from this process but slightly revised, as is apparent from Article 92 of the Charter quoted on p. 16 above. After the Preparatory Commission of the United Nations had taken the necessary administrative steps, the members of the new Court were elected in early meetings of the Security Council and the General Assembly. Their term of office commenced on 6 February 1946. At the same time parallel measures for the dissolution of the Permanent Court were put in hand. On 18 April, the new Court held its solemn inaugural meeting in the presence of a distinguished gathering at The Hague. On the same day, at Geneva, the League Assembly voted itself, and the Permanent Court, out of existence.

Over a year was to elapse before the first contentious case was to be filed in the new Court, a marked contrast to what had happened when the Permanent Court was set up in 1922. What did this portend? The answer will appear from the following pages.

PRINCIPAL ORGAN OF THE UNITED NATIONS

Apart from Articles 7 and 92 of the Charter, Article 93 gives reality to the integration of the Court in the Organization by providing, as had been proposed at Dumbarton Oaks, that all members of the United Nations are *ipso facto* parties to the Statute. States which are not members of the United Nations may become parties to the Statute on conditions to be determined in each case by the General Assembly upon the recommendation of the Security Council. The underlying assumption is that the world political organization, already possessed of organs with executive, deliberative and administrative functions, would be incomplete unless it also had a fully integrated judicial organ of its own. The San Francisco records show clearly that for many the intention was in this way to place the Court in a position in which it could play an important role, alongside the other organs, in the new organization of nations for peace and security. Their idea in making the Statute an integral part of the Charter was to secure for the Court the support of all the members, and not to continue with the anomalous situation which had existed in the structure of the League, where the international judicial community was something distinct, at least in theory, from the general political organization of the international community. On the other hand, there is nothing to indicate that the founders of the United Nations had in mind anything like the separation of powers in the sense used by Montesquieu and followed by many of today's political scientists.

This was a radical innovation made by the founders of the United Nations in 1945. Its import must not be obscured by their conservatism both in matters of form, and in the concept of the underlying basis for international litigation as it had developed during the preceding century.

What are the implications of this? The Court, as an organ of the United Nations, operates within the framework of the general purposes and principles of the United Nations as set out in the Charter. The Court's status as a principal organ imposes on it the responsibility of participating in the work of the Organization on an equal footing with the other principal organs, within the limits of its competence. This was vividly expressed by one of the judges who said that the Court, "which had been raised to the status of a principal organ, and thus more closely geared into the mechanism of the U.N.O., must do its utmost to co-operate with the other organs with a view to attaining the aims and principles that have been set forth".[3] This principle of *co-operation* has been enunciated and acted upon by the Court in various circumstances, but particularly to justify its refusal to accede to requests that it interfere in the working of the Security Council, and in rejecting challenges to its competence to give an advisory opinion. At the same time, recalling that it is not only a principal organ but also the principal *judicial* organ of the United Nations, the Court has been insistent on maintaining one general qualification regarding this duty of co-operation. It will not co-operate with the other organs blindly, but only if it is satisfied that what it is being asked to do is, in the circumstances, fully compatible with its judicial character.[4] Its judicial character and the integrity of the judicial process must be preserved at all costs. This, too, has particularly influenced its advisory competence, which is discretionary. The Court has repeatedly stressed that in principle it should not refuse to give an opinion unless overriding considerations of judicial propriety make this imperative.[5]

These conclusions of 1945 regarding the establishment of the Court were not the end of political interest in the role of the Court. Since then, the General Assembly has examined the general role and position of the Court within the United Nations system no less than five times. In addition, in specific cases, especially of treaty-drafting, the United Nations and conferences convened under its auspices have faced great difficulties provoked by strong desires to confer jurisdiction in concrete cases arising under the treaties being drafted, and equally strong opposition to that. This factor was particularly acute during the period of the "Cold War" when it dominated the work of the United Nations in the field of the codification of international law and of general treaty-making. It nearly wrecked the most important of the codification conferences that were held in 1968-69 on the codification of the law of treaties. It would be a mistake, however, to assume that this opposition is an especial feature of Marxist legal theories. It had been encountered in the League of Nations even before the Soviet Union became a member of that organization.

The first three of those discussions were dominated by the Cold War and its political and ideological tensions. The last two, which are still continuing, have become influenced by the completely changed structure of international relations following the disintegration of the group of the Socialist States of Eastern Europe.

The first examination occurred in the General Assembly of 1947. Its agenda included an item on the need for greater use by the United Nations and its organs of the International Court of Justice. The Cold War was then in its initial stages. The debate demonstrated a wide feeling of regret and concern at the prevailing indifference being manifested toward arbitral and judicial methods for the pacific settlement of international disputes. But this feeling was not universally shared. Particularly important were the statements of the Soviet Foreign Minister Andrei Vyshinski, emphasizing his country's negative attitude towards using the Court for political purposes. The resolution adopted recommended greater use of the Court, but as a practical matter had no direct effect.[6]

The second occasion was in connection with the drafting of the Declaration on Principles of International Law concerning Friendly Relations and Co-operation among States in accordance with the Charter of the United Nations. This, which was probably the most heated, ideologically and politically, of all the debates on the question, occupied the General Assembly and special intersessional committees from 1963 until 1970. The judicial settlement of international disputes was discussed in the context of the principle that States should settle their international disputes in such a manner that international peace, and justice, should not be endangered, especially in 1966 and 1967. The debate brought out extensive mistrust of the role of judicial settlement in the international situation then existing, some half-way through the decolonization process. It also drew attention to considerable dissatisfaction at certain features of the International Court itself, particularly its composition, and at the general state of international law. It became impossible to insert in the declaration any specific reference to the Court itself.[7]

One of the repercussions of this prolonged negotiation was that in 1967 the Court started to re-examine its Rules and internal practices with a view to their general revision. Those Rules and practices were practically identical with those of the Permanent Court adopted in 1936, and they were felt to require modernization. The first step toward this aim was taken in 1972.

The third discussion commenced in 1970 and lasted until the end of 1974. This was concerned with a general review of the role of the Court. The twelve sponsors of this initiative included both Western and a number of Latin American and newly-independent African States which were generally supportive of the Court and therefore wished to have an expert study of the matter conducted under General Assembly auspices. Their purpose was to reinforce the Court's position within the United Nations and to explore both existing and new possibilities for an increase in its use.

There was strong resistance to this initiative on the part of those States which were opposed to an increase in the Court's influence or to any attempt to expand its jurisdiction. That group of States, which was primarily, although by no means exclusively, composed of the Socialist States of Eastern Europe and a number of developing States in Africa and Asia, viewed an expansion of the Court's role as a potential encroachment upon their national sovereignty. Criticism was expressed at the composition of the Court from the point of view of the representation on it of the different regional groups, at the "sources" of the law which it applied, at its procedure which was felt by some States to be too formalistic and cumbersome, and at several of its judgments.

A lively debate followed, particularly in 1970 and 1971. Together with an important series of written observations by Governments and academic comments, this covered a wide range of issues pertaining to the Court's role and procedure. Many imaginative proposals were advanced for expanding the scope of the Court's activities and increasing the use of the Court both by States parties to the Statute and by the other organs of the United Nations. Some of these proposals would have required a revision of the Court's Statute (and therefore of the United Nations Charter). Others could be achieved through a revision of the Court's own Rules and practices.

By 1974 it had become clear that there was no political possibility to organize under the auspices of the General Assembly an in depth study of ways to reinforce the Court's role and influence. In the meantime, several new cases had been filed with the Court, and coupled with this the debate showed traces of a possible change in the political philosophy regarding the place of the Court within the United Nations. Finally a consensus was reached in 1974, during the 29th session of the General Assembly. The resolution was a compromise which met diplomatic necessities but which by no means satisfied either group of States. An important element in it is a paragraph in the preamble in which the General Assembly took note of the 1972 amendments to the Rules of Court, stressing that these had simplified the procedure, reduced the likelihood of undue delays and costs, and allowed for the greater influence of the parties on the composition of *ad hoc* chambers. (p. 58 below) Another paragraph in the preamble recognized the role that certain resolutions and declarations of the General Assembly might play in the development of international law.[8] There has been occasional reference by the Court since then to some of the more important resolutions of a legal character adopted by the General Assembly.

These debates provided a valuable opportunity for States to indicate aspects of the Court's activities and procedures which were of concern to them and accordingly to offer practical suggestions, many of which have found their way into the 1978 Rules.

As for the Court, it continued with its review of its Rules and practices. In 1972 it promulgated the first set of amendments of the Rules and these, as mentioned, were welcomed by the General Assembly. Two important charges in these Rules related to the composition of the *ad-hoc* chambers of the Court (p. 58 below) and to the treatment of objections to the jurisdiction of the Court (p. 81 below). In 1976 the Court adopted a new resolution on its internal judicial practice (p. 109 below). In 1978, it completed its revision of the Rules of Court and promulgated entirely new Rules, which were amended again in December 2000 with respect to the treatment of preliminary objections and counter-claims. These new Rules as amended in 2000 are reproduced in Appendix II.[8]

In response to the greatly increased workload in recent years, the Court has taken a number of other measures designed to further expedite the treatment of cases and in particular to make the written and oral pleadings more efficient. In April 1998, the

Court issued a number of recommendations aimed at limiting the volume of written pleadings and attached documentation and avoiding unnecessary length and repetition in the oral procedure. These recommendations were extended and clarified by the Court in October 2001 through the adoption, for the first time, of Practice Directions for States appearing before it. In April 2002, the Court adopted a number of further measures which further limit the length of both written and oral pleadings, provide it with a greater measure of control over the procedure and cut down the time necessary for deliberations relating to preliminary objections. These activities showed that the Court had taken account of ideas put forward in the General Assembly and of the experience and suggestions of recent years.

Meanwhile, the fourth broad discussion took place in the General Assembly within the context of the reports of the Special Committee on the Charter of the United Nations and the Strengthening of the Role of the Organization. This first started its activities in 1974. Work on a declaration commenced in 1980 at the prompting of the General Assembly, as a step towards a more cultivated programme of action in the sphere of dispute-prevention, dispute-management and dispute-settlement. This showed that a broader approach was being envisaged, including non-judicial as well as judicial methods of handling these matters. This reflected the growing influence of the non-aligned States in the General Assembly, and later, as the "Cold War" came to an end, the general reordering of the main patterns of international relations. In 1980, a draft declaration which had been submitted by a group of non-aligned States, dealing with the settlement of disputes, revealed the differences of opinion between States. This debate was continued during the sessions of the General Assembly in 1981 and 1982. It concentrated on the role of the Security Council and of the Court, and was characterized by sharp disagreement, particularly between a number of Western States and the Soviet Union, concerning the necessity and desirability of reinforcing the Court's role in the settlement of disputes. The basic positions had not altered perceptibly since the earlier debates on the matter, although the rhetoric was less shrill and the criticism of the Court from the non-aligned States of Asia and Africa was more muted. This discussion ended on a constructive note with the Manila Declaration on the Peaceful Settlement of International Disputes of 15 November 1982 (so named because the wording had been settled during a session of the Special Committee held in Manila in the Philippines in 1980). This declaration was a compromise reached on the initiative of the nonaligned States. Although it broke little new ground, it did include a restatement of important principles embodied in the Charter. The most prominent of these was that "recourse to judicial settlement of legal disputes, particularly referral to the International Court of Justice, should not be considered an unfriendly act between States".[9] This is not a new idea. It is not to be taken, however, as encouragement to States to resort too freely to the Court against an unwilling respondent, before the diplomatic process has been adequate to bring out the existence of a dispute within the jurisdiction of the Court. The item is still on the agenda of the General Assembly.

The fifth examination of the role of the Court was initiated by the then Secretary-General, Dr Boutros Boutros-Ghali, in his *An Agenda for Peace* of 1992. This was presented to the 47th session of the General Assembly in response to a meeting earlier in the year of the Security Council at head of State level. In this important document, he pointed out that the Court's docket had grown fuller. Nevertheless he still thought that the Court remained under-used as a resource for the peaceful adjudication of disputes. He recommended that the Secretary-General should be authorized to take advantage of the advisory competence of the Court - a *very* controversial proposition - and that other organs of the United Nations should turn to the Court more frequently for advisory opinions. Other recommendations were mostly of a technical nature.[10]

The General Assembly reacted cautiously. In its resolution 47/120 of 18 December 1992 with the suggestive title *An Agenda for Peace: preventive diplomacy and related matters* it took no position on the Secretary-General's proposals regarding the Court and decided to continue its examination of them. The Security Council also examined the Secretary-General's *Agenda for Peace*, but did not adopt any specific recommendation or decision directly relevant to the Court. Discussion continued within the context of the deliberations held in connection with the *Decade of International Law* which ended in 1999.

These debates have not resulted in any revision of the Statute which would expand the Court's jurisdiction or added to the "sources" of law which the Court applies. On the other hand, there are some who see the development in the Court's activities of a strain of judicial activism, to be attributed in some measure to subtle changes in national attitudes towards the Court detected through the cumulative records of these debates.

The Court is the only principal organ of the United Nations (other than the General Assembly itself) which did not submit an annual report to the General Assembly. In this respect, it followed the tradition of the Permanent Court in its relations with the League. In 1968 this was changed. In that year the Court started submitting an annual report to the General Assembly, and this appears on the agenda of the regular session of the General Assembly. The Court explained this innovation on the ground that it felt that such a report would contribute to a better understanding of its functions and of its activities within the framework of the United Nations.[11] In recent years, the President of the Court has attended the meeting of the General Assembly devoted to this item. In its turn the General Assembly has so far limited itself to taking note of the document.

THE COURT AS THE PRINCIPAL JUDICIAL ORGAN

The International Court has three main tasks.

First, and most important, the Court exists to decide disputes between States in accordance with the provisions of its Statute. This is not limited to disputes between States which are members of the United Nations. Nonmember States can also be parties in cases before the Court, as applicant or as respondent, and probably as intervener (although there has been no instance of this yet). In that sense the International Court of Justice is the World Court.

Second, the Court supplies judicial guidance and support for the work of other United Nations organs and for the autonomous specialized agencies (p. 31 below) through the provision of advisory opinions. Any of those organs and specialized agencies duly authorized may request the Court to give an advisory opinion on any legal question which arises within the scope of its activities (p. 86 below). On the other hand, other international intergovernmental organizations, and States, cannot have direct recourse to the Court's advisory competence.

Third, the Court, or more frequently its President, also engages in the performance of the "extra-judicial" activities, as already mentioned (p. 15 above).

Before the San Francisco Conference some anxiety was expressed lest too close a link between the Court and the United Nations might impair its standing and its ability to perform its judicial function dispassionately as the World Court. However, it can fairly be said that on the whole experience does not justify apprehensions of that nature, although there have been instances where the thrust of the Court's opinion has been more in the direction of the particular law of the United Nations than general international law, especially in the cases dealing with decolonization. This does not mean that world political trends, themselves reflected in the United Nations, have left the Court unaffected, but that is another matter.

The Court's status as the principal judicial organ finds reflection in the political organs when they have to take decisions relating to the Court. The influence of this is felt both in political and in administrative aspects.

From the point of view of substantive political activities, the fact that the political organs of the United Nations tend to make a sharp distinction between political matters and legal questions – some say too sharp a distinction is drawn – furnishes an explanation for the phenomenon that, unlike the experience of the League of Nations, Court procedures have not been invoked by the Security Council or by the General Assembly when dealing with the pacific settlement of a dispute, or in relation to the maintenance of international peace. The Security Council has only once, in its resolution 22 (1947) of 9 April 1947, recommended that the two States involved in a dispute brought before it -the United Kingdom and Albania should immediately refer their dispute to the Court in accordance with the provisions of the Court's Statute. That was a recommendation made in accordance with Article 36, paragraph 3, of the Charter, and it led to the *Corfu Channel* case (p. 127 below). Both the General Assembly and the Security Council have requested advisory opinions about the consequences of decisions already taken.[12] The General Assembly has several times requested advisory opinions for guidance in its future actions. Most recently, the General Assembly requested an advisory opinion on the legality of the threat or use of nuclear weapons, a question which it has been dealing with over a long period. The Economic and Social Council has requested an advisory opinion from the Court on two occasions, both of them relating to the status and immunity of Special Rapporteurs in the field of human rights.

On the other hand, care has been taken by the political organs, on receipt of an advisory opinion, not to adopt operational decisions susceptible of casting doubts on the Court's authority. Nevertheless, on at least two occasions attempts by the General Assembly to act in accordance with the Court's opinion encountered unsurmountable political obstacles and had to be abandoned – the question of the admission of new members (1955) and the financing of United Nations early peace-keeping operations (1965).

Several of the Court's judgments and advisory opinions, as well as orders indicating interim measures of protection, have in the end not been successful in terms of laying the basis for the resolution of the political difficulties in connection with which they were requested. In other instances, however, decisions on preliminary objections or on requests for the indication of provisional measures have, by their reasoning, been effective in laying the basis for an out-of-court settlement of the matter, even when the decision itself was a negative one.

Turning to administrative aspects, when, for instance, the Security Council dealt with the question of the access to the Court of States which are not members of the United Nations, the view prevailed that as the Court was a judicial organ and in consequence a non-political body, the question of access to it ought not to be influenced by irrelevant political considerations.[13] To take another administrative example: when, in 1959, the General Assembly had to examine certain matters relating to the pensions of the Members of the Court, the Legal Committee insisted that full weight should be attached to the circumstance of their election and the character and requirements of the office of Judge as expressed in the Statute. This view prevailed over a less sympathetic attitude of the General Assembly's Administrative and Budgetary Committee, approaching the matter exclusively from an administrative perspective.[14]

The fact that the Court is the only judicial organ directly established by the Charter and is the principal judicial organ of the United Nations does not mean that it is the only judicial organ that may be established, either by the United Nations as an organization or by its individual members. Article 33 of the Charter, which enumerates the various methods for the pacific settlement of international disputes, includes arbitration, judicial settlement, or other peaceful means of the parties' own choice. The principle that the parties are free to choose their own methods of peaceful settlement is firmly enshrined in the Charter. Parallel to this, Article 95 of the Charter spells out that nothing in the Charter shall prevent the members from entrusting the solution of their differences to other tribunals by virtue of agreements already in existence or which may be concluded in the future.

The General Assembly has established several other tribunals. These include the United Nations Tribunal for Libya, the powers and functions of which were transferred to the Italian-Libyan Mixed Arbitration Commission;[15] the United Nations Tribunal for Eritrea; and the United Nations Administrative Tribunal to settle disputes between members of the Secretariat and the Organization and arising out of their contracts of service for which the Court has a special role in its working (p. 149 below). In its resolution 827 of 25 May 1993, the Security Council established the International Criminal Tribunal for the Former Yugoslavia. In the following year, the Security Council established the International Criminal Tribunal for Rwanda by adopting resolution 955 of 8 November1994. Both of these bodies established by the Security Council were based on Chapter VII of the Charter, which provides for the Security Council enforcement powers for dealing with threats to the peace, breaches of the peace and acts of aggression. These tribunals were established to prosecute serious violations of international humanitarian law and other egregious violations of international law arising from the armed conflicts in the former Yugoslavia and Rwanda respectively. After an initially slow start, these tribunals have become progressively more active and have had an increasingly significant impact upon wider events and upon the further development of international criminal law.

They differ from other international adjudicatory bodies in that their function is not to settle disputes between States, but rather to determine individual criminal responsibility of persons accused of perpetrating violations of international humanitarian law. As *ad-hoc* tribunals, they have been set up for this specific purpose and their jurisdiction is limited to the territories concerned. The example of the two *ad-hoc* criminal tribunals had a significant influence on the efforts to create a permanent international criminal court. These efforts stretch back over 50 years to 1948 when the United Nations General Assembly first took the matter up and requested the International Law Commission to prepare a Draft Code of Crimes against Peace and Security of Mankind. However, further progress was impossible in the ensuing decades as a result of the political impasse which characterized the period of the Cold War and the many difficulties involved in establishing an effective international criminal tribunal which would be acceptable to the wide majority of States. In 1990 the situation had changed sufficiently to enable the General Assembly to issue a new request to the International Law Commission. The ILC resumed its work and succeeded in presenting a Draft Statute to the General Assembly in 1994, with a recommendation that a conference of State representatives be convened in order to conclude a convention on the establishment of an International Criminal Court.[16]

This was followed by the creation of a Preparatory Committee in December 1995 with the task of working out an acceptable consolidated text of a convention to establish an international criminal court. The Preparatory Committee succeeded in doing so during the period 1996-1998. In December 1997 the General Assembly adopted Resolution 160/52, which provided for the convening of a Diplomatic Conference on the establishment of an International Criminal Court. This conference was held in Rome, Italy between 15 June and 17 July 1998 to conclude a convention. After delicate and complex, if hurried negotiations, the Conference succeeded in adopting a Statute and text for the Convention within five weeks, which is a virtually unprecedented and noteworthy achievement – albeit one which is in some respects controversial. The Convention containing the Statute was opened for signature on 18 July 1998. There are currently 139 signatories to the Convention and with the necessary threshold of 60 ratifications having been reached in April 2002 the Convention will go into force on 1 July 2002.[17]

The International Criminal Court (ICC) will exercise jurisdiction over the crime of genocide, crimes against humanity and serous violations of the laws of war against individuals on the basis of complementarity. The Statute also provides for criminal jurisdiction over the crime of aggression once a provision is adopted which defines the crime and sets out the conditions for the exercise of jurisdiction.[18]

The ICC is not officially an organ of the United Nations, but rather a judicial body established by States on the basis of a treaty. It will differ in that respect both from the *ad-hoc* criminal tribunals for Yugoslavia and Rwanda which were, as stated, established by the Security Council, and from the International Court of Justice, which is, of course, a principal organ of the United Nations. As a criminal court, it will differ significantly from the International Court in that its function will be to prosecute and determine the individual criminal responsibility of persons accused of committing crimes which fall within its jurisdiction when national authorities are unwilling or unable to do so (the complementary principle). This is a wholly different function from that of the International Court of Justice whose tasks have been elaborated upon in the preceding pages. Although the seat of the ICC will also be in The Hague, not far from the Peace Palace where the International Court resides, there will be no formal institutional links between the two bodies. However, it is clear that the establishment of the ICC will have a significant impact upon the future development of international law and the future development of the international judicial system. It will be up to both bodies to ensure that their relationship is a constructive, fruitful, and where necessary, complementary one.

Throughout the whole period of the existence of the United Nations, States have shown a growing tendency to have recourse to arbitration, and sometimes Members of the Court, or former Members of the Court, are chosen to act as arbitrators. The main difference between arbitration and resort to the Court lies in the ability of the parties to exercise greater influence over the composition of the arbitral tribunal and over the law to be applied by it. This preference may exist against a political backdrop: it may just as well exist in light of the specialized nature of the arbitration. These are all *ad hoc* bodies. More recently, a number of standing tribunals have been set up by States for resolving specific types of disputes of a specialized nature. The International Centre for the Settlement of Investment Disputes, under the auspices of the World Bank, is an example of this. The Centre operates as a clearing house, offering facilities for arbitration or conciliation procedures aimed at resolving disputes arising out of the investment of foreign capital in capital importing States.[19] Other important tribunals are the European Court of Human Rights and the Inter-American Court of Human Rights, neither of which exists within the framework of the United Nations.

The Law of the Sea Convention of 1982 adopted by the Third United Nations Conference on the Law of the Sea, and which entered into force on 16 November 1994, contains the most elaborate provisions for the settlement of disputes yet envisaged. It establishes several new tribunals and commissions, with jurisdiction over the settlement of assorted types of disputes and other matters arising from the interpretation or the application of the Convention. The complex system of dispute-prevention and dispute--settlement built into the Convention offers a choice of procedures. These include the International Court, different forms of arbitration, and the new International Tribunal for the Law of the Sea. The Statute of that Tribunal is closely influenced by that of the Court. Other forms of general and specialized arbitral tribunals and commissions will deal both with questions of a general legal nature as well as specialized categories of disputes between the parties to the Convention.

One of the innovations of the Convention is the establishment of a Sea-Bed Disputes Chamber within the International Tribunal for the Law of the Sea. This is to deal with disputes involving the provisions of the Convention relating to the exploration of the mineral resources of the sea-bed beyond the limits of national jurisdiction, both disputes between States, and those between States and juridical persons including the International Sea-Bed Authority and private corporations involved in mining activities on the ocean floor. This Chamber will have truly compulsory jurisdiction over a series of specific and highly specialized types of disputes.[20]

The position of the Court, as the principal judicial organ of the United Nations, can be summarized.

Within the framework of this highly political organization the Court, although an integral part of the Organization, stands in a special and to some extent distanced position, as is indeed appropriate for a court of justice. It is not composed of the representatives of States. It reacts to the initiatives of States and other organs in a spirit of co-operation. It has no power of initiating action itself. The political organs, for their part, and the States represented on them, have on the whole been careful not to allow completely extraneous political factors to influence decisions which they have been called upon to make in relation to the Court. They have equally, on the whole, tried not to implicate the Court in the intractable political problems which they face daily.

Generally speaking, the other organs have shown awareness that the special character of the Court requires them to be cautious and not to embroil the Court directly in issues in which the political aspects predominate. Perhaps this need for caution was not always fully appreciated in the early years of the United Nations, before it had become clear that judicial techniques could not always advance the solution of a grave political problem. In particular, the advisory competence was invoked in some highly political situations and despite strong opposition.

By the same token it is the responsibility of the Court to satisfy itself that it should exercise jurisdiction in the concrete case, especially when the dispute has conspicuous political or other extra-legal factors. The Court cannot normally refuse to exercise jurisdiction for the sole reason that political and legal considerations exist side by side. To do so would inhibit the Court from acting in a situation in which it might be able to contribute to the settlement of the dispute. For as the Court has said: "legal disputes between sovereign States by their very nature are likely to occur in political contexts, and often form only one element in a wider and long-standing political dispute between the States concerned.[21] Much of the criticism of the Court's decisions in the *Military and Paramilitary Activities in and against Nicaragua* case (Chapter 5 below) is based on the view that here the Court may have overstepped the limit of judicial caution in this respect.[22]

The complicated circumstances surrounding the *South West Africa* cases (p. 137 below) illustrate the inherent dangers involved in the exercise of concurrent jurisdiction when this results in the political and judicial organs of the organization reaching incompatible conclusions. That case demonstrates how in exceptional conditions the fact that a case is *sub judice* in the International Court will not preclude the General Assembly from exercising its own responsibilities under the Charter, even to the extent of taking action which may not be compatible with the judicial pronouncements of the Court, if this is felt to be imperative for overriding reasons of policy or principle. The *U.S. Diplomatic and Consular Staff in Tehran* and the *Military and Paramilitary Activities in and against Nicaragua* cases on the other hand show that the Court will not allow the fact that a dispute has both political and legal aspects to prevent it from examining the legal questions that are involved. But these are controversial matters, on which the last word has not yet been said.

The Court has a special role in the working of the United Nations Administrative Tribunal and the ILO Administrative Tribunal. For these Tribunals, a system of recourse has been instituted. This resembles the continental *Cassation,* that is a form of review on defined questions of law, after which the Tribunal's judgment is either affirmed or revised (p. 149 below).[23]

WHAT THE COURT IS NOT

The establishment of the Court as one of the principal organs of the United Nations means that it exists on a par with the other principal organs. It is neither a position of superiority nor in one of inferiority in relation to the others.

One consequence of this is that the Court is not a general "constitutional Court" of the United Nations. There is no duty on any organ of the United Nations, on any State or on any person to seek its opinion when a legal question, including a question of the interpretation of an instrument such as the Charter or the Rules of Procedure, arises in the course of the activities of an organ. The San Francisco Conference decided that each organ of the United Nations would be free itself to interpret the Charter as and when circumstances require. This does not *prevent* the Court from giving its opinion on these matters when it is required to do so in due form. This has been applied in practice in two ways. Thus, when the President of the Security Council, the representative of the Ukraine, once explained that the Court could not be regarded as a kind of court of appeal from the decisions of the General Assembly or the Security Council, no member of the Council dissented.[24]

The Court itself has pointed out that no provision of the Statute or Rules contemplates that the Court should decline to take cognizance of one aspect of a dispute merely because that dispute has other aspects, however important. This means that if it has jurisdiction, the Court can exercise concurrent jurisdiction alongside other organs of the United Nations. It has not regarded the fact that a dispute or situation is before one of the political organs of the United Nations as *in itself* an obstacle to its examining those legal aspects of the matter as properly come within its jurisdiction, if it is requested in due form to dò so. The Court has several times pointed out that the fact that a given matter is at one and the same time before the Court and one of the political organs, albeit different aspects of the same dispute, is no bar to the admissibility of such a case. The Court applied this principle in the *United States Diplomatic and Consular Staff in Tehran* case, observing: "It is for the Court, the principal judicial organ of the United Nations, to resolve any legal questions that may be in issue between parties to a dispute; and the resolution of such legal questions by the Court may be an important, and sometimes decisive, factor in promoting the peaceful settlement of the dispute."[25]

Since the Court is not a constitutional court for the United Nations system, it has no general power of judicial review to determine the "constitutionality" of the actions or decisions of any other organ or subdivision of the United Nations. It can only act in response to a contentious or advisory case duly brought before it, although in the course of its decision on a case it may and does give interpretations of the Charter and of the compatibility of the actions of States with their obligations under the Charter. Thus, in contentious cases it has been careful not to trespass on the authority of the Security Council, for example by itself interpreting or re-interpreting previous decisions of that body or otherwise interfering in ongoing action in a matter of which the Security Council is seised.[26] In its advisory opinions it has been called upon to pronounce upon questions of general importance to the Organization. Examples include the "legal personality" of the United Nations; the question whether the cost of "peace-keeping" operations initiated by the Security Council in the Congo and in the Middle East properly were "expenses of the Organization" for budgetary purposes within the competence of the General Assembly under Article 17 of the Charter; the legal consequences resulting from the termination of South Africa's mandate over Namibia (formerly South West Africa) and the continued presence of South Africa in that territory in defiance of this termination; and questions concerning the application of the Headquarters Agreement with the United States and the Convention on the Privileges and Immunities of the United Nations.[27]

The Court is not the "guardian of the Charter" in the way that in some federal and other States a constitutional court is the "guardian of the constitution". This could not be possible in the context of international relations in their present state of development. A federal constitutional court presupposes a federal system - which the United Nations system is not.

The International Court is not a supreme court of appeal exercising superior or appellate jurisdiction from other international or national tribunals or courts, and in effect trying the case *de novo*. It can only exercise appellate jurisdiction when this is expressly conferred on it, such as is found in the constituent instrument of the International Civil Aviation Organization, the 1944 Convention on International Civil Aviation. In the exercise of its normal jurisdiction it can examine questions of the possible validity or nullity of an arbitral award and the obligation to comply with it.[28] That, however, is not an "appeal". A court of appeal has a completely different hierarchical relationship to a lower court, which is subordinated by law to the former and its judgments can be wholly or partially overturned. There is no formal international hierarchy of courts.

The International Court is not a court exercising jurisdiction in criminal cases between States (or between a State and an individual or individuals). The States that appear before it do so within the context of general international law. The cases may be and often do involve allegations of internationally wrongful behaviour, but this is wrongful behaviour in the sense of the law governing international responsibility. There are no "defendants" or "accused" States in the Court. The parties are referred to as "applicant" and "respondent". This usage reflects their status of equality both *vis-à-vis* the Court and in relation to each other. Article 34, paragraph 1, of the Statute provides that only States may be parties in cases before the Court. This, apart from any other considerations, precludes individuals from being arraigned by a State or any other body before the Court.

The recently established International Criminal Court (ICC) has been set up to prosecute and try individuals accused of committing genocide, crimes against humanity and the most serious war crimes; like its predecessors the *ad-hoc* criminal tribunals for Yugoslavia and Rwanda and more indirectly, the Nuremberg and Tokyo tribunals. However, this is a wholly different function from that of the International Court of Justice. To use an illustrative, if not wholly accurate analogy with national legal systems; if the ICC is meant to play the role of 'High Criminal Court' in the international community, the International Court of Justice is the 'Court of First and Last Instance' in relation to non-criminal matters, specifically inter-State disputes.

The International Court a not a legislative body established to formulate new rules of law. In a sense this is stating the obvious. Nevertheless, confusion persists. The Court, like all courts, applies the *existing* law. It does not "create" new rules of law either for the parties to a given dispute or for the international community at large. Of course, the Court, like any court, does not simply "discover" what the law is and deliver a judgment in some mystic way. The Anglo-American common-law fiction that the law exists ready-made in the breasts of the judges is not accepted in international law. At the same time, all courts, regardless of the legal system in which they operate, will be confronted with issues in which the law is unclear, or where there is controversy over the content or continued validity of a given rule of law. In determining such cases or applying norms and principles within a given factual context a court will clarify the law, even if only in a negative sense, by stating what is not the law. In this sense, the International Court has made a monumental contribution to the clarification and to the development of international law. It is true to say that the massive advances in the codification of international law accomplished under the auspices of the United Nations could not have occurred but for the clarification and exposition of the law by the World Court. The Court is not bound by its earlier decisions in the sense of the Anglo-American common law, nor are other international or national tribunals, although the Court's judgments do normally carry great authority and persuasive power. Indeed, it is quite rare for any other international tribunal to disregard them when relevant.

Even less is the Court an academy of international law, or a philosophical or moral society engaged in the formulation of new canons of behaviour for the international community, beyond what international law requires. The Court has included amongst its members many great authorities on international law. Its judges are almost universally persons of long experience and learned in their art. That does not make the Court an institution for research or the teaching of international law. This signifies that when engaged on the business of adjudication, the Court pronounces itself on questions relevant to the case at bar. This is not to say that philosophical or moral considerations play no role in the decision of individual cases. Far from it. But they do so only to the extent that they form part of the corpus of existing international law and are necessary for adequate reasoning of the decision by the Court.

The creative role of the Court for international law has recently been described in the following terms:

> Virtually all of them [the judges] ... recognize the creative element in the judicial function; no one thinks of himself as a phonograph playing the recording of custom and treaty. They have made us aware – if we did not already know it – of the discretionary elements in the art of judging: the selection of "relevant" facts, the need to give specific meaning to broad, undefined, concepts, the subtle process of generalizing from past cases, the uses of analogy and metaphor, the inevitable choices between competing rules and principles. These elements are to be found as well in domestic courts, and most notably in constitutional litigation. But they are more conspicuous and troublesome in international law. One reason obviously is the large area of uncertainty in international law, especially unwritten customary law, and not infrequently on the meaning of basic treaty law.[29]

The International Court then, like any other court of law, is primarily engaged in deciding legal disputes, here for a specific society, the international community, and also in the provision of legal advice to authorized organs of the United Nations. It does so by applying relatively objective legal criteria through judicial techniques. The Court, as one of the means of peaceful settlement of disputes, is part of the machinery of international diplomacy, albeit one with special characteristics. As such it does not operate outside the limits of international politics. The Court is sensitive to political developments in the international society and to the realities of the international political system of sovereign States with differing power potentials, traditions, aspirations and goals. When States are unable to resolve their disputes by the normal interplay of diplomacy, the Court is a forum in which the dispute can be determined according to the objective criteria of law. The Court can only act, however, if the parties themselves are willing to allow objective legal criteria to be applied. But that is another matter.

THE COURT AND THE SPECIALIZED AGENCIES

The United Nations does not exist alone in the world of the organized international community. It stands at the centre of a complicated system of international organizations, established by inter-governmental agreement and having wide international responsibilities in economic, social, cultural, educational, health, communications and related fields. The Charter makes it possible for these organizations to be brought into formal relationship with the United Nations by means of agreements approved by the General Assembly. These are called Specialized Agencies, and they form part of the United Nations family. These organizations are autonomous and independent. At the same time they are subject to certain overriding controls of the United Nations itself, and in major political situations are guided by United Nations decisions. Today they include the Food and Agriculture Organization

(FAO), the World Health Organization (WHO), the International Bank for Reconstruction and Development (IBRD), the International Civil Aviation Organization (ICAO), the International Development Association (IDA), the International Finance Corporation (IFC), the International Fund for Agricultural Development, the International Labour Organization (ILO), the International Maritime Organization (IMO), the International Monetary Fund (IMF), the International Telecommunication Union (ITU), the World Intellectual Property Organization (WIPO), the World Meteorological Organization (WMO), the United Nations Educational, Scientific and Cultural Organization (UNESCO), the United Nations Industrial Development Organization (UNIDO) , the Universal Postal Union (UPU), and, for some purposes, the International Atomic Energy Agency (IAEA). Most members of the United Nations are members of most of these Specialized Agencies. The United Nations exercises loose control over the relations between the Specialized Agencies and the Court through the power of the General Assembly, under Article 96, paragraph 2, of the Charter, to authorize an organization to request an advisory opinion on matters arising in the course of its activities. This is done through the *Relationship Agreements* by which an organization becomes formally associated with and part of the United Nations system.[30]

The contacts between the Court and these Agencies are spread over several dimensions.

First: Article 96, paragraph 2, of the Charter, which deals with the right to request an advisory opinion, empowers the General Assembly to authorize organs of the Specialized Agencies to request advisory opinions on legal questions arising within the scope of their activities. This point arose within the context of the request by the World Health Organization for an advisory opinion on the *Legality of Nuclear Weapons in an Armed Conflict*, where the Court declined to render an opinion on the grounds that the request fell outside the scope of that specialized agency's activities. Appropriate organs of each of the Specialized Agencies, except the Universal Postal Union (which has an internal system for settling legal disputes), are now authorized to request advisory opinions. The Relationship Agreements specify which organs of an agency may initiate a request. This authorization does not extend to questions concerning the mutual relationships of the United Nations and the Specialized Agencies, an aspect left to the exclusive competence of the Economic and Social Council in exercise of its general role of supervisor and coordinator of the Specialized Agencies, and whenever an organ of a Specialized Agency decides to request an advisory opinion, it has to inform the Economic and Social Council of its action. This seems to be a formality.

Against this, autonomous bodies within the United Nations itself, such as the United Nations Children's Fund (UNICEF), the United Nations Environment Programme (UNEP) or the United Nations Conference on Trade and Development (UNCTAD), to give some examples, are not autonomous organizations whatever degree of autonomy they have within the United Nations. None of these bodies has been authorized to request advisory opinions, and none of them has yet shown any need to request one.

Second: Article 34 of the Statute of the Court requires the Court to inform every public international organization, whether it is a Specialized Agency or not, whenever the constituent instrument of that organization or a treaty adopted thereunder is in question in a case before the Court. That provision also empowers the Court to request any public international organization to furnish it with information relevant to a case before it, and requires the Court to receive such information presented by such an organization of its own initiative. The Court has occasionally made use of this facility in contentious cases and the organizations approached have all furnished replies. These include among the Specialized Agencies the ICAO, ILO and the WHO, and from other intergovernmental organizations the Organization of American States and the Organization of African Unity.

The Relationship Agreements contain undertakings by the Specialized Agencies to furnish information requested by the Court. However, the Rules of Court give the organization concerned discretion as to its reply. Experience has shown that in some circumstances it could not be appropriate for the organization to submit observations touching upon the substance of the case before the Court.[31]

In addition, most of the constituent instruments of the Specialized Agencies, unlike the Charter of the United Nations itself, contain a provision regarding the settlement of disputes as to the interpretation or application of the instrument, and in some of these disputes the Court may be referred to. This is a normal compromissory clause and provides the basis for contentious litigation between States members of that organization. There has been no instance of this procedure being invoked. An unusual provision is found in the International Civil Aviation Convention of 1944. This envisages a complex dispute-settlement procedure through the Council of the Organization, with the possibility in given circumstances of an appeal from the Council's decision to the Court. Instances of this occurred in 1972 and 1989.

These cases were both presented as appeals from a decision of the ICAO Council. In the first India appealed from a decision of the ICAO Council on some complaints by Pakistan, and in the second Iran appealed from a decision which did not satisfy it on an issue arising out of the aerial incident of 3 July 1988 when United States armed forces accidentally shot down an Iranian civil airliner. As a result the Court has been empowered to exercise "a certain measure of supervision" over a decision of a Specialized Agency. The consent of the parties to the Court's exercise of "supervisory jurisdiction" had been conferred through their common membership in ICAO.[32]

Contrary to earlier expectations, these innovations have not led to any noticeable increase in the judicial business of the Court. Only three Specialized Agencies have availed themselves of their right to request advisory opinions, UNESCO, IMO and WHO.[33] This has led the Secretary-General, in his *Agenda for Peace* mentioned earlier, to recommend that organs duly authorized "turn to the Court more frequently for advisory opinions".

As expected, in dealing with requests from the Specialized Agencies, the Court has followed the same principle that it enunciated in relation to the United Nations itself. It has asserted its duty to co-operate in the activities of the organization concerned while preserving the strictly judicial character of its own actions.

COMPLIANCE WITH THE COURT'S DECISIONS

As mentioned in the previous chapter, the international arbitral procedure of the nineteenth century came as a matter of course to include in every arbitration agreement an implied obligation that the decisions of the arbitral tribunal would be complied with in good faith. This is also a fundamental principle of the law governing international litigation before the International Court.

When the international community was not organized on the political level, no ready-made machinery existed, or indeed could exist, to ensure compliance with the terms of an arbitral award which the judgment debtor State did not like. But when the League of Nations was established, opportunity was taken to insert in Article 13 of the Covenant a stipulation to the effect that in the event of failure to carry out a decision of the Permanent Court, the Council should be empowered to propose what steps should be taken to give effect to it. Instances of this were very rare, and in fact the problem of the execution and enforcement of the decisions of the Permanent Court did not appear to be a serious one. Since the jurisdiction of the Court was based on the consent of the parties, it may be assumed that they consented in advance to comply with the judgment. In addition, the unanimity rule for the adoption of decisions of the Council could have become a factor to deprive that provision of the Covenant of much of its practical significance.

These ideas have been included in the Charter of the United Nations.

The basic principle, that the judgment of the Court in a contentious case is final and without appeal and is only binding on the parties in respect of that particular case, is enunciated in Articles 59 and 60 of the Statute. That is supplemented by two important provisions which, having broader political implications, are contained in the Charter.

The first is Article 94, paragraph 1. That lays down shortly and simply: "Each member of the United Nations undertakes to comply with the decision of the International Court of Justice in any case to which it is a party." A State which is not a member of the United Nations but which is a party to the Statute of the Court, and a State which is not a party to the Statute of the Court but which is a party to litigation before the Court, has to give a corresponding undertaking before it is admitted to the Court.

The second appears in paragraph 2 of that Article: "If any party to a case fails to perform the obligations incumbent upon it under a judgment rendered by the Court, the other party may have recourse to the Security Council, which may, if it deems necessary, make recommendations or decide upon measures to be taken to give effect to the judgment." The underlying implication of this provision is that failure to comply with a decision of the Court creates a new political problem, and the Security Council is given wide powers to deal with the consequent situation. This type of situation would be similar to that which confronted the federal authorities in the United States in the 1950s, after the leading decision of the Supreme Court in the landmark *Brown v. Board of Education* case, when segregation in the schools was held to be unconstitutional. Local authorities in Little Rock, Arkansas, defied the Supreme Court by removing black students from a high school, requiring President Eisenhower to send federal troops to ensure compliance with that judgment.

In addition to Article 94, Article 41 of the Statute requires that notice of any provisional measures suggested by the Court should be given both to the parties and to the Security Council. This does not place the matter on the agenda of the Security Council: if either party wishes for that, it has to follow the normal procedure of the Security Council. On the other hand, if the dispute in relation to which the case was brought before the Court is also before the Security Council, whether before or after the provisional measures were indicated, no further action is required for the measures indicated to be on the record of the Security Council.

Although such "enforcement" action has never been undertaken by the Security Council until now following a failure to comply with a Court judgment, there have been a few instances of complete or alleged failure to comply with a final judgment of the Court.

In the first contentious case before the Court, the *Corfu Channel* case, the Albanian Government of the day refused to pay the damages awarded to the United Kingdom. Recourse to the Security Council was not invoked to secure compliance with this judgment. The United Kingdom resorted to other methods in an attempt to recover the sum in question, and that led to the *Monetary Gold Removed from Rome* case (p. 147 below). In May 1992, after the change of regime in Albania and the resumption of diplomatic relations between the two countries, a settlement was reached, and the judgment debt was paid in full.[34]

In the *Anglo Iranian Oil Company* case (p. 145 below), Iran rejected an order of the Court indicating provisional measures which it felt was inequitable and which had been made against the background of considerable tension in Anglo-Iranian relations. The United Kingdom complained to the Security Council about Iran's failure to comply with those provisional measures. This encountered serious political difficulties. While the Security Council was considering the matter, events both in Iran and at the Court overtook the complaint and debate and the Security Council decided to postpone the discussion of the question until the Court, "which was seized of certain aspects of the matter, had ruled on its own competence to deal with them". The Court later found in its judgment of 22 June 1952 that it had no jurisdiction in the case.

In the *Right of Passage* case in 1960 (p. 152 below), the Indian Government did not so much reject or defy the judgment of the Court as render it irrelevant by annexing Portuguese territories (Goa) in 1961. That in effect was the same thing. This, however, was perhaps a special case – it certainly was in political terms because of the process of decolonization and the prevailing attitude towards it within the United Nations. That superseded the question which Portugal had presented to the Court in the first place. Portugal brought the question of Goa before the Security Council at the end of 1961, but no substantive action was taken. In 1974 Portugal formally acquiesced in the annexation of the enclaves.

In 1975 a minor dispute between Iceland and the United Kingdom arising out of the "cod war" and the 1974 judgment in the *Fisheries Jurisdiction* case (p. 167 below) was brought before the Security Council by Iceland, but no decision was taken.

Although the Iranian Government refused to take part in the Court proceedings or to accept the Court's decisions in the *U.S. Diplomatic and Consular Staff in Tehran* case, a solution to the question of the U.S. diplomats held hostage by the revolutionary Iranian Government was ultimately reached within the context of the Algiers Accord in which the Court's rulings played a definite if indirect role. In its resolution 461 of 31 December 1979, the Security Council took account of the Court's order indicating provisional measures which should be taken, and decided in the event of non-compliance with that resolution to adopt effective measures within the framework of Chapter VII of the Charter, regarding the powers of the Security Council in face of threats to the peace, breaches of the peace and acts of aggression. That was the most far-reaching resolution of the Security Council in connection with enforcing compliance with a decision of the Court.

To the end of 1991 the United States refused to acknowledge the jurisdiction of the Court in the case brought against it by Nicaragua and refused to accept any of the decisions of the Court in that case (Chapter 5 below). Consequently, it refused to take any of the actions required of it in the executory provisions of the judgment on the merits of 27 June 1986. Nicaragua accordingly brought the matter before the Security Council in reliance on Article 94 of the Charter. This was the first direct invocation of

Article 94 in relation to a decision on the merits of a case by the judgment creditor itself. The negative vote of the United States prevented the adoption of any resolution by the Security Council. Nicaragua thereupon turned to the 41st session of the General Assembly which, without thorough examination of the matter, adopted resolution 41/31 on 3 November 1986, reading:

> *The General Assembly,*
> *Having heard* the statement made by the Minister for External Relations of the Republic of Nicaragua,
> *Recalling* Security Council resolutions 530 (1983) of 19 May 1983 and 562 (1985) of 10 May 1985,
> *Aware* that, under the Charter of the United Nations, the International Court of Justice is the principal judicial organ of the United Nations and that each Member undertakes to comply with the decision of the Court in any case to which it is a party,
> *Considering* that Article 36, paragraph 6, of the Statute of the Court provides that "in the event of a dispute as to whether the Court has jurisdiction, the matter shall be settled by the decision of the Court",
> *Taking note* of the Judgment of the International Court of Justice of 27 June 1986 in the case of "Military and Paramilitary Activities in and against Nicaragua",
> *Having considered* the events that have taken place in and against Nicaragua since the Judgment was rendered, in particular the continued financing by the United States of America of military and other activities in and against Nicaragua,
> *Emphasizing* the obligation of States, under customary international law, not to intervene in the internal affairs of other States,
> 1. *Urgently calls* for full and immediate compliance with the Judgment of the International Court of Justice of 27 June 1986 in the case of "Military and Paramilitary Activities in and against Nicaragua" in conformity with the relevant provisions of the Charter of the United Nations;
> 2. *Requests* the Secretary-General to keep the General Assembly informed on the implementation of this resolution.

Similar resolutions were adopted at the 42nd (1987) to the 44th (1989) sessions. After a change of government in Nicaragua, Nicaragua discontinued the case in the International Court, and the General Assembly at its 45th session (1990) deferred further consideration.

In relation to the situation in Bosnia-Herzegovina (p. 203 below), the Security Council, in its resolution 819 of 16 April 1993, took note of one of the three operative paragraphs of the Court's first order indicating provisional measures in the *Application of the Convention on the Prevention and Punishment of the Crime of Genocide* case. This is unusual. That paragraph had been adopted by the Court unanimously but the Russian member of the Court had dissented from the second operative paragraph. The third. which was addressed to both parties, was also unanimous. This is the first occasion on which the Security Council has picked out only one operative paragraph of a decision of the Court, and has not referred to the judgment or order as a whole. The Security Council took no action on the second order indicating provisional measures. On the other hand, the General Assembly, in its resolution 48/88 of 20 December 1993, like the Security Council before it, took note of one of the operative paragraphs of the

Court's second order indicating provisional measures.

It is clear from this survey that the efficacy of Article 94, paragraph 2, of the Charter as a backing for the decisions of the Court depends on the general functioning of the Security Council at a given moment. The instances of recourse to the Security Council in the event of non-compliance with a decision of the Court all occurred at times of great international tension. That tension was manifested amongst other things by the absence of unanimity amongst the permanent members of the Security Council, making concerted action impossible.

It is important to distinguish between the problems of compliance faced by a State which has been brought unwillingly before the Court on the basis of a unilateral application and that of compliance with decisions in cases where the parties are in agreement that the case should be resolved by the Court.

It is evident that a State will be far less likely to fail to comply with an unfavourable decision in a case which it has specifically agreed to submit to the Court's jurisdiction than in a case in which -for whatever reason -it has little interest in resolving the dispute on the basis of the existing law or legal considerations in general. Such unwillingness can stem from many factors, for example preference for a diplomatic settlement of a given dispute, dissatisfaction with elements of the existing law relevant to the case, or the conviction that the dispute is not ripe for settlement at the given moment. It should be borne in mind that unwillingness to submit a dispute to the Court is not necessarily indicative of a lack of faith in international law in general or in the Court in particular. A Minister for Foreign Affairs and a cautious legal adviser could well take the view that the risk of losing the case outweighs the disadvantage of leaving the matter unsettled.

The submission of disputes to the Court remains an exceptional if important means of resolving international problems. However, one should not and cannot in fairness surmise from this state of affairs or from the previously mentioned instances of partial or total non-compliance of States with the Court's judgments that the decisions are habitually ignored or are only accepted when the questions at issue are of marginal importance.

The Court has been presented with an appreciable – if perhaps insufficient – number of disputes, many of which involved important questions, and which touched on interests of real concern to the parties. Nor can it be assumed that those disputes which were brought before the Court on the basis of some form of agreement were of lesser importance to the States concerned. This group of cases included most of the maritime delimitation cases as well as several vexatious border disputes, which, if left unresolved, were potentially capable of seriously impairing relations between the parties.

Thus, despite the real differences involved in the manner in which the dispute can be submitted to the Court, it is important to recognize that States generally comply with the Court's decisions. Two examples, the first concerning a case which was adjudicated on the basis of an agreement between the parties and the second a case involving an "unwilling respondent", will serve to illustrate this.

In a virtually unanimous decision in November 1960, the Court decided in favour of Honduras in a frontier dispute with Nicaragua concerning the validity of an arbitral award rendered by the King of Spain in 1906 (p. 157 below). This dispute, involving sovereignty over a region extending some 500 miles in length and comprising some 5000 square miles of territory with a population of several thousand persons, had troubled relations between the two States over a long period. The dispute was brought before the Court in the guise of another dispute over the validity of that arbitral award.

The decision of the Court served as the basis for the ensuing demarcation of the frontier which was carried out with the assistance of the Organization of American States. Nicaragua withdrew from the area which was duly incorporated into Honduras.[35]

The *Temple of Preah Vihear* case between Cambodia and Thailand also concerned a question of sovereignty over frontier territory (p. 161 below). This dispute had also arisen much earlier, in this instance in the closing years of the last century when colonial expansion by a major power of the period was at its peak. Underlying the dispute was the title to a Temple complex which had been built in the heyday of the Khmer civilization, and which was of deep religious significance and a place of pilgrimage for the Khmer people. Thailand was convinced that the Temple formed part of its territory and national heritage. It laid claim to large areas of what had formerly been part of French Indochina, contending that these areas -including the Temple -had been acquired by coercion at a time when Thailand was unable to resist encroachment. The Court's judgment of 15 June 1962 was in favour of Cambodia. At first the Thai Government declared that it would not adhere to the judgment and stated that the "Temple would be defended to the last drop of blood". Thailand had even sent troop reinforcements to strengthen the armed detachment it had stationed there since 1954 when the French had withdrawn from Indochina. Nevertheless, after a week of tension inside Thailand and with its neighbour, the Thai Government announced it would respect the Court's decision and subsequently withdrew from the area.[36]

A most outstanding instance is furnished by the territorial dispute between Burkina Faso (formerly Upper Volta) and Mali, brought before a Chamber of the Court by a special agreement negotiated through the Organization of African Unity. After the judgment was rendered, the President of each country publicly thanked the Court for settling the dispute (further p. 191 below).[37] Another example from Africa deserves mention. In the dispute between Libya and Chad concerning the "Aouzou Strip", an area comprising a significant portion of Chad's territory and of considerable economic and strategic importance, the Court's decision resulted in the ending of a long and bloody conflict which had brought the two States to the brink of all out war and been the cause of outside military intervention on a number of occasions. The complete withdrawal of Libyan armed forces was carried out voluntarily and in accordance with the Court's judgment, which awarded the disputed area to Chad.

These examples show that even in cases which are emotionally charged and involve important questions of national prestige and "national honour", the Court's decisions are respected. Generally speaking, the Court's decisions, like international law in general, have been complied with, despite the lack of an effective means of ensuring compliance and notwithstanding some notable exceptions.

THE COURT'S FINANCES

Article 33 of the Statute of the Court provides: "The expenses of the Court shall be borne by the United Nations in such a manner as shall be decided by the General Assembly." These expenses include besides the normal costs of running the institution, the annual salaries and pensions of the members of the Court, the Registrar and the staff of the Registry. This remuneration is free of all taxation. The contributions of non-U.N. members which are parties to the Statute are fixed periodically by the General Assembly.

The Court's preliminary draft budget is prepared by the Registrar, and is subject to approval by a special committee comprised of Members of the Court, or by the President if the Court is not sitting. This draft budget is then sent to the UN Secretariat in New York where it is incorporated in the draft budget of the United Nations. That is examined by the Advisory Committee on Administrative and Budgetary Questions which is empowered to make enquiries and corrections. It is then submitted to the General Assembly of the United Nations, where it is adopted by a two-thirds majority after detailed scrutiny in the Budgetary and Administrative Committee. Since 1974 the budget has been drawn up on a biennial basis. The Registrar is responsible for the Court's expenditure. The Court's accounts are audited every year by a Board of Auditors appointed by the General Assembly.

For many years the Court's budget has been fixed at around 0.6% of the total United Nations budget. With the greatly increased work-load, the Court has sought and received some increased funding to provide for several additional posts in the Registry. In two years period 2000-2001, the Court's budget appropriation amounted to US$ 21,481,600. The Court remains one of the least expensive of international institutions.

The annual tax-free salaries of the Members of the Court and of the Registrar are fixed by the General Assembly, the latter on the basis of a proposal by the Court. The other members of the Registry Staff receive salaries corresponding to those of United Nations Staff members of the same rank.

The salaries of the members of the Court are currently fixed at US$ 160,000.00 annually, with the President receiving an extra allowance, and the Vice-President receiving an equivalent allowance on a *per diem* basis for every day on which he exercises the functions of President, subject to an annual maximum. The salary of the Registrar -whose diplomatic status corresponds to that of an ambassador - is fixed at the level of an Assistant Secretary-General of the United Nations. In recent years it has become necessary to make special arrangements to maintain the real level of salaries against monetary inflation and currency fluctuations. A drop in the average age of Members of the Court and the growing tendency, on account of the increased work-load, for them to establish their principal residence at The Hague, have led to the introduction in 1990 of an education grant for their minor children.

THE SECRETARY-GENERAL'S TRUST FUND

In 1989 the Secretary-General established a Trust Fund to assist States in the settlement of disputes through the Court. This is intended as a practical means of overcoming financial obstacles to the judicial settlement of international disputes by the Court. It is funded by voluntary contributions from States, intergovernmental organizations, national institutions, nongovernmental organizations and natural and juridical persons. The Financial Regulations and Rules and auditing procedures of the United Nations apply to the administration of this Trust Fund, concerning which the Secretary-General reports to the General Assembly.

Experience has demonstrated the worth of this initiative.[38]

THE SEAT OF THE COURT

Article 22, paragraph 1, of the Statute provides that the seat of the Court shall be established at The Hague. The International Court is the only organ of the United Nations the seat of which is provided for in its constituent instrument. The reasons for the choice of The Hague can be traced to the intricacies of European politics at the time of the Hague Peace Conferences (Chapter I above). This provision was not altered in 1945. In the 1970s the Court suggested amending this provision but this did not attract sufficient support in the General Assembly.[39]

Criticism that the choice of The Hague might deter States outside Europe from utilizing the Court, or that it betrays an alleged European bias of international law, is not borne out. Article 22 also permits the Court to sit and exercise its functions elsewhere whenever the Court considers it desirable. This is amplified in Article 55 of the Rules. This enables the Court to conduct all or part of the oral proceedings elsewhere than at The Hague, but before making a decision, it is to ascertain the views of the parties. So far there has been no request to hold proceedings elsewhere than at The Hague, and there have been instances in which the parties have insisted that the case should be tried at The Hague, away from local influences.

The fact that seat of the Court is in a small European country with a long tradition of support for the Court and for other institutions of international law seems to work to the advantage of the Court.

The offices of the Court and the Hall of Justice are located in the Peace Palace. This was built with funds donated by the Scots-American philanthropist Andrew Carnegie and materials contributed by many States from all over the world. It was opened in 1913. The United Nations rents the premises – for the exclusive use of the Court -from a private foundation which bears the name of Carnegie himself. In 1978 the Dutch Government presented a new building to the Peace Palace complex, providing attractive and modem office space for the judges. This office building was recently extended with a new wing in 1997 with additional funding by the Dutch Government.

The Peace Palace is shared with several other institutions devoted to the peaceful settlement of disputes, and the study of international law. These include the Permanent Court of Arbitration, the Academy of International Law, and the Peace Palace Library, a major international law library. The Small Hall of Justice is used by the Permanent Court of Arbitration, and it may be used for arbitrations not conducted within the framework of the Permanent Court of Arbitration.

Generally, the relations between the Court and its host State have been harmonious. The fact that the Court is situated in The Hague, away from New York and Geneva where the political activities of the United Nations are concentrated, has certainly contributed to maintaining the Court's independence and discreteness from the political organs of the Organization. The Hague hosts, in addition to the Court and the Permanent Court of Arbitration, the International Criminal Tribunal for the Former Yugoslavia and has been chosen as the seat for the newly established International Criminal Court. This has led to it being sometimes referred to as "the judicial capital of the world"; a designation which although not completely accurate, is not wholly unearned.

REVISION OF THE STATUTE

The Statute being an integral part of the Charter, its revision is accomplished in the same manner as the revision of the Charter. That is governed by Article 108 of the Charter. Amendments come into force for all members of the United Nations when they have been adopted by a vote of two thirds of the members of the General Assembly and ratified in accordance with their respective constitutional processes by two thirds of the members of the United Nations, including all the permanent members of the Security Council. Article 69 of the Statute adds that the participation of States which are not members of the United Nations in the process of amending the Statute shall take place on the basis of decisions of the General Assembly adopted on the recommendation of the Security Council. General Assembly resolution 2520 (XXIV) of 4 December 1969 allows such States to participate in the General Assembly in the same manner as members of the United Nations, and they are included in the calculation of the two thirds required for the entry into force of amendments to the Statute.

In addition, Article 70 of the Statute empowers the Court itself to propose such amendments as it may deem necessary. In 1969 the Court, as indicated, did propose an amendment to Article 22 of the Statute regarding the seat of the Court. This was not accepted by the General Assembly which finally decided not to continue the discussion.

3

THE JUDGES

Who are the persons in whose hands the power to decide international legal disputes is entrusted? How do they reach their position?

The Court consists of fifteen Members, each of a different nationality, elected independently by the Security Council and the General Assembly. Each Member serves for a term of nine years (commencing on 6 February following his election) and is eligible for re-election. The term of office of one third of the Members comes to an end each third year. An occasional vacancy, caused for example by the resignation or death of a Member of the Court, is filled in the same way. A Member elected at an occasional election takes office immediately and serves out the remainder of his predecessor's term.

The process by which these elections are conducted is complex, and unavoidably so.

THE JUDGES' QUALIFICATIONS

As a former President of the Court has put it, "A judge – as needs no emphasis – is bound to be impartial, objective, detached, disinterested and unbiased".[1] A clearer statement of what is required of all judges of the International Court of Justice could not be found.

Every political society faces a delicate problem when it has to determine how its judges are appointed, especially the members of the senior courts and tribunals. The international society is no exception. The natural aspiration of those having power to appoint judges in whom they have confidence, persons believed to be sympathetic to their political and social aims and ideals, is not always reconciled with equally natural desires for an independent judiciary (though it must not be assumed that there is an unbridgeable gap between the two). Conflicts between those having political power and the judiciary are always painful. In Western legal systems this type of problem is largely overcome by a tradition of good faith coupled with a delicately balanced system of checks and balances in which the representative political institutions (the Parliaments) usually have a say. But ultimately, in most countries, the responsibility for the appointment of the judiciary rests with the executive branch of the government.

The difficulty in the international field is that the international political life is structured entirely differently. There is no executive as such, responsible to a constituency for the proper conduct of its affairs. In the last resort the choice of the international judge is, as is the choice of a judge within a State, a political operation, in which an attempt has been made to impose some limitations on the free play of political aspirations. But in international affairs the nature of that political operation is fundamentally different from what it is in the internal life of a State.

These differences are reflected in the provisions of the Court's Statute regarding the qualifications of the judges and their election.

The qualifications are of two distinct kinds – those of a personal nature and those of a more general quality.

The requirements of a personal nature are found in Article 2: "The Court shall be composed of a body of independent judges elected, regardless of their nationality from among persons of high moral character, who possess the qualifications required in their respective countries for appointment to the highest judicial offices, or are jurisconsults of recognized competence in international law."

There is no international machinery to establish that a candidate possesses these qualifications. In practice, as will be seen, some safeguards have been inserted into the Statute and others have been developed in international procedures to maintain the high standards of professional competence required of the judges. This aspect is left to the good sense of the individual States. Most of them have an interest in seeing that the Court is composed of eminently qualified persons and that the reputation of the Court as a whole remains high. That interest does not only derive from the possibility, however slight it may be as a matter of political reality (keeping in mind that the Court can only decide cases when the parties consent that it should, as will be described in the next chapter), that any State may become involved in litigation before the Court, whether as applicant or as respondent. It is also connected with the natural desire of all States that authoritative pronouncements on questions of international law should be made by as "strong" a Court as possible.

REGIONAL DISTRIBUTION OF SEATS

The more general requirement appears in Article 9 of the Statute: "At every election, the electors shall bear in mind not only that the persons to be elected should individually possess the qualifications required, but also that in the body as a whole the representation of the main forms of civilization and of the principal legal systems of the world should be assured." That requirement introduces the political factor into the composition of the Court.

The formula – representation of the main forms of civilization and of the principal legal systems of the world – is a refined version of the cruder principle of "equitable geographical distribution" which the Charter incorporates to govern the allocation of elective seats in most of the organs of the United Nations. The formula has been in common use since 1920 for the international legal organs. It is found, for example, in the Statute of the International Law Commission.

Both formulas assume that the world is neatly divided into a number of clearly defined and unchanging regions and forms of civilization and legal systems (the division itself being both comprehensive and static), each of which has competent organs capable of negotiating with its partners. But the realities of the international situation are quite different, and the assumption has little justification.

In this connection, one of the results of the process of decolonization is that the earlier *relatively* clear distinction between the "principal legal systems of the world" and the "main forms of civilization" has become blurred. Most of the newly independent States maintain at least to some extent the legal system inherited from the former colonial power. As a consequence the element of "principal legal system" is losing ground to the element of regional distribution reflected in the expression "main forms of civilization" as now understood in current United Nations practice. This process has been accelerated in the 1990s by the break-up of federal States in Central and Eastern Europe, including the former Soviet Union, Czechoslovakia and Yugoslavia, and the disappearance of the Socialist regimes in that part of the world.

The election of Members of the Court encounters two sets of problems. The first concerns the manner in which the places on the Court will be allocated *to* the main forms of civilization and the principal legal systems of the world. The second concerns the manner in which, after the primary allocation has been made, the positions will be shared *within* the main forms of civilization and the principal legal systems of the world. This latter aspect obliquely introduces the factor of the nationality of the individual candidates.

These problems are resolved partly by a series of "understandings" which have either been negotiated diplomatically or have emerged *de facto* in the United Nations. These understandings are essential both for the smooth conduct of the elections and for the successful functioning of the Court. The membership of the Court must reflect the international community as it is, not in an idealized form. Nevertheless, in the last resort, if real contest ensues, the answer can only be reached through a trial of political strength in the electoral organs.

The first of these understandings is a tradition that a candidate who is a national of any one of the five permanent members of the Security Council China, France, Russia, the United Kingdom and the United States of America -will be elected to the Court.[2] This is the modern answer to the demand of the Great Powers for presence on any permanent international judicial organ -one aspect which the Hague Conference of 1907 was unable to solve in the absence of an organized international political community, and which was only solved, along approximately similar lines, by the League of Nations. Although the Republic of China (Taiwan) refrained in 1967 from pressing the issue, presumably because of the shifting opinion in the political organs concerning the question of Chinese representation (which was resolved in 1971 when the General Assembly recognized the People's Republic of China as the only representative of China in the Organization), there was no reason to believe that this practice had been modified. Indeed although there was no candidate having the nationality of the People's Republic of China until 1984, the understanding remained intact. In 1984 the Chinese candidate received the necessary majority in both the Security Council and the General Assembly, and once again one Member of the Court is a national of each one of the permanent members of the Security Council.

The second of these understandings is that the regional distribution of seats among the Members of the Court should roughly parallel the regional distribution of seats on the Security Council, also at present composed of 15 members. This does not signify that every member on the Council is correspondingly assured of having one of its nationals on the Court, but that the regional balance within the Security Council is loosely reflected in the membership of the Court.

This arrangement dates from the mid-1960s. Its origin can be traced to the decolonization which took place during the first two decades after the establishment of the United Nations. The composition of various United Nations organs, in particular the Security Council and the Court, had not initially kept pace with the changed structure of the international community. This caused much dissatisfaction on the part of the newly independent States at the time. This dissatisfaction resulted in the expansion of the Security Council from 11 to 15 members in 1965 to take account of the altered composition of the United Nations.[3] Discontent at the composition of the Court persisted and reached a peak in the General Assembly of 1966, immediately after the 1966 judgment in the *South West Africa* cases. This led to the present arrangement in which the make-up of the Court has been brought into line with that of the Security Council. Consequently the representation of the regional groupings in the United Nations among the Members of the Court has altered perceptibly since 1966. For the composition of the Court in recent years, see Appendix III.

A glance at the shifts in the regional make-up of the Court at various key moments in the Court's history from 1946 until the present time will illustrate this.

The first election of Members of the present Court in 1946 was held on the basis of decisions reached at the San Francisco Conference. This was the first – and only – general election to fill all 15 seats and not the usual third of Members as has been the case pursuant to Article 13 of the Statute in all elections since then. The absolute majority in the Security Council was six, and in the General Assembly 34.

After complicated procedural discussions and several inconclusive ballots extending over two days, the election resulted in the following "regional composition" of the Court: the Western European and other States, including the three "Western" permanent members of the Council, France, the United Kingdom, and the United States -and also including the "old Dominions" of the British Commonwealth -Australia, Canada, New Zealand and South Africa -obtained six seats. The Latin American group consisting of all of the independent Spanish or Portuguese speaking Republics of Central and South America acquired four seats. The Eastern European Socialist group consisting of the Soviet Union and the States of Eastern Europe obtained three seats. The Afro-Asian group, which then consisted of the independent States of those regions including the Republic of China with a permanent seat in the Security Council, received two seats. On this occasion, immediately after the Second World War, the former Axis Powers and most of the neutral States during the War were not yet members of the United Nations or parties to the Statute and consequently played no part in the election.[4]

When the election of 1966 was held, the process of decolonization was already in an advanced stage and had reached the point at which most of the former colonies in Africa and Asia had gained full independence and membership in the United Nations. This, together with dissatisfaction at the Court's composition felt by most formerly colonized States to be at least partly responsible for the controversial judgment in the *South West Africa* cases,[5] combined to produce a major long-term impact on the regional distribution of seats on the Court.

This was the first election in which the required absolute majority in the Security Council was eight, completely outnumbering the permanent members. The necessary absolute majority in the General Assembly had risen to 63. After numerous inconclusive ballots in both the Security Council and the General Assembly, the election resulted in a new regional distribution. The Western European and other States received five seats, including the three permanent members of the Security Council. The Eastern European Socialist States received two seats, including the USSR. Latin America retained two seats. The Afro-Asian group, without China as a result of the persistent and continuing controversy over the issue of Chinese representation in the UN, received six seats, two of which went to African States, and four to Asian States.

A comparison of this Court with that of 1946 shows a loss of one place by the Western European and related States, one seat by the Socialist States of Eastern Europe, and two seats by Latin America, all in favour of the newly independent States of Africa and Asia. While this must not lead to snap conclusions concerning any supposed radical impact upon the working of the Court and its decisions, clearly the expanded representativeness of the Court's membership reflected the changing structure of the international community.[6]

The regular election of 1969 underlined this process and demonstrated the increasing importance of the African group of States within the UN decision making process. The significance of this election in an examination of the regional distribution of seats on the

Court is that it brought the number of seats held by nationals of African States to three. The African Group has maintained this number since then. The regional distribution of seats on the Court as a result of this election was now as follows: Western Europe and Other States five seats, Eastern Europe two seats, Latin America two seats, Asia three seats and Africa three seats.[7]

This distribution showed no major shifts until the election of 1987. The relevance of that election within this context was that it saw a major effort by the English speaking States of the Caribbean, to obtain a place on the Court. This effort succeeded in having a national of an English speaking Caribbean State, Guyana, elected to the Court for the first time.

This election confirmed the operation of the understanding that, except where a candidate is a national of one of the permanent members of the Security Council, if there is a competition between two States for a single seat, the Security Council will avoid a deadlock and accept the decision of the General Assembly.

More importantly, this election saw the emergence of a new regional subgrouping, the Caribbean, within the Latin American Group of States, thereby transforming that group into the Latin American and Caribbean Group. Although Latin America currently again has two seats on the Court, it is probably safe to conclude that the election of a national of a Caribbean State in 1987 opened the way for this to occur again sometime in the future.

As a result, it is reasonable to see the Court now as being as representative of the major geographical regions and main forms of civilization as a bench of 15 members can be within the limits of political and diplomatic realities (although it should be noted that there is no national of a Pacific State on the Court). This increased representativeness is a positive development. The Court cannot be expected to gain and hold the confidence of the international community unless it is perceived as reflecting the major elements of the community.

Has this resulted in a breakdown of the second criterion of Article 9, namely that in the Court as a whole, the representation of the principal legal systems of the world should be assured?

The answer to this question is probably a qualified "yes". The nomination procedure is primarily concerned with the competence of the individual candidates and their personal suitability to exercise the office of judge in such an important and prestigious body as the Court. The election process in the United Nations is chiefly, if not exclusively, concerned with the geographical-political element in the selection process - that is the distribution of seats among, and within, the principal groupings in the United Nations. As a result, the representation of legal systems does not appear to constitute a major factor in the election process.

However, the legal systems of most States have incorporated in one form or another the fundamental tenets, both in matters of substance and in matters of procedure, of either the continental Civil Law or of the Anglo-American Common Law. Obviously, important modifications in these systems have been made, both in the countries where they originated and in the States where they have been retained. Moreover there are other meaningful influences, such as that of the cultural traditions and philosophical values of the world's major religions and ethical systems, and Marxist political-legal philosophy. At the same time it is probably true that a lawyer trained for example in Sierra Leone would find much which was familiar in the legal systems of Guyana, Sri Lanka, the United Kingdom and the United States, while the jurist from Madagascar would recognize many similarities in the legal systems of Venezuela, Algeria and France.

As a result, most of the judges are trained in either one or the other of these systems and share for the most part a thorough knowledge of public international law. The influences of Muslim, Hindu, Confucian, Bhuddist and Socialist legal thought and traditions are felt through the presence of the individuals among the membership of the Court.

The real impact of decolonization and of modern trends in international law, which is not limited to lawyers from States formerly under colonial rule, is to be found in the questioning of received conceptions and a reexamination of their applicability to contemporary conditions -that is to say in the personal outlook, experience and perception of the individual Members of the Court.

Apprehension is sometimes expressed that unless care is taken, the general criterion of Article 9 will clash with the personal qualifications required by Article 2, leading to a lowering of the standards required for the Court as a whole. On the other hand there is equal danger in exaggerating the possibility of discrepancy. Having regard for the primary purposes for which the Court exists, it seems to follow that the emphasis may rightly be placed on Article 9. Taking that as the point of departure, obviously it is most desirable that the individual Members of the Court should be reasonably competent in the theory and practice of international law (an expression which is broad enough to include both persons who have had practical experience of international law in the course of a diplomatic career and those whose qualifications are for the most part academic or whose experience is more secluded). In order to ensure a properly balanced Court for the purposes of Article 9, it is permissible to depart from that test provided, in that event, that a candidate is qualified to hold the highest judicial offices in his or her own country.

In fact there are usually found amongst the Members of the Court at any given moment judges who are highly qualified and experienced international lawyers as such, judges who have had considerable diplomatic experience at a high level of responsibility (including one or two former Foreign Ministers), and judges whose main experience has been in domestic judicial and administrative spheres. There is no doubt today that membership in the International Law Commission is an advantage to a candidate for election to the Court, although the number of Members who had been members of the Commission has varied considerably from time to time. It is not necessary that every judge be highly familiar with the whole of present-day international law (a virtual impossibility!). But out of a Court of fifteen Members, there should be no difficulty in finding a sufficient number of judges who can speak with authority on all the problems which arise in a given case. The practical exercise of the judicial function undoubtedly requires a high level of statesmanship and practical wisdom in addition to knowledge of the law, and this mixture of talents is generally speaking adequate and meets the international requirements.

Yet the problem of combining an equitable distribution of seats and at the same time ensuring a high level of professional competence has by no means completely disappeared. While the imbalance that existed during the years immediately following decolonization has been largely redressed, the fact that the Court's composition reflects the distribution of seats in the Security Council along the lines of the regional groupings within the United Nations does not necessarily satisfy everyone. Regardless of whether the composition of the Court is a significant barrier for some States to make use of its services, the fact remains that a number of States and noted authorities on international law continue to name this as a reason for the relative underutilization of the Court.

There is also concern that the prevalence of political considerations, too powerful to be ignored (and which in domestic legal systems play just as much a role in the selection of judges as on the international level -albeit in a more disguised form in some cases), may make it difficult to maintain the high standards of professional qualifications required.

As a solution to this problem, the suggestion has been made for a slight increase in the number of Members of the Court. Although this could lead to a more unwieldy and cumbersome decision-making process, it would also certainly tend to diminish the rivalry both within and between the various groups for a place on the Court. In 1956 the Institute of International Law adopted a cautious resolution for increasing the membership of the Court to eighteen,[8] and the item appeared on the agenda of the General Assembly in 1956, 1957 and 1958, without any substantive action being taken. The new International Tribunal for the Law of the Sea will have 21 elected members. There is today little sign of political support for an increase in the size of the Court, and that issue is being kept distinct from the possible increase in the size of the Security Council. Any increase in the size of the Court means amending the Statute which, being an integral part of the Charter, requires the formal ratification of all five of the permanent members of the Security Council (see p. 41 above). Under the present political circumstances this is considered to be unlikely for the foreseeable future.

The complicated system by which candidates are nominated and elected is designed to ensure that the double test laid down by the Statute is applied in practice. In this connection, it is obvious that the primary responsibility for attaining the desired standards rests with those who *nominate* candidates, especially when they have reasonable prospects of seeing their nominees elected. For the electors can only perform *their* task in the light of the objective situation placed before them. Their role is limited to choosing from among the candidates presented.

NOMINATING CANDIDATES

In an attempt to ensure that the candidates will possess the desired personal qualifications, the Statute adopts the principle not of direct nomination by governments, but of indirect nomination by existing or specially constituted "National Groups" in each country. The original idea, when the Statute was first drafted in 1920, was that the national groups of four persons chosen by a country as its members on the panel of the Permanent Court of Arbitration (see p. 5 above) would nominate candidates for the Permanent Court of International Justice. Where a country is not a party to the Hague Convention, it is to constitute a national group along the same lines. As a further check on the candidates' qualifications, the Statute recommended each of these groups to consult with its highest court of justice, its legal faculties and schools of law, and its national academies and national sections of international academies devoted to the study of law.

How this may work in practice may be illustrated by the functioning of the American National Group in nominating candidates for the election of 1961. A letter was sent to the Chief Justice of the United States Supreme Court, the American Society of International Law, the Chairman of the International Section of the American Bar Association, the Chairman of the American Branch of the International Law Association and the Deans of the principal American law schools among others. On the basis of the advice received, four individuals were nominated, nationals of Italy, Japan, Pakistan and the United States. Three of these were elected in 1961, the fourth being elected in the following elections of 1964. In short, advice was given by a wide section of non-governmental expert opinion. Many of the national groups follow a similar procedure. An American Member of the Court has demonstrated the value of this system of nomination. He has pointed out that had the practice of direct nomination by governments been followed, "two of the most distinguished American judges who have sat on the Court would not have been elected [Judges Jessup and Baxter]".[9]

When the Statute was revised in 1945, there was a strong move to alter these provisions. It was argued that the system had not worked as intended, and that the same results would be attained by direct nomination by governments, especially if they would undertake a series of consultations such as were enjoined on the national groups. But in the end it was decided to retain the previous system. Nevertheless today, out of the total of 186 parties to the Statute (including the non-members of the United Nations), 78 were at the end of 1992 parties to the Hague Convention of 1899 or 1907. This means that the nominations are in most instances made by specially constituted nominating colleges.

At least three months before the date of the election, the Secretary-General of the United Nations communicates with the national groups (not directly, but through the Foreign Minister of each country), and invites them to undertake the nominations. Each national group may nominate not more than four persons, of whom not more than two may be of its nationality; and in no case may the number of candidates nominated by a group be more than double the number of seats to be filled.

On receipt of the nominations, the names, in alphabetical order, are presented to the General Assembly and the Security Council, by which the elections themselves are conducted. Only persons on these lists are eligible for election, save in the case of a complete deadlock between the Security Council and the General Assembly. In addition to the list, the Secretary-General customarily circulates biographical particulars of the candidates. This is a useful practice which enables the electors to make their choice in full knowledge of the qualifications of each candidate.

Although at times there may be an element of artificiality in the nominating process, especially since, in the present circumstances, a readymade national group does not exist for most parties to the Statute, the decision of 1945 to retain the existing system was wise. The International Court is the only principal organ of the United Nations empowered to make decisions binding upon States which is composed of individuals not representing States. While it is true that a person is elected a Member of the Court not only on the basis of his personal qualifications but also having regard to his nationality, the present nominating system, if conscientiously applied, does offer the best possibility of ensuring that the candidates will be duly qualified.[10]

THE ELECTIONS

As stated, the Members of the Court are elected jointly by the Security Council and the General Assembly. They serve for a period of nine years and may be re-elected. Furthermore, there is no age-limit or compulsory retirement. For the Permanent Court, all the Members of the Court were elected simultaneously for each nine-year period, and elections accordingly took place in 1921 and 1930, those due to be held in 1939 being postponed on account of the Second World War.

In 1945 a fundamental change was introduced. At the San Francisco Conference it was decided that the term of office of five of the judges would come to an end each third year, the initial choice of three, six and nine year terms being made by lot.

As a consequence, all the fifteen Members of the Court were elected in February 1946. Since then, partial elections of five Members of the Court at a time have been held every third year during the regular sessions of the General Assembly, starting in 1948, the last such election taking place in 2003. The proposal for this change was made by the Washington Committee of Jurists, which felt that the previous system presented serious drawbacks principally on the ground that while it preserved continuity *during* the nine-year period, it did not maintain it *beyond* the nine-year period.. It was thought that the new system would therefore overcome that deficiency, while allowing for reasonable change in the personnel of the Court each third year.

It is not clear on what that assumption was based. Of the Members of the Permanent Court in office in 1939, who continued in office until the dissolution of that Court in 1946, five had first been elected before the general election of 1930. Two others had been deputy judges (a position which was abolished in 1936). Three had been continuously Members of the Court from its first election in 1921, serving two full terms plus the further six years of the War. Of the fifteen Members of the present Court elected in 1946, only three remained after the election of 1960, and only one served until the election of 1967. The late Judge Lachs, who was a Member of the Court from 1967 until his death in January 1993, was the longest serving Member of the Court. The present system of partial election of five Members of the Court every third year seems to have increased the turnover of Members of the Court. In turn, this has led many observers to the view that it has had an unsettling effect on the work of the Court.

On the other hand, the San Francisco Conference rejected proposals to alter the system of elections, by entrusting them to the General Assembly alone. Accordingly, the League system has been retained, and Members of the Court are elected by the General Assembly and the Security Council, which proceed "independently of each other".

To be elected, a candidate has to receive an absolute majority of votes in each of these two organs.

In the General Assembly, States parties to the Statute which are not members of the United Nations (there are no longer any States in that category) participate on a footing of equality. The absolute majority of 50% plus one is calculated on the basis of the total membership in the United Nations plus the non-member State which is a party to the Statute on the day of the election, regardless of whether any particular delegation is present or not, or is entitled to participate in the work of the General Assembly or to vote. In the election of 1993, the absolute majority required was 94 out of a total of 186 electors, nearly three times the absolute majority required at the first election of 1946. In calculating that quorum, two States not participating in the work of the General Assembly – South Africa and Yugoslavia (this latter by virtue of an express decision of the General Assembly) – were included.

This is a change from the practice in the League Assembly, where a simple majority, that is one half plus one of the votes cast, was the rule. The "absolute majority" rule now practiced in the General Assembly has several times been decisive in excluding a candidate who received a simple but not an absolute majority on the first ballot in the

General Assembly.

In the Security Council, no distinction is made between the permanent and the non-permanent members, that is the so-called "veto" does not apply. But although the permanent members do not have a privileged position as regards voting (which is secret), they can ensure the election of candidates of their own nationality – something which, as has been emphasized, is essential for the successful functioning of the Court – though it is doubtful if they can today do much more than that. Nor does it appear that the non-permanent members of the Security Council (they are ten in number) secure any particular advantage for themselves through their double votes. Recent experience indicates that on the whole, apart from the candidates of the nationality of the permanent members, if there is protracted balloting through differences between the Security Council and the General Assembly, the candidate clearly preferred by the General Assembly will finally be elected also by the Security Council, thus avoiding a deadlock.

The Statute contains elaborate provisions to overcome a deadlock, but there has been no need to apply them yet. The prolonged phases through which an election may go before it is clear that a deadlock is really developing are usually sufficient to allow the normal processes of diplomacy to produce a solution.

How are the elections conducted?

As stated, the two organs act independently of each other. The meeting of each organ proceeds until the *exact* number of candidates to fill the vacant places has received the required majority. Balloting will be continued in each meeting until that result is reached. As soon as the General Assembly has elected the required number to fill outstanding vacancies, each electoral organ formally communicates its list to the other, and comparison of the two lists shows which candidates have simultaneously received the required absolute majority in each organ. One meeting may therefore have an indefinite number of ballots. In both organs the counting of the votes is supervised by tellers from among the delegations. As the process of counting the ballots in the General Assembly naturally takes a long time, the meeting itself may be suspended for as much as twenty-four hours, and although that is a matter of the personal convenience of the delegations, it is at the same time useful in permitting further consultations between delegations for the eventuality that no candidate will receive the necessary majority. The counting process has been accelerated by the introduction of electronic equipment. The two sets of elections are carried out by secret ballot in separate public meetings, but in the Security Council the ballots are not counted until all the ballot papers in the General Assembly have been collected.

If places remain to be filled after the first meetings, the process continues for a second and a third meeting of each organ, and again each of the meetings continues for as many ballots as may be necessary.

Comparison of the votes in the two organs takes place after each has completed its meeting, and the President of the General Assembly announces the names of the candidates who have received the required majority in each electoral organ and are therefore elected.

Only after three meetings have been held in this way, with still not all the vacant places filled by both the Security Council and the General Assembly, will the machinery for resolving the deadlock be put into operation. This machinery consists of a joint conference of three members of each of the Security Council and the General Assembly for the purpose of choosing by absolute majority one name for each seat still vacant.

That name is submitted to the Security Council and the General Assembly for their acceptance. If the joint conference is unanimous it may choose a person whose name does not appear on the original list of candidates. As a final safeguard, if the joint conference is unsuccessful, the Members of the Court already elected are empowered, within a period to be fixed by the Security Council, to fill the vacant seats by selection from among the candidates who have obtained votes either in the Security Councillor in the General Assembly, the eldest judge (and not the President) having a casting vote in the event of a tie.[11]

An occasional vacancy is filled by the same process, in accordance with Articles 14 and 15 of the Statute. Such elections take place during the next convenient meeting of the General Assembly following the creation of the vacancy consistent with the time limits, the person elected taking office immediately. If a triennial election is due at the same time as an occasional election to fill a vacancy, the two are kept distinct, both as regards the nomination and as regards the election. Likewise, if there is more than one vacancy to be filled, each requires a separate process of election.

It goes without saying that the whole process of election is accompanied throughout by a considerable amount of diplomatic negotiation which frequently commences even before the nominating phase. Sometimes an individual who wants to become a Member of the Court will himself start by canvassing his chances on his own account. The results of that phase will enable him to open negotiations with his own national group. Sometimes a government will initiate its diplomatic overtures well in advance -as much as a year or two. It is not unknown for a candidature to go forward to election without real chance of immediate success, simply to provide a jumping-off point for a sustained diplomatic effort leading to a renewal of the candidature at a later date with better prospects.

The reaction to these early steps is important for the nomination phase. It enables all concerned (including the candidate himself) to assess the probabilities. After the list of candidates is published, and especially after the session of the General Assembly begins, the diplomatic contacts become much more intense, and there is little doubt that at times a delegation is instructed to vote for a given candidate in return for promises of support on another matter of close concern to it, whether its own candidature in another election or a matter of substantive concern. It is difficult to see why such bargains should be deprecated (except out of an exaggerated regard for legal purism), because both the General Assembly and the Security Council are political bodies and it is not expected of them, or of the States of which they are composed, to exclude political considerations when they come to perform the very important function of electing the Members of the Court. These diplomatic contacts are also valuable in maintaining the desired professional standards of the Court. Through them, influential governments are able discreetly to indicate their view whether a given candidate is qualified for the duties, and there is reason to believe that this too is a factor which influences the final outcome of the elections.

THE INDEPENDENCE OF THE JUDGES

The Statute does not content itself with the general provision of Article 2 that the judges shall be "independent", but clothes it with other provisions to give it reality.

The underlying principle is laid down in Article 16 of the Statute: "No Member of the Court may exercise any political or administrative function, or engage in any other occupation of a professional nature." Any Member of the Court who, immediately before his election, was in the service of a government or an international organization has to resign his office before his term of office as a Member of the Court commences. Any doubt is to be settled by the Court. By Article 20 of the Statute and Article 4 of the Rules, every Member of the Court before taking up his duties has to make a solemn declaration in open Court that he will perform his duties and exercise his powers honourably, faithfully, impartially and conscientiously. It is also understood that a Member of the Court having financial holdings which could lead to a conflict of interest should divest himself of those holdings.[12] No Member of the Court may act for one of the parties in any case before the Court, and if, before he became a Member, he had previously advised one of the parties, or had served as a member of a national or international court or commission of enquiry or in any other capacity in connection with the case, he has to stand down and refrain from participating in the decision of that case by the Court. Membership in the Court is a full-time and exclusive occupation and has priority over all other activities of a Member.

The provision of the Statute regarding the incompatibility of a Member of the Court acting as agent, counsel, or legal adviser in any case does not automatically extend to the participation of Members of the Court as members of arbitral tribunals or conciliation commissions. During the period of the Permanent Court, several of its Members acted as sole arbitrator in important cases which the parties had submitted to arbitration. Several Members of the present Court have acted similarly.[13] The basic condition is that there is no likelihood, at the time of the appointment of the arbitrators, of the case coming before the Court, whether on appeal or in some other way. Criticism is sometimes heard of this practice, but there would seem to be no good reason why the Members of the Court who are invited by the parties to a dispute to offer their services as arbitrators should not do so. Obviously, both the judges concerned, and the Court as a whole, must exercise caution that such activities in no way impair the efficiency or standing of the Court as an institution or as a principal organ of the United Nations. Again, by Article 17 of the Statute any doubt is to be settled by the Court.

This principle also applies to former Members of the Court.

Judges are granted security of tenure during their term of office (but have no right to automatic re-election), and are offered reasonably attractive financial terms and pension rights. By Article 18 of the Statute, a judge can only be dismissed if, in the unanimous opinion of his colleagues, he has ceased to fulfil the required conditions (no other organ, institution, or State has the right to impeach a judge).

Every judge should participate in each case unless he is on leave or is prevented by sickness; a State is entitled to have its case determined by the full complement of Members. Subject to these provisions, the Statute contains a specific provision which corresponds to the general system of *recusation,* that is a renunciation by a judge of his powers in a case because of a conflict of interest, or an objection to the participation of a judge in a case, on ground of relationship or known personal bias towards one or other of the parties. If the President considers that for some special reason one of the Members should not sit in a particular case, or if one of the Members himself reaches that conclusion, he may be excused from participation.[14]

These provisions have worked reasonably well in practice, and no instance is known, whether from the history of the Permanent Court or in that of the present Court, in which doubt has been cast on the independence of the Court as a whole.[15]

THE PRESIDENT

The Court elects its President and Vice-President by an absolute majority of votes. Each holds office for three years. These elections take place following each triennial partial election of Members of the Court. The President is responsible for directing the work of the Court and for its proper administration. He also performs important diplomatic and representative functions, both *vis-à-vis* the Netherlands Government as host to the Court and in relation to others and to the organs of the United Nations, especially the General Assembly. When the Court is not sitting, the President has extensive powers to make orders for the procedure in pending cases. He directs the Court's deliberations, and is *ex officio* a member of the Drafting Committee unless he does not share the majority opinion. In that situation his place is taken by the Vice-President, unless he is ineligible for the same reason, when the next senior member of the Committee presides. However, if the President is not a member of that Committee, the draft must be discussed with him before it is submitted to the Court, and if he proposes amendments which the Drafting Committee does not find it possible to adopt, it shall submit those proposals to the Court together with its own draft. The President and the Vice-President are also *ex officio* members of the Court's Chamber of Summary Procedure.

In two matters the President (and this includes an Acting President in appropriate cases) has a wide and unfettered discretion. By Article 55, paragraph 2, of the Statute, in the event of an equality of votes the President has a casting vote. He can exercise this casting vote as he thinks fit. By Article 74, paragraph 2, of the Rules, when a request for the indication of provisional measures is made, the President may, before the Court meets, call upon the parties to act in such a way as will enable any order made by the Court on the request to have its appropriate effects. It is therefore not surprising that provision has to be made to ensure at the seat of the Court the continuous discharge of the duties of the office of President either by the President or by the Vice-President.

The President signs all formal orders, judgments and advisory opinions and other formal texts emanating from the Court, his signature being countersigned by the Registrar. This is for purposes of authentication and does not commit the signatories to their contents.

In return for their onerous duties, the President and the Vice-President (when he is acting as President) receive a special non-pensionable allowance (p. 39 above).

The President and Vice-President take precedence over all the other judges. After them, judges elected at the same time take precedence according to seniority of age, serving Members of the Court who are reelected retaining their original precedence. In public sessions of the Court, the Vice-President sits to the President's right, and the other judges take their seats to his left and right in order of precedence. In the closed deliberations of the Court, the judges vote in inverse order of precedence, as is usual in judicial bodies.

If the President is a national of one of the parties in a contentious case before the Court, he has to abstain from acting as President for that case, and hands over his duties to the Vice-President or, of he is unable to act, to the next senior Member of the Court who is not disqualified.

Very frequently the "extra-judicial activities" of the Court (p. 15 above) are confided to the President. In carrying them out he will observe similar principles.

JUDGES *AD HOC*

What happens when one Member of the Court is a national of one of the States which is a party to a case? Several solutions are possible: the nationality of the judges could be ignored on the ground that they do not "represent" States; or the "national judge" (or judges) could be asked to stand down; or, when only one party has a national judge, the other party could be entitled to appoint a judge of its own for the occasion. The answer given in Article 3.1 of the Statute is a combination of the first and third solutions.

Firstly, judges of the nationality of the parties retain their right to sit in all cases before the Court. A Member of the Court is not disqualified from exercising his rights merely because he is a national of one of the parties. The Statute lays this down specifically.

Secondly, if the Court includes upon the Bench, that is the body actually trying a case, a judge of the nationality of one of the parties, the other party may choose a person to sit as judge. That person is known as a judge *ad hoc.* That person takes part in the decision on terms of complete equality with his colleagues. A judge *ad hoc* may be appointed not only to equalize the situation when the Bench already includes a judge of the nationality of one of the parties, but also when it includes no judge having the nationality of *either* of the parties. But if the Court finds that there are several parties in the same interest and that none of them has a judge of its nationality upon the Bench, the Statute provides for those parties acting in concert to choose one judge *ad hoc.* So far the Court has adopted a formal attitude in the few instances in which this problem has arisen.[16]

These provisions have given rise to controversy, principally on the grounds that they distort the "international character" of the international magistrature and that they conflict with the principle that no man should be judge in his own cause. (*Nemo judex in sua causa*). From the theoretical point of view this is undoubtedly true. However, as seen, the notion of "national arbitrators" is deeply rooted in the practice of international arbitration, and indeed the facility to appoint them is probably a *sine qua non* for the success of the whole idea. The important thing for ensuring third-party judgment is not that national arbitrators or judges should disappear, but that the balance in the tribunal should be held by neutral judges. This is the conception which has been incorporated in the Statute, for in practice the outcome is rarely likely to be influenced by the views of the judges having the nationality of the parties who, in the nature of things, tend to cancel each other out. The justification for the presence especially of judges *ad hoc* is to be found in more general and psychological grounds connected with the nature of international relations and the special function performed in that context by international litigation: it is not to be sought in any strained concepts of legal theory, with which, indeed, it may conflict.

What is the role of a judge *ad hoc?* It is sometimes said that they perform a useful function in supplying "local knowledge and a national point of view", and objection is then taken that if the parties cannot do that in their pleadings, so much the worse. But clearly, it is not their function to continue the pleadings through the deliberations of the Court. Their task would seem to be more to participate in the formulation of the judgment than to influence the actual decision (except, perhaps, when the division in the Court is very close). A State is not only interested in the operative part of a judgment: and even when the decision goes against it the wording of the reasons of the judgment may be of no less significance for it. Once the pleadings are closed, the parties have no further opportunity of bringing their points of view to bear on the Court, and it rests with the judge or judges *ad hoc* not to continue to plead their countries' cases (that would be virtually impossible), but to represent their countries' interests in the wording of the decision. If their role could, then, be more accurately designated as that of assessors, the grant to them of the status of judge represents a concession to diplomatic susceptibilities.

In most cases in which they have been appointed, the judges *ad hoc* have voted in favour of their country's point of view, although they have not always agreed with the arguments put forward, and have appended a separate opinion or a dissenting opinion if the majority decided against it, although there have been notable exceptions. Indeed, so prevalent is this that one may be tempted to speculate whether a judge *ad hoc* is not expected to act in this way, and whether it is not in the long-term interests of the Court as an institution that he should do so. The reason is that having regard to the fragile foundations of international adjudication, the presence of a judge *ad hoc* on the Bench, and the inclusion of his opinion appended to the text of the judgment itself, lends reality to the dictum that justice must not only be done but that it must be seen to be done. It makes it easier for a government to decide to entrust its affairs to the International Court.

Although judges *ad hoc* display a clear tendency to find in favour of the countries that have appointed them, one must not blindly assume that they will always do so. For example, in the Application for Revision and Interpretation of the Tunisia/Libya *Continental Shelf* judgment, the judge *ad hoc* for Tunisia, who, incidentally, was the first woman to sit on the International Court, voted with the rest of the Court in dismissing the Tunisian requests.[17]

The voting record of national judges (Members of the Court whose countries appear in a contentious case before the Court) is less marked in favour of their countries, and there have been some notable instances of national judges finding against their own countries even in cases of major importance. One of the best-known examples was Lord McNair's rejection of the British Government's contentions in the *Anglo-Iranian Oil Co.* case, but this is far from being a unique instance. More recently, the voting and the dissenting opinions of Judge Schwebel (U.S.A.) in the various phases of the *Nicaragua* case were by no means wholly in sympathy with the position of the U.S. Government in that case. On the other hand, there has been no case of a national judge or a judge *ad hoc* dissenting from a majority decision in his country's favour.

A judge *ad hoc* has to possess all the personal qualifications required of the Members of the Court, and any doubt is to be settled by the decision of the Court. A judge *ad hoc* also has to make the same solemn declaration. On the other hand, they are *appointed,* and are not subject to any form of international election. They need not be nationals of the State appointing them, and several instances have occurred in which one or both judges *ad hoc* themselves came from "third" countries. Indeed, this practice is coming more frequent today. They sit supernumerary to the Members of the Court taking part in .the case, which means that the bench may include up to seventeen judges. They take precedence after the titular judges. They do not have to give up their normal activities, but they have to give preference to the requirements of the Court.

The failure or unwillingness of a State to exercise its right to choose a judge *ad hoc* does not obstruct the Court in trying a case. States sometimes agree between themselves that no judges *ad hoc* will be appointed.

By Article 25 of the Statute a quorum of nine Members of the Court is sufficient to constitute the Court: this excludes the judges *ad hoc*. The number of judges who participate in a case is not unduly large considering the nature of the issues that come before the Court, though it is larger than is customary for the supreme courts of the common law countries.

In 2001, the Court adopted a number of "Practice Directions" designed to increase the Court's efficiency in the handling of cases and contribute to the sound administration of justice (see p. 91 below). Two of these related to the institution of the judge *ad hoc*, and direct the parties in a case to refrain from choosing a person to serve as a judge *ad hoc* who has served as an agent or counsel in another case, or was a regular judge on the Court or who served as a member of the Court's Registry within three years of his or her appointment as judge *ad hoc*.

CHAMBERS OF THE COURT

The Statute allows the Court to sit in smaller chambers. Three types of chambers are envisaged.

The first is the Chamber of Summary Procedure, which Article 29 of the Statute requires the Court to set up each year. This now consists of the President and the Vice-President *ex officio,* and three other Members of the Court together with two substitutes. The object is to maintain in existence a small court especially attuned to the speedy dispatch of business. However, States have shown no disposition to avail themselves of this facility, and during the whole of the combined existence of the Permanent Court and the present Court, only one case was in fact referred to the Chamber of Summary Procedure, and that was in 1924.

The second type is envisaged in Article 26, paragraph 1, of the Statute, a so-called special chamber. The Court may establish a chamber, consisting of three or more judges as the Court may determine, for dealing with particular categories of cases. Labour cases and cases relating to transit and communications are mentioned as examples. The Court first made use of this power in 1993, when it established a special chamber, consisting of seven Members of the Court, to deal with what it termed "any environmental case falling within its jurisdiction". Previously the Court had thought that it was unnecessary to establish special standing chambers of this kind, preferring to rely on its ability to constitute an *ad hoc* chamber as required, to be next described.

The third type is the so-called *ad hoc* chamber. By an amendment made in 1945 in Article 26, paragraph 2, of the Statute, the Court may at any time form a chamber for dealing with a particular case, the number of judges being determined by the Court with the approval of the parties.

These *ad hoc* chambers were hardly mentioned in the 1946 Rules of Court. However, the revisions of the Rules in 1972 and 1978 introduced important substantive and procedural changes, designed to facilitate recourse to this kind of tribunal in appropriate circumstances. These measures met the demand which had been articulated in the different discussions in the General Assembly and elsewhere for allowing the Court to take greater account of the wishes of the parties regarding both the composition of a Chamber and the procedure to be employed, thereby combining many of the advantages of judicial settlement and arbitration. In November 1981, the first case involving an *ad hoc* Chamber was referred to the Court by Canada and the United States concerning the maritime boundary in the Gulf of Maine (p. 179 below). This was followed in 1983 by the notification of a special agreement by Burkina Faso (formerly Upper Volta) and Mali referring the delimitation of a portion of the land frontier between these two African States to an *ad hoc* Chamber (p. 181 below). Two further cases have since been submitted to the Court for determination by an *ad hoc* chamber, one between El Salvador and Honduras concerning a dispute regarding land, island and maritime delimitation off the Pacific coast (p. 184 below), and the other between the United States and Italy arising out of the requisition of some American assets by the Italian authorities (p. 185 below).

THE REGISTRAR AND THE REGISTRY

The Statute confers on the Court power to appoint its Registrar and such other officers as may be necessary. The Court's staff is recruited specially and is technically not part of the United Nations Secretariat.

The Registrar, who is elected by secret ballot and by an absolute majority of votes from among candidates proposed by Members of the Court, serves for a period of seven years and is eligible for re-election provided that his candidature is again proposed by a Member of the Court. A Deputy-Registrar is appointed in the same way. The other officers of the Court are appointed by the Court on the proposal of the Registrar.

The Registry Staff consists of approximately 60 officials, who form a highly trained cadre which can be supplemented whenever necessary by temporary assistance. Their duties have been officially classified under four heads, which in fact overlap: judicial, diplomatic, administrative and linguistic. They are specified in greater detail in the Court's Instructions for the Registry. Apart from the Registrar and Deputy-Registrar, the other officers are accorded the usual diplomatic titles.[18]

DIPLOMATIC PRIVILEGES

The Members of the Court and the Registrar, when engaged on the business of the Court, enjoy full diplomatic privileges and immunities. In addition, the agents, counsel and advocates of the parties before the Court, and the Court's officials, enjoy the privileges and immunities necessary to the independent exercise of their functions. The details are regulated in an exchange of notes between the President of the Court and the Minister for Foreign Affairs of the Netherlands of 26 June 1946, which was approved, and slightly supplemented (with the consent of the Netherlands) by the General Assembly in its resolution 90 (I) of 11 December 1946.

A question which lay unresolved for many years during the existence of the Permanent Court concerned the relative precedence of the Members of the Court and the diplomatic corps accredited to the Netherlands. In 1971 it was agreed by the Dutch Government that the President of the Court takes precedence over the heads of the diplomatic missions, including the Dean of the Diplomatic Corps, who himself is immediately followed by the Vice President of the Court. Thereafter, the precedence proceeds alternately between Heads of Mission and the Members of the Court, each according to his own seniority. Despite some isolated objections, this arrangement has been generally accepted, and there is much relief that an old difficulty has been removed.[19]

How the Court Works

Considering the arguments of the parties, appraising the evidence produced by them, establishing the facts and declaring the law applicable to them – the definition by the Court of how a judicial organ works, in an advisory opinion of 13 July 1954.

The Deliberation Room (Photo: PE Fotostudio, Wassenaar)

The Peace Palace, Front (Photo: PE Fotostudio, Wassenaar)

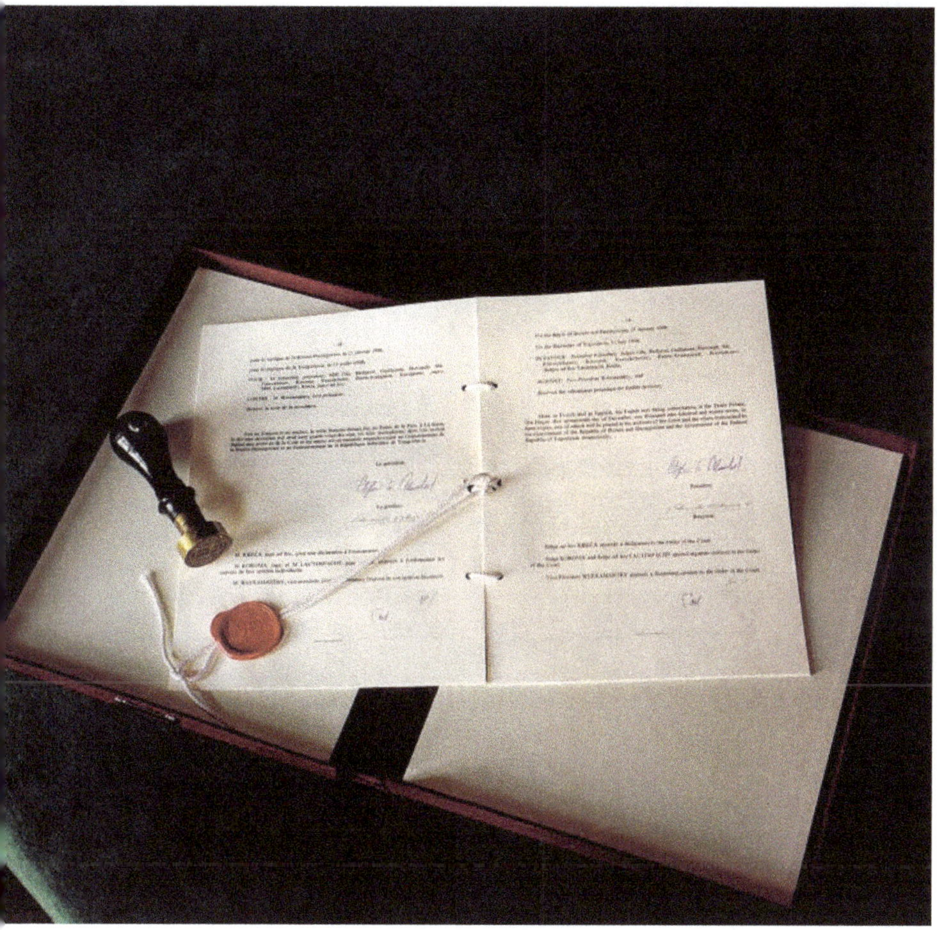

A Judgment of the Court with the Court's official Seal (Photo: PE Fotostudio, Wassenaar)

JURISDICTION

The term "jurisdiction" is used in two different senses.

Its primary meaning refers to the power or authority of the Court to render a binding decision on the substance or merits of a case placed before it. This is sometimes called "mainline jurisdiction". The secondary meaning of 'jurisdiction" relates to what is often called "incidental jurisdiction". That comprises a series of miscellaneous and usually interlocutory matters that can arise during the conduct of a case. These include; the power of the Court to decide a dispute as to its own jurisdiction in the case, its general power to control the proceedings, its power to indicate provisional measures of protection, its ability to consider requests by third States to intervene in pending proceedings, and its ability to deal with counter-claims and with the discontinuance of a case. Although these different matters appear to have no connection with one another, common to them all is that their parameters are fixed by the mainline proceedings, and that is what gives them their *incidental* character. In addition, after a judgment has been delivered, the Court has the power to interpret or to revise it under certain circumstances. None of this incidental jurisdiction depends on the direct consent of the parties. It always derives from the Statute of the Court itself. By becoming a member of the United Nations or a party to the Statute, a State agrees to the exercise of that jurisdiction in accordance with the Statute.

The International Court receives its power to decide mainline proceedings only from the consent of the States parties to the case that it should so act. Inherent in that consent is, by virtue of Article 36, paragraph 6, of the Statute, recognition that if a dispute arises as to whether the Court has jurisdiction, the matter shall be settled by the Court. Neither the Charter of the United Nations, nor any general rule of present-day international law, imposes on States the obligation to refer their legal disputes to the Court – but once consent has been given, the decision of the Court is final and binding and without appeal, and the States parties to the litigation are obliged to comply with that decision. The San Francisco Conference rejected all proposals to make some form of compulsory jurisdiction over certain defined types of legal disputes a condition for membership in the world organization.

By the same token, the finality and binding quality of the Court's judgments and the obligation to comply with a judgment are written into the Charter of the United Nations and the Statute of the Court, through the combination of Article 94 of the Charter and Articles 59 and 60 of the Statute.

Jurisdiction based upon consent, and the binding nature and finality of the decision, are thus the two basic principles underlying international adjudication in the Charter of the United Nations. The general principle that the Court's jurisdiction depends on the consent of the parties is equally clearly enunciated in Article 36, paragraph 1, of the Statute: "The jurisdiction of the Court comprises all cases which the parties refer to it and all matters specially provided for in the Charter of the United Nations or in treaties or conventions in force."

Although the San Francisco Conference did not accept the principle of compulsory adjudication of legal disputes as a condition for membership in the United Nations, it did accept the *political* principle that, as a general rule, legal disputes should be referred by the parties to the Court, in accordance with the provisions of its Statute. This appears in Article 36, paragraph 3, of the Charter.

The fact that the Court receives jurisdiction to decide a concrete case only from the consent of the States concerned means that the decision to have recourse to the Court is, in all cases, a deliberate political decision.

The Court has defined in clear terms its role in the settlement of international disputes by peaceful means: "the judicial settlement of international disputes, with a view to which the Court has been established, is simply an alternative to the direct and friendly settlement of such disputes between the Parties; consequently it is for the Court to facilitate, so far as is compatible with its Statute, such direct and friendly settlement, and any negotiation between the parties with a view to achieving a direct and friendly settlement is to be welcomed."[1] Article 33 of the United Nations Charter contains a general obligation on the members to seek a peaceful settlement of their disputes which could constitute a threat to international peace and security, and lists different means for that purpose. They include both arbitration and judicial settlement. The choice of means is left to the parties, and the Court has warned against hampering the free play of that provision by, for instance, drawing strict legal conclusions from actions and positions taken by parties with a view to resolving their disputes.[2] That attitude is not an expression of undue modesty on the part of the Court: it is rather a fair assessment of the place of the judicial settlement of international disputes among the available diplomatic techniques. It serves notice that the Court will not make excessive claims for its particular method of pacific settlement, while at the same time adhering firmly to the duties imposed upon it by its Statute.

But to say that the jurisdiction of the Court depends upon the consent of the States concerned, can, through an excess of brevity, be misleading. There are many ways in which States can confer jurisdiction on the Court, and some of these are undoubtedly moving in the direction of compulsory jurisdiction in the sense that proceedings can be instituted unilaterally. As a result of this probably most States have accepted the jurisdiction of the Court in one way or another, even if only for very limited types of dispute. The Court has facilitated the development of this process. Some of these ways will now be described more fully (while avoiding technicalities), because it is only through the advances in the techniques of conferring jurisdiction on the Court that the practice of international adjudication can make any headway at all.

A COURT FOR STATES

The primary rule, laid down in Article 34 of the Statute, is that only States may be parties in cases before the Court. This is axiomatic, and it excludes as parties in cases both international intergovernmental organizations on the one hand, and individuals (including non-governmental organizations) on the other. This is a matter of deliberate choice. The Court has been established to decide disputes between States, and not for other purposes. What this means is that the Court's procedures can only be set in motion by governments in exercise of their responsibilities, and that the judgment, the *res judicata,* itself can only be directly and formally binding upon States. This does not mean that the interests of an individual cannot be the subject of international litigation: on the contrary. But before the Court can deal with such a case the individual's government has to take it up and make of it an international claim in accordance with international law (espouse the claim in the exercise of its right of diplomatic protection of its nationals, to use the technical expression). When that happens, the litigation is conducted exclusively between the two governments concerned, and the individual has no *locus standi* in the Court itself. Both the Permanent Court and the present Court have seen several instances of this.[3]

The fact that only States may be parties in contentious cases excludes the possibility that the United Nations, the Specialized Agencies, and other international intergovernmental organizations may be parties in that kind of litigation, whether with other international organizations or with States. The San Francisco Conference refused to change this rule. All it did was to insert paragraph 2 into Article 34. This entitles the Court to request relevant information from public international organizations, and entitles those organizations to submit information to the Court on their own initiative. Since that idea itself does not accurately describe present-day international law, the perpetuation of the traditional concept of international litigation is criticized. This criticism has gained in strength since 1949, when the International Court itself in the *Reparation* advisory opinion (p. 131 below) held that the United Nations possesses international personality, and can advance an international claim against States, whether or not members of the Organization.

On the other hand, to allow international organizations to bring cases against States, or to be sued by States, would change the very character of international judicial settlement. It is not clear what the advantages would be. Experience since 1946 does not encourage the idea that the intergovernmental organizations *need* access to the contentious jurisdiction for the better performance of their tasks.

The question of disputes between a State or States and an international organization or between organizations has been partly dealt with in the United Nations Convention on the Law of Treaties between States and International Organizations or between International Organizations of 21 March 1986.[4] Article 66 of that Convention provides for a relatively complex dispute settlement procedure which includes the possibility of recourse to the Court, either through the contentious jurisdiction if the dispute is only between States, or through a request for an advisory opinion, initiated by a State through or by any organ of the Organization empowered to make such a request, if the dispute is one between a State or States and an international organization. Following precedents, the Convention provides that all parties undertake to accept an advisory opinion given under these conditions as "decisive", that is "binding". The Convention, again following precedent, also provides for arbitration of certain kinds of treaty disputes, with arrangements to prevent deliberate frustration of the arbitration.

Every State, whether or not member of the United Nations, may be a party in a case with other States. The Court is established as Court for the entire world. A State which is not a member of the United Nations may become a party to the Statute of the Court, on a footing of complete equality with the members of the United Nations, on conditions laid down by the General Assembly on the recommendation of the Security Council. Since 1945 five States have done this before they became members of the United Nations: Japan, Liechtenstein, Nauru, San Marino and Switzerland – which only became a member in September 2002.

A State which is not a party to the Statute may be a party in a case if it accepts the conditions laid down by the Security Council in its resolution 9 (1946) of 15 October 1946. In brief, that resolution places those States, for the purposes of the case at hand, in a position of equality with the States parties to the Statute, as far as concerns the obligations deriving from recourse to the Court, including the Charter obligation to comply with the Court's decision.

Now that the United Nations is to all intents a truly universal organization, the question of access to the Court by the independent States which are not parties to the Statute has lost much of the practical importance it once might have had. The focus is shifting to the position of semi-independent States enjoying a degree of autonomy in the conduct of their foreign affairs, as a matter of deliberate choice in the process of their decolonization.

The fact that a State – whether or not a member of the United Nations – is a party to the Statute means that it is *qualified* to be a party in litigation. It does not mean that it has agreed to confer mainline jurisdiction on the Court for a specific dispute. To confer mainline jurisdiction requires a separate act altogether, one directed specifically towards a defined, or ascertainable, State in respect of a defined, or ascertainable type of, dispute.

HOW JURISDICTION IS CONFERRED

There are two primary ways, and many variations, by which this mainline jurisdiction over a contentious case is conferred on the Court or, to put it more conveniently, by which a title of jurisdiction may be created. The first is by specific agreement between two or more States. The second is by unilateral declaration made by a State, accepting the jurisdiction of the Court for defined types of legal disputes, in accordance with a special procedure contained in the Statute. This is sometimes called the "compulsory jurisdiction" – a phrase which is misleading since it causes the voluntary nature of the acceptance of the jurisdiction to be overlooked.

Another form of compulsory jurisdiction exists whenever a treaty, whether multilateral or bilateral (or a collateral instrument), whatever its subject-matter, contains a compromissory clause, that is a stipulation by which a dispute arising out of that treaty may be referred to the Court by one of the parties to that dispute unilaterally. A State may initially invoke more than one title of jurisdiction, and in those cases the Court will, if necessary, choose the title of jurisdiction which it finds to be the most suited to the case before it.

There are no formal international requirements for a treaty conferring jurisdiction on the Court. The internal law of the different States may, however, require the observance of internal formalities before the government can conclude a treaty with this type of clause in it. For its part the Court has deliberately kept this aspect flexible as part of its general policy of facilitating recourse to the judicial process. The important thing is for the Court to be satisfied that the parties have agreed that it should decide the case, and not how that agreement is expressed. In fact this question will only arise should one of the parties challenge the jurisdiction of the Court on the ground that no such agreement exists, a process for which a special procedure is established.

At least four systems of conferring jurisdiction on the Court by way of international treaty are found.

Firstly, two or more States may conclude a special agreement – *(compromis)* – limited to referring a defined question or issue to the Court (see p. 94 below). This is similar to the early type of a special agreement to submit a dispute to arbitration, but is now usually much simplified thanks to the existence of the provisions of the Statute and Rules of Court governing all the procedural aspects.

The special agreement was a relatively important method of conferring jurisdiction on the Permanent Court (no less than 11 cases were so brought before it). In the early years of the present Court it suffered a decline (only three cases were brought before the present Court by this method during the first twenty years of its existence).[5] Lately, the special agreement appears to have regained its old importance, particularly -but not exclusively – for land and sea frontier delimitation cases.[6] An interesting feature of this method of recourse to the Court – the *North Sea Continental Shelf* cases are the first instance of this – is that the parties can request the Court to lay down and define in a final and binding judgment the applicable legal principles, leaving to the parties to negotiate the definitive settlement. This method of dividing a dispute into segments, with the Court determining with binding force the legal issues leaving to the parties the closing settlement on the basis of that decision, combines some of the best features of both judicial and diplomatic means of dispute settlement. It is quite probable that this method of submitting portions of disputes by mutual agreement to the Court (or variations on this theme) will prove to be of continuing and increasing importance because of the advantages it offers by combining authoritative and binding legal guidance with the freedom of the parties to negotiate the conclusive settlement between themselves.

It is not always easy for States engaged in a dispute to agree on a precise definition of the dispute to form the basis of a joint approach to the Court. Modern diplomatic requirements have therefore introduced a refinement into the special agreement. This consists in a formal agreement that a dispute exists and that it should be settled by the Court, without, however, defining the precise point in dispute. This type of agreement, sometimes called a "framework agreement", leaves to the parties to concretize the dispute through a unilateral application or a pair of applications. This manner of conferring jurisdiction originated in Latin America. Its value is that through the framework agreement to invoke Court procedures (which can also deal with the implementation of the Court's decision), the later unilateral reference to the Court cannot be castigated as an inimical act. On the other hand, by not defining accurately or fully the substance of the dispute, it may prevent the Court from reaching a conclusive decision, as occurred in the *Asylum* case (p. 134 below). Three cases have come before the Court in this way.[7] This development in diplomatic techniques – which could be combined with the power of the Security Council or of a regional organization such as the African Union (formerly the Organization of African Unity) or the Organization of American States to recommend recourse to the Court – is only possible thanks to the existence of a permanent international judicial organ: it is inconceivable for *ad hoc* arbitration.

A second method of conferring jurisdiction on the Court is by a compromissory clause in a treaty. That is a provision by which any dispute arising out of the application or interpretation of the treaty may be referred to the Court by any of the parties to the dispute. This, too, originated in nineteenth century arbitral practice. Here the scope of the disputes that may be referred to the Court is defined in advance by reference to the treaty, while the number of States who can be potential litigants is limited to the parties to the treaty. Compromissory clauses of this kind are found in both multilateral and in bilateral treaties.

During the period of the League of Nations and in the early days of the United Nations a compromissory clause of this nature was included almost as a matter of course in most multilateral conventions of a general character drawn up under the auspices of the international organization. A large number of these treaties are presently in force, although in the United Nations period reservations have been made to these jurisdictional clauses going a long way towards depriving them of practical effect (the 1950 confrontation over reservations to multilateral conventions was partly provoked by reservations of this character, see p. 143 below).

But a marked change of international sentiment has taken place. According to a view which was advanced with persistence by the Soviet Union and is shared by many other States, rules of substance are one thing, and rules for the settlement of disputes are another thing, and the inclusion of rules for the settlement of disputes *as a matter of course* in treaties dealing with substantive matters could jeopardize the efficacy of the substantive provisions and make it difficult for States to accept the treaty. This is not an absolute or a question of principle, and there are instances – the law of the sea is an outstanding example of this – where agreement to a new rule of international law or to a precise written formulation of a customary rule may depend upon the establishment of adequate procedures for the settlement of disputes arising out of the treaty in question.

The issue has become acute with the advances made in the codification and progressive development of international law in treaty-form. The clash of principle came to a head in the first United Nations Conference on the Law of the Sea of 1958, the first "codification" Conference to work on the basis of draft articles prepared by the International Law Commission. The Commission had pointed up the difficulty of affirming what was "codification" of international law and what was "progressive development" as envisaged in Article 13 of the Charter. The solution then adopted consisted in placing the dispute-settlement provisions in a separate "Optional Protocol" which States are free to accept at will. Optional Protocols of this character were also adopted in connection with the Vienna Conventions of 1961 and 1963 on Diplomatic and Consular Relations respectively, and constituted the title of jurisdiction in the *U.S. Diplomatic and Consular Staff in Tehran* case. Nevertheless, this compromise is widely regarded as unsatisfactory. In the Convention on the Law of the Sea of 1982, acceptance of one or other part of the "package deal" was made conditional on acceptance of binding third-party dispute settlement, not necessarily by the International Court; and accordingly provisions on the settlement of disputes are an integral part of the new law of the sea. Inherent in this approach is the inclusion of the permissible reservations to the dispute settlement provisions as an integral part of those provisions. This approach, regretted by some, reflects contemporary international realities, including the fact that many States, of all political hues, are not willing to accept in advance the judicial settlement of undefined disputes. This is coupled with a conviction that judicial settlement leading to a final and binding decision is not necessarily always the only or even the best means of settling every dispute. The provisions of the 1982 Law of the Sea Convention for various types of special arbitration and conciliation fill gaps for different types of highly technical or politically charged disputes not necessarily amenable to the type of judicial settlement which the Court provides, at least under present political conditions and with the limitations inherent in the Statute preventing individuals from having direct access to the Court.

Compromissory clauses in treaties, whether bilateral or multilateral in nature, are an important source of business for the Court. Many persons think that this type of dispute is on the whole well suited to judicial settlement. Experience shows, however, that this operates more effectively with the Court in the background acting as a reserve, so to speak, and being available should diplomatic means fail. A distinction could possibly be made between cases which are brought on the basis of a genuine disagreement concerning the interpretation of a treaty, or allegations of a breach of a treaty which are clearly related to the subject matter of that treaty on the one hand, and cases involving allegations of illegal conduct which have little or no relationship to the subject matter of the treaty on the other. In the latter type of case, the Court will be unable to entertain the claims due to the lack of relationship between the claims and the substance of the treaty. However, the existence of a relationship between the allegations of illegal conduct and the substance of a treaty is not always readily apparent and is subject to the Court's appreciation. A large number of cases have been brought before the Court on the basis of a compormissory clause in a treaty; many of which have been of major political importance.[8]

The third way of conferring jurisdiction is through a treaty for the pacific settlement of disputes either on a regional level or on a bilateral level. In this kind of treaty arbitration or judicial settlement of disputes is the very substance of the agreement. Here the scope of the litigation is limited to the parties to the treaty and materially, by the terms of the treaty.[9]

This too is a system which originated in nineteenth century arbitration practice. It was greatly encouraged by the League of Nations and the Permanent Court, and has continued to be popular in the present time. There are undoubtedly hundreds of these clauses in existence conferring jurisdiction on the Court. Several cases which originated in this way have been ultimately settled out of court and the judicial proceedings discontinued.

Finally, and this is a particularity of judicial procedure proper (it being almost impossible for *ad hoc* arbitration procedure), the International Court recognizes that its concern is with the substance of the agreement that it should exercise jurisdiction and not with the form in which the agreement is expressed. Consequently, consent may be given even after the proceedings have been started. The commonest example of this is where the respondent waives any irregularities in the way in which the proceedings were instituted or otherwise pleads to the case on the merits while formally refusing to recognize the title of jurisdiction invoked by the applicant State. Once the issues on the merits have been joined, the respondent State cannot be heard to deny the jurisdiction of the Court. This kind of agreement is a useful mechanism for perfecting the jurisdiction of the Court when, for any reason, the case in the course of the pleadings extends beyond the strict letter of the title of jurisdiction.

This form of conferring jurisdiction achieved some prominence in 1948 as a result of the manner in which the Court originally held that it had jurisdiction in the *Corfu Channel* case. During the 1950s a number of attempts were made to bring cases before the Court through a unilateral invitation to the respondent to confer jurisdiction on the Court, contained in an application instituting proceedings. Most of these cases were instituted by the United States in connection with various claims against the Soviet Union and its Allies arising out of incidents involving American military aircraft. Two cases were also instituted by the United Kingdom against Argentina and Chile relating to the disputed sovereignty over the Falkland Islands (Malvinas) and Antarctic territories.[10] In none of these cases did the respondent State accept the invitation, and in the absence of any jurisdiction whatsoever, the Court ordered the cases to be removed from the list. The fact that these attempts were made, and that the practice of the Court permits them, demonstrates new possibilities in opening up ways of access to the Court.

On the other hand, some regarded this type of proceeding as politically motivated and an abuse of Court procedures. In the 1978 revision of the Rules of Court (Article 38, paragraph 5) the Court decided that in future it would not take any step in the proceedings or enter a case of this nature in its general list until the respondent had notified its consent thereto. The first instance of this under that new Rule occurred in 1992, when Hungary filed a unilateral application against what was then called the Czech and Slovak Federal Republic over a projected diversion of the River Danube. The respondent did not accept that invitation to adjudicate the dispute. However, in 1993, Hungary and Slovakia concluded a special agreement bringing the *Gabčíkovo-Nagymaros Project* case before the Court.

For its part, the Court will satisfy itself that what it is being asked to do is compatible with its status and that its essential characteristics as a judicial organ are not being impaired.

JURISDICTION BY UNILATERAL DECLARATION (THE COMPULSORY JURISDICTION)

The most noteworthy advance in the techniques of conferring jurisdiction on the Court introduced by the Statute of the Permanent Court, and maintained in 1945, is the possibility of conferring jurisdiction over legal disputes, as defined in the Statute, through a unilateral declaration. Under this form of jurisdiction, a case can be instituted unilaterally against any other State which has made a similar declaration that is in force on the day the proceedings are instituted. This is the "compulsory jurisdiction" or the system of the optional clause (it being optional for States to make such a declaration). It is embodied in Article 36, paragraph 2, of the Statute as follows:

> The states parties to the present Statute may at any time declare that they recognize as compulsory *ipso facto* and without special agreement, in relation to any other state accepting the same obligation, the jurisdiction of the Court in all legal disputes concerning:
> a. the interpretation of a treaty;
> b. any question of international law;
> c. the existence of any fact which, if established, would constitute a breach of an international obligation;
> d. the nature or extent of the reparation to be made for the breach of an international obligation.

A declaration may be made unconditionally or subject to reservations which are not incompatible with the purposes of the optional clause. Reciprocity is inherent in the system, and where two declarations are in different terms, jurisdiction exists only to the extent that they coincide. A declaration may be limited or unlimited in time. There are no aspects of form to be followed beyond the requirement that a declaration be deposited with the Secretary-General of the United Nations. Such a declaration enters into force with its deposit, unless it itself prescribes another date.

The description of "legal dispute" for which jurisdiction can be conferred in this way is virtually identical with that which appeared in Article 13 of the Covenant of the League of Nations (see p. 9 above).

The introduction of this type of jurisdiction in 1920 was a compromise between those who wanted true compulsory jurisdiction over legal disputes as was proposed by the Committee of Jurists who prepared the draft Statute of the Court and those who wanted to retain the exclusively consensual basis of the jurisdiction. It was a major innovation in international practice, and time was required for diplomatic techniques to adjust themselves to it. It was not until about 1929 that the Great Powers of the League of Nations finally decided to translate the abstract principle into reality by themselves making declarations under the optional clause. However, they did so only in a halfhearted manner, by recognizing the jurisdiction subject to many reservations and safeguards. The effect of this was to reduce its scope within limits narrower than seem to have been originally contemplated.

Nevertheless, this initiative encouraged many other States to follow, and it has been estimated that at its height, in 1934, there were in force 42 declarations accepting the compulsory jurisdiction of the Permanent Court, this being the equivalent of 861 bipartite agreements.[11] Eleven cases came before the Permanent Court on the basis of declarations of this nature, ten after 1930. Clearly this was a method of conferring jurisdiction on the Court of potential importance, and it was taken over, virtually unchanged (save in some technical details), when the Statute was revised in 1945.

The reservations and exclusions which are made in these declarations fall into several common patterns, and most of them are reasonable. They include, for instance, reservations limiting the acceptance of the jurisdiction to disputes arising after a given date, to disputes for which a solution is not reached through diplomatic means or for which the parties have not agreed on some other method of settlement, on excluding disputes relating to events occurring in time of war, or in time of compulsory action by the Security Council, and so on. When necessary, individual States have inserted special conditions appropriate to their particular international situation.[12]

A common form of reservation excludes disputes which come within the domestic jurisdiction of States. Legally speaking, such a reservation is probably not necessary, because if the subject of the dispute falls within the domestic jurisdiction of a State according to current international law, it cannot be a legal dispute governed by international law and therefore in the nature of things cannot come within the scope of the compulsory jurisdiction. Accordingly, this type of reservation is inherent in the system of compulsory jurisdiction itself, at least when such a reservation is not further qualified by the inclusion of such words as *solely* or *essentially.* The inclusion of these reservations is probably governed less by legal considerations than by political factors reflecting the general reluctance of States to entrust their interests to third parties beyond their control. Article 15, paragraph 7, of the League Covenant excluded from the competence of the League disputes arising out of a matter which "by international law is solely within the domestic jurisdiction" of a party, and in this form this exclusion was taken into the compulsory jurisdiction of the Permanent Court. In the corresponding provision of Article 2, paragraph 7, of the United Nations Charter the words "by international law" have been omitted. This may have led some countries, headed at the time by the United States of America, to exclude from their acceptances of the compulsory jurisdiction of the present Court disputes with regard to matters essentially within their domestic jurisdiction *as determined by* that State itself.[13] Arguably a subjective reservation in these terms nullifies wholly or partially the acceptance of the jurisdiction and may not be compatible with Article 36, paragraph 6, of the Statute, which lays down that if a dispute arises as to whether the Court has jurisdiction, the matter shall be settled by the decision of the Court. In the Court this view was advanced with great vigour by the late Sir Hersch Lauterpacht, as well as by other judges.[14]

However, the Court has continually avoided making a definitive pronouncement on the issue. The Court's decision of 26 November 1984 in the jurisdictional phase of the *Nicaragua* case may be taken as implicitly rejecting the view that these reservations vitiate the acceptance of the compulsory jurisdiction. There is little doubt that the withdrawal of this reservation by several States has been prompted by that earlier criticism. On the other hand, some more recent declarations have included a self-judging reservation. This suggests that the factors which led to this practice in the first place are not altogether dormant. Surprisingly, perhaps, the Court has not yet had to decide such a dispute as between litigating States. In two instances in which the Court exercised its jurisdiction to decide its own jurisdiction in cases brought against a State (in each instance a permanent member of the Security Council) whose acceptance of the compulsory jurisdiction contained a subjective reservation, each of those States refused to take part in the Court proceedings and later withdrew its acceptance of the compulsory jurisdiction. This occurred in the *Nuclear Tests* and the *Nicaragua* cases. *Fiat justitia...* !

The facts that the United States qualified its acceptance of the compulsory jurisdiction in this manner between 1946 and 1985, that of the other permanent members of the Security Council China and France have allowed their earlier acceptances of the compulsory jurisdiction to lapse, and that the USSR or Russia has never yet accepted it at all (a striking repetition of the attitude of the permanent members of the League Council in the period 1920 to 1929) are probably largely responsible for the present situation regarding the compulsory jurisdiction. Out of the 191 parties to the Statute in December 2002, 63 are presently bound by a declaration in force accepting the compulsory jurisdiction. This represents a low point in the joint history of the Permanent Court and the present Court, of the percentage of members of the compulsory jurisdiction, although there are signs of a slight improvement in recent years.[15]

This relatively small number of States which have made declarations under Article 36, paragraph 2, of the Statute, coupled with the practice of including in the declarations many and far-reaching reservations, or the non-renewal of declarations after the Court has exercised jurisdiction without the specific consent of the respondent State, do not give much reason for complacency regarding the current state of affairs. These are regrettable facts which would seem to point to a tendency by States to prefer to base the jurisdiction of the Court on express agreement relating to a defined dispute, or at any rate to circumscribe carefully their acceptance of the Court's jurisdiction within relatively strict limits.

Despite this unfavourable political atmosphere, the compulsory jurisdiction remains an important potential source of contentious judicial business for the Court today, and politically speaking in terms of long-term judicial policy, very significant. Not only has it served as the basis of jurisdiction in a significant number of cases brought since 1946, but included in these are some of the politically most important cases *(Fisheries, Anglo-Iranian Oil Co., Nuclear Tests* (partly), the cases brought by Nicaragua against the United States, Costa Rica, and Honduras; and more recently, *Land and Maritime Boundary between Cameroon and Nigeria*, *Armed Activities* (Congo v. Uganda) and *Arrest Warrant of 11 April 2000* (Congo v. Belgium)).[16]

The significance of the compulsory jurisdiction ought not to be measured solely by the number of States which have accepted it, or by the number of cases that have been based on it. It also has an important psychological value. It has been a useful instrument for disseminating the idea that judicial settlement of international disputes is both possible and desirable. If States are agreed, on the political level, to have recourse to the Court, the fact that they have both accepted the compulsory jurisdiction may make it unnecessary for them to take any further steps in order to bring their dispute before the Court thus, from the political point of view, facilitating recourse to the Court. There is reason to believe that something like this occurred in the diplomatic phase of the fisheries dispute between the United Kingdom and Norway which was decided by the Court in 1951 (p. 132 below). On the other hand, if the political agreement is not present and the respondent State challenges the jurisdiction of the Court, the Court will have to decide, on the basis of law, whether the dispute comes within the scope of the acceptance of the jurisdiction, or how it will deal with the dispute. The Court's decision on this issue, or the decision of the respondent to waive objections to the jurisdiction, will then become an important factor leading to the solution of the dispute. But if the respondent persists in its unwillingness, an eventual decision by the Court on the merits may aggravate rather than calm the dispute. Experience has shown that for the most part the Court will display prudence and caution in dealing with that type of situation, and not allow the system of the compulsory jurisdiction to be abused so as to compel a State to submit to the jurisdiction when it is clearly not obliged to do so. Yet some of its decisions on this kind of issue have proved to be highly controversial and probably detrimental to its general standing in the eyes of many observers.[17]

CONTINUITY OF JURISDICTION BETWEEN THE PERMANENT COURT AND THE PRESENT COURT

Most of these ways of conferring jurisdiction became established for the Permanent Court. When the San Francisco Conference decided to replace the Permanent Court by the present Court, the question arose of the future of all the various instruments in force conferring jurisdiction on that Court. As part of the general policy of maintaining continuity in the administration of international justice the Conference decided to make every effort to retain these instruments as conferring jurisdiction on the new Court, at least as between the States parties to the new Statute. This would prevent the reorganization from adversely affecting the achievements in this sphere.

To that end, two stipulations were inserted into the new Statute. The first, in Article 36, paragraph 5, provides that declarations accepting the compulsory jurisdiction of the Permanent Court which were still in force should be deemed, as between the parties to the new Statute, to be acceptances of the compulsory jurisdiction of the new Court for the period which they still had to run and in accordance with their terms. The second, in Article 37, lays down that whenever a treaty or convention in force provides for reference of a matter to the Permanent Court, the matter should, as between the parties to the new Statute, be referred to the new Court.

The Court has given two interpretations of the first of these provisions. It has held that a declaration accepting the jurisdiction of the Permanent Court could only be deemed to be an acceptance of the jurisdiction of the present Court in the case of an original member of the United Nations, and not in the case of a State admitted to the United Nations or to the Statute of the Court after the dissolution of the Permanent Court (18 April 1946). Secondly, a declaration accepting the jurisdiction of the

Permanent. Court which had not been ratified and was therefore not in force could, in the case of an original member of the United Nations which had participated in the San Francisco Conference, become perfected and take effect as an acceptance of the jurisdiction of the present Court through the ratification of the Charter, of which the State is an integral part.[18] The second of these interpretations is the more controversial. The significance of these two cases, however, must not be exaggerated, as in both of them only one declaration was involved and the Court's decision had no effect for any other country.

As for Article 37 of the Statute, the Court has been more emphatic in asserting its jurisdiction if the treaty had been continuously in force and both States were parties to the 1945 Statute and to the treaty when the proceedings were instituted.[19]

MUST A STATE APPEAR? THE "UNWILLING RESPONDENT"

The present Court, particularly since the 1970s, has been confronted with the problem that in contentious cases instituted unilaterally by one State, the respondent State has refused to acknowledge the competence of the Court or to take part in the proceedings in any way. Sometimes a State has not taken part in an initial phase of the proceedings, participating in a later phase. In other instances the respondent has withdrawn from the case before the final decision has been given. This is frequently termed "non-appearance". The Statute makes provision for this. Article 53, paragraph I, provides: "Whenever one of the parties does not appear before the Court, or fails to defend its case, the other party may call upon the Court to decide in favour of its claim." The primary sign of non-appearance is the non-appointment of an agent to represent the State in the Court, although this is not conclusive.

Perhaps the best known instance of a State initially not appearing in an earlier phase but coming in later was in the *Anglo-Iranian Oil Co.* case. Iran did not participate in the provisional measures phase of the case. Iran later appointed an agent and filed preliminary objections while denying that the Court had jurisdiction. After full pleadings on this issue the Court upheld the objections. Another case where this occurred was *Nottebohm.* Here the respondent initially did not appear, but later participated. In both *Corfu Channel* and *Nicaragua,* the respondent appeared in the initial phases but subsequently withdrew. Cases in which the respondent failed to appear at any point of the proceedings include: *Fisheries Jurisdiction, Nuclear Tests, Pakistani Prisoners of War, Aegean Sea,* and *U.S. Diplomatic and Consular Staff in Tehran.*

Non-appearance in whatever guise has received increasing attention both in political circles and in learned societies and legal literature.[20] It has also given rise to much criticism and anxiety that the Court is not being accorded the respect due to an institution of its standing and, more important, that a State's failure to enter in judicial proceedings brought against it poses a threat to the international legal order. While there is certainly room for criticism of much of this conduct, several considerations should also be borne in mind.

Firstly, the refusal of a party to appear is not a bar to the continuation of the proceedings. Nor does it mean that the Court cannot ascertain the facts and law at issue. However, the categoric language of the Statute means that there is no automatic presumption in favour of the applicant – no judgment by default. The Court "must satisfy itself, not only that it has jurisdiction", but also that the claim "is well founded in fact and law". While the Court's task is frequently more difficult as a result of non-appearance, the difficulties are not unsurmountable, and the Court has shown itself capable of carrying out its task of reaching a decision despite the absence of formal pleadings and evidence by one of the parties.

The words "formal" pleadings and "formal" evidence are used intentionally. In nearly all the cases of non-appearance to date, the unwilling respondent *has* found a way to make its views known to the Court. For its part the Court is prepared to accept these informal statements at their face value, and hear the arguments of the other party on them. Nevertheless the Court has always expressed regret at being faced with this situation, and has stated forcefully that a State which decides not to appear "must accept the consequences of its decision". This is most conspicuous when the facts are in dispute, for the non-appearing party is not in a position to challenge evidence produced by the other side – for instance, it cannot cross-examine the other side's witnesses.

Secondly, even assuming that the States parties to the dispute should in principle co-operate with the Court, Article 53 of the Statute can leave no doubt that a party to a case is under no legal obligation to take an active part in the proceedings. In failing to appear, the unwilling party is acting on the basis of a policy decision, not whimsically, and, as in the case of any such decision, it is taking a calculated risk – just as it does when it takes part in the formal proceedings. A State is free to decide how it will conduct its case, and in the nature of litigation between States this includes a decision not to appear. Obviously, a decision not to take advantage of all the procedural openings such as the submission of formal evidence, examination of the opponent's witnesses in Court (if there are any) and fully to develop the possible arguments and take advantage of any weaknesses in the opponent's arguments, will have an impact on the proceedings and on the judgment.

The real challenge which non-appearance presents to the Court is for the Court to ensure that neither side profits from the non-appearance of the other. The Statute requires the Court to "satisfy itself", and not merely "be satisfied", that the claim is well-founded in fact and in law.

A State's decision not to take any part in the proceedings in a case in which it is properly a party does not in itself affect the final and binding quality of the Court's decisions, or the Charter obligation of compliance with them.

PROVISIONAL MEASURES OF PROTECTION

Article 41 of Statute gives the Court power to indicate, if it considers that circumstances so require, any provisional measures which ought to be taken to preserve the respective rights of either party. (These are sometimes called *interim measures.*) This enables the Court to take steps roughly corresponding to an interim injunction which domestic courts are frequently empowered to issue pending the final determination. As such a decision by the Court is likely to have political implications, the Court has to give notice of measures indicated not only to the parties, but also to the Security Council.

A request for an indication of provisional measures may be made at any time in the course of the proceedings. The Court will normally only indicate such measures if it is satisfied of their urgency and that there is the possibility that the object of the litigation will be prejudiced if appropriate measures are not indicated – for example if there is a danger that economic assets which are the object of the claim may be lost. In indicating provisional measures, the Court is free to suggest conduct different from that requested by either of the parties. An order indicating measures of protection will remain in force so long as the Court is dealing with the case, unless it is made for a fixed period of time, or is revoked or amended.

Because of the factor of urgency, a request for the indication of provisional measures has priority over all other cases. A pending hearing will be interrupted to enable the Court to deal fully with a request for provisional measures.

The present Court has had thirty-four requests for provisional measures.[21] In *Anglo-Iranian Oil Co.,* during a period of great tension, the Court indicated provisional measures, but Iran did not acknowledge the jurisdiction of the Court (its preliminary objection was later upheld), and the Security Council, in which political considerations predominate, was unable to take any effective steps in the matter. In *Interhandel* the Court upheld its jurisdiction to indicate provisional measures even though its jurisdiction was going to be contested, but found that there was no need for them at the time. In *Fisheries Jurisdiction,* the Court upheld its jurisdiction to indicate provisional measures despite the respondent's intimation that it did not recognize the Court's jurisdiction and that in its view provisional measures would be unnecessary.

A similar attitude was followed in *Nuclear Tests.* In *Pakistani Prisoners of War* the request was withdrawn after the hearing, the attitude of the applicant showing that there was no urgency about the matter. In *Aegean Sea,* the Court found that there was no need for the indication of provisional measures because the activities complained of by the Applicant (seismic exploration of the sea-bed) could not – in its opinion – cause irreparable harm to Greek rights or interests which could not be subsequently redressed by compensation. In *U.S. Diplomatic and Consular Staff in Tehran* and *Military and Paramilitary Activities in and against Nicaragua* measures were indicated in periods of tension and confrontation involving the risk of an armed clash or incident between the parties. By unanimous or near unanimous votes the Court called on the parties to cease and desist from actions which were the cause of these tensions and to avoid the possibility of armed confrontation. In the former case, the respondent State (Iran) ignored the order calling for the release of the diplomatic hostages. That led the United States to attempt an abortive military rescue of its diplomatic personnel in Iran in 1980. In the latter case, the order was partially complied with. The Court refused to deal with a second request by Nicaragua. In the *Frontier Dispute* case which was submitted by special agreement by Burkina Faso and Mali, when fighting broke out in December 1985, the Chamber succeeded through a carefully balanced order, and with the assistance of mediation by the Organization of African Unity, in restoring the *status quo ante* thereby enabling the Chamber to continue with the proceedings in a calmer atmosphere. In 1988 Nicaragua's request for provisional measures against Honduras was withdrawn almost as soon as it was filed. In the *Arbitral Award* case between Guinea-Bissau and Senegal, the Court dismissed a request by Guinea-Bissau. In the *Passage through the Great Belt* case, the Court declined Finland's request for the indication of provisional measures. In the *Lockerbie* cases too the Court found that it could not grant the requests; and in the Application of the Genocide Convention (Bosnia v. Yugoslavia) case it only granted the applicant's request in part. A second request led to a reaffirmation by the Court of its earlier order. These last two cases were attempts by the applicant States to use the Court as an instrument for exercising control over the Security Council acting under Chapter VII of the Charter – a role the Court has to date wisely refused to play. In the *Nigeria Cameroon Boundary* case, the Court issued provisional measures directed at both Parties aimed at preventing a recurrence of armed incidents in the disputed border area.

In the cases brought by Yugoslavia against ten NATO member States, Yugoslavia unsuccessfully sought provisional measures which would have ordered a cessation of NATO bombing of Yugoslavia, due to a lack of *prima facie* jurisdiction. In both the *Breard* and *LaGrand* cases, the applicant States petitioned the Court for an indication of provisional measures directing the United States to refrain from carrying out death sentences against their nationals pending the outcome of the proceedings. Although the requests were granted; the latter under somewhat exceptional circumstances, they were not successful in preventing the executions from taking place. In the *LaGrand* case, this led Germany to claiming that the United States failure to observe the provisional measures constituted a breach of the Statute. This posed the question – for the first time – directly to the Court as to whether provisional measures are binding upon the Parties. This had been a matter of longstanding controversy which the Court resolved once and for all, by ruling that provisional measures have binding legal effect. In *Armed Activities in the Congo*, the Court directed both Parties to abstain from any incident which could further aggravate the dispute and enjoined them to carry out their obligations under the relevant humanitarian law. Finally, in the *Arrest Warrant* case, the Court rejected a request by the Congo to withdraw an arrest warrant issued by a Belgian judge against its (former) Foreign Minister, due to lack of urgency.

Since the power to indicate provisional measures is exceptional, the Court is strict upon insisting the observance of the proper procedure. It will not indicate provisional measures unless it is satisfied that it possesses at least a *prima facie* jurisdiction over the mainline proceedings. The Court will not give general instructions to the parties to abstain from any measure capable of having a prejudicial effect on the subject matter of the case or which might bring about an aggravation or extension of the dispute, unless the power to indicate provisional measures is expressly invoked. In this connection it has to be recalled that the Court does not have direct responsibility for the maintenance of international peace. That responsibility is expressly confided on the Security Council by Article 24 of the Charter. On the other hand, the Court is entitled to rely on the general good faith of the parties not to exacerbate a dispute with which it is dealing.

JURISDICTION OR ADMISSIBILITY DISPUTED: PRELIMINARY OBJECTIONS

There is a basic rule of international law and a principle of international relations that a State is not obliged to give an account of itself on issues of merits before an international tribunal which lacks jurisdiction or whose jurisdiction has not yet been established. A State – usually the respondent in a case brought unilaterally – is not obliged automatically to accept the case as formulated by its opponent, neither the title of jurisdiction as it has been invoked nor the case as it has been presented. It may challenge the competence of the Court to entertain the case. It may contest the jurisdiction of the Court or the admissibility of the case as a whole or of a claim made in it. For this purpose a special procedure – the preliminary objection procedure – exists.

In addition, the parties may agree, or the Court may require these questions to be argued and decided at an early stage in the proceedings and before any pleadings on the merits are filed.

The Court's decision on these matters, if in the form of a judgment, attracts all the consequences of a judgment, even if it is not the final decision in the case. This follows from the rule that a judgment is final and binding and is not subject to appeal, contained in Articles 59 and 60 of the Statute, and the obligation imposed by the Charter on all parties to the Statute to comply with the decision of the Court (see p. 34 above). It is possible to say that as regards jurisdiction to determine the merits - a major example of the "incidental jurisdiction" of the Court - true compulsory jurisdiction exists once a case has been properly instituted.

It has been seen (p. 7 above) that nineteenth century arbitral procedure had reached the position that disputes over the jurisdiction of an arbitral tribunal should normally be settled by the tribunal itself and not be referred back to the parties, unless the arbitration agreement provided otherwise. When the Permanent Court was established, a specific power was inserted in Article 36, paragraph 6, of the Statute of the Permanent Court, which has been carried over in the corresponding provision of the present Statute. The procedure regulating the raising of preliminary objections is worked out further in Article 79 of the Rules of Court, which has been recently amended to assist in the more efficient handling of cases. This provision empowers the Court to decide on all disputes concerning its jurisdiction or the admissibility of a claim, or any other objection the decision on which is requested before any further proceedings on the merits. This is a specific statutory power which the Court shares with most other international tribunals, and is sometimes referred to by the French term *'compétence de la compétence'* or the German *'Kompetenz Kompetenz'*. Essentially, this means that the Court is the final arbiter of its jurisdiction.

The inclusion of this provision was an innovation at the time. It has since become one of the fundamental principles governing its work and of international adjudication in a more general sense. Any submission by Parties purporting to override it would be held to be inconsistent with the Statute and the Court's functioning as an independent international judicial organ.

The main feature of the preliminary objection procedure is that if a party wishes to dispute the Court's jurisdiction or the admissibility of a case, it must do so *before* it pleads to the merits (substance of the dispute). Of course, it will almost always be the respondent State which disputes the Court's jurisdiction. However, in very exceptional circumstances the applicant State may raise a preliminary objection. If a preliminary objection is raised, the proceedings on the merits are suspended until the matter is decided. This is a categoric rule. In those circumstances, the preliminary questions of jurisdiction or admissibility are pleaded in independence of the main proceedings (indeed, in some cases the parties' roles are reversed, the respondent on the merits appearing as the applicant on the objection),[22] in the form of an interlocutory proceeding. An interlocutory proceeding of this kind does not determine the merits of the action. If the Court finds it cannot entertain a case or part of a case due to lack of jurisdiction or inadmissibility, that will bring the proceedings, or part of the proceedings to an end.

There are three possible outcomes to the raising of preliminary objections:
If the Court finds at least one of the objections is well founded, the proceedings will come to an end or in some cases will proceed on the basis of a narrower scope of jurisdiction if the objection only relates to one of several possible bases for jurisdiction. If the Court rejects all of the objections, the proceedings on the merits will be resumed. The same result will follow if the Court decides that in the circumstances of the case, the objection does not possess an exclusively preliminary character. These possibilities

are spelled out in Article 79 of the Rules of Court. There are minor variations to these possibilities and this general order of the proceedings. For example, the respondent State can withdraw its objections at any point. Another variation is that the respondent State can contest the Court's competence to rule on the merits without formally raising a preliminary objection. The Court will deal with this issue to the extent necessary within the context of its judgment on the merits. The parties can also agree to request the Court to join the preliminary objections to the merits, which the Court would probably be bound to do. The possibility also existed for the Court to join preliminary objections to the merits prior to the revision of the Rules of Court in 1972. However, this option is no longer open to the Court on the basis of the revised Rules of Court. Nevertheless, it would appear that the Court probably retains an inherent power to postpone any decision on preliminary objections which are very closely related to the merits, until the decision on the merits is made. Finally, the Court may consider a preliminary question on its own initiative which has not been raised as an objection by one of the parties. The reason for this is that the Court must always be satisfied that it has jurisdiction. In the most recent amendment of the Rules of Court of 5 December 2000, the Court has laid down the requirement that preliminary objections must be raised within three months after the filing of the [Applicant's] written memorial. The purpose of this is to further expedite the conduct of the proceedings.[23]

Broadly speaking, preliminary objections fall into three classes.

One type of objection argues that the instrument invoked as the title of jurisdiction simply is not in force or does not exist, for instance that it is a treaty, or a declaration accepting the compulsory jurisdiction, which is not yet in force or which has terminated or is for some reason void. Clearly, this kind of objection is the most remote from the merits. Indeed, normally it has no direct connection with the merits.

Another class of objection does not contest the existence of the title of jurisdiction as such, but argues that on the facts the concrete dispute does not come within its scope. For instance, if jurisdiction is accepted only as regards disputes arising after a certain date, the argument that the concrete dispute arose before that date should be raised as a preliminary objection. It may be difficult to separate examination of this issue from the merits, but how the Court will deal with it will depend on all the circumstances of the case, all variants appearing in the combined practice of the Permanent Court and the present Court. This is not an easy matter.

The third category is not really an objection to the jurisdiction at all, but is normally treated procedurally in the same way. Accepting the jurisdiction of the Court, the objecting State argues that the claim cannot be admitted, is "inadmissible", often on the ground that some other applicable rule of general international law has not been complied with – for instance the substantive condition of the law for the exercise of the right of diplomatic protection, such as the failure to exhaust local remedies before the institution of the proceedings. Questions of admissibility can also include such matters as the failure to attempt to reach an agreement through diplomatic negotiations where this is called for in a treaty or under rules of general international law. "Admissibility" can also isolate such matters as whether the dispute in question is a "legal" dispute capable of being settled by judicial means, or whether it involves questions which fall within the exclusive competence of the Security Council. These types of objection involve questions of judicial policy as much as they do issues of strict law.

Preliminary objections are a prominent feature of the work of the Court. In the Permanent Court, objections were raised in 13 out of a total of 66 cases. With the advent of the present Court in 1946, preliminary objections have become more frequent. In cases other than those brought through the mutual consent of the parties to submit a dispute to the Court on the basis of a special agreement, it is more likely than not that preliminary objections or other related preliminary points will be a factor which the Court will have to deal with in the proceedings. With the increased complexity and political importance of the cases before the present Court in comparison to those brought before the Permanent Court, coupled with the expansion of the international judicial community, it is completely logical that States will not necessarily wish to have a sensitive dispute submitted to the Court at a time and in a manner chosen by another State. Most cases involving preliminary objections have been of high political importance, involving potentially far-reaching issues relating to the policies and interests of the States concerned. In a significant number of these, the States concerned have been involved in a confrontational relationship which has even included the clear possibility or actual occurrence of the use of armed force. Under such circumstances, the bringing of a case by unilateral application against the will of the respondent party will almost inevitably lead to the raising of preliminary objections or similar moves aimed at challenging the Court's jurisdiction.

Coupled with the increased frequency with which the Court's jurisdiction is challenged is another development, namely, that it is rare for it to be challenged on a single, simple ground. Instead, multiple objections, often falling into all the categories previously mentioned, are put forward. When this happens, and especially when the objections relate both to the jurisdiction and to the admissibility, it will be difficult to unravel the preliminary objections from the merits, even if the overlap is only indirect. Under those circumstances, it would be an oversimplification to regard a judgment declining jurisdiction as being necessarily a merely technical matter, or to assume that because of the objections, the Court has been prevented from making an effective contribution to the settlement of the dispute. There have been a number of cases in which the formal decision of the Court declining jurisdiction has served to ease tensions and in fact has assisted the parties in reaching a negotiated solution of their difficulties.

Because of the prevalence of raising multiple objections in cases introduced unilaterally, the Court has come to rely on a new form of proceedings relating to preliminary objections. In the exercise of its general control over a case, the Court orders the first pleading to address the questions of jurisdiction and admissibility. This throws on the applicant the duty of satisfying the Court positively that the court has jurisdiction and that the case is admissible. In preliminary objections proceedings prior to 1972, it was the normal practice that the respondent took the initiative and had to satisfy the Court that the Court lacked jurisdiction, or that the case was not admissible. Since then, however, the Court has relied on this new form of proceeding in the large majority of cases, especially where the respondent does not appear. This new form of proceeding is not regulated by any specific provision of the Rules of the Court, but falls within the scope of Article 48 of the Statute.

Impatience is often expressed at the prevalence of the practice of raising preliminary objections and at the apparent frequency with which the Court has accepted them. But such impatience is misplaced. A State -as any private litigant – is fully entitled, without abusing the due process of law, to adopt any litigation strategy and tactics allowed by the law to prevent judgment being given against it. Every State is entitled to intimate, through whatever procedure it deems appropriate and compatible with the Statute of the Court, that it is not willing for a concrete dispute implicating it to be decided by the

Court. The State's subjective willingness is something quite different from its objective legal obligation to submit to the jurisdiction, on which the Court will pronounce itself in the decision on the objection. Every State has the right that the existence of that obligation be judicially determined before it joins issue on the merits. There have even been cases where the respondent Government has felt itself constitutionally obliged, or because of a domestic situation politically compelled, to have its obligation to accept the jurisdiction of the Court judicially established. This result can only be attained by raising preliminary objections, and the judicious handling of them by the Court will be useful in assuaging local opinion. So long as the international community is not prepared to accept the principle of compulsory jurisdiction over legal disputes, the Court is certainly justified in the prudence and circumspection with which it deals with questions of its own jurisdiction, and in its refusal to attribute to States intentions which they themselves have not clearly formed. On the rare occasions on which the Court's action has been badly received politically, the consequences have been grave.

The institution of preliminary objections serves both a political as well as a legal function and is itself a reflection of the decentralized nature of the international legal system and the consensual nature of the adjudication of inter-State disputes. In terms of the legal function, it serves as a means to safeguard the rights of the litigants, while at a more political level, it serves as a means whereby a State can signal its opposition to having a particular dispute submitted to the Court at a time, or in a manner, which it finds unfavourable and can nevertheless provide a useful face-saving instrument by which it becomes acceptable to submit to adjudication on the merits should its attempts to block jurisdiction fail.

As a consequence of the importance and function of the preliminary objections, the Court will exercise due caution in all questions regarding jurisdiction and will neither assume jurisdiction where it is lacking, nor take over the role of pleading the issue which properly falls to the litigants themselves. It will also be careful not to prejudice the rights of third States not parties to the litigation.

APPEALS AND REFERENCES TO THE COURT

Provided that it has mainline jurisdiction under the principles already described, the International Court of Justice may act as an instance of appeal or other reference from other international judicial or quasi-judicial bodies.

The first case of this kind to come before the Court was the *ICAO Council* case. Here India appealed to the Court from a decision of the ICAO Council on complaints by Pakistan. The possibility of such an appeal is expressly regulated in the Chicago Convention on Civil Aviation of 1944. The Court took the opportunity to explain that in this type of case, the appeal to the Court must be regarded as an element in the general regime contemplated by the basic agreement, and that the provision for judicial recourse gives member States, and through them the organ in question, the possibility of ensuring a certain measure of supervision by the Court over the decisions of that organ. To that extent, the treaty enlists the support of the Court for the good functioning of the Organization. This is a useful clarification of the principles on which the Court will entertain appeals from jurisdictional or quasi-jurisdictional organs within the United Nations context. It is a further illustration of the general policy of the Court to co-operate with the other organs in the implementation of United Nations policy -using here the term "United Nations" in its broadest sense.

In the 1978 revision of the Rules of Court Article 87 changed the emphasis from "appeals" to "special reference to the Court" when, by virtue of a treaty in force, a contentious case is brought before the Court concerning a matter which has been the subject of proceedings before some other international body. Given the structure of international intergovernmental organizations and their relationship to each other, this probably provides a better framework than the concept of "appeal".

The suggestion is heard that the Court should be available in some appropriate form to advise national courts on questions of international law, especially questions of treaty interpretation, much in the way that the Court of Justice of the European Communities can give "preliminary rulings" to the national courts of the member States. But the analogy is false. The Luxembourg Court is in one sense integrated in the judicial system of the member States and the community law is part of the legal order of the member States. Given the political tensions in today's world, it is easy to imagine abuse of the International Court of Justice should national courts be enabled to request rulings from The Hague. It might also be noted that the International Court has never shown any inclination to seek the opinion of any national court on a question of the internal law of any State, and indeed it is not easy to see how this could be organized in a way that would be satisfactory in providing justice for the litigating parties.[24]

Appeal implies that the body exercising appellate jurisdiction may hear the case "*de novo*". This has to be distinguished, as far as international litigation is concerned, from recourse to the Court to challenge the validity or opposability of an arbitral award. A case of that nature does not imply that the International Court can determine "*de novo*" the issues put to the arbitral tribunal. What it means is that the Court, applying the rules of international law governing the impugned arbitral award, is called upon to determine whether the arbitral award complies with those rules. Two cases of that nature have come before the Court, the *Arbitral Award Made by the King of Spain on* 23 *December 1906* case, and the *Arbitral Award of 31 July 1989* case. In neither instance did the Court express any opinion on the substance of the award in question.

THE ADVISORY OPINIONS OF THE COURT AND ITS ADVISORY COMPETENCE

The principle underlying the advisory competence is that a qualified international intergovernmental organ, and not an individual State or a group of States, may ask the Court for an advisory opinion on legal questions, that opinion itself not constituting *per se* a "decision" with which anyone is legally bound to comply.

In several national legal systems the Executive has power to request a higher court to render an advisory opinion of this nature: though other legal systems look askance on the idea of a court rendering advisory opinions, on the ground that it distorts the true function of a court of law, which is to render binding decisions on disputes. For instance, in the United Kingdom the Judicial Committee of the Privy Council may be asked to give an advisory opinion. On the other hand, in 1793 the United States Supreme Court refused to give an advisory opinion to President Washington.[25] The introduction into the Covenant of the League of Nations of a discretionary power for the Permanent Court to render advisory opinions was thus a controversial innovation.

After considerable hesitation and experimentation, the main lines of the international advisory practice were clarified by the late 1920s. Its features include the following: *(a)* the right to request advisory opinions should be retained only by collegiate organs of international organizations, which would be expected to weigh the interests of the organization as a whole before making the request; *(b)* although the advisory jurisdiction opened up new ways of access to the Court, its existence should not be taken to authorize the surreptitious introduction of compulsory jurisdiction to decide concrete disputes between States; *(c)* the Court, in the exercise of its discretion to render advisory opinions, would remain faithful to its character as a court of justice, and as the supreme international tribunal, incorporate into its advisory practice such of the basic principles of its contentious jurisdiction as were appropriate; *(d)* subject to this, the *procedure* for dealing with advisory matters would be assimilated as far as possible to that for dealing with contentious matters. Indeed, from the procedural point of view the main difference between the two classes of case is that in advisory matters there are technically no "parties" and no binding "decision". The role of individual States in advisory cases is essentially to supply "information" – an *amicus curiae* function so to speak. In 1929 the Statute of the Permanent Court was amended by the introduction of these concepts in Articles 65 to 68. In this connection it is recalled that decisions in the Assembly and the Council of the League of Nations were adopted on the basis of the unanimity rule for voting then current. This supplied an additional hurdle in the way of excessive use of the advisory procedure.

Since the organs authorized by the Covenant to request advisory opinions were the Council and the Assembly of the League alone, on which only States were represented, it follows that the advisory competence did not constitute any departure from the basic nature of the Court, as a tribunal established by and for States. Only States, working through the duly qualified organs, could initiate an advisory case. The difference between access to the contentious jurisdiction, and access to the advisory competence, is that in the first type of case a State could go to the Court on its own responsibility, while for the second it required the concurrence of other States, expressed in the form of a resolution requesting the Court to give the opinion. It is sometimes suggested that individual States, or at least pairs of States, might be authorized to request advisory opinions. This has so far been rejected, for to accept it would mean to make possible the substitution of the advisory jurisdiction for the contentious – a real distortion of the true function of the Court. This has not prevented the Court from stating, in the form of a final and binding judgment, what the relevant legal principles are, leaving it to the parties to apply that judgment concretely.

The San Francisco Conference approved the patterns of advisory practice as they had evolved. It contented itself with a few technical and drafting changes which have, however, had the effect of accentuating the formal differentiation between the advisory and the contentious competences. This has been carried further by the general developments within the United Nations as they have unfolded over the last half century.

Accordingly, Article 96 of the Charter gives the Security Council and the General Assembly the right to request an advisory opinion on "any legal question". It further extends to other organs of the United Nations and Specialized Agencies, which may at any time be so authorized by the General Assembly, the right to request advisory opinions on legal questions arising within the scope of their activities. At the same time Article 65 of the Statute confirms that the Court "may give" – that is, has a discretionary power – an advisory opinion on any legal question at the request of any duly authorized body.

All of the principal organs of the United Nations (except the Secretariat) and the Specialized Agencies are now authorized to request advisory opinions. In addition, the Interim Committee of the General Assembly (now defunct), and the Committee on Applications for Review of Administrative Tribunal Judgments have also been given the necessary authorization.

Notwithstanding the degree of continuity in the conception of the basic function of the advisory competence and in the procedure utilized by the Court in rendering advisory opinions between the Permanent Court and the present Court, there are a number of important differences. The most important of these are of a political and institutional (or constitutional) nature. They relate in part to the manner in which the different organs of the United Nations and the Specialized Agencies operate, in comparison with the League's organs. They also relate in part to the difference in the scope of activities of the present day organs and agencies authorized to request advisory opinions, in comparison to their predecessors in the League-era. They also probably reflect a different perception of the present Court in relation to the rendering of advisory opinions to the organs of the United Nations, than that of the Permanent Court in relation to the League.

During the League era, unanimity, or virtual unanimity was required for reaching decisions on substantive issues, while a simple majority sufficed for decisions on procedural matters. Although the Permanent Court never clearly stated whether a decision to request an advisory opinion was substantive or procedural, it was extremely careful not to give advisory opinions over the opposition of one of the parties as expressed in the debate leading to the request.[26] In one case, the Court declined to give an advisory opinion over the opposition of a State which was not then a member of the League on a question which involved its interests.[27]

In the United Nations the situation has been quite different. One reason for this is the replacement of the unanimity rule on substantive issues by the rule requiring a two-thirds majority on 'important questions' in the General Assembly. It is unclear whether a request for an advisory opinion constitutes an important question, but it would be possible for a simple majority to determine that it did not. In any case, the abandonment of the unanimity rule has made it possible for a decision on a request to be made over the strong opposition of a sizeable number of States, including the States directly concerned with a particular issue. This has resulted in a number of requests of a controversial nature on sensitive issues.

This has been compounded by the previously mentioned perception of the present Court of its role in relation to the other organs of the United Nations and the rendering of advisory opinions to those organs. Unlike the Permanent Court, the present Court is an integral part of the Organization whose organs are empowered to request advisory opinions. Consequently, it sees itself as under an obligation to cooperate with the other organs to the maximum extent possible. Consequently, it will be heavily inclined in the direction of providing an advisory opinion, even if the request is made over strong opposition, so long as the requesting organ is competent to make the request. This has led on a number of occasions to its advisory opinions being a somewhat marginal element in the political evolution of a given issue.

However, the advisory procedure has sometimes been politically useful and of real legal significance in obtaining answers of general international concern. A number of its opinions have had a major impact upon the development of international law and international relations. Examples of these include the *Reparations for Injuries* opinion relating to the legal personality of the United Nations, the *Certain Expenses* opinion relating to the legal status of UN peace-keeping operations, the *Reservations to the Genocide Convention* opinion relating to the permissibility of reservations to multilateral conventions and others. Such cases could not have come before the Court but for the advisory procedure.

To date, the Court has given 21 advisory opinions in response to requests made by duly qualified organs and Specialized Agencies. This relative underutilization of the advisory competence prompted a former UN Secretary General to recommend that the Secretary-General himself be authorized to take advantage of the advisory competence, and that the other organs which already enjoy the necessary authorization should turn to the Court more frequently for advisory opinions.[28] These are controversial proposals, both politically and legally. Nevertheless, there is undoubtedly room for an increased, if judicious, use of the advisory procedure by the organs which are presently authorized to do so, and at least serious consideration of some of the possibilities of expanding the advisory competence to bring it more into line with the developments in international law since it was first conceived in 1920.

5

HOW A CASE IS TRIED

Procedure in the International Court is mostly governed by fundamental principles and rules enunciated in the Statute itself, and by the Rules of Court made under Article 30 of the Statute, supplemented by the accumulated practice since 1922. The current Rules were promulgated in 1978 and subsequently amended in December 2000. More recently, the Court adopted a number of "Practice Directions" in October 2001, as a part of its ongoing review of its procedure, with the object of expediting proceedings in view of its increased workload in recent years. In addition, these Practice Directions address issues related to the sound administration of justice, that is to say the perception of the parties that the proceedings are conducted in a way which contributes to their transparency and legitimacy. Neither the Court, nor the Parties can override the provisions of the Statute. There is more flexibility in the application of the Rules, and procedural precedents are a useful although not decisive guide.

These procedural requirements, however, are little more than a framework addressed to those responsible for the conduct of a case. It would not be appropriate for an international court to attempt to regulate its procedure in the precise and detailed manner which is necessary for national tribunals. Litigation in an international court – and especially in the International Court of Justice – cannot be approached on the same basis as litigation in a national court. Suggestions to model the International Court's procedure more closely on that of the Supreme Court of the United States or of any comparable constitutional court in a federal country overlook essential features of international litigation. The litigants are sovereign States which do not easily accept outside interference in how they conduct their affairs. Speed in the conduct of the proceedings is not always appropriate and the saying "justice delayed is justice denied" not always pertinent, since proceedings can be significantly affected by diplomatic developments outside the control of the Court, or even of the parties themselves, and diplomacy can have its own time-table. The nature of the international system is fundamentally different from the domestic constitutional and legal order pertaining to individual States and the role of the International Court within that system cannot be compared to that of a national constitutional court within a wholly different legal and political context. The legal relations of States are highly complex and generally can have far-reaching repercussions. Time and patience are required in the preparation of cases. The arguments of the parties have to be developed in a way that will convince a majority of the Bench and take account of the fact that the judges are the product of widely differing legal and general cultures. Finally, the Court is essentially based on consensus and its very jurisdiction and power to entertain a case derive from the litigants themselves. Consequently, the general approach of the Court is, subject to the Statute and the more flexible Rules and Practice Directions, to intervene as little as possible in the presentation of their cases by the parties. The parties even have the possibility, within the limits imposed by the Court's general control over the proceedings, to propose procedural modifications to suit their particular circumstances, although instances of this are rare.

On the other hand, the workload of the Court has increased substantially in recent years. As a result, the Court has decided that an efficient and sound administration of justice requires it to exert more control over the conduct of the proceedings than it was prone to do previously. The Court has always had the power to do so on the basis of the Statute and its own Rules. However, with the increase in its workload, it has found it necessary to balance the need to accommodate the wishes and interests of the parties with the interests of efficiency, specifically the necessity to avoid unnecessary delay and repetition in the proceedings. Furthermore, the Court must ensure that the interests of all parties in the wide variety of cases before it are given due consideration. This would be difficult to achieve, if the Court were to allow the litigants unlimited freedom in the presentation of their cases. Consequently, it appears likely that the Court will increasingly make use of its power to exert control over the conduct of the proceedings, while taking into account the special requirements and considerations in litigation between sovereign States referred to above.

There are three characteristic features of the Court's contentious procedure.
The first is the sharp division of the proceedings into two distinct phases, the written proceedings and the oral proceedings. Although the Court might accept differences in the quantity of pleadings in each phase, Article 43 of the Statute insists on the maintenance of the two phases themselves. The essential difference between them is that the documents of the written proceedings are composed by each party on its own, so-to-speak, not yet face-to-face. The written proceedings are conducted in confidence, the documents only being made available to other States with the consent of the parties, and only being made public after the oral proceedings have commenced. On the other hand, the oral proceedings, where the parties confront each other before the Court itself for the first time, are in principle public.

The second feature is the reticence of the Court in giving directions as to the contents of written pleadings, although as will be seen (p. 106 below) the Court may be stricter in controlling the themes in oral pleadings. This is above all a reflection of the fact that the litigants are sovereign States.

Thirdly, noteworthy is the complete secrecy which attends the deliberations of the Court itself. On only one unfortunate occasion has there been a "leak", not of the Court's deliberations themselves but of a decision.[1] The rule of judicial secrecy is considered so important that formerly it was difficult, sometimes impossible, to know how a judge had voted on a case unless he attached an individual opinion to the judgment (see p. 113 below). Since 1978, Article 95, paragraph 1, of the Rules of Court requires the names of the judges constituting the majority to be indicated. This relates to the final vote on the operative clause of the judgment, advisory opinion or order. It does not refer to voting during the Court's internal deliberations..

To demonstrate how a case is tried the *Military and Paramilitary Activities in and against Nicaragua* case is taken as a model. This case, which was tried under the current Rules of Court of 1978, was before the Court from 1984 until 1991. Needless to say, this was prior to the amendment of the Rules in 2000 and the adoption by the Court of its Practice Direction in 2001. Where these would affect the conduct of proceedings in a case brought before the Court since these developments, this will be pointed out. The *Nicaragua* case, as it is often referred to, also came before the General Assembly and the Security Council. In one form or another it raised nearly every problem encountered in international litigation.[2] As will be pointed out (see p. 125 below), revelations since the case was discontinued indicate that Nicaragua was misleading in its presentation of evidence and sworn statements relating to certain key factual aspects of the case. This clearly had an effect upon the outcome of the case and is a relevant factor which should be taken into account in assessing the value of the case as a "precedent", particularly with regard to the handling of some of the facts and the conclusions of law on the use of force in situations of indirect aggression.

This is without doubt one of the most significant cases to have come before the International Court. It is important for several reasons. It is concerned with the central and most controversial element in public international law today, issues relating to the prohibition on the use of force laid down in Article 2, paragraph 4, of the United Nations Charter and in other multilateral conventions such as the Charter of the Organization of American States and in general international law. In that context it also raised questions about the role of law in instances of the use of force and the relations between the Court and the Security Council. Secondly, the case brought up a series of complex and highly important matters relating to the entire system of the compulsory jurisdiction of the Court and its operation in a politically charged case. Thirdly, the decision of the United States, whose position on the facts regarding Nicaraguan involvement in El Salvador has since been vindicated, to withdraw from further participation in the proceedings in January 1985 and its subsequent withdrawal from the compulsory jurisdiction, has had and will continue to have a significant impact upon the position and role of the Court in modern international relations. The Court's actions are characterized by an unusual display of judicial activism following the inactivity of the Security Council after the "veto" of the United States of America, the respondent in that case. That activism, applauded by some and bitterly criticized by others, has raised acute controversy. It may have turned the attention of the majority of the Bench at the time away from a dispassionate view of the situation in the area.

MILITARY AND PARAMILITARY ACTIVITIES IN AND AGAINST NICARAGUA: BACKGROUND

This case arose out of the complicated situation in Central America during the 1980s. In July 1979 a revolutionary government, dominated by the Sandinista National Liberation Front, came to power in Nicaragua with important backing from the United States. This changed, however, and it soon found itself faced with growing United States opposition to many of its internal. and external policies. That opposition centred around what was claimed to be its increasingly undemocratic policies internally and its support for insurgent movements in neighbouring Central American States, especially El Salvador. For its part, Nicaragua argued that its internal policies were neither undemocratic nor of any concern of the United States. It also strongly denied any direct involvement in the internal strife in El Salvador or elsewhere in the region, despite significant indications to the contrary. The situation can be fairly summed up as a fundamental clash between a major world power concerned about its security interests, prestige and influence in a neighbouring region in which it has long exercised heavy influence, and a revolutionary government which views the United States policies in the area as a continuation of traditional regional dominance and interference in the domestic affairs of both Nicaragua and its neighbours.

These diametrically opposed positions soon led to a critical confrontation between the two States. In response to what it regarded as increasing interference in the regional *status quo,* in 1981 the United States cancelled its aid programme to Nicaragua and began covert backing for Nicaraguan opponents of the Sandinista Government, known as the *Contras*. This included financial support, training, and the provision of military equipment – ostensibly to inhibit the flow of material support from Nicaragua to the insurgents in El Salvador, but apparently also with the aim of bringing pressure on the Nicaraguan Government to change its domestic and foreign policies fundamentally.

Late in 1983 and continuing into 1984, the United States Government increased its backing for the *Contras* through limited direct support for their activities. This took the form of the mining of several of Nicaragua's harbours and armed raids on Nicaragua's port facilities and oil depots. These were carried out by personnel in the direct employ of the United States Central Intelligence Agency. The aim was to disrupt Nicaraguan exports and prevent the flow of much needed foreign currency into the country.

These operations led to major negative reactions both within the United States itself, in the Congress and amongst the public and press, and in Latin America and Western Europe. Nicaragua reacted to this with a major diplomatic offensive. Its principal thrust was toward the Security Council, as a conduit to public opinion in the United States and generally. In the Security Council a draft resolution submitted by Nicaragua on 4 April 1984 was not adopted following the negative vote of the United States. This, which it may be assumed was expected, triggered Nicaragua's decision to take the case to the Court. On 9 April 1984, Nicaragua filed an application instituting proceedings against the United States.

That application closely followed the resolution which had not been adopted in the Security Council. It set out a long list of alleged violations by the United States of numerous provisions of the Charter of the United Nations and the Charter of the Organization of American States and other treaties and of customary law, principally by direct action and indirectly through support for the *Contras*. Nicaragua also claimed a large sum by way of compensation for the loss and damage it had suffered.

Simultaneously with its application instituting the proceedings, Nicaragua requested the Court to indicate provisional measures of protection on the basis of Article 41 of the Statute (see p. 79 above). The measures requested included a cease and desist order against the United States with regard to the *Contras* and with regard to military and paramilitary activity by its own personnel.

THE INSTITUTION OF THE PROCEEDINGS

The institution of proceedings is governed by Article 40 of the Statute. Cases may be begun in one of two ways. One is by notification to the Court of a special agreement. The other is by unilateral filing of an application instituting proceedings. The choice is a matter for the States concerned, and is determined by the general state of their relations and the extent to which they have or are deemed to have conferred jurisdiction on the Court to determine the specific dispute. In this case Nicaragua considered that the Court had compulsory jurisdiction through declarations of each State accepting the jurisdiction under Article 36, paragraphs 2 and 5, of the Statute (see p. 94 above).

A special agreement both defines the dispute or question which the Court is requested to decide and confers on the Court jurisdiction to answer that question or decide that dispute. For example, the special agreement of 7 April 1993 between Hungary and Slovakia stated:

(1) The Court is requested to decide on the basis of the Treaty [of 1977] and rules

and principles of general international law, as well as such other treaties as the Court may find applicable,
(a) whether the Republic of Hungary was entitled to suspend and subsequently abandon, in 1989, the works on the Nagymaros Project and on the part of the Gabčíkovo Project for which the Treaty attributed responsibility to the Republic of Hungary;
(b) whether the Czech and Slovak Federal Republic was entitled to proceed, in November 1991, to the "provisional solution" and to put into operation from October 1992 this system, described in the Report of the Working Group of Independent Experts of the Commission of the European Communities, the Republic of Hungary and the Czech and Slovak Federal Republic dated 23 November 1992 (damming up of the Danube at river kilometer 1851.7 on Czechoslovak territory and resulting consequences on water and navigation course);
(c) what are the legal effects of the notification, on 19 May 1992, of the termination of the Treaty by the Republic of Hungary.
(2) The Court is also requested to determine the legal consequences, including the rights and obligations for the Parties, arising from its Judgment on the question in paragraph 1 of this Article.

When a case is started in this way the Court's decision will normally consist of a formal reply to the precise question.

The position is different when the case is introduced unilaterally, by application. The institution of the proceedings is a unilateral act (there have been instances where diplomatic requirements have led to what looks like a unilateral application to the Court, although in fact the action was agreed beforehand). Theoretically there is no agreement between the parties either that the or indeed any case should be brought, or what the claim should be. For this reason, an application must indicate the two parties and the subject of the dispute. It must also specify *as far as possible* the provision on which the applicant founds the jurisdiction of the Court, state the precise nature of the claim, and give a succinct statement of the facts and grounds on which the claim is based, these being further developed in later pleadings.

Accordingly Nicaragua's application defined the subject of the dispute as concerning the responsibility for military and paramilitary activities in and against Nicaragua, claiming that the United States was using military force against Nicaragua and intervening in Nicaragua's internal affairs, in violation of Nicaragua's sovereignty, territorial integrity and political independence and of the most fundamental and universally-accepted principles of international law.

This was followed by a succinct statement of the facts, showing that the United States was "directing military and paramilitary actions in and against Nicaragua" and a summary of the law applicable. That was the subject of the dispute. The Court was asked to judge and declare that the United States was in breach of a series of international obligations towards Nicaragua, and was accordingly under an obligation to pay Nicaragua, in its own right and as *parens patriae* for its citizens, reparations in a sum to be determined by the Court.

As mentioned, the declarations accepting the compulsory jurisdiction were invoked. In this case, this was not a simple matter.

Nicaragua, on 29 September 1929, signed the Protocol of Signature of the Statute of the Permanent Court of International Justice. At the same time it made a declaration accepting "unconditionally" the jurisdiction of that Court. That Protocol of Signature required ratification. However, there is no record of any instrument of ratification ever having been received by the Secretary-General of the League of Nations as depositary, or by the Secretary-General of the United Nations, although the necessary internal formalities for ratification required by Nicaraguan law had been completed in 1938. Nicaragua was to argue that this declaration was covered by the transitory provision of Article 36, paragraph 5, of the Statute – in the circumstances a highly technical matter.

The United States accepted the compulsory jurisdiction of the present Court in 1946. Its declaration contained several reservations, one of which, called the "Multilateral Treaties Reservation" or the Vandenberg Reservation (after the Senator who had proposed it), excluded "disputes arising under a multilateral treaty, unless (1) all parties to the treaty affected by the decision are also parties to the case before the Court, or (2) the United States of America specially agrees to the jurisdiction". (This text is obscurely drafted, so much so that it is given in English in the non-authoritative French text of the judgment of the Court.) That declaration also required six months' notice to terminate it. On 6 April 1984, in anticipation of the Nicaraguan move, the United States filed with the Secretary-General an instrument (commonly known as "the Schultz letter") purporting to modify the 1946 declaration by excluding "disputes with any Central American State or arising out of or related to events in Central America..." That modification continued:

> Notwithstanding the terms of the [1946] declaration, this proviso shall take effect immediately and shall remain in force for two years, so as to foster the continuing regional dispute settlement process which seeks a negotiated solution to the interrelated political, economic and security problems of Central America.

At the outset, therefore, it was clear that a major issue of jurisdiction would arise, namely, whether the Court had jurisdiction on the basis of the optional clause of the Statute of the Permanent Court and its transfer to the present Court through the operation of Article 36, paragraph 5, of the Statute, and whether the Schultz letter effectively excluded the situation in Nicaragua from the jurisdiction of the Court. Other issues relating to the jurisdiction of the Court and the admissibility of the application came out later.

THE BENCH

The composition of the Court for deciding a case -that is the Bench -is fixed on the date of the opening of the hearings in each phase. If a case goes through several phases, and a triennial election (see p. 50 above) takes place while the case is pending (as occurred here), changes in the composition of the Court may result, since a different composition of the Bench will deal with each successive phase. This practice, which has been followed consistently by the present Court, has been criticized on the ground that changes in the composition of the Court while a case is pending is not conducive to the good administration of international justice. Nevertheless, the Court formally incorporated this interpretation in the 1978 Rules of Court. Article 13 of the Statute, which forms the basis for this practice, simply provides that judges who are replaced "shall finish any cases which they may have begun". The Court has interpreted the word "cases" here as meaning any procedurally self-contained phase of a "case".

The rules about replacement do not apply if the change takes place while the oral proceedings are in progress or before the decision in that phase has been delivered.

While no doubt efforts will be made to avoid commencing proceedings close to the end of the term of office of Members of the Court, it is not always possible to ensure this, or to ensure that the decision will be rendered before the term of office of sitting Members of the Court comes to an end.

The possibility that judges will be replaced at a relatively late stage of a case – for regardless of how it is phased it is and remains one case for the parties – creates uncertainties. The composition of the Court is one of the factors which the parties have in mind when they plan their litigation (and political) strategy.

If the President of the Court is the national of one of the parties, he may not exercise any of the functions of president for that case. His place as President of the Bench will be taken by the Vice-President, or if he is disqualified for any reason, by the next senior member of the Court (designated "Acting President"). The replacement of the President during the pendency of a case is treated in a similar way as the replacement of any other member of the Court.

Our case was before the Court for no less than seven years. Triennial elections took place in 1985 and 1988. When it started the Court was in its thirteenth period (see Appendix III). The President was Judge Elias of Nigeria and the Vice-President Judge Sette-Camara of Brazil. The fourteenth period began on 6 February 1985, with Judge Nagendra Singh (India) as President and Judge de Lacharrière (France) as Vice-President. In September 1985 Judge Morozov (USSR) resigned. He was replaced by Judge Tarassov from December, but as the hearings in the merits phase of the case had been completed before his election to the Court, he could not take part in that phase. In March 1987 Judge de Lacharrière died and was replaced, in September, by Judge Guillaume. Judge Mbaye (Senegal) was elected Vice-President. In 1991 the Court entered its fifteenth period, with Judge Ruda (Argentina) as President and Judge Mbaye as Vice-President.

Nicaragua exercised its right to appoint a judge *ad hoc*. It chose Professor Claude-Albert Colliard, Professor emeritus and honorary dean in Paris. He took part only in the jurisdiction and admissibility and the merits phases of the case.

OFFICIAL LANGUAGES

The official languages of the Court are English and French. The parties may agree to use one or other language exclusively, in which case the judgment too shall be delivered in that language. In the absence of agreement, each party is free to employ whatever official language it prefers. The Court may also authorize a party to use a language other than English or French. In that case an English or French translation has to be attached. If a party conducts its oral pleadings in a language other than English or French, it must make its own arrangements for the interpretation into one of the official languages.

In the present case, there was no agreement between the parties regarding language. All the written pleadings were in English. In the oral proceedings, the Nicaraguan representatives used both languages, and one of the witnesses in the merits phase gave his evidence in Spanish. The United States delegation used English. The authoritative text of all the orders and judgments in this case is English.

REPRESENTATION OF THE PARTIES

The person entrusted with the formal representation of a party in international litigation is called the Agent. He is assisted by counsel and advocates and other experts as required.[3] The Court, however, has, in Article 58 of the Rules, reserved the right itself to determine the number of counsel and advocates who will address it in the oral phase. It is sparing in the use of this power.

The status of Agent is roughly equivalent to that of a head of a special diplomatic mission. He is empowered to bind his country in all that concerns the conduct of the case in the Court. In that capacity, he has to sign every important document relating to the case, and he has to confirm every important and binding statement made in his government's name in the course of the proceedings.

There are no formal qualifications for the position of Agent. States show two tendencies. They appoint either a high-ranking member of their diplomatic service (for example, their Ambassador at The Hague), or the Legal Adviser (or a member of his staff) of the Ministry for Foreign Affairs. However, this is not invariable, and occasionally a practising lawyer or leading professor is appointed.

An application should be signed by the Agent. If he is not the accredited diplomatic representative of his country at The Hague, that diplomatic representative has to authenticate the signature. The respondent government should appoint its Agent when acknowledging receipt of the application, or as soon as possible thereafter, although these provisions must not be read too literally in the event that the respondent Government, not acknowledging the jurisdiction of the Court, should decline to appoint an Agent or otherwise be represented before it. The non-appointment of an agent is frequently, but not invariably (in the earliest stages of a case) a sign that the Government concerned does not intend to take part in the proceedings.

In the present case, Nicaragua appointed as its Agent its Ambassador at The Hague. The United States appointed the Legal Adviser of the Department of State.

Similarly, there are no formal qualifications for counsel and advocates. These are frequently chosen from experienced members of the national bar. In addition there has grown up over the years a small group of international lawyers, drawn mainly from the legal professions of Belgium, France, Italy, Switzerland, the United Kingdom and the United States who have specialized in practice in the International Court.

Nicaragua availed itself of the services of American, British and French professors of international law. The United States was represented exclusively by United States attorneys and professors of international law. Thus, in addition to the Agent, Nicaragua was represented in one or other phase by Professors A. Chayes of Harvard, I. Brownlie of Oxford, and A. Pellet of Paris together with members of a Washington firm of Attorneys, the legal advisers in the United States of the Government of Nicaragua. The United States was represented, alongside the Legal Adviser of the Department of State and members of his staff, by Professors Myres McDougal of Yale University, John Norton Moore of the University of Virginia, Fred I. Morisson of the University of Minnesota, Stefan Riesenfeld of the University of California (Berkeley), and Louis B. Sohn of the University of Georgia, together with a large staff of attorney-advisers and others.

Two strong and well-equipped teams were to be ranged against each other.

STEPS FOLLOWING THE INSTITUTION OF THE PROCEEDINGS

As soon as the Registrar receives an application, he has to carry out a series of statutory duties.

First, after satisfying himself of the formal compliance of the application with the procedural requirements of the Statute and Rules, he assigns the case a number and opens a folio in the Court's General List (this case was No. 70). Article 40 of the Statute requires him then to communicate the application to all concerned. This includes first of all the respondent Government, and secondly the members of the Court. Standing arrangements exist for the direct transmission of communications to the designated organ of each State party to the Statute, usually the Ministry for Foreign Affairs or the Embassy at The Hague. Once the Agents have been appointed, with an address for service at The Hague, they are the sole channel of communication between the Court and that party, for all matters connected with the case.

Second, all members of the United Nations have to be notified of the institution of the proceedings, through the Secretary-General, and all other States entitled to appear before the Court. This is done through the circulation of the instrument instituting the proceedings, accompanied with a translation into the other official language. The purpose of this communication is to serve general notice to all governments of the institution of the proceedings, and what they are about. This enables them to consider whether they wish to intervene in the case. In addition, for more general reasons, governments should have exact knowledge of all cases pending in the Court. The Registry also issues a Press communiqué about the new case, and further communiqués as necessary announcing the progress of the case.

The case is then given a name (if the parties have not yet done so themselves). This is normally a matter for the President and the Registrar. The naming of a case is not an easy matter, especially as the title should be unprejudicial to either side and has to be reasonably similar in English and French. The parties' names are included. If the case is introduced by application, the form *A* v. *B* is used, indicating applicant and respondent respectively. If the case is introduced by special agreement, the form *A*/*B* is normally used, the States being named in alphabetical order in each language, unless circumstances make this undesirable. Normally no parties are indicated in the title of advisory cases. The name of the case is chosen to indicate in neutral and non-prejudicial terms what the case is about. In the present case, it was taken from a passage in the application instituting the proceedings. In a letter to the Court of 27 April 1984, the United States stated that it regarded the title given to the case as "prejudicial", but the Court took no action to change it.[4]

After these communications have been made, and the two Agents duly appointed, the next step is for the President to ascertain the Parties' views regarding the future procedure. He does this both by modern electronic communication and by summoning the Agents to meet with him to establish time limits at least for the filing of the first round of written pleadings. The summoning of that meeting is obligatory, and the agreements regarding procedure reached at it can only be altered by later agreement and are subject to the control of the Court. If the consultations with the parties reveal persistent disagreement between them on questions of procedure, the Court, or if it is not sitting the President, will decide the matter.

In this case, on 13 April the United States appointed its Agent. At the same time it informed the Court of its "firm conviction" that the Court was without any jurisdiction and requested the Court to remove the case from its list. On 23 April it reiterated this request, asking for an immediate decision which would preclude further proceedings. The Court, however, on 24 April decided that it then had no sufficient basis for acceding to the requests of the United States.

The major question of the jurisdiction of the Court, on the ground that Nicaragua had not accepted the jurisdiction of either the Permanent Court or the present Court, was in that way raised at the very earliest stage of the proceedings.

THE PROVISIONAL MEASURES PHASE

A request for the indication of provisional measures, which may be made at any time by either party, takes precedence over everything else. The adverse party is given an opportunity to submit written observations. The time limits for a provisional measures phase will be fixed to some extent taking account of the views of the parties, but there is an inherent element of urgency in such a request.

Nicaragua's request at this stage was for an order requiring the United States immediately to cease and desist from providing directly or indirectly any support including training, arms, ammunition, supplies, assistance, finances, direction or any other form of support to any nation, group, organization, movement or individual engaged or planning to engage in military or paramilitary activities in or against Nicaragua, that the United States should immediately cease and desist from any military or paramilitary activity by its own officials, agents or forces in or against Nicaragua and from any other use of force in its relations with Nicaragua, and should take no action which would have the effect of extending or aggravating the situation pending further consideration of the case by the Court. For its part, the United States believed that the Court lacked jurisdiction *in limine* and raised this plea "as a plea in bar of fundamental importance". It submitted that the Court should not proceed on Nicaragua's application and "most certainly should not indicate provisional measures". It reiterated its request that these proceedings "be terminated for once and for all".

Public hearings on the provisional measures took place between 25 and 27 April 1984. They further emphasized the principal jurisdictional questions as then seen. Nicaragua challenged the "Schultz letter" purporting to modify the 1946 declaration of the United States.

On 10 May the Court issued its order. It outlined the major issues of jurisdiction which had been raised. Recalling its low threshold jurisdiction to indicate provisional measures, it found that the two declarations of Nicaragua and the United States "do nevertheless appear to afford a basis on which the jurisdiction of the Court might be founded". The Court was unanimous in rejecting the request of the United States for the immediate removal of the case from the list. It was also virtually unanimous in indicating a series of provisional measures which the parties ought to take pending its final decision. There was a joint separate opinion by Judges Mosler and Sir Robert Jennings, and a dissenting opinion by Judge Schwebel.

In that order the Court also decided unanimously that the written proceedings should first be addressed to the questions of the jurisdiction of the Court to entertain the dispute and of the admissibility of the Application. Outlines of those issues already appeared in the body of the order.

On 28 June Nicaragua submitted another request for provisional measures on the ground that the United States had failed to comply with the earlier order. The Court decided that this should await the outcome of the examination of the jurisdiction and admissibility phase of the case.

THE WRITTEN PROCEEDINGS

Traditionally, there are two methods for the filing of the written pleadings (briefs), consecutive filing and simultaneous filing.

In cases instituted by unilateral application, consecutive filing has always been the rule with the applicant filing first. The simultaneous filing of pleadings, which is taken over from international arbitration practice, was traditionally reserved for cases brought before the Court by special agreement, unless the agreement specified consecutive filing. The idea behind simultaneous filing was that it took into account the formal equality of the States appearing as parties and the absence, as in arbitration, of a formal relationship between them of plaintiff and defendant, or of applicant and respondent. However, experience has shown this to be an inconvenient mode of pleading, both for the parties and for the Court and can lead to unnecessary delay. Consequently, the Court in adopting its new Practice Directions (see p. 91 above), has indicated that it wishes "to discourage the practice of simultaneous deposit of pleadings in cases brought by Special Agreement".[5] While this may not rule out the simultaneous filing of pleadings altogether, it would appear likely to reduce it to a bare minimum, subject to the approval of the Court.

There are no detailed rules for the form of written pleadings. This is a matter in which States are guided by their national traditions and their sense of good taste and of what is appropriate in the circumstances. The fact that the pleadings are all usually published and remain on permanent record should influence the presentation of a case in the pleadings.

The Rules of Court and practice regulate to some extent the content of the pleadings. Article 49 of the Rules requires the Memorial, as the first written pleading is called, to contain a statement of all the relevant facts, a statement of law, and submissions. Copies of all relevant documents should be annexed. This is followed by the Counter-Memorial, which should contain more: an admission or denial of the facts stated in the Memorial, additional facts if any, observations concerning the statement of law in the Memorial, a statement of law in answer thereto, and submissions. Again, copies of all relevant documents should be annexed. In consecutive pleading, the Memorial and the Reply are filed by the applicant, and the Counter-Memorial and Rejoinder by the respondent. The Rules of Court prescribe that the Reply and Rejoinder should not merely repeat the party's contentions, but should be directed to bringing out the issues that still divide them. If pleadings are filed simultaneously, they are usually limited to Memorials, Counter-Memorials and Replies, although occasionally the Court may also authorize Rejoinders. A second round of written pleadings, if authorized, consists of a Reply and a Rejoinder. A second round of written pleadings is not usual in preliminary objection or other interlocutory phases.

It frequently happens that the issues are not fully brought out until the Counter-Memorial is filed. It is only when the argument and submissions of the Memorial and those of the Counter-Memorial are compared that it is possible to see what the case is really about, for only then does its presentation cease to be unilateral. That is why the

Reply and, where needed the Rejoinder, are usually important stages of pleading in the International Court.

A document raising preliminary objections should set out the facts and the law on which the objections are based and the objecting party's submissions relating to that issue. The Court has provided in its new Practice Directions that such a document should be normally filed within four months of the raising of objections. Copies of all relevant (supporting) documents should also be annexed. The Court has also strongly advised parties in one of its Practice Directions to be selective in their choice and use of annexed documents and to avoid the overproliferation of annexes.[6] Other than these Directions, there are no formal rules for other interlocutory applications. How they are presented and how the Court will deal with them will depend upon the circumstances.

The original of every written pleading is signed by the Agent and filed in the Registry together with a number of copies, now usually fixed at 125. The Registrar delivers one certified copy and a sufficient number of plain copies to the other party and circulates the document to the members of the Court and other interested persons, including governments which have been authorized to receive them. He also prepares an unofficial translation of the pleading into the other official language. Unlike the procedure commonly found in international arbitration, the parties do not communicate their pleadings to each other. The Court has recently determined in one of its new Practice Directions, that this shall also apply to the communication of full or partial translations by one party of any part of its pleadings, or of any annexed documentation. These must be passed to the Registry, which will examine them and communicate them to the other party, providing at the same time any further necessary information relating to the manner in which they were prepared. In cases of urgency, the Court will accept a pleading sent to it by electronic methods of communication if it is received before the expiration of the time limit, and the original signed text may be filed later in the normal course. This procedure is naturally rare.

The written pleadings are not usually accessible to the public until the opening of the oral proceedings (if both parties consent) or even until after the termination of the case. This is to avoid prematurely exposing them to public, and perhaps polemical, discussion which, it is considered, would not be conducive to the good administration of international justice. However, any government may apply to the Court and ask for the pleadings to be made available to it, and this will normally be granted after enquiry of the Agents. Once they are in the public domain, a set of the pleadings is placed in the Library of the Peace Palace at The Hague and in other United Nations libraries.

Parties are normally granted equal time for their various pleadings. This may not always fully apply to the first round of written pleadings, because it is fair to assume that, except perhaps in cases of great urgency, before a Government decides to institute proceedings, it has carefully considered the case it wishes to present and has at least the outlines of the Memorial prepared. Indeed, since there is a close relation between the Application instituting the proceedings and the Memorial, it is difficult to see how an Application can be properly drafted if this is not the case. When the Court is satisfied that a Government is not taking part in the proceedings, it may not maintain exact symmetry in the time limits. However, it will always give the non-appearing Government an opportunity to submit its views to the Court.

THE PHASE OF JURISDICTION AND ADMISSIBILITY

In this case, after having ascertained the views of the parties in light of the order of 10 May, the President on 14 May fixed time limits for the written proceedings on the questions of jurisdiction and admissibility: 30 June for the Memorial of Nicaragua and 17 August for the Counter-Memorial of the United States – quite short time limits considering the complexity of the issues which had already been raised. Since this was not an instance of preliminary objections in the formal sense, but of the Court's requirement that the issues of jurisdiction and admissibility should be pleaded first, Nicaragua, as applicant, filed the first pleading. The roles of the parties would have been reversed had the United States raised formal preliminary objections at this stage.

This procedure of the Court deciding separately on its own initiative, the issues of jurisdiction and admissibility within the context of its general control over a case is, as was pointed out earlier (see p. 84 above) increasingly prevalent and has been used in the majority of cases where jurisdiction and/or admissibility were contested since 1972. It differs from the formal *preliminary objection* procedure, governed by Article 79 of the Rules of Court, in that in the former, the proceedings on the merits are not formally suspended and the roles of the parties are not normally reversed, as is the case when the formal procedure is invoked.

Once the written memorials relating to preliminary objections have been filed; with either the applicant filing first in the case of the informal procedure under the control of the Court or the respondent filing first in the case of the formal preliminary objection procedure, the next step will normally be a hearing. It is highly unusual for multiple rounds of written pleadings to occur in relation to questions of jurisdiction and admissibility. The same order of appearance will normally be used during the hearings, as was used to determine the sequence for the filing of memorials.

As was pointed out earlier, preliminary objections, whether following the formal or the informal procedure, play an important role in litigation at the International Court (see p. 81 above). They are far from constituting mere "technicalities" and among other things enable both parties and the Court to gain a better understanding of the facts and issues as well as the motivations and objectives of the respective parties. Given the political ambiance in which much international litigation is conducted, a Government which loses a case on jurisdictional grounds is likely to have an easier task in reconciling its public opinion to the outcome.

In our case the pleadings were duly filed within the time limits fixed. In the Memorial, Nicaragua introduced an additional basis for jurisdiction, namely the Treaty of Friendship, Commerce and Navigation between the two countries of 24 May 1958.

THE CASE READY FOR HEARING

On 17 August 1984, with the filing of the Counter-Memorial of the United States on the issues of jurisdiction and admissibility, the Court decided that no further written pleadings were needed. The case then became "ready for hearing". There are two consequences of a case becoming ready for hearing.

The first is that it is entered into the list for oral proceedings.

If more than one case is ready for hearing at the same time, the Court will determine the order in which they will be heard, due regard being given to the relative urgency of the cases, and in particular whether any pending case should receive priority. When this phase of our case became ready for hearing, there was no other pending case in the same position. On the other hand, the five-man Chamber of the Court hearing the *Gulf of Maine* case, in which the hearings had been interrupted by the provisional measures phase of the present case, was still deliberating.

The second consequence of a case being ready for hearing is that no further documents may be filed except with the consent of the other party and with the authorization of the Court. The Court does not like the belated submission of documents unless this is unavoidable. The Court will decide the matter, in accordance with Article 56 of the Rules, after hearing the views of the parties. This was strengthened recently in one of the Court's new Practice Directives, in which it is provided that in the absence of consent of the other party, the Court will only authorize the submission of new documents in exceptional circumstances. However, the Court is not governed by a formalistic attitude and it may be possible that a new document only comes to light after the closure of the written proceedings. In such a case, the Court will determine the issue on its merits and has the power to admit a new document if it considers this necessary and justified.

In our case, no further documents were filed after the closure of written proceedings and the Court decided to commence hearings after its summer recess.

THIRD PARTY INTERVENTION IN CONTENTIOUS PROCEEDINGS

The Statute grants two possibilities of intervention by a third State in contentious proceedings.[7]

By Article 62 of the Statute, whenever a State considers that it has an interest of a legal nature which may be affected by the decision in a case, it may submit a request for permission to intervene. The application for permission to intervene is given the same wide circulation as the original application instituting proceedings. The Court decides whether to admit the application. If the permission is granted arrangements are made for the intervening State to participate in the proceedings.

A number of instances of attempted intervention of this kind have occurred before the present Court. The first two were attempts by Fiji to intervene in the *Nuclear Tests* cases in 1973. After the Court had found that the principal proceedings had lost their object, it did not find it necessary to deal with these requests (see p. 169 below). These were followed by an attempted intervention by Malta in the *Continental Shelf* case between Tunisia and Libya and by Italy in the subsequent *Continental Shelf* case between Malta and Libya. In neither of these instances was permission to intervene granted. However, in both cases the Court was careful not to prejudice the interests of the would-be intervening States, having obtained sufficient indication of what their concerns were during the proceedings on the applications of permission to intervene. Nicaragua's request to intervene in the *Land, Island and Maritime Frontier* case between El Salvador and Honduras was granted in part, with Nicaragua being given a standing of a "non-party intervener" and as such was not bound by the judgment. More recently, Australia, Samoa, The Solomon Islands, the Marshall Islands and the Federated States of Micronesia attempted to intervene in the *Request for an Examination of the Situation in Accordance with Paragraph 63 of the Court's Judgment of 20 December1974 in the Nuclear Tests* (New Zealand v. France) case. This request was denied, as was the attempt by the Philippines to intervene in the *Pulau Litigan and Pulau Sipidan* case between Indonesia and Malaysia. In the *Land and Maritime Boundary* case between Cameroon and Nigeria, neither of these States objected to Equatorial Guinea's request to a limited intervention as a non-party intervener, and this request was accordingly granted.

The second kind of intervention has its roots in the Conventions for the Pacific Settlement of Disputes of 1899 and 1907. Article 63 of the Statute deals with the contingency that the interpretation of a multilateral treaty is in question. In those circumstances the States parties to the convention other than those involved in the case, have the right to intervene (subject to the condition that the intervention is admissible). If they do so the interpretation of the treaty contained in the judgment will be equally binding upon the intervening State or States.

This so-called intervention as of right does not require the formal permission of the Court. However, the Court will examine whether the intervention is admissible. There have been three instances of this type of intervention before the present Court. The first was in the *Haya de la Torre* case, where it was granted after the terms of intervention had been narrowed and clarified by the intervening State (see p. 134 below). The third was in the *Request for and Examination of the Situation in Accordance with Paragraph 63 of the Court's Judgment of 20 December 1974 in the Nuclear Tests* (New Zealand v. France) case which not admitted. The second was in the present case.

On 15 August 1984, just before the filing of the Counter-Memorial, El Salvador filed a declaration of intervention. It was followed by two letters of 10 and 17 September. The United States raised no objection. Nicaragua's attitude was ambiguous, and was open to the interpretation that Nicaragua opposed the intervention. That opposition would have brought into play Article 84, paragraph 2, of the Rules, requiring a hearing before the Court decided on the admissibility of the declaration of intervention.

In its order of 4 October 1984, the Court, by the close vote of nine to six, decided not to hold a hearing, and then by fourteen to one went on to decide that the declaration of intervention was inadmissible at that stage. The order was virtually unreasoned, but it seems that the underlying feeling was that the attempted intervention dealt more with the merits of the case, that is with Nicaragua's backing of the guerillas in El Salvador, than with the issues of jurisdiction and admissibility. There was a separate opinion by Judge Nagendra Singh, a joint separate opinion by Judges Ruda, Mosler, Ago, Sir Robert Jennings and de Lacharrière, separate opinions by Judges Oda and Bedjaoui and a dissenting opinion by Judge Schwebel.

Although he had been appointed, the judge *ad hoc* of Nicaragua did not sit in this phase of the case. The vote of nine to six was the closest of all the votes in the Court throughout the case. Moreover, in the merits phase, two of the judges constituting the majority stated that they had second thoughts. Be that as it may, as will be seen the impact of this decision on the future developments in this case was far-reaching. It prevented the Court from receiving any indication of the facts beyond what had appeared in the earlier phases of the case. This, in the view of many, distorted the issues of "justiciability" which were central to the decision of the Court on the admissibility of the case.

THE HEARING

The public hearing occupied the Court from 8 to 18 October. There were two rounds of oral statements by each side, divided between different members of the teams. Nicaragua simply asked the Court to declare that jurisdiction existed in respect of its application and that the application was admissible in its entirety. The United States submitted that the claims set forth in the application were not within the jurisdiction of the Court and were inadmissible. The case of each party was argued by five qualified advocates.

Nicaragua, as stated, introduced in its Memorial a second basis of jurisdiction, namely the bilateral Treaty of Friendship, Commerce and Navigation concluded between the two countries in 1958. This was an added complication.

The oral proceedings, in principle held in public (in exceptional circumstances the public may be excluded), take place in the dignified setting of the Great Hall of Justice in the Peace Palace at The Hague. The members of the Court and the Registrar wear their judicial robes. The Agents (if they are members of the legal profession), counsel and advocates dress as they would if they were appearing before the Supreme Court of their own country. In addition to the Registrar and his professional assistants, the official recorders, interpreters and other members of the staff on duty are also present. The press and the electronic media are ubiquitous. The speaker's rostrum is immediately facing the President: to its right sits the applicant government's Agent and his delegation, and to the left those of the respondent State.

At the appointed hour the Chief Usher, after making sure that all is ready (and in particular that the representatives of the parties are present), gives the traditional cry *La Cour*. All rise. The judges proceed with measured tread to their seats. At a sign from the President they are seated, and the others follow. The atmosphere is subdued and forensic. The Great Hall of Justice at the Peace Palace is bigger than many court-rooms, and discreetly placed microphones carry the voices to all corners. The remarks of the President and his colleagues are immediately interpreted. Speeches, which are now usually delivered from prepared texts (as in other United Nations principal organs), are simultaneously interpreted into the other official language of the Court. While this may to some extent be necessary it does tend to have a deadening effect upon the presentation of the arguments. This notwithstanding, it is still the hearing which has the most direct impact. The written pleadings lay the necessary foundations – of fact and of law – on which good oral pleadings can be based. One cannot fail to be struck by the close attention with which the judges follow the oral statements, for they act as the focusing point for the work of the Court in deciding the case, and accordingly can have a great impact on the case. Skilful pleading may not win a bad case, but it can mitigate the effect of a negative decision. While clearly there is no room for flamboyant advocacy appropriate for a trial by a jury, the effect of intonation, of inflexion, of command of language and a cultivated presentation of the case, of personal integrity and candour, mastery of complicated issues, and, where appropriate, a touch of humour, of drama, a well-timed quotation – all this is concealed in the lifeless printed version of the oral pleadings which is subsequently circulated and published. Above all, it is in the hearings that the two parties first meet face-to-face. Their cases emerge from the remote tranquillity of Counsel's chambers and clash head-on in the hands of highly skilled lawyers, each of whom knows the strength, and the weakness, of his own and of his opponent's cases, and before a Court of equally skilled and experienced personalities.

The pleading is strenuous. The Rules require that the oral statements shall be as succinct as possible within the limits of what is requisite for the adequate presentation of that party's contentions. They should be directed to the essential issues that divide the parties. They should not traverse the whole ground covered by the written pleadings nor simply repeat facts and arguments those contain. Furthermore in the 1972 Rules, the Court first spelled out its power (previously only implicit) to indicate to the parties any points or issues to which it would specially like them to address themselves as well as points or issues on which it feels there has been sufficient argument. This is designed to avoid prolixity and repetitiousness in the oral phase. A provisional record of the day's proceedings is prepared and distributed, together with an unofficial translation by the Registry, each evening. This is known as the C.R. (*compte rendu*). Subject to correction under the control of the Court, these become the formal minutes of the proceedings and are later published by the Registry in the series of *Pleadings, Oral Arguments and Documents*.

The President and other members of the Court endeavour to maintain a courteous and businesslike atmosphere, respecting the traditions of forensic civility, both inside and outside the Court during the proceedings. Indeed the atmosphere is notable for its general lack of polemics or heated exchanges, although this does not exclude the forensic equivalent of "points of order" when appropriate. There is little "playing to the gallery" which sometimes occurs during the public meetings of political bodies like the Security Council and the General Assembly. At the same time, the press is everywhere. Immediately before a hearing begins a short time is allowed for television crews to record the scene.

The normal order for addressing the Court (unless the parties agree otherwise) is that first the applicant presents its oral argument, followed by the respondent State. After a short interval, perhaps a day or perhaps the weekend, the second round of oral statements takes place, delivered in the same order. In cases introduced by special agreement and with simultaneous written pleadings, if no agreement is reached about the order of speaking, the matter will be decided by the Court (or perhaps by the flip of a coin.)

Witnesses and expert-witnesses as to facts or opinions are still relatively infrequent in proceedings in the International Court, despite a slight increase in their frequency in recent years and a significant increase in comparison to the practice in the Permanent Court. Witnesses and experts have been called in a number of cases, including our case under discussion. There is also the possibility that evidence can be submitted in the form of a signed affidavit in which the witness provides evidence in written form which is duly entered into the records of the proceedings, without the witness physically appearing in Court. However, in filing an affidavit, the deponent implicitly acknowledges his or her readiness and responsibility to undergo cross-examination in Court, if this is requested by the other party and/or the Court finds it necessary. On the other hand, the International Court, unlike the ad-hoc criminal tribunals for Yugoslavia and Rwanda and the recently established International Criminal Court, has no power to issue subpoenas or otherwise compel witnesses to appear in Court due to the difference in nature and function between it and a criminal tribunal. The only sanction open to it would be to exclude evidence provided in an affidavit, if the witness refused to undergo cross-examination when so requested.

In the cases in which witnesses or experts have appeared the procedure for examination has differed slightly in accordance with the circumstances and the functions of the disputed facts or expert opinion as a whole. However, a general practice resembling Anglo-American procedure in this respect has emerged, with its three phases of examination-in-chief, cross-examination and re-examination, although the rules of evidence in international procedure are less strict and formalistic than in common-law countries. The examination of a witness is usually entrusted to one member of each team, not necessarily the same person if there is more than one witness.

With regard to the burden of proof, the general rule is that a party putting forth a claim has the burden of establishing the elements of fact and of law on which the claim is based. How this is done will vary from case to case. Here too the Court's procedure is flexible. The Court will not allow itself to be encumbered by formalism or by a legalistic approach. Although the Court has the power to make an inspection *in loco* (the locality of a dispute) on the basis of the Statute and Rules, it has made sparing use of it up to the present.[8]

The Court itself, through the President, may ask questions of the parties, although this is rare. It is more usual for individual judges to exercise their right to put questions to the parties and to witnesses if there are any. In recent years, the judges on the Court have made increased use of this right in comparison to previous years, and the current Rules of Court, and practice directives stimulate a more active posture of the Court and more interaction between the Bench and the parties. Nevertheless, there is much less interaction than is the case in courts in common law systems and practice in this regard is closer to that in civil law systems. The relative passivity of the International Court in comparison to courts in common law countries has on occasion been the subject of criticism. However, it should not be forgotten that proceedings in the International Court differ from proceedings before national courts in that the litigants are sovereign States and the proceedings do not mirror the traditions of any one legal system. In its recent Practice Directions, the Court has made clear that it will, in any case, exert more control than in the past in the interests of efficiency, without losing sight of the specific characteristics of international litigation at the inter-State level.

In our case, there were no interventions by the judges during the jurisdictional phase, but there was vigorous questioning from the Bench of the witnesses during the merits phase of the proceedings. At the end of their argument each agent will present his or her "final submissions" (see p. 119 below).

CLOSURE OF ORAL PROCEEDINGS

After the parties have completed their presentation of the case, the President formally declares the hearing closed. He may do this at the end of the last hearing on the case, or he may wait a few days, depending on the circumstances. Once the oral hearings are closed, the Court withdraws to consider the judgment. No further evidence or pleading may be submitted by either party (unless the Court calls for it). The parties can now relax. The initiative passes to the Court.

THE COURT'S DELIBERATION

The following are the basic rules governing the manner in which the Court deliberates. Article 56 of the Statute requires the judgment to state the reasons on which it is based.

All questions are decided by a majority of the judges present. By Article 55 of the Statute the President (or Acting President) has a casting vote in the event of a tie. Two contentious cases and one advisory opinion have to date been decided by a casting vote of the President. In the two contentious cases *Lotus* (in the Permanent Court in 1927) and *South West Africa* (in the present Court in 1966), the decision was unacceptable politically, and led to political action to undo the effect of the judgment. The Court deliberates in private, only the judges and the Registrar or his substitute being present. The President is generally responsible for the conduct of the deliberations, which are held in strict secrecy.

Within that framework, a long evolution in the Court's internal procedure has taken place. Initially the Court followed the internal practice of its predecessor, the Permanent Court, which had been first formalized in 1931 and later revised in 1936. That practice was provisionally adopted by the present Court in 1946.[9] On 17 April 1976 the Court adopted the current resolution regarding its internal judicial practice.[10]

An authoritative description of how a judgment is prepared has been given by the Registry, and is reproduced here (with some omissions and explanations) with permission:

> Once the public hearings are over Members of the Court have a short time in which to study the arguments of the parties, following which there is a brief exchange in writing of their preliminary views. The President orally outlines to the Members of the Court the issues that in his opinion will require decision and they may comment thereon and make any suggestions of their own. At their private meetings to deliberate on the case the judges sit as a committee *in camera,* in a room of the Peace Palace in the new wing. No one else is allowed to be present except the Registrar and a few officials of the Registry to service the meetings. The minutes of these meetings, which are intended for the internal use of the Court alone, simply state the date, those present and the subject discussed, without any comment.
>
> Each judge then has several weeks in which to prepare a written note giving his tentative views on the answers to the questions put by the President and any other judge and on the way in which he considers the case should be decided. The notes, which are in English or French, are translated by the Registry and distributed to all judges composing the Court for the case in question. They enable Members of the Court to gain a first idea of where the majority opinion may lie. The notes are strictly for the use of Members of the Court and, after the end of the case, they are destroyed by the Registry.
>
> In 1998, the Court announced that in preliminary phases of the proceedings (e.g. objections to its jurisdiction or admissibility of an application), it would, on an experimental basis and where it considered it necessary, deliberate without such written notes. In April 2002, the Court decided to maintain the traditional practice of preparing written notes in phases of the proceedings relating to the merits, but to continue also with the recent practice of deciding, on a case by case basis, whether to dispense with written notes in a preliminary phase of a case. The Court also decided that in the interests of expediting the work of the Court, the written notes should be as concise as possible, and the periods for their preparation would be shortened.
>
> The deliberations resume after the members of the Court have examined any written notes, or without the use of notes as indicated above, and the deliberations

can extend over several meetings. At these, the judges express their views orally and usually in inverse order of seniority, i.e. beginning with any judges *ad hoc* there may be and ending with the Vice-President and President. They answer such questions as their colleagues may put to them. The sense of the coming decision and the make-up of the future majority now become more clearly discernible, but no vote is normally yet taken on any specific point. On the conclusion of this deliberation, a drafting committee of three Members of the Court is constituted. Two of its members are elected by secret ballot from among those judges whose personal views most closely reflect the opinion of the apparent majority, whilst the third is the President *ex officio*, unless it seems that his views are in the minority, in which case the Vice-President takes his place; should both of them hold minority views, the third member of the drafting committee is also elected.

The drafting committee then prepares a preliminary draft judgment in English and French, with the assistance of the Registry for drafting the introductory passages of the judgment that summarize the proceedings, translation from one language to the other and the checking of statements of fact. The preliminary draft, which like the judges' notes is secret, is circulated to Members of the Court. They then have a short time in which they may make written suggestions for formal or substantive amendments relating to the English or French texts or to any discrepancies between the two languages. The drafting committee considers whether or not to accept these amendments and issues a fresh draft. The Court then gives this a first reading, during which it is discussed at several private meetings. Each paragraph is read aloud in both languages and, after discussion, is either left unchanged, amended or sent back to the drafting committee. Finally an amended draft judgment is distributed to Members of the Court, which is then given a second reading, shorter than the first reading, at which it is taken page by page and adopted with or without minor amendments.

At the end of the second reading, a final vote is taken on the answers that it is proposed in the final judgment the Court should give to the points raised by the parties in their submissions [see p. 119 below]. Members of the Court vote "yes" or "no" orally, in inverse order of seniority. Each decision is taken by an absolute majority of the judges present. No abstentions are allowed on any point voted upon. A judge who has failed to attend part of the oral proceedings or the deliberations but who has nevertheless not missed anything essential may participate in the vote. If the judge is in a fit condition to vote and wishes to do so but is physically incapacitated from attending the meeting, measures may be taken to enable him to participate, if necessary by correspondence. Should the votes be equally divided, which may happen when there is a judge *ad hoc* or a regular Member of the Court is not sitting, the President or the member of the Court acting as President has a casting vote. The results of the vote and any explanations relating thereto are recorded in the minutes.[11]

This method of composing the collegiate decision of the Court shows that the text later determined to be "authoritative" (whatever that may mean) is itself the product of a bilingual intellectual process regularly encountered in diplomatic and United Nations practice. While the text is being put together in one of the Court's official languages -the choice of which at that stage is presumably very much a matter of chance depending on the composition of the drafting committee – a "translation" is being prepared by the

Registry into the other working language. The Court in fact formulates its decision in both official languages simultaneously, and it adopts both texts before determining which version is "authoritative". A contention that the double-version format is essentially for the use of the Court and international lawyers is based on a misreading of the Statute and on a misconception of the real and substantive nature of the bilingualism that is an integral part of the judicial process. Anyone who has to have recourse to these materials, whether as judge, advocate, arbitrator, codifier or teacher, or even as layman, will always be alert to the possibility that he may have to interest himself in the second text when considering any judicial pronouncement of the Permanent Court or of the present Court. This would not be the plaything of an excessive virtuosity.

When all is ready, the parties are notified of the date of the public meeting at which the judgment will be delivered, in accordance with Article 58 of the Statute. At the public meeting the judgment is read in its authoritative text, a translation also being read of its operative clause. Signed and sealed copies are handed to the Agents (a further signed and sealed copy is retained in the archives of the Court). A copy of every judgment is sent officially by the Registrar to every member of the United Nations, to the Secretary-General of the United Nations and to every State entitled to appear before the Court.[12] The text is immediately made available to the press together with an unofficial summary prepared by the Registry.

The judgments, advisory opinions and orders are published consecutively throughout each year. At the end of the year they are collated, indexed and bound, and form a series of *Reports* similar to domestic series of Law Reports. Apart from official distribution to governments, these texts (as the other publications of the Court) are also placed on sale to the general public and can be obtained through the local United Nations Sales Agency in every country.

The texts are in English and French, face-to-face, the authoritative text on the left (verso). The pagination of the facing pages is identical. Since 1969 the Court has adopted the practice of numbering the paragraphs, making references to the material easier.

THE JUDGMENT OF 26 NOVEMBER 1984

The deliberations of the Court in this phase lasted from 19 October to 26 November, a relatively short period considering the complexity of the issues that had be decided. The judgment is long, over 50 printed pages, of which under six are devoted to the formal parts.

In this judgment, by eleven votes to five the Court found that it had jurisdiction on the basis of the declarations accepting the compulsory jurisdiction. By fourteen votes to two it found that it had jurisdiction under the Friendship Treaty. By fifteen votes to one it found generally that it had jurisdiction to entertain the case, and it was unanimous in finding that the application was admissible. Separate opinions were appended by Judges Nagendra Singh, Ruda, Mosler, Oda and Sir Robert Jennings, and a dissenting opinion by Judge Schwebel.

The jurisdictional questions considered by the Court related to the following aspects: the acceptance of the compulsory jurisdiction by Nicaragua and the United States, the "multilateral treaties" reservation of the United States (which it deferred to the merits), the effect of the Schultz letter, jurisdiction under the newly invoked Friendship Treaty, and, as regards the admissibility of the case, contentions that Nicaragua had failed to bring before the Court all the parties whose presence and participation was necessary (this related particularly to Costa Rica, El Salvador and Honduras), and that the fundamental claim of Nicaragua came within the competence of the Security Council and not of the Court, since it related to the on-going use of force and individual and collective self-defence.

This judgment was an impressive achievement for Nicaragua. At the same time it is one of the most significant judgments on ostensibly technical questions of jurisdiction and admissibility to have been rendered by the present Court.

What had Nicaragua gained?

Nicaragua's forensic triumph had powerful political resonances, largely concealed by the technicalities of this judgment. From the point of view of the Court proceedings, Nicaragua was now assured that its grievances would be fully ventilated in the Court and in that way brought before a wider public. The political objective of the exercise, commencing with the approach to the Security Council, would be met. In litigation terms, the Court had established the broadest possible base for its jurisdiction.

THE AFTERMATH OF THE JUDGMENT

To say that this judgment caused the greatest dismay to the Administration in Washington is no understatement. On 18 January 1985 the State Department issued two statements. One was a critical analysis of the judgment. The other was to announce that the United States had, "with great reluctance, decided not to participate in further proceedings in the case". On 7 October 1985 the United States withdrew completely its acceptance of the compulsory jurisdiction of 1946, and has not replaced it.

The United States gave several reasons for these steps. On the major jurisdictional issue of whether Nicaragua could have been held to have accepted the compulsory jurisdiction of the Permanent Court, transferred to the present Court in 1945, the United States found the decision "erroneous as a matter of law and ... based on a misreading and distortion of the evidence and precedent." It was critical of the decision holding inadmissible El Salvador's declaration of intervention, and mentioned also the "haste" with which the judgment was prepared. The United States also implied that the Court had become politicized like many other organs of the United Nations, and that this decision created the impression "that the Court is determined to find in favor of Nicaragua in this case".

With regard to the withdrawal of the acceptance of the compulsory jurisdiction, in the statement of 7 October 1985 the State Department pointed out that the United States had never been able to use its acceptance of the compulsory jurisdiction to bring other States before the Court, although itself it had been sued three times. In 1946 it had assumed that "the Court's own appreciation of the need to adhere scrupulously to its proper judicial role would prevent the Court's process from being abused for political ends". Those assumptions had been proved wrong. As a result, the President (Reagan) had determined that continuance of acceptance of the compulsory jurisdiction "would be contrary to our commitment to the principle of the equal application of the law and would endanger our vital international interests".[13]

This did not affect the jurisdiction of the Court to continue to hear the case.

THE SEPARATE AND DISSENTING OPINIONS

Article 57 of the Statute allows any judge to append a separate opinion if the judgment does not represent in whole or in part the unanimous opinion of the judges. An opinion given by a judge who supports the view of the majority is called a separate or concurring opinion, and one given by a judge who disagrees with the view of the majority is called a dissenting opinion. This is a formal distinction which refers primarily to the attitude adopted by the individual judge on the final vote and the operative clauses of the judgment. The term "individual opinion" covers both types of opinion. Individual opinions are found in judgments, advisory opinions, and when necessary also in orders.

The system for the preparation and promulgation of judgments (as well as advisory opinions, and, where necessary, orders of substance) is a combination of the continental approach and the common-law approach. The continental approach prefers a single judgment given anonymously in the name of the Court as a whole and without any indication of dissentient views. This form of judgment is used by the Judicial Committee of the Privy Council in London and by the Court of Justice of the European Communities at Luxembourg. The approach of the common law jurisdictions allows every judge to make his own decision and to give his own reasons for it, even if this means criticizing the majority and his colleagues. The judgments of the International Court are themselves collective. Until 1978 they were anonymous in the sense that their author remained unknown, as well as how each judge voted on the final vote on the operative clause. This last aspect is now made public.

Many people think that the right of each judge to append his own opinion is essential for the effective working of the Court. A former President of the Permanent Court of International Justice, Dr. Max Huber (Switzerland), stated in 1929 that this right was "a guarantee against any subconscious intrusion of political considerations", and that through its existence 'judgments were more likely to be given in accordance with the real force of the arguments submitted". In 1956 he went on record as saying that he would hardly have accepted the office of Member of the Court if the Statute had not taken over the Anglo-American system of dissenting opinions. A Member of the present Court has pointed out that this system "has come to be regarded as a safeguard of the individual responsibility of the Judges as well as of the integrity of the Court as an institution. It precludes any charge of reliance on mere alignment of voting and lifts the pronouncements of the Court to the level of the inherent power of legal reason and reasoning". In 1987 the Court itself went on record in a strong passage in favour of the "wise practice" of the United Nations Administrative Tribunal, following its own example, "not only to permit such expressions of opinion but to publish them appended to the judgment".[14]

At the same time, the collective and anonymous drafting of the majority opinion has drawbacks. The opinion tends to be colourless and lack "character" and even cohesion, although there are exceptions. It is the outcome of compromise over concepts, words and phrases between a group of persons who may be united only in their determination to reach a formally binding decision in the concrete case, but who remain divided between themselves. In such circumstances questions of semantics loom large. When this happens the opinion will appear excessively brief, for it will do no more than reflect the common denominator of the divergent views of the judges and exclude everything redundant. The problem which arises is the following: Should the Court strive for the largest possible majority for its decisions, at the cost of eliminating every word and thought that gives rise to controversy; or should it place the general cogency of the reasoning at the head of its concern, voting only on the operative clauses of the judgment, and leaving the reasons to the skill and energy of the individual judges?

The Court has chosen the first course. While this was probably a wise choice, it adds to the general significance of the individual opinions.

Individual opinions, whether concurring or dissenting opinions, perform several functions. Thanks to the greater freedom of expression and emphasis enjoyed by the individual judges, many concurring opinions do little more than underpin the anonymous collective opinion of the majority, which cannot always articulate fully and expressively the underlying principles which were applied. In other cases, the opinion may indicate other general underlying principles which its author believed could or should have been more appropriately applied in the concrete case. Such an opinion may have a value of its own as a counter-balance to the majority opinion, although it must be used with caution since the views it expresses did not persuade the majority. In other instances, the international judge may differ from his colleagues on what the facts are, what facts are relevant, and what weight is to be attached to different facts. When some ideas only appear in a separate opinion, it does not mean that the Court as a whole *rejected* them. It means nothing more than that the Court did not find it necessary to adopt them for its decision – something quite different. In another direction, there are concurring opinions which flatly contradict both the underlying principles and their application by the majority. Here, dependent on the author's general reputation and the cogency of his reasoning, the individual opinion may in the course of time come to be seen by enlightened and informed opinion as expressive of better law. Above all, the publication of these opinions focuses attention on the nature of the discussion in the Council Chamber. For a full understanding of the real implications of any judgment, the discerning reader will consult both the pleadings and the individual opinions appended to the judgment. The pleadings will show how the parties presented the issues. The individual opinions, concurring and dissenting, will show the main issues on which the Court concentrated in its deliberation.

Nevertheless, in the present Court the individual opinions have become excessively prolix, sometimes reading more like articles than as expressions of judicial opinion. This leads to the possibility of abuse, especially when they go beyond the limits fixed by the Court in its judgment. Successive Presidents have not been able to bring this aspect under tighter control. The Court's *Reports* since 1946 are replete with instances of this, and of warnings against the perpetuation of this practice.

There is another factor to be noticed. The figures of the final voting by the judges can be deceptive. In most instances of international litigation, the balance between the parties' cases, from the point of view of abstract legal merit, is fine. Countries do not become involved in international litigation, and certainly not applicant governments, if their case is not reasonably arguable! The fact that in the *Military and Paramilitary Activities in and against Nicaragua* case the three operative paragraphs of the judgment on jurisdiction and admissibility, and the 16 operative paragraphs of the judgment on the merits, were reached by very large majorities is no test whatsoever of the strength of the United States' case, which was much more plausible than a *cursory* reading of the judgments would suggest.

How, then, is this phenomenon, of the large majorities in this, and in other cases, to be explained? The answer is in the overriding compulsion of the Court to reach a decision which will be final and authoritative. This means that in the end a *choice* must be made – a choice which must be in accordance with the professional skill and the conscience of the individual judge. The care with which the issues are sifted by the Court during its deliberations, even before the writing of the judgment is taken in hand, is designed to enable the normal processes of free and equal discussion and persuasion to take their course. The right of each judge to express his own view of the case in the form of his individual opinion is thus an important residuary power, and even a stimulus to the formation of large majorities on which the ultimate acceptability of a decision will depend. A government, and public opinion, will the more easily acquiesce in a decision reached by a large majority than in one reached by a small majority.

Not all these aspects are fully illustrated by the decisions in this case.

The Court reaches its decision by applying international law. In the case of the preliminary objections in the present matter, the law applied was a limited and highly technical aspect of the law governing the compulsory jurisdiction of the Court. Broader issues of this character came out in the merits phase of the case, and that will therefore be the most convenient place to discuss this aspect of the Court's working.

THE PROCEEDINGS ON THE MERITS

After the judgment of 26 November 1984, the President convened the usual meeting of the Agents to discuss the next procedure. It is not known, however, what was agreed at that meeting, since intervening events, as described above, led to an abrupt change in the proceedings.

On 18 January 1985 the United States informed the Court of its decision not to participate further in the proceedings. On 22 January, Nicaragua notified the Court that it was maintaining its application and would avail itself of Article 53 of the Statute (see p. 78 above). The Court agreed that the time had come to fix time limits for the written proceedings on the merits. In an order of 22 January 1985 it fixed 30 April 1985 for Nicaragua's Memorial on the merits, and 31 May 1985 for the United States' Counter-Memorial. Since the United States had announced its withdrawal from the proceedings, the Court did not find it necessary to grant equal time for the two pleadings. It simply left an opening for the United States to reconsider its position. If there were no change, the case would become ready for hearing on 31 May, and the Court began to make the necessary logistical preparations for that. As was to be anticipated, there was no change in the attitude of the United States towards the case.

The Memorial on the merits was accordingly filed on the date fixed. No further formal pleading having been filed by the United States, the hearings on the merits commenced on 12 September and continued to 20 September 1985.

In the Memorial, Nicaragua claimed relief under eight heads. The Court was asked to adjudge and declare that the United States had violated its obligations of international law and that in particular respects was in continuing violation of those obligations. Nicaragua went on to request the Court to state in clear terms the obligation which the United States bore to bring to an end those breaches of international law. Thirdly, Nicaragua asked for a declaration that, in consequence of the violations of international law, compensation was due to Nicaragua, both on its own behalf and in respect of wrongs inflicted upon its nationals, and to determine in a later phase the quantum of damages to be assessed as the compensation due. Nicaragua also sought an immediate award of $370,200,000.00, the "minimum valuation for the direct damages, with the exception of damages for killing Nicaraguan nationals, resulting from the violations of international law". With reference to that request, Nicaragua reserved the right to present further evidence at a later stage. This part of the case was rejected by the Court.

Those submissions were maintained in the oral proceedings. They thus became what are known as the "final submissions" of Nicaragua.

Although the United States did not file a Counter-Memorial, the Department of State published a brochure entitled *Revolution beyond our Borders: Sandinista Intervention in Central America.* This had been circulated as an official document of the General Assembly and of the Security Council. Copies were also sent by the United States Embassy at The Hague to the Registry of the Court.[15]

The oral proceedings were short, but dramatic. Nicaragua called five witnesses. Among them were a former officer of the U.S. Central Intelligence Agency, the Nicaraguan Minister of Finance and the Vice-Minister of the Interior. Nicaragua's case was presented by the same team that had argued the jurisdiction and admissibility issues. These representatives also examined the witnesses. Questions were put to the witnesses by Members of the Court, and especially and vigorously by Judge Schwebel, but in the absence from the proceedings of the United States, there was no cross-examination in the true sense. Although the Judge was able to establish that the facts of Nicaragua's behaviour were significantly different from what had been presented by Nicaragua, the Court did not accept that. In its Judgment the Court said that it could not, by its own enquiries, entirely make up for the absence of one of the parties, and in particular it stressed the inability of the absent party to "counter the factual allegations of its opponent".

THE JUDGMENT OF 27 JUNE 1986

The deliberations took a long time. The judgment was not delivered until nine months later, on 27 June 1986. It is one of the Court's most controversial judgments. The operative provisions contain no less than 16 different paragraphs, since the Judgment considered the claims of Nicaragua under each of the two titles of jurisdiction recognized in the previous phase.

The Court first disposed of a new question of jurisdiction which came to light, namely the deferred effect of the "multilateral treaties reservation" (p. 111 above) of the United States acceptance of the jurisdiction. By eleven votes to four the Court found that this was applicable. That excluded all the claims that were based on the four multilateral treaties mentioned in the application, namely the Charter of the United Nations, the Charter of the Organization of American States, the Havana Convention of 1929 on the Rights and Duties of States, and the Montevideo Convention of 1933 on the Duties and Rights of States in the event of Civil Conflict (the last two are American regional treaties). That, however, did not dispose of Nicaragua's case, since the Court also found that most of the allegedly wrongful acts were also breaches of international customary law, and thus came within the reach of the compulsory jurisdiction.

By twelve votes to three the Court then rejected the justification of collective self-defence, which had been raised by the United States in the previous phase as a ground for its objection to the Court's entertaining the case. That opened the way to the different decisions on the substance of Nicaragua's claims set out in the Memorial.

By twelve votes to three the Court decided that the United States had committed a series of violations of customary international law not to intervene in the internal affairs of Nicaragua; had violated its obligations under customary international law not to use force against Nicaragua; had violated Nicaragua's sovereignty; had violated its obligations not to interrupt peaceful maritime commerce. The Court then went on to consider the violations of the Treaty of Friendship, Commerce and Navigation. By fourteen votes to one on three heads, and by twelve votes to three on another three heads, it found a series of violations of that Treaty. The Court then turned to the consequences of its findings.

By twelve votes to three it held that the United States was under a duty immediately to cease and to refrain from all such acts as might constitute breaches of the legal obligations thus found. By the same vote it decided that the United States was under an obligation to make reparation to Nicaragua for all injury caused to Nicaragua by the breaches of obligations under customary international law; and by fourteen votes to one that the United States was under a similar obligation regarding breaches of the Friendship Treaty. By another similar vote it decided that the form of such reparation, failing agreement between the parties, should be settled by the Court after further proceedings. Finally the Court was unanimous in recalling to both parties "their obligation to seek a solution to their disputes by peaceful means in accordance with international law".

That was the decision, and the majorities were impressive. At the same time, separate opinions were appended by the President, Nagendra Singh, and by Judges Lachs, Ruda, Elias, Ago, Sette-Camara and Ni, together with dissenting opinions by Judges Oda, Schwebel and Sir Robert Jennings. The dissenting opinion of Judge Schwebel is scathing and unrelenting in its detailed critique of the majority. It brings out fully the facts elucidated largely by him through his questioning of the witnesses. The other dissenting opinions are equally severe.

This brief survey is sufficient to indicate the wide range of issues covered in this judgment. It has since been subject to the most minute examination by international lawyers and political scientists of all shades of opinion. It has had a long-term impact on the development of international law, especially through its holding that many of the obligations of the Charter are at the same time obligations under general international law. The consequence was that although through the application of the Vandenberg reservation the Court had no jurisdiction to consider alleged violations of the Charter (as a multilateral treaty), this did not deprive it of jurisdiction over alleged breaches of general and customary international law. Some take the view that the judicial activism which this Judgment displays, after the inaction of the Security Council following the "veto" of the United States, would not be acceptable to the majority of States. The other view is that if the Court had not acted in the way it did, it would have put itself out of business for all but the minority of "Western" States. That view may reflect the majority's misunderstanding of the facts of Nicaragua's conduct.

This is not the place for further discussion of this judgment.[16] Suffice it to say that in the short term, it does not appear to have seriously affected one way or the other the willingness (or reserve) of States to have recourse to the Court. Nevertheless, in the longer term, there are signs that the non-aligned States, individually and collectively, are showing more interest in the possibility of invoking Court procedures for their purposes.

THE FINAL PHASE

The Court left the way open to negotiations between the parties for the settlement of the dispute. This was unlikely to occur having regard for the emotions that had been aroused on both sides,[17] as well as by the unprecedented sum of damages demanded by Nicaragua. Immediately after the judgment Nicaragua informed the United States of its willingness to discuss the matter of reparation, but received a negative reply. In May 1987 Nicaragua made another approach to the United States, and again the reply was negative. Political jousts accompanied this correspondence, first in the Security Council and then in the General Assembly. Nicaragua had recourse to the Security Council on 27 June, 12 July and 9 December 1986, but the Security Council took no action. At the same time Nicaragua had recourse to the General Assembly. On 3 November 1986 the General Assembly adopted resolution 41/31, reproduced on p. 36 above. Similar resolutions were adopted in 1987, 1988 and 1989.

On 7 September 1987 Nicaragua informed the Court that no agreement had been reached as to the form and amount of reparation, and that it wished to take advantage of the opportunity afforded by the Court to satisfy the Court that the nature and the amount of the reparation claimed was well founded in fact and in law. Nicaragua, recalling that the case remained within Article 53 of the Statute (in the continued absence from the proceedings of the United States), asked the Court to arrange for the further proceedings. The United States was informed of this, and of the intention of the President to convene a meeting of the parties for the purpose of ascertaining their views on the procedure to be followed. On 13 November the Deputy-Agent of the United States replied that the position of the United States was unchanged, and that the United States would not be represented at the meeting which was held on 17 November. On 18 November the President fixed time limits for the written proceedings on the question of the form and amount of reparation. Nicaragua was given until 29 March 1988 to file its Memorial on that question, and the United States until 29 July for its Counter-Memorial.

The Memorial was then duly filed. Under different heads, the total amount claimed, as quantified in that Memorial, came to $11,216,000,000.00 – probably the largest amount ever advanced in a single international claim. Moreover, some of the figures, relating to continuing damages, were tentative. Nicaragua also asked for costs (on this, see p. 123 below) and post-judgment interest from date of judgment to date of payment.

No Counter-Memorial was filed by the United States. Accordingly, this phase became ready for hearing on 29 July 1988.

On 22 June 1990 the President called a meeting to ascertain the views of the parties on the date for the opening of oral proceedings on the issue of reparation. There had been a change of government in Nicaragua, and the Agent indicated to the Court that it was studying its different cases then pending in the Court (see pp. 183 below). The instant case was very complex and there were "special circumstances which would make it extremely inconvenient for it to take a decision" on the procedure during the coming months. This was reported to the Court which took no action for the time being.

In 1990, too, Nicaragua halted its action in the General Assembly regarding compliance with the judgment on the merits. On 12 September 1991 Nicaragua informed the Court that the Government had decided to renounce all further right of action based on the case and requested the Court to record the discontinuance of the proceedings and the removal of the case from the General List.. In accordance with the procedure for discontinuance (see p. 123 below), a time limit was fixed for the United States to state whether it opposed the discontinuance. On 25 September the United States welcomed the discontinuance, and the next day the necessary order was made. The *Military and Paramilitary Activities in and against Nicaragua* case was removed from the Court's General List.

FINAL SUBMISSIONS

It has been mentioned that certain written pleadings – including all those which have been filed in our case – have to contain "submissions". In the course of the oral pleadings, the parties must present what are commonly called their "final submissions", following Article 48 of the Statute. The submissions are so important that the judgment must recite fully each party's submissions.

A submission is a concise statement of what a party wants the Court to decide. The pleading explains the party's view on the relevant reasons of fact and of law in support of its case. The submissions should be drawn up in the form of the operative clause of the decision requested, and show in concrete terms exactly what the party is asking the Court to decide. They should not recapitulate the arguments. When a case is introduced by application, the decision of the Court is given on the final submissions. When a case has been introduced by special agreement that, as we have seen, defines what it is that the Court has to decide. The final submissions, therefore, are the ultimate concretization of the dispute and as such have to be regarded as an act of State. The outcome of the case will depend on their formulation, and the interpretation of the final submissions may in turn depend upon a comparison with the earlier submissions in the case.

For this reason, and to assist the clarity of the discussion, the Court has, in the course of its judicial experience, come to require certain attributes of the final submissions. They should be worded in the form of a positive statement: if they are worded negatively, or interrogatively, they may not provide a satisfactory basis for the decision, and the Court may not be able to give effect to them. At one time it had been fairly common for States to commence their final submissions with a series of preambles, "Whereases" – in which the whole case was epitomized with the maximum of succinctness. This practice is deprecated as being inconsonant with the proper function of a submission. In some cases, however, it may be justified if the diplomatic role of the judicial settlement of international disputes is kept in mind. For its part the Court will ignore .the irrelevant parts of submissions. In this case the final submissions, in all phases, were drawn up in accordance with the Court's requirements.

The submissions should stand in direct relation to the original statement of the claim as it appears in the application (or preliminary objection). They do not have to be identical with it, and through the normal processes of pleading modifications, sometimes far-reaching, will appear in the shape of the case through the successive developments in the pleadings. The Court will watch this carefully. There are two reasons for this. One is to guard against a change in the character of the case which might affect the basis of its jurisdiction. The second is to ensure that, by reason of such change, circumstances have not arisen in which notice should be given to third States to alert them to the possibility that they may have grounds to intervene. As between the parties, however, the principle that consent to the jurisdiction can be given tacitly means that when they file submissions they are taken to accept any possible irregularities in the jurisdiction which might exist up to that stage. Submissions which "match" will normally confer jurisdiction on the Court, at least unless some clear reserve to the competence of the Court is expressed.

Having regard to their importance, the final submissions are signed by the Agent, and written copies, signed by him, should be communicated to the Court and to the other party. Submissions may always be modified up to a party's last statement, and the party against whom they are filed is always given the opportunity of commenting on them, even if that involves a modification of that party's own final submission.

THE LAW APPLIED BY THE COURT

The Court is an international court designed to serve the international community of States. In the nature of things, the law which it applies is international law. The Statute of the Court therefore contains general directions on this aspect. By Article 38, the Court, whose function is to decide in accordance with international law such disputes as are submitted to it, shall apply: *(a)* international conventions, whether general or particular, expressly recognized by the contesting States; *(b)* international custom, as evidence of a general practice recognized as law; *(c)* the general principles of law recognized by civilized nations; and *(d)* judicial decisions and the teachings of the most highly qualified publicists of the various nations as subsidiary means for the determination of the rules of law..

For theoretical reasons this has given rise to much controversy. In practice, however, it is found to be generally satisfactory, and indeed is frequently repeated in international arbitration agreements. Difficulty is nevertheless experienced on two points. The first is the word "civilized" in head *(c)*. In current political thinking the word is supererogatory and meaningless. The second relates to the place of the so-called "law-making resolutions" of United Nations organs. This is a very intricate and perplexing matter. To include these as part of the law to be applied by the Court would attribute to them a status which does not flow either from the Charter or from the rules of international law itself concerning the creation of legal norms applied in international relations. This does not mean that the Court should not be responsive to the trends registered in those resolutions. In a consensus resolution 3232 (XXIX) of 12 November 1974, the General Assembly also recognized that the development of international law may be reflected, *inter alia,* by declarations and resolutions of the General Assembly which may, to that extent, be taken into consideration by the Court. Although technically General Assembly resolutions are usually not "binding" in the legal sense, that cautious wording reflects a growing practice on the matter.

Heads *(a)* and *(b)* refer to the rules of law itself. The real innovation that was introduced when the Statute was first drafted in 1920 relates to head *(c)*. Its purpose was to remove any danger that the Court would be unable to give a decision on the mere ground that it could find no rule of law to govern the case. The technical name for this kind of finding is *non liquet* – literally "it is not clear" – a term borrowed from Roman law. It is now generally accepted that an international tribunal in principle may not bring a finding of *non liquet.* This useful provision enables the Court to deal with entirely unprecedented situations, and through its pronouncements to keep the law abreast of the constantly changing developments.

Head *(d)* refers to two distinct aspects which are not on the same level. One element is "judicial decisions" (not limited to decisions of the International Court itself). The second is "teachings of the most highly qualified publicists". This is a guide to explain how the law may be ascertained. However, it is far from exhaustive. It is an interesting compromise between two approaches. One is that of the continental jurist, who freely makes use of *doctrine,* theoretical literature, of publicists of repute and who attaches no formal *binding* authority to judicial decisions. The other is that of the common law which on the whole refuses to employ the writings of publicists in this way and indeed would even tend to look askance at their citation in a pleading or in a judgment, but which gives to judicial decisions the formal authority of a binding precedent. Nevertheless, the practical difference between these two schools of thought is not great. The continental jurist will tend to recognize the inherent as distinguished from the formal authority of a judicial precedent, especially when the higher courts are consistent in their decisions (the French call this *une jurisprudence constante).* The lawyer trained in the Anglo-American common law is second to none in his ability to "distinguish" one precedent from another, a characteristic which the International Court is beginning to develop, and will be assiduous in studying relevant literature.

International thinking tends to prefer the continental approach in theory, and the common law approach in practice. One reason for this is that in comparison with domestic litigation, international litigation is sparse. The approximately two hundred and fifty substantive decisions over a period of 80 years given by the Permanent Court and the present Court cannot be compared to the non-stop inflow of judicial decisions, from all levels of the judiciary inside a State. All international judicial and arbitral decisions put together do not make a data-base of case-law constituting a bottomless well of judicial precedents. It would place a great strain on the concept of the binding force of judicial precedent, in the common-law sense, to give the same quality to international judicial decisions, including those of the International Court.

There are several other fundamental reasons for rejecting in international law the Anglo-American theory of the binding force of judicial precedents. One is the particularism of the international judicial system and its unintegrated character. A second is the absence of an international legislature able at short notice to adopt legislation which a judicial decision may require. A third is the absence of automatic enforceability of the decisions of the Court, especially advisory opinions or orders indicating interim measures of protection, and to some extent even judgments. We therefore find that the International Court has refrained from saying that it was *obliged* to follow previous judicial decisions – of itself, of the Permanent Court, or of authoritative Arbitration Tribunals. At the same time it has been very careful not to upset established jurisprudence unless it was convinced that there was good reason. For example, in the order indicating provisional measures and the two judgments in the *Military and Paramilitary Activities* case, there are frequent references to earlier decisions, which are sometimes followed and at others distinguished. Citation of passages from earlier judgments is a convenient form of legal composition, and does not necessarily mean that the Court thought it was bound by the earlier decision.

As far as it is possible to establish, neither the Permanent Court nor the present Court has ever cited an individual writer by name. The opinions of the individual judges are, naturally, freer in this regard, and the parties' pleadings even more so. However, the non-citation of an earlier judgment or of important works of reputable publicists does not imply that the Court was unaware of them or wilfully ignored them. The experience of the International Law Commission has shown that to cite writers by name, at all events in its final report which constitutes a collective *exposé des motifs* for decisions reached, is a delicate matter. In 1966, after carefully weighing the issues, the Commission decided to omit citations from *doctrine* from its final report on the law of treaties.[18]

The use of judicial decisions as precedents is subject. to one important qualification. Article 59 of the Statute is specific in laying down that a judicial decision itself has no "binding force" except between the parties and in respect of that particular case. There is, however, no real contradiction. The "decision" which is only "binding" on the parties to a particular case is found in the operative clauses of the judgment, and in the facts which support that decision. If one of those parties is involved in another case based on similar facts, it cannot take those facts as proved for the second case. The Court's reasoning in law – its statement of what it regards as the correct legal position *and why* – enters into the general storehouse of public international law. That is why the decisions of the International Court have become one of the most important reservoirs today for the rules of international law, and indeed one of the law's most powerful instruments for adaptation to the constantly changing conditions.

The Court also has power, if the parties agree, to "decide a case *ex aequo et bono"*. The words mean "right and equitable". What this connotes is that if the parties expressly confer that power on the Court, it may lay down, in the form of a binding decision, a reasonable adjustment of the relations between the two parties, and not limit its decision to a statement of what those relations are on the basis of the law as it is. This concept, of which instances are very rare in international practice, must not be confused with the English concept of "equity", at least in its modern form, or with any rule of international law which itself incorporates equitable principles. No instance has occurred of States asking the International Court to decide a case on this basis. The reason probably is that it is the normal function of diplomacy to bring such adjustments about, and the normal processes of diplomacy have developed special machinery, such as conciliation and mediation procedures, to assist it. This does not exclude the application of equitable principles when these are inherent in the rule of law itself.

In the merits of the *Military and Paramilitary Activities* case several significant general issues regarding the law applied by the Court arose.

The most important of these was the Court's holding that even if customary rules of law have been adopted in international treaties, the exclusion of those treaties from the jurisdiction of the Court does not prevent it from deciding on the basis of the same rules as rules of customary law. This is probably the most controversial part of the legal reasoning in the judgment on the merits of this case, especially as the Court relied partly on instruments which themselves are not binding as such.

ASSESSORS AND EXPERTS

Article 30 of the Statute empowers the Court to appoint assessors to sit with it or with one of the chambers, without the right to vote. Article 50 *inter alia* empowers it to appoint experts. The Court has never yet appointed assessors. On the other hand, experts have been appointed in different circumstances.

The Court's decision is normally produced without outside assistance. But cases can arise where the Court will require, or the parties may desire, expert assistance in formulating the decision, especially if it involves matters of high technicality (such as maritime delimitations), or if technical elucidation of facts is required. In such circumstances the Court will appoint an expert or experts to assist it in this.

The present Court made use of this power in the *Corfu Channel* case in connection with disputed facts (see p. 127 below). In other cases it has appointed an expert to assist in drawing a maritime boundary. In the 1984 judgment in the *Gulf of Maine* case the technical report of the expert appointed by the Chamber at the parties' request was annexed to the judgment (see p. 179 below). The Court found no need for any outside assistance in the merits phase of the *Military and Paramilitary Activities* case, although the matter was raised during the deliberations. Doubtless, had the compensation phase led to a decision, an expert examination of the accounts submitted would have been required.

This must be distinguished from the appointment of experts by the Court to assist the parties in putting a judgment into effect, for instance where the Court has indicated how a frontier is to be drawn. These would normally not be experts of the Court, the Court's appointment being merely action designed to assist the parties in compliance with the decision to reach a final settlement of their dispute. The first instance of this occurred in the *Frontier Dispute* (Burkina Faso/Mali) case, where the Chamber was able to give general directions about part of the frontier, leaving to the experts appointed by it at the parties' request to effect the correct demarcation on the ground.

SETTLEMENT OUT OF COURT

Since the case had been introduced by unilateral application, Nicaragua could at any time have discontinued the proceedings by giving the Court notice to that effect. Before effecting the discontinuance, the Court would have consulted the United States to see whether it had any objection to it. (The reason for this is in case the respondent has advanced a counter-claim which it would like to see decided by the Court.)

In addition to this, the two parties could have settled the case out of Court by agreement. If necessary the Court could place the terms of the settlement on record. Articles 88 and 89 of the Rules regulate this aspect.

Instances of both these procedures are fairly common. One of the most notable examples of an out-of-Court settlement was the agreement between Iran and the United States of America settling the *Hostages* dispute and related matters. That was concluded through the mediation of the Algerian Government on 19 January 1981, through what is known as the "Algiers Accords". This agreement embraced the release of the American diplomats and nationals held hostage in the U.S. Embassy in Tehran and the transfer of Iranian funds and bank assets which the U.S. Government had impounded by Executive Order in retaliation. The agreement provided for the establishment of the Iran/United States Claims Tribunal in The Hague (not connected in any way with the Court). Its function is to settle a series of claims and counterclaims between the two Governments and between their nationals and one or other Government, and other matters.[19] Nicaragua discontinued the present case in 1991 (see p. 118-9 above).

COSTS

Article 64 of the Statute gives the Court a general power to award costs, although the normal principle in international litigation is that each party bears its own costs. This principle is an expression of the sovereign equality of the States at bar. There has been no instance in the International Court in which costs have been awarded. A discussion about costs in international legal proceedings is found in the *Application for Review of Judgement No.* 158 *of the United Nations Administrative Tribunal* (Fasla case) Advisory Opinion.[20]

In its Memorial on compensation in the *Military and Paramilitary Activities* case, Nicaragua asked for costs. In the absence of any judicial experience, however, it reserved its position until the Court should find it convenient to indicate its views on the precise procedural implications of the claim for costs. Nicaragua thought that it would be inappropriate for it to present a claim in the absence of adequate knowledge of the procedural framework. The case was discontinued before this aspect could be carried further.

INTERPRETATION AND REVISION OF A JUDGMENT

By virtue of Articles 59 and 60 of the Statute, each judgment, and especially the judgment on the merits, became binding on the parties with its delivery, and there is no appeal. The judgment on the merits of 1986 finally decided the issues between them with the force of *res judicata.* But what happens when the judgment refers to future conduct and the parties encounter difficulties is trying to put it into effect?

The Statute anticipates that possibility. By Article 60, if a dispute arises over the meaning or scope of a judgment, the Court has jurisdiction to construe it on the request of either party. Such a request may be submitted either by special agreement or by unilateral application, and the Court will decide on it by judgment. The Court has called this a "special jurisdiction" which derives directly from the Statute. Therefore, the right of a party to invoke it overrides any provisions in a special agreement regarding interpretation.[21] This does not give the Court an unlimited power to re-open the case (for the judgment is final and without appeal), and how far the Court can go through interpretation is limited. The reason is to prevent a new dispute being submitted to the Court in the guise of a request to interpret an earlier judgment, for the jurisdiction to interpret derives directly from the Court's jurisdiction to decide the merits of the original case, and is not, to that extent, an independent jurisdiction. No encouragement must be given to its abuse, at all events so long as the international community does not accept the legal principle of compulsory jurisdiction.

The present Court has had two cases of interpretation (see pp. 135 and 178 below). Experience shows that even if formally the Court regards a request for interpretation as inadmissible, its reasons for that decision will in fact give an interpretation of the matter in question.

The Court also has general power under Article 61 of the Statute to revise the judgment, under the same conditions as to jurisdiction, if some new fact of a decisive nature which was unknown to the Court and to the party producing it (provided that such ignorance was not due to negligence) is discovered within the period of ten years from the date of the judgment. To date, the Court has had two applications for revision, one of which is currently pending at the time of writing (see p. 178 and 205 below). The cases on interpretation and revision indicate that such an attack on the finality of the *res judicata* will not be easily entertained.

THE EXTRA-JUDICIAL FUNCTION

As seen (p. 15 above), from the start the President of the Court has performed different "extra-judicial functions". No question arose in this case of inviting the Court to employ its extra-judicial function to assist the parties in reaching a settlement of their dispute.

POSTSCRIPT

An explosion in a car repair shop in Managua on 23 May 1993 led to the discovery of a weapons cache containing, among other things, a number of surface-to-air missiles, large quantities of ammunition and military weapons, and plastic and other explosives. Many documents were also found, including 300 passports of different nationalities. This was established as belonging to the Salvadorean guerillas, material assistance to whom had been denied before the Court by Nicaragua. As part of the agreements of 1987 and later for the establishment of a firm and lasting peace in Central America and particularly for the settlement of hostilities in El Salvador, the Salvadorean geurillas had undertaken to declare and surrender all these arms and war material to the United Nations Observer Mission in El Salvador (ONUSAL) for destruction. The cache, which had not been declared, both demonstrated the violation of the agreements by the Salvadorean guerillas and Nicaragua's involvement in aiding and abetting them. This cannot be reconciled with statements made in Court on behalf of Nicaragua.

The revelations that followed this explosion led to a grave crisis of confidence between the Secretary-General of the United Nations and the Salvadorean guerillas, who later acknowledged their deception of the Secretary-General and of ONUSAL and apologized to the Secretary-General. This incident gave rise to prolonged correspondence duly reported to the Security Council, which adopted two resolutions on the matter.[22]

To a very large extent these revelations brought to light a situation closely resembling that which had been described by the State Department in the brochure noted on p. 116, above, and confirmed facts elucidated by Judge Schwebel in his questioning from the Bench.

This is not the first time that an international tribunal has been misled by one of the parties in its appreciation of the facts.[23] It remains to be seen how far these later revelations, following on an accidental explosion in Managua, will affect the different assessments that have been made of this case and its value as a precedent, especially where the unwilling respondent withdrew from further participation in the proceedings before the merits were reached.

THE WORK OF THE COURT

This chapter gives a rapid survey of the cases that have come before the present Court since 1946. Avoiding the technical aspects, a summary indication of a case's significance is given. Each case has produced detailed commentaries and literature, most of which is listed in the classified *Bibliographies* produced by the Court's Library. For the composition of the Court and its Chambers at any time, see Appendix V below.

THE CORFU CHANNEL

On 22 October 1946 a squadron of British warships sailed through a previously swept minefield in the Corfu Channel, which separates Albania from Greece. In the course of the mission, two of the ships, HMS *Saumarez* and HMS *Volage,* struck mines, subsequently established to have been "recently laid", and were badly damaged. Forty-four officers and men were killed and forty-two injured. The British Government held Albania responsible and, after the failure of diplomatic negotiations to settle the matter, referred the dispute to the Security Council in January 1947. A long and complicated discussion followed, during which the Soviet Union vetoed one draft resolution. On 9 April 1947, the Security Council recommended that the two governments should "immediately" refer the dispute to the International Court of Justice, in accordance with the provisions of the Statute of the Court. The resolution was adopted by eight votes to none, with two abstentions (Poland and the USSR), the United Kingdom not participating in the vote in accordance with Article 27 paragraph 3 of the Charter.

During these proceedings Albania had accepted the formal invitation from the Council under Article 32 of the Charter to participate without vote in the discussion, on condition that it accepted all the obligations which a member of the United Nations would have to assume in such a case. After the resolution was adopted, the President of the Council observed that although Albania could not be compelled to appear before the Court, by accepting the obligations of a member it was obliged to comply with the provisions of the Charter and the Statute.

On 22 May, the United Kingdom filed in Court an application instituting proceedings. In July the Albanian Government informed the Court of its view that in proceeding unilaterally the United Kingdom was not acting in conformity with the Statute, as required by the Security Council's resolution, and that accordingly Albania would be within its rights in holding that the case could not be brought without a special agreement. However, this notwithstanding Albania, accepting the recommendation of the Security Council, was prepared to appear before the Court. When the time came to file the Counter-Memorial, Albania raised a preliminary objection which, in effect, repeated that attitude regarding the consequences of the initial irregularity of the manner in which the case had been instituted. In a judgment of 25 March 1948 – the first delivered by the present Court – the objection was dismissed by fifteen votes to one, only the Albanian judge *ad hoc* separate, and the proceedings on the merits were resumed. A joint dissenting opinion was appended by Judges Basdevant, Alvarez, Winiarski, Zoričić, de Visscher, Badawi Pasha and Krylov, and a dissenting opinion by Judge *ad hoc* Daxner.

Immediately before that judgment was delivered the parties had concluded a special agreement by which they decided to put two questions to the Court. The first asked the Court to decide whether Albania was responsible under international law for the explosions which occurred on 22 October 1946 in Albanian waters and for the damage and loss of human life which resulted therefrom, and whether there was any duty to pay compensation. The second enquired whether the action of the United Kingdom in sending its warships through the Corfu Channel on 22 October, and whether its later action in re-sweeping the Channel on 12 and 13 November, violated Albanian sovereignty, and whether there was any duty to give satisfaction. The Court thereupon recognized that this special agreement constituted the basis for the future conduct of the case.

The pleadings showed – as had also been evident in the Security Council – that there were serious divergences between the parties on questions of fact. It become necessary for the Court to hear witnesses and experts called by the parties. This was the first occasion on which witnesses had been heard in the International Court. Five witnesses and two witness-experts were called by the United Kingdom, and three witnesses and two experts by Albania. Since the first witnesses were called by the British delegation, they were examined along the lines of British examination of witnesses, with its three phases of examination-in-chief, cross-examination and re-examination, with the possibility of questions from the Bench. This has remained the pattern for the examination of witnesses in the International Court.

As the differences of fact were not easily resolved, the Court decided to obtain an expert opinion on a number of contested points. It therefore appointed a committee of experts, consisting of senior officers of the Netherlands, Norwegian and Swedish Navies. Their first report did not sufficiently clarify matters, and the experts were requested to proceed to the scene, there to make further investigations. Although it was never fully established who had laid the mines which had damaged *Samaurez* and *Volage,* the Court in its judgment of 9 April 1949 found sufficient evidence to hold, by eleven votes to five, that in law Albania, as the territorial State, was responsible, and by ten votes to six was under the duty of making compensation for the consequent loss and damage. On the second question the Court, by fourteen votes to two, found that the passage of the British warships through the Corfu Channel on 22 October was not a violation of Albanian sovereignty. It was unanimous in declaring that the mine-sweeping activities of November "violated the sovereignty of the People's Republic of Albania, and that this declaration by the Court constitutes in itself appropriate satisfaction". Declarations were made by the President, Judge Basdevant and by Judge Zoričić; Judge Alvarez appended an individual opinion and Judges Winiarski, Badawi Pasha, Krylov and Azevedo, and Judge *ad hoc* Ečer dissenting opinions.

There had been no pleadings on the question of the amount of compensation to be paid – indeed Albania proceeded to argue that on a proper interpretation of the special agreement the Court did not have jurisdiction to assess the amount of compensation. In its judgment of 9 April the Court had rejected that argument, and decided on a third phase of the case, limited to the question of compensation. Albania did not present any pleadings in that phase of the case and, although duly notified, did not participate in the Court's hearing devoted to that question. This led the Court to apply the procedure of the non-appearance of a party (see p. 78 above), the first instance of this. However, the figures advanced by the United Kingdom were found to raise questions of a technical nature requiring an expert opinion. The Court accordingly appointed another committee of experts consisting of two senior officers of the Royal Netherlands Navy to examine the claim. The experts reached the conclusion that the amount claimed by the United Kingdom could be taken as a fair and accurate estimate of 'the damage sustained. In its judgment of 15 December 1949, the Court gave judgment in favour of the United Kingdom for the sum of £843,947. This decision was reached by twelve votes to two, a declaration by Judge Krylov and a dissenting opinion by Judge *ad hoc* Ečer being appended.

The People's Republic of Albania never paid the reparation awarded to the United Kingdom. Echoes of this were to be heard in the Court later (see p. 147 below). Diplomatic relations between the two countries were broken, only to be resumed after the collapse of the People's Republic of Albania when the outstanding claim was settled (see p. 148 above).[1]

The incidents in the Corfu Channel – among the earliest incidents of .the Cold War – gave rise to much tension, which had been exacerbated by the debates in the Security Council. The Security Council by itself was unable to remove the friction and therefore enlisted the aid of the Court by recommending the parties to refer the case to it. The special agreement opened the way to proceedings which could take account of Albania's complaints against the United Kingdom (in fact Albania could always have introduced its complaints in the proceedings, by way of a counter-claim), and the Court was enabled to deliver a judgment which gave partial satisfaction to both sides. To that extent, the combination of Court proceedings with those of the Security Council was a successful innovation, and it may be regretted that neither the Security Council nor the General Assembly has been able to repeat it since.

This case raised expectations in some circles that with the emergence of the Soviet Union as a major power, the earlier attitude of reserve manifested towards the Permanent Court might be relaxed, at least to the extent that the Soviet Union would be prepared to conclude special agreements for referring specific disputes to the Court. However, later developments were to show that any such hopes were premature.

In its judgment the Court made some important pronouncements on the right of innocent passage through the territorial sea and through international straits. These were to form an impulse for the reconstruction of the international law of the sea, culminating in the United Nations Convention on the Law of the Sea of 1982.

MEMBERSHIP IN THE UNITED NATIONS

Article 4 of the Charter lays down how new members can be admitted to the United Nations. Paragraph 1 specifies the conditions for membership – that the applicant State shall be peace-loving, have accepted the obligations contained in the Charter, and be able and willing to carry out those obligations. Paragraph 2 indicates the procedure –that admission to membership shall be effected by a decision of the General Assembly on the recommendation of the Security Council. Both these provisions have been interpreted by the Court.

From 1946 there had been a deadlock in the Security Council over the question of the admission of new members. Candidates proposed by the Socialist States of Eastern Europe did not receive the necessary majority of votes (at that time seven). Those proposed by the West encountered the veto. This gave rise to sharp discussions in the Security Council and later in the General Assembly which, on 17 November 1947, by

40 votes to eight, with two abstentions, decided to ask the Court for an advisory opinion on the interpretation of the first paragraph. The question put to the Court was whether a member which is called upon to express itself by its vote, either in the Security Council or in the General Assembly, on the admission of a State to membership, was juridically entitled to make its consent to the admission dependent on conditions not expressly provided for in paragraph 1. In particular, could such a member, while recognizing the conditions to be fulfilled, subject its affirmative vote to the additional condition that other States would be admitted together with that State? This was designed to obtain a ruling on the "legality" of a possible "package deal", by which all outstanding applications for membership would be accepted.

The competence of the Court to give the advisory opinion was challenged on the grounds that the question was a political one and therefore fell outside the jurisdiction of the Court, that it was abstract, and that the Court is not entitled to interpret the Charter. The Court, in its advisory opinion of 28 May 1948, rejected these arguments. By nine votes to six, it answered both questions in the negative. However, two of the judges forming part of the majority, Judges Alvarez and Azevedo, appended individual opinions, and Judges Basdevant, Winiarski, McNair, Read, Zoričić and Krylov dissenting opinions. These together indicated that despite the *judicial* answer, political considerations could not be regarded as irrelevant. That led to considerable confusion over what the opinion of the Court was, and why. Nevertheless, the General Assembly, in resolution 197 (Ill) of 8 December 1948, recommended that each member of the Security Council and of the General. Assembly, in exercising its vote on the admission of new members, should act in accordance with the Court's opinion. This opinion was not addressed to the Security Council, which did not act upon it.

In practice, the Court's opinion did not mean very much because all States could fully comply with it simply by explaining their negative vote on the basis of their view that the applicant State did not meet the conditions of paragraph 1. The political problem of the admission of new members did not originate in the explanations given for the negative vote, but in the underlying political situation for which those votes were merely an expression. The request for the advisory opinion did not, and indeed could not, bring out that aspect, and the practical wisdom displayed by the General Assembly in requesting the opinion and in trying to tie its hands (and those of the Security Council) on the question of the "package deal" is therefore questionable. On the other hand, the Court's decision rejecting the challenges to its jurisdiction rests on solid and convincing grounds.

The advisory opinion did not contribute to resolving the *political* problem of the admission of new members. A move developed in the General Assembly urging that when the Security Council made no recommendation at all, the General Assembly could decide to admit new members. Although the language of Article 4, paragraph 2, of the Charter seems clear enough, the General Assembly decided to put the question to the Court by resolution 296 J (IV) of 22 November 1949, adopted by 42 votes to nine with six abstentions. In a brief and clear advisory opinion of 3 March 1950 the Court gave its opinion that admission to membership cannot be effected by a decision of the General Assembly when the Security Council has made no recommendation for admission, by reason of the candidate failing to secure the requisite majority or of a veto in the Security Council. The Court reached this decision by a majority of twelve votes to two. Dissenting opinions were written by Judges Alvarez and Azevedo. The Court summarily rejected challenges to its jurisdiction, similar to those which had been advanced in the first *Admission* case.[2]

There has been criticism of the General Assembly in putting the question to the Court, on the ground that it did not raise a difficult point of law. That criticism is not justified. The putting of the question to the Court resulted from political considerations, and not from legal difficulties. The Court's opinion prevented extravagant claims being put forward in the General Assembly and performed a valuable function in keeping the dispute confined within given limits.

The deadlock over the admission of new members continued until the end of 1955 when the USSR and the United States were able to agree on the means for bringing it to an end. A "package deal" was negotiated. By resolution 995 (X) of 14 December 1955, 16 new members were admitted "en bloc". The advisory opinion of 1948 had been interpreted as excluding a package deal, and many people consider that this resolution of the question of the admission of new members was not in conformity with the legal interpretation of the Charter given by the Court. On the other hand, there was a general relief that a solution had at last been found, and there is no serious disposition now to query its legality.

The Council of the League of Nations had adopted all its requests for an advisory opinion from the Permanent Court of International Justice unanimously. That was in accordance with the voting practice of the League of Nations. The Charter of the United Nations abolished that unanimity rule and replaced it by an absolute majority for most cases in the General Assembly and a qualified majority in the Security Council. These two requests for advisory opinion were the first occasions on which the request for the advisory opinions had been adopted on a divisive vote. The fact that a request can be adopted on a majority vote and over important political opposition has opened the door to new and unforeseen employment of the advisory procedure, as can be seen in later cases.

THE LEGAL PERSONALITY OF THE UNITED NATIONS

Following the assassination in Israel of Count Bernadotte, the United Nations Mediator in Palestine, and the killing of other United Nations agents in Jordan and Egypt during the latter part of 1948, the question arose whether the United Nations could claim from the responsible governments reparation for the injuries it had suffered. The Secretary-General placed this matter on the agenda of the General Assembly which unanimously decided at the end of 1948 to refer a series of complicated legal questions to the Court for its opinion. The advisory opinion of 11 April 1949 is one of the Court's major opinions of general international law. In it the Court was unanimous in holding that the United Nations has the capacity to bring an international claim against the responsible *de jure* or *de facto* government of a member or non-member State with a view to obtaining the reparation due to it in respect of the damage caused to the United Nations in the event of an agent of the United Nations, in the performance of his duties, suffering injuries in circumstances involving the responsibility of that State. The Court divided eleven to four on questions relating to the capacity of the United Nations to make the international claim on behalf of the State of which the victim was a national. The opinion also indicated how to reconcile claims brought on behalf of the United Nations itself and those brought on behalf of States injured by the acts, and mentioned the safeguards necessary to protect a respondent State against the possibility that it would have to pay double damages. Judge Winiarski declared his dissent. Judges Alvarez and Azevedo added concurring opinions, and Judges Hackworth, Badawi Pasha and Krylov dissenting opinions.[3]

On the basis of that opinion, the Secretary-General made proposals for the method by which the United Nations would claim the reparation due. The General Assembly gave its approval in resolution 365 (IV) of 1 December 1949. The Secretary-General then proceeded to present the claims against the responsible governments. None of the respondent governments at any time contested the right of the United Nations to present these claims, although only the Government of Israel paid the damages claimed, the others contesting the way in which they had been calculated.

This opinion has supplied important underpinning for the development of the concept of the legal personality of international intergovernmental organizations in international law, now a standard feature of the law.

FISHING ZONES IN THE NORTH SEA

On 28 September 1949 the United Kingdom filed an application instituting proceedings against Norway, basing itself on the compulsory jurisdiction. The subject of these proceedings was the validity or otherwise, under international law, of the Norwegian system of delimitation of a fisheries zone by a Decree of 1935. Although disputes between British and Norwegian fishermen had existed in one form or another for several centuries, it was only since the beginning of the twentieth century, with the introduction of modern methods of fishing and the increasing economic pressures on the world's fish stocks, that Norway began to take more stringent measures to protect its own fisheries interests in the sea areas adjacent to its coast. After the Decree of 1935 the dispute became more acute and there was talk of referring it to the Permanent Court, but those negotiations had not been completed when the Second World War broke out. After the War, the danger of depletion of the fish stocks through over-fishing had brought to a head a number of fishing disputes, in both the North Sea and the North Atlantic, and in other parts of the world. Although the United Nations has only been obliquely concerned with these disputes, the prolonged discussion on the law of the sea, and the major conferences of 1958, 1960 and 1973-82 and the instruments they produced have been closely influenced by them, and by a succession of major cases in the International Court itself, as will be described later (see pp. 165, 167, 177, 179, 184, 187 and 213 below) and international arbitrations. The *Fisheries* case was therefore partly the first test case on a matter of great and general international interest.

Before the Norwegian Decree of 1935, it had been generally believed that the low-water line along the coast is the baseline from which the breadth of the territorial sea (over which the coastal State has exclusive fishing rights) is measured, with special rules for bays, gulfs, estuaries and other indentations. In such cases, if straight baselines are drawn, they should be based on points on the mainland and as far as possible follow the sinuosities of the coast, even if the coast is deeply indented by fjords and lochs, as is the coast of Norway. The Decree of 1935, however, proceeded on a different principle. It joined by straight lines a series of base-points, 48 in all, many of them not being points on continental Norway at all but on rocks out at sea and visible at low tide (drying rocks, or low-tide elevations). The total length of these lines, which did not follow the sinuosities of the coast but at most its general direction, was some 600 miles.

From these baselines an exclusive fishing zone, four miles wide, was claimed. This Decree affected some 6,900 square kilometres of sea, with important stocks of cod, saithe, haddock, halibut, plaice, herring, mackerel, seal and some types of whale.

The case was introduced unilaterally by the United Kingdom. However, it appears that although the parties were unable to draw up a special agreement, there was diplomatic understanding to refer the dispute to the Court in this way. The proceedings took their course without any complications. On 18 December 1951 the Court rendered its judgment. By ten votes to two, it upheld the Norwegian contentions and by eight to four found that the baselines also were not contrary to international law. Judge Hackworth made a declaration. Separate opinions were made by Judges Alvarez and Hsu Mo, and dissenting opinions by Judges Sir Arnold McNair and Read.[4]

This is commonly regarded as one of the most important judgments rendered by the present Court. The issues far transcended the bipartite dispute of which the Court was seized, for since the end of the Second World War, as stated, questions of fishing rights have become a major international, issue, and the implications of a judgment admitting that the new conception of baselines on this extended scale was not contrary to international law, and even more so the reasons adopted by the Court, were general. In 1950 the General Assembly had decided to take up the whole question of the codification of the law of the sea, and the first phases of the work were entrusted to the International Law Commission. It soon became clear that the question of generalizing the rules applied by the Court in the *Fisheries* case for the delimitation of baselines, and those applied earlier in the *Corfu Channel* case relating to the right of innocent passage through the territorial sea in general and through straits used for international navigation in particular, would encounter major political obstacles. In the end, the First United Nations Conference on the Law of the Sea, which was in session for two months in Geneva in the spring of 1958, succeeded in achieving agreement on these vital aspects. That agreement has been incorporated virtually unchanged in the United Nations Convention on the Law of the Sea of 1982.[5]

There can be little doubt that but for the Court's decision in 1951, the 1958 Conference would not have been able to complete its work. The Court, in deciding the concrete case, had expounded the principles which were applicable. Those principles were then taken up first by the International Law Commission (with political guidance from the General Assembly and from individual governments), and in that way generalized, and later finally approved, on the political level, by the 1958 Conference. Here is an important instance of the manner in which the Court, by its decision on a concrete dispute, makes a significant contribution to the development of international law, which itself is the basis for the prevention, or the settlement, of other international disputes.

On a point of clarification, the Court was not asked to decide in this case what is the breadth of the territorial sea recognized by international law. That was not in issue in 1951. The sole question was the manner in which the inner, or landward, limit of the area of territorial sea may be fixed in cases where the coastline presents the special features of the coast of Norway incidentally, features which are not so unique as is sometimes alleged. On the other hand, the Court treated the Norwegian fishing zone in this case as territorial sea. It was only later that a fishing zone began to be accepted as something lying adjacent to but beyond the outer limit of the territorial sea.

This was the second of the series of major cases concerning the law of the sea. Later cases concerned fishing rights and the determination of the boundaries of maritime spaces under national jurisdiction in different types of geographical formation.

FRENCH NATIONALS IN EGYPT

In October, 1949, France filed an application against Egypt, based on the Montreux Convention of 1937 for the abrogation of the Capitulations, asking for compensation for the damage suffered by a number of French nationals and protected persons, in their persons, property, rights and interests, as a result of measures taken by the Egyptian Government in May, 1948, in connection with the hostilities which broke out on the termination of the Mandate for Palestine. The proceedings were instituted after 15 months of diplomatic negotiations had been in vain. In February, 1950, the impugned measures were lifted. In those circumstances the proceedings were discontinued.[6]

A CASE OF DIPLOMATIC ASYLUM

On 3 October 1948, an unsuccessful military rebellion broke out in Peru at the instigation of a political party led by the well-known Peruvian politician, Señor Victor Raúl Haya de la Torre. Judicial proceedings were then opened against him, but he managed to evade arrest. On 3 January 1949 he sought and was granted political asylum in the Colombian Embassy in Lima. This was done on the basis of certain Latin American customs and conventions regulating diplomatic asylum. The next day, the Colombian Ambassador made the usual demand for a safe-conduct so that Haya de la Torre could leave the country. That was refused on the ground that he was not charged with political offences, and a dispute ensued between the two countries. On 31 August 1949 they concluded an agreement, called the Act of Lima, to refer the dispute to the Court. However, they were unable to concur on the terms of the reference, and accordingly agreed that either party might institute the proceedings unilaterally without that being regarded as an unfriendly act towards the other. This was the first of this form of "framework agreement". On 15 October, Colombia, on the basis of that agreement, filed an application instituting the proceedings. This was to lead to three judgments in what became technically three separate cases.

In the application the Court was asked to decide, on the basis of the various legal rules binding the parties, whether Colombia was legally entitled, for the purpose of granting the asylum, to qualify the offence as a political offence and not as an ordinary offence (for which no asylum should be granted), and whether Peru as the territorial State was bound to give the necessary safe-conduct to enable Haya de la Torre to leave the country. In the course of the proceedings, Peru submitted a counter-claim, asking the Court to declare that the grant of asylum was in violation of the Havana Convention on Asylum of 1928. In the judgment of 20 November 1950, the Court found on a vote of fourteen to two that Colombia was not entitled unilaterally, and in a manner binding on Peru, to qualify the nature of the offence, and by fifteen to one it rejected the Colombian claim that Peru must give the necessary safe-conduct. On the other hand, while partly rejecting the Peruvian counter-claim by the same vote, it nevertheless found by ten votes to six that the grant of asylum was not made in conformity with the Havana Convention. Dissenting opinions were filed by Judges Alvarez, Badawi Pasha, Read and Azevedo, and Judge *ad hoc* Caicedo Castilla, and Judge Zoričić made a declaration.

This judgment left things as they were. This was not the fault of the Court, but was the consequence of the manner in which the parties presented and pleaded the case. The agreement in principle to refer the dispute to the Court did not go so far as to include any underlying agreement about the real issues on which the Court's decision could lay the basis for the political settlement.

On 20 November, the day on which the judgment was delivered, Colombia filed an application for interpretation. The purpose of this was to obtain a decision from the Court on the manner of the termination of Haya de la Torre's continued enforced residence in the Colombian Embassy in Lima. In a judgment of 27 November 1950 the Court found by twelve to one that the request for interpretation was inadmissible on the grounds that no dispute as to the meaning and scope of the judgment had been disclosed, and that new questions were raised, and not questions of the meaning of statements appearing in the judgment. Judge *ad hoc* Caicedo Castilla declared his dissent.

The next day, Peru demanded the surrender of the refugee on the basis of the judgment of 20 November. Colombia refused on the ground that neither of the judgments had dealt with the question of the surrender. This led to a new dispute between the two countries, and on 13 December 1950 Colombia filed a further application asking whether or not Colombia was bound to deliver Haya de la Torre to Peru. Jurisdiction was based on the Treaty of Friendship between the two countries of 24 May 1934. Colombia was willing to have a decision by the Court *ex aequo et bono* (see p. 148 above), but Peru did not agree to this. On 13 March 1951 Cuba, as party to the Havana Convention of 1928 the construction of which was again in question, intervened under Article 63 of the Statute (see p. 127 above), but the admissibility of the intervention was contested.

By a judgment of 13 June 1951, Cuba's intervention was first admitted, limited, however, to the new questions that had arisen, and not covering the interpretation of the Havana Convention which had been given in the first judgment. On the merits, the Court found unanimously that it was unable to give effect to submissions of both parties asking it to declare how the judgment of 20 November should be executed. The Court's reason for this was that a submission couched in an interrogative form implied a political choice which only the parties were in a position to appreciate. It was not part of the Court's judicial function to make such a choice. The Court went on to find by thirteen votes to one that Colombia was not obliged to surrender the refugee to Peru, and unanimously that the asylum itself ought to have ceased after the judgment of 20 November. A declaration was made by Judge *ad hoc* Alayza y Paz Soldán.[7]

This had cleared up one point, but still left outstanding the major issue of how to bring the asylum to an end. This aspect reverted to the diplomatic channel. The reason for this again was the fact that the parties had been unable to agree what was the dispute to be referred to the Court. The Court, for its part, and consistent with its usual caution, did not feel itself empowered to do any more than declare the legal position between the parties. It nevertheless expressed the hope that after their mutual relations had been made clear the parties would be able to find a practical and satisfactory solution by seeking guidance from those considerations of courtesy and good-neighbourliness which, in matters of asylum, have always held a prominent place in the relations between the Latin-American republics. Over three more years were to elapse before Haya de la Torre was able to leave the Colombian Embassy, and the virtual stage of siege under which it had been placed was lifted.

This case involved questions of regional law in Latin America. It is the first case involving exclusively regional law to have come before the Court. It was also the first case in the present Court in which a third State intervened under Article 63 of the Statute.

QUESTIONS OF HUMAN RIGHTS IN CERTAIN PEACE TREATIES OF 1947

From 1948 the General Assembly had been discussing the observance of the human rights clauses of the Peace Treaties with Bulgaria, Hungary and Romania. Those countries, not then members of the United Nations, were being accused of grave violations of those provisions. The Peace Treaties each contained a clause for the settlement of disputes which provided, amongst other things, for the reference of a dispute to a three-man Commission of which the third member should be appointed by the Secretary-General of the United Nations in the event of disagreement. Attempts to refer the disputes to the Commissions failed owing to the refusal of Bulgaria, Hungary and Romania to appoint their commissioners, and in 1949 the question arose whether the Secretary-General could make the third appointment. In October, 1949, the General Assembly decided to ask for an advisory opinion on four legal questions: *(a)* Was the existence of disputes disclosed by the diplomatic correspondence? *(b)* If so, did the provisions of the Peace Treaties for the settlement of disputes come into operation? If the answer to those questions was in the affirmative, and if, after a delay of one month, the national commissioners had not been appointed, *(c)* was the Secretary-General authorized to proceed to the appointment of the "third" commissioner; and *(d)* if so, would such a Commission be competent? The General Assembly had adopted this resolution by 47 votes to three, with seven abstentions. That was the third instance of an advisory opinion being requested after a politically divisive vote.

In its first advisory opinion of 30 March 1950 the Court answered the first two questions in the affirmative, each time by a vote of eleven to three. A separate opinion by Judge Alvarez, and dissenting opinions by Judges Winiarski, Zoričić and Krylov were appended. In its second opinion of 18 July, by eleven votes to two it answered the third question in the negative, and therefore did not consider the fourth question. Here there were dissenting opinions by Judges Read and Azevedo, and a declaration by Judge Krylov.[8]

As in the previous advisory opinions which originated in Cold War issues, here, too, the competence of the Court was challenged, on the ground, essentially, that if there were concrete disputes, the invocation of the advisory procedure was in fact an attempt surreptitiously to introduce a form of contentious case, and the Court was not authorized to deal with such a case in the absence of the consent of all the parties. The Court rejected these contentions in the present case. Its principal reason was that the advisory opinion as such was not binding, representing the participation of the Court in the work of the United Nations. The object of the request for the advisory opinion was to obtain enlightenment for the General Assembly, and in the present circumstances the advisory opinion would not be substantially equivalent to deciding the questions in dispute between the parties.

The General Assembly had no alternative but to take note of the two advisory opinions, and in resolution 385 (V) of 3 November 1950 in effect dropped the matter.

As in a previous case, it may be considered that here too the questions put to the

Court were on the whole not difficult from the legal point of view. The disputes were rooted in a more intractable political situation at an early stage of the Cold War, which all the organs of the United Nations were unable to solve. The real significance of this experience was that it showed once and for all that the Soviet Union and its Allies were not prepared to enable the advisory procedure to be employed to handle disputes relating to or arising out of the tensions of the Cold War.

These opinions had delayed consequences. They encouraged the international community to develop new forms of political and arbitral procedures which it is hoped would not be frustrated in this way. On the other hand, it may be regretted that through this opinion the Court in effect withdrew from an active role in the sphere of human rights for a considerable period of time.

SOUTH WEST AFRICA AND NAMIBIA

Questions relating to the Mandates system established under Article 22 of the Covenant of the League of Nations had come before the Permanent Court in one instance only – the *Mavrommatis Palestine Concessions* cases of 1924, 1925 and 1927. Although the Mandates system did not survive the liquidation of the League, being replaced by the International Trusteeship System set out in Articles 75 to 91 of the Charter, the new Court has had before it six cases to do with the legal status of the former mandated territory of South West Africa (now independent Namibia), four requests for an advisory opinion, and two contentious cases which were joined. On this question it has rendered four advisory opinions and two judgments, all in the period 1950 to 1971.

On 17 December 1920 the League Council conferred this Mandate on South Africa and confirmed its terms. It was what was called a "C" class Mandate. The mandatory had full powers of administration and legislation over the territory as an integral portion of its own territory, subject to a number of obligations, and the League was to supervise the administration and see to it that the obligations were fulfilled. Difficulties over the interpretation and application of the Mandate had appeared already in the days of the League. However, they only came to a head in the United Nations. South Africa refused to convert the Mandate into a Trusteeship agreement, despite repeated urgings by the General Assembly. In 1949 the General Assembly by 40 votes to seven, with four abstentions, decided that for its further consideration of the question, the Court's opinion on a number of legal questions on the status of South West Africa was desirable. On 11 July 1950 the Court gave an opinion on five questions related to the status of the territory. It found unanimously that the Mandate was still in force. By twelve votes to two it found that the obligations arising under the Mandate were still binding on South Africa. It was unanimous in concluding that under the Charter the territory could be placed under the Trusteeship system but by the close vote of eight to six that there was no legal obligation on South Africa to do so. Finally the Court was unanimous that South Africa, acting alone, did not have the competence to modify the international status of the territory, but that modifications in its international status could only be made with the consent of the United Nations. Declarations were made by the Vice President Guerrero and by Judges Zoričić and Badawi Pasha, separate opinions by Judges Sir Arnold McNair and Read, and dissenting opinions by Judges Alvarez, de Visscher and Krylov were added. The competence of the Court to give this opinion was not challenged.

The General Assembly then adopted the advisory opinion and commenced a long series of efforts to implement it. In the course of these efforts further questions arose on the meaning of certain passages in the 1950 Opinion in which the Court had stated that the degree of supervision over the territory by the General Assembly should not exceed that which had previously been applied by the League and should conform as far as possible to the procedure of the League Council. On that basis the General Assembly had established the Committee on South West Africa, broadly analogous to the Permanent Mandates Commission of the Council of the League. South Africa refused to co-operate with this Committee and to submit the annual reports which had been required by the League. This deprived the Committee of information necessary to enable it to discharge its functions. Other difficulties had arisen, because it was contended that the substitution in the United Nations of the two-thirds majority for the unanimity previously current in the League implied an increase in the degree of supervision, against which the Court in 1950 had uttered a warning. To meet this criticism the General Assembly adopted a special rule of procedure requiring a two-thirds majority for decisions of the General Assembly on questions relating to reports and petitions concerning the territory, and also decided to ask the Court for an advisory opinion on what voting procedure should be followed, if that interpretation of the 1950 advisory opinion was not correct. This decision was adopted by 25 votes to 10 with 21 abstentions. In its advisory opinion of 7 June 1955 the Court unanimously replied that the voting rule was a correct interpretation of the advisory opinion. A declaration was made by Judge Kojevnikov, and separate opinions by Judges Basdevant, Klaestad and Lauterpacht.

After accepting this opinion the General Assembly continued its efforts, and the next year found it necessary by 32 votes to five with 14 abstentions to ask the Court whether it would be consistent with the 1950 opinion for it to authorize the Committee on South-West Africa to grant hearings to petitioners (under the original Mandates system, petitioners could only submit their petitions in writing, and the question was whether oral petitions would constitute an excess in the degree of supervision). The underlying purpose in granting these hearings was to supplement the Committee's information on the situation in South-West Africa. In its opinion of 1 June 1956 the Court, by a vote of eight to five, answered the question put to it in the affirmative. Here there were declarations by Judges Winiarski and Kojevnikov, a separate opinion by Judge Sir Hersch Lauterpacht, and a joint dissenting opinion by Vice-President Badawi and Judges Basdevant, Hsu Mo, Armand-Ugon and Moreno Quintana.

These opinions had certainly gone a long way towards clarifying the legal situation, but being advisory opinions they were not technically binding on South Africa. The opinions had all been requested and rendered before the process of decolonization had changed the character of the United Nations. Nevertheless, the political conflict between the majority in the General Assembly and South Africa started to grow sharper. At its eleventh session (1956) the General Assembly decided to look for new ways to ensure that South Africa fulfilled the obligations incumbent on it under the Mandate. After detailed consideration of this aspect, the General Assembly, in resolution 1361 (XIV) of 17 November 1959, drew the attention of member States to the possibility of their bringing a contentious case against South Africa, based on the submission to the jurisdiction contained in the Mandate. The question was then discussed at the Second African States Conference held at Addis Abeba in June 1960. On this occasion Ethiopia and Liberia announced their intention of initiating contentious proceedings, as recommended. The Conference established a steering committee of four African States, including Ethiopia and Liberia, to determine the procedure and tactics incident to the conduct of the case.

In November 1960, two contentious cases were accordingly instituted, by Ethiopia and Liberia respectively, against South Africa, jurisdiction being based upon the compromissory clause contained in the Mandate instrument. This action met with strong approval by the General Assembly, which also refused to see in the subsistence of the contentious proceedings at The Hague any reason to cause it to refrain from exercising its own responsibilities for the supervision of South-West Africa, as defined in the previous three advisory opinions of the Court.

The contentious cases were to give rise to one of the most complicated and, in the view of many, frustrating pieces of litigation ever decided by any international tribunal.

After the two Memorials (in substantially identical terms) had been filed the Court noted that the two applicant governments were "in the same interest" before the Court. It therefore joined the two proceedings. The immediate consequences were that the two applicant governments were to act in concert to choose a single judge *ad hoc,* and that joint pleadings were filed in the subsequent phases.

In due course South Africa filed a series of preliminary objections. The first objection was to the effect that the Mandate itself had not survived the dissolution of the League of Nations and was no longer in force, and at any event its compromissory clause was no longer in force. The second, which was related, argued that since the compromissory clause conferred jurisdiction in respect to another member of the League of Nations, with the dissolution of the League the two applicant States had lost that quality. The third objection consisted of the proposition that the dispute brought before the Court was not a dispute as envisaged in the compromissory clause, since it did not affect any material interests of the applicant States or their nationals. The fourth was to the effect that if the dispute was one which came within the scope of the compromissory clause, it was not one which could not be settled by negotiation with the applicants, and that there had been no such negotiations with a view to its settlement. After heavy pleading the Court, in its judgment of 21 December 1962, by eight votes to seven found that it had jurisdiction to adjudicate upon the merits. There were separate opinions by Judges Bustamante y Rivero and Jessup, and Judge *ad hoc* Sir Louis Mbanefo, and dissenting opinions by President Winiarski and Judges Basdevant, Sir Percy Spender and Sir Gerald Fitzmaurice (jointly), Morelli and Judge *ad hoc* van Wyk. The Court did not pronounce itself on each objection individually in the operative clause of the judgment, contrary to usual practice.

The first two objections to a large extent raised issues which the Court had previously considered in its advisory cases, especially the principal one of 1950. The third and fourth, however, broke new ground. The third objection, in particular, raised fundamental issues of the kind of rights which can be protected by the international judicial process. As will be seen, it was on this issue that the contentious proceedings were ultimately to founder.

The cases continued, therefore, in accordance with the normal procedure, and after more extremely heavy pleading became ready for hearing on 23 December 1964. The hearings commenced in March 1965. At their commencement, South Africa made an application relating to the composition of the Court for the purposes of the case. A closed hearing took place, after which the Court decided by eight votes to six not to accede to that application. No further details of this step have been officially published, and it is believed that the motion related to one or more of the judges who, previously to their election, had been responsible members of their countries' delegations at the General Assembly of the United Nations when the South West Africa issue had been discussed. In the decisive periods of this case, the Court was to sit fortuitously with an even number – fourteen – of judges.

Hearings lasted from March to November 1965, with a break for the summer vacation. During these hearings, South Africa proposed that the Court should carry out an inspection *in loco* in South West Africa, and that it should also visit South Africa, Ethiopia, Liberia and one or two other countries of the Court's own choosing south of the Sahara. In an order of 29 November 1965 the Court, by eight votes to six, decided not to visit South West Africa and South Africa, and by nine votes to five it decided not to visit the applicant States and sub-Saharan African countries. Again there is no information about individual voting.

Fourteen witnesses and experts were called by South Africa and subjected to examination, cross-examination and re-examination by the parties, and to questions put by members of the Court.

The complicated submissions by Ethiopia and Liberia covered all of the grievances of the African States against South Africa. They seem to have had two major ends in view – a pronouncement by the Court to the effect that the policy of *apartheid* (which had been extended to South West Africa) was contrary to international law, and that the breaches of the Mandate perpetrated by South Africa should be remedied. For its part South Africa contended that the Mandate was no longer in force, and in the alternative that it was not in breach of any of its provisions.

On both sides, then, the submissions were directed to the merits of the dispute. The Court, however, found that there was one matter which appertained to the merits but which had an antecedent character, namely the question of the applicants' standing in the present phase of the proceedings. The Court defined this as meaning their legal right or interest regarding the subject-matter of the claim as set out in their final submissions. On this the Court found that the applicants could not be considered to have established any legal right or interest appertaining to them in the subject-matter of the present claims, and accordingly, by the President's casting vote – the votes being equally divided – it decided to reject the claims. There were declarations by the President, Sir Percy Spender, separate opinions by Judge Morelli and Judge *ad hoc* van Wyk, and dissenting opinions by Vice-President Wellington Koo, Judges Koretsky, Tanaka, Jessup, Padilla Nervo and Forster, and Judge *ad hoc* Sir Louis Mbanefo.[9]

The explanation of this apparent reversal of the 1962 decision is that there the Court was solely concerned with the question of *jurisdiction,* while here the issue was the applicants' entitlement to bring the claim over which, in other respects, the Court would have jurisdiction.

Needless to say, this surprising result, reached after such prolonged and expensive proceedings, sent shock-waves through the international community. The General Assembly, in its resolution 2145 (XXI) of 27 October 1966, decided that South Africa was in breach of the Mandate which was accordingly terminated. The General Assembly assumed direct responsibility for the Territory until its independence. It took various dispositions designed to persuade South Africa to withdraw from the territory, but these were to no avail.

Early in 1968 the African States brought the question of South West Africa before the Security Council. On 25 January 1968 the Security Council adopted resolution 245

(1968) in which it backed the General Assembly's 1966 decision. This was followed by resolution 246 (1968) of 14 March, censuring South Africa for its refusal to abide by the earlier resolutions. Further resolutions were adopted in 1969, and on 30 January 1970, in resolution 276 (1970), the Security Council established an *ad hoc* subcommittee to study ways and means for the effective implementation of the Council's resolutions. One of the recommendations of this subcommittee was for a further advisory opinion to be requested of the Court, and on 29 July 1970, in resolution 284 (1970), the Security Council decided to ask the Court what were the legal consequences for States of the continued presence of South Africa in Namibia, notwithstanding Security Council resolution 276 (1970). The Court was asked to transmit its opinion to the Security Council at an early date. That resolution was adopted by twelve votes to none, Poland, the USSR and the United Kingdom abstaining.

A large number of written statements were filed by the end of November, but before the public hearings could commence, a series of questions relating to the composition of the Court had to be solved. South Africa objected to the presence of three judges on the Court. In respect of two of these, the President Sir Muhammad Zafrulla Khan and Judge Padilla Nervo, the Court was unanimous in rejecting the objection. In the third case, relating to Judge Morozov, the Court reached a similar decision by ten votes to four. These objections all related to previous activities by the Members of the Court concerned in their national delegations in the General Assembly. In the third case, the Member concerned had also been one of his country's representatives at the Security Council when the relevant resolutions had been adopted. In addition, the South African government applied for the appointment of a judge *ad hoc*. In a closed hearing (the record of which was subsequently made public) the application was heard, to be rejected by ten votes to five. Judges Sir Gerald Fitzmaurice, Gros and Petrén appended a joint declaration to that order.

Apart from the questions relating to the composition of the Court, South Africa raised other objections. These included political pressure to which the Court might have been subjected, invalidity of the resolution of the Security Council by which the opinion was requested, that the opinion related to a dispute to which South Africa was a party and the consent of South Africa to the giving of the opinion should have been obtained, and procedural irregularities in the Security Council. All these objections were rejected by the Court.

Hearings lasted for six weeks in February and March, 1971. During the course of these South Africa requested that a plebiscite under the joint supervision of the Court and South Africa be held in the territory, and that South Africa should be permitted to adduce a considerable amount of evidence on factual issues. In May the Court announced its negative decision on these requests.

The advisory opinion was delivered on 21 June 1971. After explaining its reasons for its decisions on the composition of the Court it proceeded to reject a series of objections by South Africa to the giving of the opinion. It then turned to the substance of the matter, to a large extent covering ground previously traversed in the earlier opinions and judgments. By thirteen votes to two, the Court was of opinion that the continued presence of South Africa in Namibia being illegal, South Africa was under the obligation to withdraw its administration from Namibia immediately and thus put an end to its occupation of the territory. By eleven votes to four, the Court indicated that States members of the United Nations were under the obligation to recognize the illegality of South Africa's presence in Namibia and the invalidity of its acts on behalf of or concerning Namibia, and to refrain from any such acts and in particular any dealings with the Government of South Africa implying recognition of the legality of, or lending support or assistance to, such presence and administration. It was also incumbent upon States which were not members of the United Nations to give assistance in the action which had been taken by the United Nations with regard to Namibia. There was a declaration by the President, Sir Mohammad Zafrulla Khan, and concurring opinions by the Vice-President Ammoun and Judges Padilla Nervo, Petrén, Onyeama, Dillard and de Castro, and dissenting opinions by Sir Gerald Fitzmaurice and Gros.[10]

In resolution 301 (1971) of 20 October 1971 the Security Council, by 12 votes to none, with France and the United Kingdom abstaining, *inter alia* took note with appreciation of that opinion and expressed agreement with it. Both the Security Council and the General Assembly continued their efforts to find a satisfactory solution to the problem. In 1988 agreement was reached between the interested parties by which Namibia would become independent in 1989. By General Assembly resolution S-18/1, 23 April 1990, Namibia was admitted as a member of the United Nations.

This history well illustrates the extraordinary complications which can plague a dispute, in which there are important legal elements, between the majority of the United Nations, in the Security Council and in the General Assembly, and a member State. It also demonstrates the inherent limitations of the judicial process, especially the advisory competence, as an effective instrument for the resolution of these problems in the absence of the real consent of the parties concerned. The abstract and generalized consent to the functioning of the Court implicit in the bare fact of membership in the United Nations is insufficient as consent to the exercise of the judicial function in a concrete case. The purpose underlying the recourse to the contentious procedure in 1960 was to remove the ambiguity characteristic of the formally non-binding advisory opinions, and to obtain a binding decision on broadly similar grounds in the form of a judgment which could be brought before the Security Council for "execution".

The inability of the Court to meet this problem is due above all to institutional causes and the fragile basis on which modern international litigation rests. This, and the legalistic nature if not pure sophistry which many purport to see in some of the Court's pronouncements, gave in their turn rise to profound disappointment and misgivings. These reactions were not limited to the African States immediately concerned. With the 1966 judgment, the standing of the Court in political circles in the United Nations fell to its lowest point. It is significant that the profound changes in the geographical distribution of seats on the Court, bringing it into line with the composition of the Security Council, were felt after that date, and that the Court itself, after the elections of 1966, took in hand a re-examination of its internal practices, leading firstly to the 1968 and later 1976 resolutions on its internal judicial practice (see p. 109 above) and to the 1972 amendment and the 1978 revision of the Rules of Court (see p. 21 above).

There is a tendency in some quarters to attribute South Africa's change of policy over Namibia to the impact of this series of judicial decisions. This is a speculative assessment. In the broader context of South Africa's relations with its African populations and the process of dismantling the *apartheid* State, however, the grant of independence to Namibia can be seen in another light. It will not be possible to reach a viable assessment of the impact of the Court's decisions on South African policy until all the relevant archives are open to public inspection.

RIGHTS OF U.S. NATIONALS IN (FRENCH) MOROCCO

On 28 October 1950 France began proceedings against the United States, on the basis of the compulsory jurisdiction, and asked for a definition of the rights of United States nationals in Morocco. The dispute originated in measures of currency and import controls introduced in 1948. It also raised complicated questions concerning the extent to which United States citizens enjoyed rights of exterritoriality under the system of capitulations, and the method of evaluating imports for customs purposes under the Act of Algeciras of 1906, and other related topics.

The United States made a formal reservation about the applicability of the compulsory jurisdiction in this case, but nevertheless agreed to the questions being decided by the Court. The United States also raised a technical objection designed to ascertain whether the judgment would be binding not only on France but also on Morocco. After this point had been cleared up, the objection was withdrawn. In a long and complicated judgment of 27 July 1952, the Court gave its decision on the various issues presented to it. There was a declaration by Judge Hsu Mo, and dissenting opinions by Judges Hackworth, Badawi, Levi Carneiro and Sir Benegal Rau.[11]

The Court's decision in this case had no long-term significance after Morocco gained its independence in 1956.

RESERVATIONS TO MULTILATERAL TREATIES

The Convention on the Prevention and Punishment of the Crime of Genocide which was opened for signature on 9 December 1948 provided that it would come into force after twenty States had become parties to it. On the eve of the fifth session of the General Assembly in 1950 the Secretary-General was confronted with a novel problem: the number of States parties to the Convention was growing, but some of these had made reservations to which other States had entered objections. It seemed likely that he would run into difficulties in deciding whether, in those circumstances, the reserving States could be included in the twenty necessary to bring the Convention into force. On that basis he asked the General Assembly for directions.

For practical purposes his difficulties were overcome on 14 October 1950 when five States ratified the Convention, bringing the total number to twenty-four. Only two of these were affected by reservations, so there was no difficulty in determining the entry into force of the Convention. However the incident had disclosed great differences of opinion among the members about the applicable rules of law in circumstances such as these (which are fairly common), and the General Assembly decided, by 47 votes to five, with five abstentions, to ask the Court for an advisory opinion on the basic question whether a reserving State could be regarded as being a party to the Convention if some of the other parties object to the reservation, but not others. Although the immediate problem of the Genocide Convention was therefore to some extent solved in fact, the questions were asked in relation to that Convention in order to enable the Court to consider the problems against a concrete background, and not entirely in the abstract. For the Court this became a normal question of treaty interpretation, of ascertaining the intentions of the negotiators, even though the issues involved were novel. On 28 May 1951 the Court gave its opinion, which is mainly of technical interest to the professional international lawyer. The vote in the Court was close and clear-cut, seven to five. Vice-

President Guerrero and Judges Sir Arnold McNair, Read and Hsu Mo appended a joint dissenting opinion, and Judge Alvarez a dissenting opinion of his own. The General Assembly subsequently gave appropriate instructions to the Secretary-General.[12]

The underlying issues of this case, relating to highly technical matters of the law of international treaties, are important for the smooth conduct of international affairs. These issues had greatly troubled the responsible organs of the League of Nations as well as the General Assembly and the International Law Commission of the United Nations. This, indeed, had vacillated in its approach to the matter, between the attitude which was current in the League of Nations and the position adopted by the International Court in this case. Ultimately, that position prevailed, and is adopted, in a refined form, in articles 19 to 23 of the Vienna Convention of 23 May 1969 on the Law of Treaties.[13]

A GREEK CITIZEN'S CLAIM FOR DAMAGES FOR BREACH OF CONTRACT

In 1919 a Greek shipowner, Nicholas Ambatielos, contracted with the British Government for the purchase of some steamships then under construction. However, the ships were not delivered as soon as anticipated and Mr Ambatielos became indebted to the British Government for a considerable sum of money, part of which was secured by a mortgage on the ships. In the course of legal proceedings in London in 1920, some interdepartmental minutes were not produced by the British Government – a fact which later gave rise to a claim by Ambatielos for "denial of justice". Ambatielos lost his case in the Court of Appeal in London, and made no attempt to take it to the House of Lords. The Greek Government then took up the case in exercise of its right of diplomatic protection of one of its citizens. Diplomatic correspondence ensued, and at one time there was talk of referring the dispute to the Permanent Court, but the British Government took the position that there was no international dispute and did not consent to referring the matter to that Court. Proposals for arbitration were finally rejected by the British Government at the end of 1939. After the War the discussion was resumed, but without result. On 9 April 1951 Greece instituted proceedings against the United Kingdom, basing the jurisdiction on a Treaty of Commerce and Navigation of 1926. That Treaty provided for the reference of certain disputes to the Permanent Court. The Court was asked to declare that by virtue of agreements between the parties, the United Kingdom was obliged to co-operate with Greece in establishing an Arbitration Commission to determine the merits of the dispute.

The United Kingdom first challenged the jurisdiction of the International Court even for this limited purpose. In its judgment of 1 July 1952 the Court held, by thirteen votes to two, that it was without jurisdiction to decide on the merits of the Ambatielos claim. By ten votes to five it went on to find that it did have jurisdiction to decide whether the United Kingdom was under an obligation to submit the claim to arbitration. There were individual opinions or declarations by Judges Levi Carneiro and Alvarez, and by Judge *ad hoc* Spiropoulos, and dissenting opinions by the President Sir Arnold McNair and Judges Basdevant, Zoričić, Klaestad and Hsu Mo. The issues that arose in this phase of the case were mostly technical issues of international treaty law.

In a second judgment of 19 May 1953 the Court found that the United Kingdom was under the obligation to submit the dispute to arbitration. The vote here was ten to four. A joint dissenting opinion by the President Sir Arnold McNair, and Judges Basdevant,

Klaestad and Read was appended.

In the third phase of the proceedings before the arbitration commission (containing three "neutral" members), the final award was in favour of the United Kingdom.[14]

It will be noted that the role of the International Court here was limited to deciding upon the "arbitrability" of the dispute, and its own jurisdiction to decide that issue. Since the parties had not agreed that it should decide the merits of the dispute, it was extremely careful in both its judgments not to encroach on the jurisdiction of the arbitral commission. The final judgment is important for the law of international arbitration proceedings.

THE ANGLO-IRANIAN OIL CO.

Tension between Iran and the United Kingdom over the affairs of the Anglo-Iranian Oil Company had persisted throughout the first half of the present century. The original D'Arcy Concession was granted in 1901, and after the First World War the Iranian Government complained that the Company was not paying sufficient attention to Iran's national interests. In 1932 the dispute reached such a pitch that the United Kingdom Government contemplated referring it to the Permanent Court. In 1933 a new concession agreement was negotiated between Iran and the Company through the Council of the League, to which the United Kingdom had referred the dispute, and in 1949 a supplemental agreement, designed to increase Iran's benefits under the concession, was not ratified by the Iranian Parliament. Matters took a dramatic turn in March 1951, when the Iranian Parliament enacted legislation, which received the Imperial assent on 1 May, for the nationalization of the oil industry throughout the country. The dispute became serious, and the British Government even started to make preparations for sending its armed forces into Iran in the event of danger to British nationals there.[15] Later, however, it decided to refer the dispute to the Court. The British application instituting the proceedings was filed on 26 May. The jurisdiction was based on the declarations accepting the compulsory jurisdiction, which, on account of reservations in both declarations and the application of the principle of reciprocity (see p. 74 above) was said to be applicable by virtue of a somewhat complicated construction given in the document instituting the proceedings.

The filing of this application did not arrest the rapid deterioration in the situation, and there was a danger that the Company's installations would be damaged. Accordingly, on 22 June 1951 the British Government filed an urgent request for an indication of interim measures of protection designed to protect the Company and its installations. On 23 June the President of the Court appealed to the Government of Iran to take no action which might aggravate the dispute. The Iranian Government immediately denied that the Court had jurisdiction to deal with this request, and did not take part in the oral proceedings held on 30 June (nor was an Iranian judge *ad hoc* appointed at this stage). On 5 July the Court, being satisfied that it had jurisdiction for this purpose, without the customary indication of the vote, made an order as requested. Judges Winiarski and Badawi Pasha made a joint dissenting opinion.

Iran did not comply with this indication, and in September the United Kingdom referred to the Security Council the question of its enforcement, with the inconclusive results described earlier (p. 35 above).

In due course, the Iranian Government appointed its agent and also designated a judge *ad hoc*. When the time came, Iran filed preliminary objections. In a judgment of 22 July 1952 the Court, by nine votes to five, found that it had no jurisdiction in the case. Most of the grounds for this decision were technical. At the same time, in the course of explaining its reasons, it had to deal with one facet of the dispute which was complicating the legal relations between the parties. As stated, the concession agreement of 1933 had been negotiated between the Iranian Government and the Company through the good offices of the Rapporteur appointed by the Council of the League of Nations. In consequence it was argued that the concession agreement itself could be regarded as an international convention. The Court decided that question in the negative.

Almost simultaneously with the filing of the British Government's application in this case, the Anglo-Iranian Oil Company applied to the President, asking him to appoint an umpire for the arbitration tribunal between the Company and the Iranian Government, in accordance with a provision in the 1933 concession conferring that power on the President of the *Permanent* Court. The President deferred his decision until after the termination of the British Government's case. Then, in the absence of the necessary consent on the part of the Iranian Government, he found that he was not authorized to make the appointment.[16]

This was the first case in the Court involving a revolutionary government in Iran. Here Iran was the respondent. In later cases in the 1980s and 1990s Iran was involved in litigation with the United States, in one case being the respondent and in two others the applicant.

WHOSE ARE THE CHANNEL ISLETS: MINQUIERS AND ECREHOS?

On 5 December 1951 the United Kingdom filed the text of a special agreement concluded a year earlier with France by which a dispute over the sovereignty of these two islets lying between Jersey and the French coast was submitted to the Court. Underlying this dispute were not only fishing interests of the two countries – for the area contains valuable oyster beds – but also other economic interests including certain French plans to exploit the tides for the purpose of generating electricity. Furthermore, the interested party on the British side was not the United Kingdom itself, but one of the Channel Islands, Jersey, technically not part of the United Kingdom although it is one of the British Isles. Jersey's parliamentary authority had approved the submission of the case to the Court as far back as 1948, after diplomatic negotiations had broken down. The United Kingdom delegation included the Attorney-General of Jersey. On 17 November 1953 the Court gave a unanimous judgment in favour of the claim of the United Kingdom. Judge Alvarez attached a declaration, and Judges Basdevant and Carneiro individual opinions. A notable feature of this case is the opinion of Judge Basdevant in favour of the United Kingdom, a worthy illustration of judicial independence.[17]

By a separate agreement of 30 January 1951, made independently of the special agreement to submit the case to the Court, the British and French Governments had reached accord on the question of the fishing rights without prejudice to the question of sovereignty over the groups of islands. This case was an instance of the two parties appearing before the Court "arm-in-arm", in the words of the Attorney-General of the United Kingdom.

A GERMAN NATIONAL CLAIMS RESTORATION OF HIS SEQUESTERED PROPERTY

Herr Friedrich Nottebohm was born at Hamburg in September 1881, of German nationality. In 1905 he established himself in Guatemala, where he continued to have his fixed abode until 1943 when, Guatemala having declared war on Germany in 1941, he was arrested, deported to the United States, and interned, and his substantial property sequestered under the equivalent of the trading with the enemy legislation. In March 1939, he had paid a visit to Germany. In October, shortly after the outbreak of the War, he visited Liechtenstein where he applied for, and was granted, Liechtenstein nationality after undertaking to make certain annual payments by way of "naturalization tax". He then applied for a Guatemalan visa on his new passport with which he returned to Guatemala and resumed his business activities.

After the War, Liechtenstein, exercising its right of diplomatic protection, attempted to recover the sequestered property. On the failure of the diplomatic negotiations Liechtenstein, not then a member of the United Nations but a State which had become a party to the Statute, filed an application in Court on 17 December 1951, on the basis of the compulsory jurisdiction. Further negotiations were unsuccessful, and the pleadings commenced. In due course Guatemala filed a preliminary objection to the effect that since Guatemala's acceptance of the compulsory jurisdiction had expired after the institution of the proceedings, the Court no longer had jurisdiction. By a judgment of 18 November 1953 the Court unanimously (there was no judge *ad hoc* for either party in this phase) dismissed the plea, which many lawyers believe to have been unarguable (a rare instance of this). There was a declaration by Judge Klaestad.

In the next phase of the case, Guatemala contended that the claim was inadmissible on the ground that Liechtenstein was not entitled to rely against Guatemala on the nationality thus conferred for the purposes of exercising its right of diplomatic protection, so as to transform enemy (German) property into neutral property. The Court, in its judgment of 6 April 1955, by eleven votes to three, upheld this contention. Judges Klaestad and Read, and Judge *ad hoc* Guggenheim, filed dissenting opinions.[18]

This was the first case in the present Court concerning aspects of economic warfare of the Second World War.

MONETARY GOLD LOOTED FROM ROME IN 1943

This was the second case arising out of events occurring during the Second World War.

In September 1943, the Germans looted from a bank in Rome nearly 2,340 kilograms of monetary gold belonging to the National Bank of Albania and transferred it to Germany. The Paris Act on Reparation of 1946 provided that monetary gold found in Germany by the allied forces should be pooled for distribution as restitution proportionately among the countries which had lost gold through looting during the War. Both Italy and Albania were parties to the Paris Act, which established a Tripartite Commission, consisting of the United States, France and the United Kingdom, to pass upon claims to a share out of the pool. Both Italy and Albania had claims, and since the Tripartite Commission was unable to solve them the Three Powers decided to submit that question to arbitration. On 20 February 1953 the arbitrator decided that the gold belonged to Albania.

At this point a complication appeared. The gold was in the hands of the Tripartite Commission, and the three Powers had agreed between themselves that if the arbitrator were to decide that the gold was Albanian, they would hand it over to the United Kingdom in partial satisfaction of the unpaid judgment debt in the *Corfu Channel* case, unless within a period of 90 days, either Albania or Italy instituted appropriate proceedings against them in the International Court. For that purpose they agreed in advance to accept the Court's jurisdiction as respondents.

Having lost before the arbitrator, the only way by which Italy could protect its claim to the gold was, therefore, by turning to the Court. Italy commenced the proceedings on 19 May 1953 against the three Governments. Albania refused either to institute proceedings of its own or to intervene in the Italian suit. Before filing its Memorial the Italian Government asked the Court to decide the preliminary question of whether, in such circumstances, it could exercise jurisdiction. In its judgment of 15 June 1954 the Court, by two votes, one unanimous and the other of thirteen to one, answered that question in the negative, on the ground that in the absence of Albania, a directly interested party, it could not decide a case directly involving the international responsibility of Albania. The President, Sir Arnold McNair (he had not presided over these proceedings), made a declaration, Judge Read an individual opinion and Judge Levi Carneiro a dissenting opinion. The future of the gold was therefore returned to the diplomatic channel. It remained in a vault in London in the name of the Tripartite Commission until it was restored to Albania on 8 May 1992, VE-Day, when the judgment debt arising from the *Corfu Channel* case was also discharged (see p. 35 above). By that time it was probably worth much more than the judgment debt.[19]

The importance of this case is not so much in the pronouncement of the Court, interesting though that is from the legal point of view, as in the action of the three Powers in developing novel procedures for securing satisfaction of a judgment debt previously awarded to one of them by the International Court. This was an instance of the adoption of measures of economic self-help, in which provision was made for the application of judicial controls at the request of interested parties, including possible competitive claimants.

FRANCE'S DIFFICULTIES IN THE LEBANON

On two occasions, in 1953 and again in 1959, France has referred to the Court disputes with the Lebanon arising out of Lebanese attempts to modify concession agreements with French companies. The first concerned the public services concession of the Electricité de Beyrouth Company, and the second the Compagnie du Port, des Quais et des Entrepôts de Beyrouth and the Sociéte Radio-Orient. In the first case a settlement was reached after the Memorial had been filed, and the case was accordingly discontinued. In the second, after the Memorial had been filed, preliminary objections were raised and observations thereon filed and that case was ready for hearing. Negotiations for the settlement of the two disputes nevertheless continued outside the Court, and upon being notified the Court placed on record the settlement of the case.[20]

These are instances of the contentious jurisdiction being invoked to bolster diplomatic negotiations aiming at the settlement of a dispute.

THE ADMINISTRATIVE TRIBUNALS

The United Nations and the International Labour Organization have each established Administrative Tribunals (UNAT and ILOAT) to deal with disputes between members of the staff and the internal administration. Between them, these Tribunals are available to all the specialized agencies (except the financial agencies going under the name of the World Bank, which has an Administrative Tribunal of its own). Five cases involving judgments of the UNAT and ILOAT have come before the Court for an advisory opinion. The operation of both Tribunals, especially when they have found against the administration or awarded to a staff member damages or other payments in exceptional cases, led to the introduction of a system of limited recourse to the International Court through the advisory competence. This limited recourse now consists of a review of defined questions of law decided by an Administrative Tribunal, with the effect of either confirming that decision, or requiring its reform in light of the advisory opinion of the Court on the issues of law involved. This process resembles the continental system of *cassation* – *review* and not *appeal* – and no question relating to the facts can be brought in.

The first two cases had a similar background. They concerned the rights of former staff members of the organization concerned, who had been discharged by the organization's administration because of their refusal to answer questions put to them by an investigating committee of the United States Senate relating to membership in the Communist Party or subversive activities in the United States. All the staff members were United States nationals. After their discharge, they sought redress from the appropriate Administrative Tribunal which, in many instances, found that the circumstances of the discharge gave rise to a claim for compensation. The three other cases were instances of recourse from UNAT judgments, the first on the initiative of the aggrieved staff member and the second and third on the initiative of a State, in accordance with the provision for recourse contained in the Statute of UNAT. This recourse is strictly limited to the review of defined questions of law connected with the interpretation of the Charter and the good administration of justice. So far the Court has always upheld the judgments of the Administrative Tribunal which it has been asked to review.

In the first case, in accordance with normal practice, the Secretary-General had included, in the 1953 budget, appropriations to meet the compensation that had been awarded. This was challenged on the ground that the General Assembly was entitled to override the judgment of the Administrative Tribunal. The General Assembly by 41 votes to 6 with 13 abstentions then decided to seek an advisory opinion on the legal issues. In its advisory opinion of 13 July 1954, the Court reached the conclusion that the General Assembly did not have the right on any grounds to refuse to give effect to an award of compensation made by the Administrative Tribunal in favour of a staff member whose contract of service had been terminated without his assent (this unusually broad language simply corresponds to the question as formulated by the General Assembly, and obviously need not to be taken literally!). The Court adopted its advisory opinion by nine votes to three, with Judge Winiarski attaching an individual opinion, and Judges Alvarez, Hackworth and Levi Carneiro dissenting opinions.

In the light of that advisory opinion the General Assembly decided to introduce the system of review by the Court of the judgments of the Administrative Tribunal (see p. 28 above).

In the second case, the recourse to the Court was initiated in 1955 by the Executive Board of UNESCO which wanted to avail itself of the procedure for review already existing under the Statute of ILOAT and challenge decisions of that Tribunal confirming its own jurisdiction. This was the first occasion on which this form of recourse had been employed, and it enabled the Court to indicate the kind of procedure which would be appropriate and how the Court would ensure that it had adequate information to enable it to give its opinion. In its advisory opinion of 23 October 1956, the Court by nine votes to four first decided to comply with the request for the opinion. It then went on to decide by ten votes to three that ILOAT was competent to hear the complaints of the staff members of UNESCO concerned, and by the same majority that the validity of the decisions of ILOAT "is no longer open to challenge".

The important feature of this case is that the procedure adopted by the Court enabled the interested staff members who had already obtained judgments in their favour in ILOAT to present their views to the Court. When the Executive Board of UNESCO adopted the request for the advisory opinion, it decided to enable the staff members to submit their statements to UNESCO which would annex them to its own statement without comment, and this was done. The Court decided not to hold oral proceedings, but instead to make provision for a second round of written pleadings in which both UNESCO and the interested persons could comment briefly on the statements made in the first round of statements. The problem which the Court then faced was whether it could give the advisory opinion and remain faithful to the requirements of its judicial character as a Court in which only States can litigate their differences. Without prejudice to its future action, the Court found that in the circumstances it could, and that if there was any inequality between the "parties" – UNESCO on the one hand and the staff members on the other – it was purely nominal and did not affect the exercise by the Court of its judicial functions.

The remaining three cases of recourse from UNAT were formally requested by the Committee on Application for Review of Administrative Tribunal Judgments, and in all cases the challenges to the decisions of the Tribunal failed. The issues are highly technical involving appreciation of relevant staff regulations.[21]

This accumulated experience has led to doubts as to the appropriateness of recourse to the International Court in this way. Increasing criticism has been expressed by Members of the Court. On the other hand, the care evinced by the Court to safeguard the judicial character and integrity of the Administrative Tribunals, and to ensure a form of procedural equality in the advisory proceedings between the administration and the aggrieved staff member, are seen as an important contribution towards the creation of an independent international civil service on which the effective functioning of the system of international organizations depends. Certainly this work is innovative and useful. But it is not without risks for the general standing of the international judicial function for the settlement of international disputes. The Administrative Tribunals do not apply general international law as set out in Article 38 of the Court's Statute, and there are doubts whether the Court is the most appropriate organ to perform any necessary judicial supervisory functions.

THE IRON CURTAIN OVERFLOWN (I) – MILITARY AIRCRAFT

It has been seen (p. 73 above) that nothing in the Statute prevents a State from instituting proceedings in the Court even though there is at the time no basis for the Court to exercise jurisdiction. The application instituting proceedings contains an invitation to the respondent to confer jurisdiction on the Court to decide that concrete dispute. The first instances of this occurred on 3 March 1954, when the United States filed identical applications against the USSR and Hungary relating to the treatment of aircraft and crew of the United States in Hungary. These applications referred to an incident which had occurred in 1951, when a United States military aircraft had been shot down over Hungary and its crew subjected to treatment which the United States regarded as contrary to international law. Attempts to reach a solution of these differences through the diplomatic channels had been unsuccessful.

The respondent governments declined the invitation to adjudicate the dispute, and the Court was left with no alternative but to order the two cases to be removed from the list.

There were more incidents of this kind, and in September 1954, the United States asked the Security Council to deal with a situation which it thought could constitute a danger to the maintenance of international peace and security. The debate, in the Council's 679th and 680th meetings on 10 September, was inconclusive, and no resolution was proposed. Subsequently, the United States instituted three similar cases against the Soviet Union and one against Czechoslovakia, between 1956 and 1959. In no case did the respondent government consent to confer jurisdiction on the Court, which could therefore take no action except to order the cases to be removed from the list.[22]

In the 1978 Rules, the Court decided that such cases will no longer be entered in the Court's general list until the respondent has given its consent. For the first attempt to invoke this new rule, see p. 225 below.

THE FALKLANDS (MALVINAS) DEPENDENCIES CLAIMS

The United Kingdom took similar action when it commenced separate proceedings against Argentina and Chile on 4 May 1955. In these applications the Court was asked to declare that the sovereignty over the disputed Falkland Islands Dependencies in the areas of the Antarctic belonged to the United Kingdom and that the claims of Argentina and Chile to those territories were, as against the United Kingdom, invalid. After the proceedings were instituted, the United Kingdom continued to make strenuous efforts to obtain the consent of the respondent governments to litigate the dispute, but finally conceded that the Court did not have jurisdiction, and the cases were accordingly removed from the list.[23]

As in the *Aerial Incident* cases, the effect of this action is to place the claim, and the main grounds on which it is based, on public record. The action of the United Kingdom may be regarded as a diplomatic phase in a dispute which has been in existence for some time.

SOME NORWEGIAN LOANS

The origins of this dispute lie in a flotation of loans by Norway at the turn of the last century on various foreign markets, including that of Paris. The bonds contained a “gold clause". During the financial instability of the First World War, and again in the financial crisis of 1931, the convertibility of the notes was suspended, and remained so. Diplomatic correspondence between France and Norway claiming fulfilment of the gold clause proceeded intermittently since 1925, in the course of which Norway rejected all proposals to submit the dispute to arbitration or adjudication on the ground that the matter came within its exclusive jurisdiction. On 6 July 1955 France instituted proceedings on the basis of the compulsory jurisdiction, and in due course Norway raised four objections to the jurisdiction and to the admissibility of the suit. The parties agreed to postpone the decision on these objections until the merits.

The French declaration accepting the jurisdiction then in force contained a clause (since revoked) by which France excluded from the jurisdiction disputes relating to matters which are essentially within the national jurisdiction as understood by the French Government (see p. 75above). One of the Norwegian objections was that the loan contracts were governed by domestic law and not by international law, and in the course of pleading that objection the Norway had sought to rely, in a subsidiary manner, on the subjective element of the French declaration (which Norway was entitled to invoke on the basis of reciprocity), and thus exclude the jurisdiction. In its judgment of 6 July 1957, the Court upheld that contention and found that it was without jurisdiction. The vote here was twelve to three. There was a declaration by Judge Moreno Quintana, separate opinions by the Vice-President Badawi and Judge Sir Hersch Lauterpacht, and dissenting opinions by Judges Guerrero, Basdevant and Read.[24]

The ability of the parties to agree that objections can be heard with the merits has since been incorporated in the Rules of Court of 1978.

PORTUGUESE ENCLAVES IN INDIA

In the Indian Peninsula are situated the three districts of Goa, Daman and Diu. In 1955 these were Portuguese territory. Daman also included two enclaved parcels, Dadra and Nagar-Aveli, at the time entirely surrounded by Indian territory. It was in respect of communications between these enclaves and Daman and between each other that the question of a right of passage in favour of Portugal through Indian territory arose. Commencing in 1950, India had been trying to annex all those districts, in pursuance of its policy of expelling the last vestiges of European colonialism from the Peninsula. In 1954, an internal insurrection overthrew Portuguese authority in Dadra and the enclaves, and in the light of the tension produced by those events in the neighbouring Indian territory, the Indian Government then suspended all passage over its territory to and between them. That suspension had remained in force, and it prevented Portugal from restoring its authority. At that point the legal dispute between the two countries crystallized.

In 1954 Portugal was not a member of the United Nations and not a party to the Statute of the Court. The only way in which it could then have brought its dispute with India before the Court was by making an appropriate agreement with India. Portugal's application to become a member of the United Nations was first submitted in 1946, but the Security Council and the General Assembly only completed their action on 14 December 1955, when Portugal was admitted into the United Nations. Portugal at no time requested to become a party to the Statute without being a member of the United Nations.

India had accepted the compulsory jurisdiction of the Permanent Court by a declaration of 28 February 1940 which excluded from the jurisdiction disputes with regard to questions which by international law fall exclusively within the jurisdiction of India; and the acceptance was limited to disputes arising after 5 February 1930 – the date upon which India had first accepted the compulsory jurisdiction – with regard to situations or facts subsequent to that date (this was a common form of reservation). That declaration had remained in force in accordance with the arrangements contained in the present Statute for preserving continuity in the administration of international justice (see p. 77 above). On 19 December 1955, five days after admission into the United Nations, Portugal deposited with the Secretary-General of the United Nations a declaration accepting the compulsory jurisdiction of the present Court. That declaration contained the following condition, which was subsequently to play an important role in the *Right of Passage* case:

> 3. The Portuguese Government reserves the right to exclude from the scope of the present declaration, at any time during its validity, any given category or categories of disputes by notifying the Secretary-General... and with effect from the moment of such notification.

Three days later, on 22 December 1955, Portugal filed an application instituting proceedings against India. This was at the end of a session of the General Assembly and during the period of the Christmas holidays in New York. When these proceedings were instituted, India had no knowledge of the Portuguese acceptance of the compulsory jurisdiction. India received information about the Portuguese action not from the depositary, but from the Court itself.

When the time came, India filed six preliminary objections. The first two related to the circumstances of Portugal's acceptance of the jurisdiction. These objections were rejected by fourteen votes to three. The third objection was based on the absence of diplomatic negotiations before the claim was filed. That was rejected by thirteen votes to one. The fourth was also based on India's ignorance that Portugal had accepted the jurisdiction. That was rejected by fifteen votes to two. The fifth objection, based on India's reservation, argued that the facts and law set out in Portugal's Memorial led to the conclusion that there was no reasonably arguable case that the claim was outside the domestic jurisdiction of India. This objection was, by a vote of thirteen to four, joined to the merits. The sixth objection was based on the temporal limitation of India's acceptance of the compulsory jurisdiction, and was joined to the merits by fifteen votes to two. In its judgment of 26 November 1957, therefore, the Court resumed the suspended proceedings on the merits. There was a declaration by Judge Kojevnikov, and dissenting opinions by Vice-President Badawi and Judges Klaestad (with concurrence of Judge *ad hoc* Fernandes), and Judge *ad hoc* Chagla.

The proceedings accordingly continued in the normal way. Judgment on the merits was delivered on 12 April 1960. By thirteen votes to two the Court rejected the outstanding fifth objection, and by eleven votes to four it rejected the outstanding sixth objection. On the merits, by eleven votes to four it held that Portugal had in 1954 a right of passage over intervening Indian territory between the enclaves and the coastal district, and between the enclaves, but limited to the extent necessary for the exercise of Portuguese sovereignty over the enclaves and subject to the regulation and control of India, in respect of private persons, civil officials and goods. By eight votes to seven it held that this right did not extend to the armed forces, armed police and arms and ammunition. Finally, it decided by nine votes to six that India had not acted contrary to its obligations with regard to Portugal's right of passage for private persons. There were declarations by President Klaestad. and Judges Basdevant, Badawi, Kojevnikov and Spiropoulos, a separate opinion by Judge Wellington Koo, a joint dissenting opinion by Judges Winiarski and Badawi. and dissenting opinions by Judges Armand-Ugon, Moreno Quintana, and Sir Percy Spender, and by Judges *ad hoc* Chagla and Fernandes.

This was a pyrrhic victory for Portugal. The right of passage was limited to civilian purposes and did not extend to the armed forces. In 1961 India annexed the territories. Portugal's recourse to the Security Council led to no result.[25]

WHO SHALL APPOINT A GUARDIAN OVER AN INFANT?

This dispute between the Netherlands and Sweden did not reflect any political tension between the two countries. It arose out of a family squabble between two branches of a mixed Dutch-Swedish family about the right to appoint a guardian over an infant born in May 1945. The girl, who was the issue of a marriage between a Dutchman and a Swedish woman and was of Dutch nationality, had lived all her life in Sweden. After the mother's death in 1953, the father became guardian by Dutch law, but later a female guardian was appointed by a Dutch civil Court dealing with children. About the same time a Swedish Court instituted measures of protective upbringing based on a Swedish Law of 1924 for the protection of children. The Swedish authorities refused to allow the child to be transferred to the Netherlands.

The dispute was then taken up through the diplomatic channels, without result. On 9 July 1957, when the child was already 12 years old, the Netherlands instituted proceedings against Sweden on the basis of the compulsory jurisdiction. The legal questions at issue related to the Hague Convention of 1902 on the Guardianship of Infants. In its judgment of 28 November 1958 the Court by twelve votes to four rejected the claim of the Netherlands, and decided to leave the existing arrangements untouched.

There were declarations by Judges Kojevnikov and Spiropoulos, individual opinions by Judges Badawi, Sir Hersch Lauterpacht, Moreno Quintana, Wellington Koo (in which Vice President Zafrulla Khan agreed generally) and Sir Percy Spender, and dissenting opinions by Judges Winiarski and Cordova, and Judge *ad hoc* Offerhaus.[26]

The view is sometimes expressed that a case of this nature is trivial for the International Court. Such opinions must be examined with care. There is no doubt that the dispute raised difficult issues of interpretation of the Guardianship Convention of 1902, and there is no reason why the Court should not have been asked to decide it. Although the dispute had no political implications, it involved conflicting decisions of the competent judicial authorities of two friendly States, and it seems clear that international legal proceedings are especially appropriate for overcoming that kind of difficulty. On the other hand, in most legal systems the welfare of the child is a major consideration, and the preferences of a child over twelve years old are also carefully considered. The Court does not seem to have taken any steps of its own to ascertain the child's views before it decided to maintain the existing situation.

THE INTERHANDEL COMPANY'S ASSETS

This was another case arising out of the economic aspects of the Second World War.

In 1942 the United States Government, acting under the Trading with the Enemy Act, vested in itself nearly all the shares of the General Aniline and Film Company, incorporated in the United States, on the ground that in reality they belonged to or were controlled by the I.G. Farbenindustrie of Frankfurt. Until 1940 I.G. Farben certainly controlled General Aniline and Film through a company incorporated in Switzerland, later known as Interhandel. The Swiss Government, acting in exercise of its right of diplomatic protection, alleged that in 1940 Interhandel severed its links with the German company, so that the General Aniline assets became Swiss, and neutral, and were not enemy property when they were seized. Towards the end of the war, property of Germans in Switzerland was blocked following an agreement between Switzerland and the Western Allies, but the Swiss Compensation Office accepted the view that Interhandel was Swiss, and its assets there were not blocked. An agreement of 1946 provided for the unblocking of Swiss assets in the United States, and further discussions ensued regarding the character of Interhandel.

No agreement was reached, and in 1948 Interhandel began proceedings in the United States Courts. One of the obstacles to those proceedings was the refusal of Interhandel to produce certain documents on the ground that their production would be a violation of Swiss law. In the course of the diplomatic correspondence between the two governments, the United States informed Switzerland (prematurely, as it later transpired) that in fact Interhandel had failed in its suit. Accordingly, on 2 October 1957 Switzerland instituted proceedings in reliance on the compulsory jurisdiction. The claim was for the restoration of Interhandel's assets. The next day Switzerland requested interim measures of protection asking the United States Government to take no steps to part with the property and in particular not to sell the shares which were being claimed as Swiss property. The United States immediately made a determination that the matters referred to came within the domestic jurisdiction of the United States, in accordance with the condition appearing in its acceptance of the compulsory jurisdiction (see p. 75 above).

Oral proceedings on the request for measures of protection were held on 12 and 14 October 1957. On 16 October the United States informed the Court that the Supreme Court had, on the 14th but many hours after the International Court had terminated its meetings, issued an order readmitting Interhandel into its suit. The United States stated that it would not be proceeding to the sale of the shares. In those circumstances, and holding that there was no urgency, the Court, by an order of 24 October 1957, found without a vote that although it had jurisdiction there was no need for it to indicate interim measures of protection. There were declarations by Judges Wellington Koo and Kojevnikov, and separate opinions by Judges Klaestad (with the concurrence of the President, Judge Hackworth, and Read) and Sir Hersch Lauterpacht.

In due course the United States filed four preliminary objections, three arguing that the Court lacked jurisdiction, and one contending that the suit was inadmissible on the ground that Interhandel had not exhausted the local remedies provided by the law of the United States before Switzerland instituted the proceedings at The Hague. In the judgment of 21 March 1959 the Court, by ten votes to five, rejected the first objection, which was to the effect that the dispute arose before the date on which the United States accepted the compulsory jurisdiction. It was unanimous in rejecting the second objection, that the dispute had arisen before the date of entry into force of the Swiss declaration. By fourteen votes to one it rejected part of the fourth objection that the matter came within the domestic jurisdiction of the United States, and by ten votes to five held that it was not necessary to adjudicate on another part of that objection to the same effect. The Court then, by the same vote upheld the third objection based on the non-exhaustion of the local remedies available, which it reclassified as an objection to the admissibility (cf. p. 83 above), since the legal proceedings in the United States were continuing. Declarations were appended to this judgment by Judges Basdevant and Kojevnikov, and Judge *ad hoc* Carry. Judges Hackworth (with the concurrence of Vice-President Zafrulla Khan), Córdova, Wellington Koo and Sir Percy Spender made separate opinions, and President Klaestad with the concurrence of Judge *ad hoc* Carry), and Judges Winiarski, Armand-Ugon, Sir Hersch Lauterpacht and Spiropoulos dissenting opinions.[27] Again the Court was able to avoid pronouncing itself on the subjective condition in the United States acceptance of the compulsory jurisdiction.

The protracted domestic litigation came to an end in 1965 after proceedings in the United States Court of Appeals and the Supreme Court. Agreement in principle was reached between the principal parties for the settlement of the litigation, the intervention of the courts, however, being still required on certain matters of detail.

THE IRON CURTAIN OVERFLOWN (II) – CIVIL AIRCRAFT

On 27 July 1955 an Israel civil aircraft on a scheduled commercial flight was shot down by the Bulgarian aerial defence service, having inadvertently penetrated into the Bulgarian airspace. All its 58 occupants were killed. The victims were nationals of Israel, Austria, Belgium, Canada, France, Germany, South Africa, Sweden, the United Kingdom and the United States. A few days later the Bulgarian Government announced that its armed forces had shot the aircraft down, those armed forces having acted in haste and without taking all the necessary measures. The Bulgarian Government undertook to identify and punish the culpable persons, and to pay the compensation due. Negotiations and diplomatic correspondence followed in attempts by the various claimant governments to reach a friendly solution, but to no avail. On 16 October 1957, Israel instituted proceedings against Bulgaria with regard to the destruction of this aircraft. On 28 October and on 21 November, the United States and the United Kingdom also instituted separate proceedings in respect to the damage suffered by their nationals arising out of the destruction of the aircraft.

Each one of the applicant Governments invoked the compulsory jurisdiction, relying on a Bulgarian declaration of 1921 and the provisions contained in the present Statute for maintaining continuity in the domain of international jurisdiction (see p. 77 above). These were three separate proceedings, and no question of joining them arose. Although each case arose out of the same incident, each Government represented different interests. Israel, in addition to claiming on behalf of its injured nationals, which included both the airline and the Israeli passengers and crew, was also interested in protecting its flag. The other Governments were interested in protecting the rights of their injured nationals. As a consequence, each case took a separate course. They were never all at the same procedural stage.

When the time came for Bulgaria to reply to Israel's Memorial, it filed five preliminary objections. Two related to the jurisdiction and concerned the transfer of jurisdiction from the Permanent Court to the present Court and the condition of reciprocity, and the other three contested the admissibility of the claim on different grounds. One of the objections was that since Bulgaria had become a member of the United Nations and a party to the Statute of the Court ten years after the Charter had come into force (Bulgaria was admitted to the United Nations on 14 December 1955) the clause in the Statute providing for the maintenance in force of declarations accepting the jurisdiction of the Permanent Court did not apply to it. In its judgment of 26 May 1959, the Court by twelve votes to four upheld that objection to its jurisdiction. There was a declaration by Vice-President Zafrulla Khan. Separate opinions were added by Judges Badawi and Armand-Ugon. Judges Sir Hersch Lauterpacht, Wellington Koo and Sir Percy Spender wrote a joint dissenting opinion, and Judge *ad hoc* Goitein added his dissenting opinion.

Following that judgment, the United Kingdom, without prejudice to its international claim, decided to discontinue its suit against Bulgaria. The United States, however, on the basis of the rule that the judgment in the Israel case was only binding as between Israel and Bulgaria (see p. 34 above), continued with its case, and in due course Bulgaria filed four preliminary objections, one based on the very ground which the Court had upheld in the Israel case. Another of these objections pleaded, on the basis of reciprocity and following the Court's decision in the *Norwegian Loans* case, that Bulgaria was entitled as against the United States to determine that the matter came within the domestic jurisdiction of Bulgaria, and that the Court had no jurisdiction. The United States was originally prepared to contest this plea, but shortly before the case became ready for hearing had second thoughts, and entered notice of discontinuance.[28] After further diplomatic negotiations Bulgaria made small payments in respect of the victims of the disaster.

BAERLE-DUC AND BAARLE-NASSAU – BELGIAN OR DUTCH?

On 26 November 1957 a special agreement between the Netherlands and Belgium was filed. It requested the Court to decide whether sovereignty over certain parcels of land on the frontier, about 14 hectares (35 acres) in area, belonged to the Dutch Commune of Baarle-Nassau or the Belgian Commune of Baerle-Duc. In a judgment of 20 June 1959, by ten votes to four the Court found in favour of Belgium.[29] There were declarations by Judges Sir Hersch Lauterpacht and Spiropoulos, and dissenting opinions by Judges Armand-Ugon, and Moreno Quintana. Neither side appointed a judge *ad hoc.*

Underlying this seemingly insignificant dispute was an important conflict of economic interests which the two governments were unable to resolve themselves. The invocation of the Court procedures opened the way to the settlement.

THE FRONTIER BETWEEN HONDURAS AND NICARAGUA

This was the first case to come before the Court as a result of actions for the settlement of a difficult territorial dispute undertaken by a regional organization, here the Organization of American States.

The roots of this dispute go back to the period of Spanish colonial rule in South America. In 1906 the King of Spain was asked to arbitrate the differences between the two countries, and in his award he fixed the frontier, for the greater part to the advantage of Honduras. That frontier was not delimited, however, and from about 1912 onwards Nicaragua began to challenge the regularity of the arbitration proceedings before the King of Spain and the validity of the arbitral award that he had rendered. Various attempts to reach a settlement of this dispute failed, and in 1957 hostilities broke out between the two countries over the disputed territory. This incident was brought before the competent organs of the Organization of American States. Through its good offices the parties, in July 1957, agreed to submit their dispute to the International Court. Honduras would submit its claim that the arbitral award should be carried out, and Nicaragua would answer the claim in the normal course. On 1 July 1958 Honduras accordingly instituted the proceedings by application based on the Washington Agreement of 1957. The pleadings in this case were heavy, but proceeded without complication, and judgment was given on 18 November 1960. The Court by fourteen votes to one decided that the award of the King of Spain was valid and binding, and that Nicaragua was under an obligation to give effect to it. There was a declaration by Judge Moreno Quintana, a separate opinion by Judge Sir Percy Spender, and a dissenting opinion by Judge *ad hoc* Urrutia Holguín.

After this judgment, negotiations proceeded between the parties for the demarcation of the new frontier and the transfer of the population of the ceded territories. It was found that parts of the original award were obscure, and Nicaragua, the judgment debtor, referred the matter to the Inter-American Peace Committee. A Mixed Commission was set up, and its neutral chairman was granted certain powers of decision. He gave a reasoned decision on 5 August 1961 on the outstanding matters, after which the dispute was settled.[30]

This case is the first of its kind in two major respects. It is the first instance before either the Permanent Court or the present Court which was exclusively concerned with a territorial dispute between States outside Europe and is not Eurocentered in any way. Secondly, it is the first instance of the interplay of a regional international organization – the Organization of American States and its various bodies – and the International Court of Justice in the settlement of a grave dispute which had led to acts of hostility. The Organization deployed its efforts first to bring the acts of hostility to an end, then to persuade the parties to submit their differences to the International Court, and finally to assist them in executing the decisions binding upon them with the force of *res judicata.*

Another innovation here was that both parties appointed a judge *ad hoc,* but neither of them was a national of the country by which he was chosen. One of the judges *ad hoc* was not even a national of any of the Latin American States.

THE AFFAIRS OF THE BARCELONA TRACTION, LIGHT AND POWER COMPANY

This company was established in Toronto in 1911, but into the inter-War period most of its shares came into Belgian hands. The Belgian Government took up the case in exercise of its right of diplomatic protection. It claimed that the company had been subjected to a variety of vexatious measures by the Spanish authorities, and was subsequently, in 1948, adjudicated bankrupt in Spain, and that in the measures of liquidation it was despoiled of its assets which were transferred to a Spanish group. The diplomatic negotiations were unsuccessful, and on 23 September 1958 Belgium instituted proceedings against Spain, founding jurisdiction on the Treaty of Conciliation, Judicial Settlement and Arbitration between the two countries of 19 July 1927. In that application, Belgium asked for the restoration of the despoiled assets or alternatively for compensation for damage allegedly caused to the company on account of acts said to be contrary to international law committed by organs of the Spanish State.

After the Memorial was filed Spain raised three preliminary objections. However, negotiations between the private interests concerned continued, and as part of those negotiations, and at the request of the private interests, the Belgian Government served notice of discontinuance of those proceedings, to which Spain agreed.

The negotiations led to no result, and in 1962 Belgium filed a new application instituting proceedings against Spain. This case differed from the previous application in that Belgium now limited its claim to reparation for the damage allegedly sustained by Belgian nationals, shareholders in the company, on account of acts said to be contrary to international law committed in respect of the company by organs of the Spanish State. The amount of compensation claimed was of the order of $78,000,000 plus costs and interest, being the equivalent of 88% of the assets of the despoiled company. The impugned acts of the Spanish State come within the general rubric of "denial of justice" as a ground for a diplomatic claim put forward by a State in exercise of its right of diplomatic protection of its nationals abroad.

Against this new application Spain filed four preliminary objections. The first was new and related to the legal consequences of the discontinuance of the earlier case. The remainder were adaptations of the objections raised in the first case. The first objection to the jurisdiction was to the effect that the discontinuance of the earlier proceedings precluded the renewal of the case later. The second was to the effect that the compromissory clause on which the jurisdiction was based, namely the 1927 Treaty, had lapsed on the dissolution of the Permanent Court, Article 37 of the Statute notwithstanding. The third was an objection to the admissibility and really embraced the nub of the case. It was to the effect that Belgium was not entitled to exercise its right of diplomatic protection in favour of Belgian nationals who held shares in a Canadian registered commercial corporation. The fourth, also an objection to the admissibility, and also raising issues central to the whole dispute on the diplomatic level, was to the effect that the application to the Court was premature having regard to the well-known rule of international law requiring exhaustion of the local remedies before an international claim for denial of justice can be brought. The issues involved in the third objection had been thoroughly discussed in the diplomatic phase prior to the institution of the first proceedings, and Belgium had even intimated willingness for the Court to decide the point. No agreement had been reached, however, on submitting the dispute to the Court and, as stated, it was submitted unilaterally and without any agreement by Spain.

In its judgment of 24 July 1964 the Court dismissed the first objection by a vote of twelve to four and the second by ten to six. By nine votes to seven it joined the third objection to the merits, and by ten votes to six it did the same for the fourth objection. President Sir Percy Spender and Judges Spiropoulos, Koretsky and Jessup appended declarations, Vice-President Wellington Koo and Judges Tanaka and Bustamante y Rivero separate opinions, and Judge Morelli and Judge *ad hoc* Armand-Ugon dissenting opinions. This is the first instance in the present Court of the appointment as judge *ad hoc* of a former Member of the Court.

Strenuous written and oral pleading on the merits followed (no less than 64 public hearings were held in this phase between April and July 1969, and the Court required the best part of six months to frame its judgment). In its judgment of 5 February 1970 (delivered on the eve of the expiry of the term of office of the judges not re-elected in the election of 1969), the Court found that the Belgian Government had no *locus standi* in this case, and therefore rejected the claim. There was a joint declaration by Judges Petrén and Onyeama and another declaration by Judge Lachs. President Bustamante y Rivero, and Judges Sir Gerald Fitzmaurice, Tanaka, Jessup, Morelli, Padilla Nervo, Gros and Ammoun appended separate opinions and Judge *ad hoc* Riphagen a dissenting opinion.[31]

This case, coming relatively soon after the 1966 South West Africa judgment (where too the Court had decided the case on "antecedent" grounds related to the *locus standi* of the applicants), gave rise to similar misgivings, in both political and professional circles. It was widely felt that the particular issue was a question of law which could and should have been decided in the first phase. Criticism was also levelled at the prolixity of the pleadings, both written and oral: it was widely felt that the Court should have exercised more control over them. Another ground of reserve was that by joining the question of the *locus standi* of Belgium to the merits after it had been fully pleaded as a question of law in 1964, the parties had been put to much unnecessary expense. Not all this criticism is justified, and the fact that Spain had raised no less than four preliminary objections, and then fought them with tenacity, was a signal for caution. Nevertheless, there is no doubt that some of the revisions of the Rules of Court of 1972 designed to reduce the cost of international litigation and to reduce its delays were inspired by the experience of this case. This applies particularly to the revision of the rules regarding preliminary objections, now Article 79 of the 1978 Rules of Court (see p. 83 above). On another level, the case has had a lasting influence on international law by introducing the concept of obligations *erga omnes*, certain fundamental rules in relation to which all States have, in principle, an interest in their being upheld.

THE MARITIME SAFETY COMMITTEE

The original Constitution of the Intergovernmental Maritime Consultative Organization (IMCO), since renamed the International Maritime Organization (IMO), established the Maritime Safety Committee as one of the main organs of the Organization. Among the members of the Organization to be represented on it were the eight largest ship-owning nations. At the first meeting of the IMCO Assembly in 1959 the question of the meaning of that phrase arose -whether it meant the nations possessing the largest amount of registered tonnage or those beneficially owning the largest amount of tonnage. Beneath this formal dispute lay the vexed question of "flags of convenience", i.e. the registration of ships in a foreign country, usually for purposes of tax relief or for other reasons. If the first interpretation were adopted, Liberia and Panama, under whose flags over ten million and over four millions of tons of merchant shipping respectively were registered at that time, would have been entitled to be members of the Maritime Safety Committee. In the elections held in January 1959, neither of those countries had been elected to the Committee. At the same time the Assembly, recognizing that differences of opinion had arisen regarding the correct interpretation of the Constitution, unanimously adopted a proposal by Liberia to request an advisory opinion.

In its opinion of 8 June 1960, the Court by nine votes to five gave a negative answer to the question whether the Committee which was elected in January 1959 was properly constituted. This meant that the proper criterion was registered tonnage, and that Liberia and Panama were entitled to be elected. Only President Klaestad and Judge Moreno Quintana added dissenting opinions, so it is impossible to know how the Court divided in this case.[32]

During the proceedings Liberia had agreed that if the Court should make such a finding, it would nevertheless raise no question as to the validity of the work of the Committee during the period prior to the date on which Liberia should become a member. Following the advisory opinion the Assembly decided to dissolve the Committee as previously elected, and to constitute a new one in accordance with the Court's interpretation of the Constitution. Later the constitution of the Organization was revised. The name was changed to *International Maritime Organization* and the Maritime Safety Committee became open to all members of the Organization.

The significance of this case is that it is the first instance in which the International Court has held that action taken by an international organization was not in conformity with the constituent instrument of that organization. On the other hand, the advisory opinion makes no attempt to solve the legal problems arising from the existence of flags of convenience: the Court's opinion was for the most part based on a textual analysis of the relevant clause of the constituent instrument as it then stood. The question of flags of convenience, on the other hand, was left to the political organs. The general topic of the nationality of ships is now covered by article 92 of the 1982 Convention on the Law of the Sea, the United Nations Convention on the Conditions for the Registration of Ships of 1986, and the FAO Agreement to Promote Compliance with International Conservation and Management Measures by Fishing Vessels on the High Seas of 1993.

THE TEMPLE OF PREAH VIHEAR

On 6 October 1959 Cambodia, invoking the compulsory jurisdiction, instituted proceedings against Thailand alleging violation on the part of Thailand of Cambodia's territorial sovereignty over the region of the Temple of Preah Vihear and its precincts. In a judgment of 26 May 1961 the Court was unanimous in rejecting challenges to its jurisdiction by Thailand. Vice-President Alfaro and Judges Wellington Koo, Sir Gerald Fitzmaurice and Tanaka appended declarations and Judges Sir Percy Spender and Morelli dissenting opinions.

Proceedings on the merits were then resumed. In a judgment of 15 June 1962, the Court found, by nine votes to three, that the Temple was situated in territory under the sovereignty of Cambodia, and made various consequential findings. There was a joint declaration by Judges Tanaka and Morelli, separate opinions by Vice-President Ammoun and Sir Gerald Fitzmaurice, and dissenting opinions by Judges Moreno Quintana, Wellington Koo and Sir Percy Spender.

This decision caused great disappointment to Thailand. However, on 3 July 1962 the Government of Thailand announced that despite its profound sorrow at the result of the case it considered that "as a member of the United Nations, Thailand is bound to honour its obligations under the United Nations Charter. It will do so under protest and with reservation of her intrinsic rights".[33]

This was the first case to come before the Court involving exclusively two Asian States.

It grew out of the dissolution of the French overseas possessions in Indo-China, and the local tension has to be viewed against the wider background of the crisis in South-East Asia. The case itself turned on the interpretation of boundary settlements made in the period 1904-8 between France, which at that time conducted the foreign relations of Cambodia, and Thailand.

Neither side chose a judge *ad hoc* in this case.

Witnesses and experts were called by both parties, and at one point the Court assembled in private, in the presence of the representatives of the parties, to attend a film of the place in dispute.

The judgment is of importance for its discussion of two legal issues, namely the effect of subsequent conduct on a State's legal position (sometimes loosely known as "estoppel" or "preclusion" in international law) and the effect of error in a treaty. The Court's statements on these points were later consolidated in the codification of the law of treaties, as articles 45 and 48 respectively of the Vienna Convention on the Law of Treaties of 1969.

THE NORTHERN CAMEROONS

This was the first "decolonization" case relating to the African Continent to come before the Court.

After the First World War the former German colony of Kamerun was placed partly under British Mandate and partly under French Mandate by the League of Nations. After the Second World War these were transformed into Trusteeship Agreements. With the decolonization in the 1960s, the independence of the territory under British Trusteeship came into question. Under United Nations supervision a plebiscite was held. This showed that part of the population wished to join the Republic of Cameroon, the former French Trusteeship territory which had gained its independence on 1 January 1960. Others, in the north, wished to join the Federation of Nigeria which had gained its independence on 1 October 1960. In resolution 1608 (XV), 21 April 1961, the General Assembly endorsed the result of that plebiscite. The Republic of Cameroon was dissatisfied with the British administration of the Northern Cameroons and with the organization of the plebiscite, but its criticisms were rejected both by the United Kingdom and by Nigeria. On 1 May 1961 it proposed a special agreement to bring the dispute before the Court, an idea which the United Kingdom rejected on 26 May. On 30 May 1961 Cameroon filed an application instituting proceedings against the United Kingdom, basing the jurisdiction on the compromissory clause of the Trusteeship Agreement for British Cameroons, which itself was terminated, as far as concerned the Northern Cameroons, on 1 June 1961.

The Republic of Cameroon alleged failure by the United Kingdom to respect certain obligations directly or indirectly flowing from the Trusteeship Agreement for the Territory of the Cameroons under British administration. Although the question of the disposition of the Northern Cameroons is longstanding, the present case grew out of dissatisfaction felt by the Republic of Cameroon, i.e. the successor of the Territory formerly under French administration, at the manner in which that Trusteeship had been terminated. This had led to the Northern Cameroons being joined to Nigeria.

Nigeria was not impleaded in these proceedings. The Court was simply asked to make a series of general declarations, without redressing any alleged injustice or detaching any territory from Nigeria. The United Kingdom filed a series of preliminary objections. In its judgment of 2 December 1963 the Court, by ten votes to five, found that the circumstances of this case and what it was being asked to do raised antecedent issues of whether the limits of the judicial function permitted it to entertain the claims submitted. That question it answered in the negative, primarily because any judgment which it might pronounce would be without object. For that reason it found that it could not adjudicate upon the merits of the claim. Declarations of dissent were filed by Judges Spiropoulos and Koretsky. and another concurring declaration was made by Judge Jessup. Judges Wellington Koo, Sir Percy Spender, Sir Gerald Fitzmaurice and Morelli appended separate opinions, and Judges Badawi and Bustamante y Rivero, and Judge *ad hoc* Beb a Don dissenting opinions.[34]

It is believed that despite this curious result, this is an instance in which the judicial pronouncement, removed from the substance of the issues though it might have been, nonetheless performed a useful function in facilitating the acceptance of a decision of the General Assembly of the United Nations (regarding the termination of the Trusteeship Agreement) which was politically unpalatable. From the point of view of the development of the Court's jurisprudence and its own concepts of its functions, the judgment is important for its discussion of the limits of judicial propriety when the Court is asked to render a declaratory judgment.

THE UNITED NATIONS BUDGET – PEACE-KEEPING OPERATIONS

After the crisis in the Middle East at the end of 1956, the General Assembly established the United Nations Emergency Force (UNEF I). The financing of this Force presented what the Court called "perplexing problems". In the middle of 1960, the United Nations commenced its activities in the Congo, for which purpose it established another Force known under the French acronym of ONUC. The expenses of these two Forces became very heavy and the question of how to meet them gave rise to serious difficulties, both for political and for legal reasons. In the summer of 1961, a Working Group appointed by the General Assembly reached the conclusion that, having regard to the differences of opinion which had been expressed about the legal nature of the financial obligations arising out of the peace-keeping operations, the General Assembly should request an advisory opinion from the Court, the precise formulation of the question being for the General Assembly to decide. In a resolution of 21 December 1961, adopted by 52 votes to 11 with 32 abstentions, the General Assembly asked the Court whether certain expenditures authorised in a series of designated resolutions relating to ONUC and to UNEF constituted "expenses of the Organization" within the meaning of Article 17, paragraph 2, of the Charter. The significance of this question is that by Article 19 of the Charter, a member of the United Nations which is in arrears in the payment of its financial contributions to the Organization shall have no vote in the General Assembly if the amount of its arrears equals or exceeds the amount of the contributions due from it for the preceding two years. Two permanent members of the Security Council – France and the Soviet Union – were coming within this provision.

The power of the Court to give the opinion in the terms requested was challenged both in the General Assembly and before the Court, although it will be noted that these challenges did not, as had been the case in the years 1948-50, question the power of the Court to interpret the Charter itself. In its advisory opinion of 20 July 1962 the Court dismissed all the challenges to its competence and, by nine votes to five, answered the question put to it in the affirmative. The Court found that it was required to answer a concrete question and, contrary to the practice adopted in all previous advisory opinions on the interpretation of the Charter, proceeded to deal with almost all the major legal contentions which had been advanced in the previous discussions. Separate opinions were attached to the advisory opinion by Judges Sir Percy Spender, Sir Gerald Fitzmaurice and Morelli, and dissenting opinions by President Winiarski and Judges Basdevant, Moreno Quintana, Koretsky and Bustamante y Rivero.[35] This case provided the first occasion since the establishment of the Permanent Court of International Justice for participation by a representative of the Soviet Union in oral proceedings.

The problem arose out of the fact that this type of peace-keeping operation is not foreseen in the Charter. This advisory opinion did not lead to a speedy solution of the crisis, which was at the same time financial and constitutional. Indeed, in the view of many it only served to aggravate it, since in the context of the tensions of the Cold War it introduced intractable questions of prestige into the issue. In resolution 1954 (XVII) of 19 December 1962 the General Assembly accepted the advisory opinion after a bitter debate. That resolution was adopted by a vote of 76 to 17, with 14 abstentions, two of the permanent members of the Security Council being among those who voted against. At the same time the General Assembly adopted other resolutions for dealing with the financial aspects.

Expectations that the advisory opinion and this resolution would lead the States concerned to change their attitude were unrealized, and in 1964 some of these States were two years in arrear in their payments found by the Court to be due to the United Nations. This brought into play Article 19 of the Charter, theoretically depriving them of their vote in the General Assembly. The nineteenth session of the General Assembly (1964) was held in the shadow and unreal atmosphere produced by that crisis. It conducted no substantive business, and the matters of routine with which it had to deal were solved without the necessity for a vote, that is by consensus (in many respects this session of the General Assembly provided the jumping-off point for the evolution of the concept of "consensus"). This ridiculous state of affairs was later rectified through diplomatic channels (although the financial aspect of the crisis was left unresolved), and in 1965 the General Assembly was able to resume its routine, albeit with reduced prestige. In the view of many, this exercise was an instance of abuse of the General Assembly and the advisory process by some of the Great Powers, and it did nothing to enhance the standing of the judicial process in the United Nations.

Although this opinion was not successful in solving the immediate crisis which led to its request and in that respect, as had happened to the 1948 *Admission* opinion (p. 130 above), its consequences had to be abandoned, its long-term effect was more positive. It was to provide a solid legal backing for the development of the peace-keeping activities of the United Nations in a form not foreseen in the Charter. In 1988 those activities earned for the "Casques bleus", the blue-helmeted United Nations peace-keeping forces, a well-deserved Nobel Peace Prize. "Peacekeeping" in that sense is now an accepted activity of the United Nations. In principle the Security Council decides upon the activity, and the General Assembly is responsible for the financing with the Member States providing troops on a voluntary basis.

THE NORTH SEA CONTINENTAL SHELF DELIMITATION

The discovery and exploitation of mineral resources in the bed of the North Sea during the 1960s intensified competition amongst the littoral States – Norway, Denmark, the Federal Republic of Germany, the Netherlands, Belgium, France and the United Kingdom – over the delimitation of the sea bed between them and the areas of the sea-bed over which each would exercise sovereign rights within the terms of the Geneva Convention on the Continental Shelf of 29 April 1958. As between most of these countries delimitation was effected through negotiations. However, difficulties arose between Denmark and the Federal Republic, and between the Federal Republic and the Netherlands. In February 1967 two special agreements, in identical terms, were concluded between those two pairs of States. The Court was asked to decide what principles and rules of international law were applicable to the delimitation as between the parties of the areas of the continental shelf in the North Sea which appertain to each of them beyond boundaries previously determined. The words "appertain to them" here and in other cases safeguard the rights and position of third States not parties to the litigation. At the same time the parties undertook to delimit the continental shelf between themselves by agreement in pursuance of the decision requested from the Court. Although the cases were somewhat different, the parties were agreed on their joinder, which the Court effected. In its judgment of 20 February 1969, adopted by eleven votes to six, the Court answered the question put to it and gave the requested indications. There were declarations by Judges Sir Zafrulla Khan and Bengson, separate opinions by the President Bustamante y Rivero and Judges Jessup, Padilla Nervo and Ammoun, and dissenting opinions by the Vice-President Koretsky and Judges Tanaka, Morelli and Lachs and Judge *ad hoc* Sørensen.

After further negotiations, agreement was reached on the ultimate delimitation of the continental shelf of the North Sea.[36]

This case presents two interesting features. Firstly, although the Court was not asked to decide any concrete dispute or to effect any delimitation of the areas in question, this exercise of the judicial function was directly related to the negotiations between the parties. This gave the judgment an object and a purpose. It was final and binding on the parties and attracted all the consequences of any other judgment of the Court. It was not a disguised advisory opinion between the States concerned. Secondly, much turned on the Court's interpretation of the 1958 Geneva Convention on the Continental Shelf, to which the Federal Republic was not a party, not having ratified it although it was subject to ratification. This Convention was one of four adopted at the first United Nations Conference on the Law of the Sea – the first United Nations codification conference working on the basis of a draft prepared by the International Law Commission. Discussion of this question led to an examination of whether that particular convention was "codificatory" or not. The significance of this was that if the answer was affirmative, the rules embodied in it, and especially the rules for the delimitation of areas of continental shelf of States whose coasts are opposite or adjacent to each other, might be held to be applicable notwithstanding that the Federal Republic was not a party to the Convention. On this point, after close analysis of the history of the Convention, the Court gave a negative answer.

This was the first time that the Court had to consider the quality of a multilateral treaty drawn up through the codifying machinery of the United Nations as "codification" or "progressive development" of the law. This was a central issue in a case before it. With the increase in the number and scope of treaties coming out of these processes, this type of issue is becoming more frequent. The criteria established by the Court are important for understanding the interaction of the two processes – of application of the law by the Court and its codification by States through the International Law Commission and international conferences. It may be added that the Court has since clarified that if it is satisfied that a rule embodied in such a treaty is codificatory, it will probably apply it as a rule of customary international law even as regards a State not a party to the codificatory instrument (this will not necessarily extend, however, to procedural rules).

This case is the first, and in some respect the most important, of the long series of cases dealing with the delimitation of maritime spaces, initially the continental shelf, and later also fisheries zones and single multi-purpose delimitation lines. That became a "hard core" issue in the Third United Nations Conference on the Law of the Sea. The particular significance of this case, however, lies in another direction. It pointed up the deficiencies in the definition of the term "continental shelf' in the 1958 Convention. That in turn set in motion the long process which was to lead to the new definition now found in article 76 of the United Nations Convention on the Law of the Sea of 1982.

This was also the first instance in which two formally separate cases were 'joined" to produce a single set of pleadings after the joinder and a single judgment. This was done at the request of the parties, The Court itself recognized that the cases were distinct and that their joinder for the purposes of the determination of the issues did not carry any further implication.

INDIA, PAKISTAN AND BANGLADESH: AIRCRAFT HIJACKING AND PRISONERS OF WAR

Following a serious incident of hijacking of an Indian civil aircraft to Pakistan and in the tension existing between those two countries throughout their long smouldering dispute India, in February 1971, suspended overflights of Indian territory by Pakistani civil aircraft. This placed a major obstacle in the way of mutual access between what were then East and West Pakistan. Pakistan thereupon complained to the Council of the International Civil Aviation Organization, before which it laid its dispute with India on this question of overflying. This Council has a quasi-judicial competence, under the Convention on Civil Aviation (the Chicago Convention) of 1944, in this type of case, subject to a right of appeal from its decision to the Court (exercising a transferred jurisdiction from the Permanent Court). In the Council proceedings, India raised some preliminary objections, which the Council rejected. India thereupon immediately filed in the Court an application instituting an appeal from the decisions of the Council. The proceedings in the Court did not touch upon the merits of the dispute brought before the Council, but only the Council's decision to reject India's preliminary objections. In the Court, Pakistan also objected to the Court's jurisdiction, but did not raise this as preliminary objections. In its judgment of 18 August 1972 the Court first, by thirteen votes to three, rejected Pakistan's objections and then, by fourteen votes to two, dismissed India's appeal. President Zafrulla Khan and Judge Lachs appended declarations, Judges Petrén, Onyeama, Dillard, de Castro and Jiménez de Aréchaga separate opinions, and Judge Morozov and Judge *ad hoc* Nagendra Singh dissenting opinions.[37] The President of the Court was a Pakistani national, and he therefore ceded the presidency to the Vice-President. For its part India appointed a judge *ad hoc.*

The question of overflying Indian territory in 1971 was closely connected with what emerged later as a triangular relationship between India, Pakistan and Bangladesh. In that context, the tension provoked by the initial hijacking and by the subsequent litigation was marginal. This does not detract from the importance of the case as brought before the International Court.

On 11 May 1973 Pakistan instituted proceedings against India relating to a number of Pakistani Prisoners of War taken by India in the 1971 fighting. From a joint statement by India and Bangladesh it appeared that 195 of these were to be handed to Bangladesh for trial for alleged acts of genocide and crimes against humanity. Pakistan contested the legality of that action which it saw as a violation of the 1948 Convention on the Prevention and Punishment of the Crime of Genocide. That Convention was invoked as the title of jurisdiction. At the same time Pakistan applied for provisional measures of protection to the effect that the repatriation of prisoners of war should not be interrupted because of these charges, and that the persons should not be handed over to Bangladesh while the action was pending in the International Court. India contested the jurisdiction of the Court and was not represented at the hearings in June 1973.

By this time there was an Indian member of the Court, and Pakistan appointed a judge *ad hoc* who, however, withdrew shortly before the hearings began. After the hearings, Pakistan intimated that as negotiations were continuing, the request for interim measures had lost its urgency. In its order of 12 July 1973 the Court, by eight votes to four, did not indicate interim measures and arranged for the case to proceed, with the issue of jurisdiction being tried first. There was a separate opinion by Judge Nagendra Singh and a dissenting opinion by Judge Petrén. Otherwise, this is another judicial pronouncement in which the voting was not made public.[38] The case was later discontinued.

ICELAND'S FISHERIES JURISDICTION

Following the failure of the First United Nations Conference on the Law of the Sea (1958) to reach agreement on the breadth of the territorial sea or on the proposed concept of exclusive fishery zones which had been strongly propagated by a number of coastal States with a heavy dependence upon the fishery reserves in their adjacent waters, Iceland issued new regulations, establishing a 12-mile exclusive fisheries zone around its coasts. It stated publicly that it viewed this measure as a first step towards its objective of ultimately reaching a fishery zone which would extend over its whole continental shelf.

This step led to difficulties with a number of States with fishery interests in the region -in particular the United Kingdom and the Federal Republic of Germany. They contested the validity of the Icelandic measures. When the Second United Nations Conference on the Law of the Sea (1960), also failed to reach agreement on the same two questions, in 1961 the United Kingdom and the Federal Republic concluded provisional agreements by which they each recognized Iceland's preferential rights in return for Iceland's acknowledgement of certain fishing rights in the zone. These agreements provided for recourse to the Court in given circumstances.

On 14 July 1971, Iceland declared that those agreements were terminated, and unilaterally extended its exclusive fishery zone to fifty miles measured from the baselines. The new fishing regulations were to become effective on 1 September 1972. This step met with strong opposition from both the United Kingdom and the Federal Republic of Germany, whose fishermen had been operating in the area for a long time. Negotiations failed to provide a solution, and the United Kingdom began proceedings in the Court on 14 April 1972, followed by the Federal Republic on 5 June of the same year. Iceland's reaction to the applications and the requests for provisional measures was that there was no basis for the Court to exercise jurisdiction and that considering that its vital interests were involved, the Icelandic Government did not recognize any role for the Court in the dispute. Consequently Iceland did not take any part in the proceedings. There was a judge of British nationality among the members of the Court. Iceland made no request to appoint a judge *ad hoc* and made no objection to the German request to appoint one. But the Court, by a vote of eight to five, held that the Federal Republic had a common interest with the United Kingdom justifying refusal to allow a German judge *ad hoc* in the jurisdictional phase. The Federal Republic did not find it necessary to appoint one in the later phases of the case.

As the date for the implementation of the new Icelandic regulations approached, the two States requested the Court to indicate provisional measures in August 1972. The Court acceded to these requests in two orders of 17 August. These orders, which were adopted by fourteen votes to one, went into some detail of catches which each applicant State could take for a period of one year, subject to review in 1973. They were accompanied with a joint declaration by Vice-President Ammoun and Judges Forster and Jiménez de Aréchaga, and a dissenting opinion by Judge Padilla Nervo. These orders were followed on 18 August by two orders fixing time limits. They were unusual in that for the first time the Court decided, by nine votes to six, that the first pleadings should be addressed to the question of the jurisdiction of the Court to entertain each dispute. The Court did not wait for formal preliminary objections, but reached this decision considering the particulars which were before it, including the communications from the Government of Iceland. Here there was a joint dissenting opinion by Judges Bengzon and Jiménez de Aréchaga.

This was the first in the spate of cases of unwilling and non-appearing respondents, where the non-appearance went beyond merely refusing to take a formal part in the proceedings since the respondent rejected the Court's jurisdiction completely. However, the Court did take account of various public statements and communications to the Court made by the Icelandic Government.

Iceland's refusal to participate in the proceedings did not prevent the Court from examining the question of its jurisdiction. By two separate but substantially identical judgments of 2 February 1973, the Court ruled by fourteen votes to one that it possessed jurisdiction to deal with the merits of the disputes. There were declarations by the President Sir Zafrulla Khan, separate opinions by Sir Gerald Fitzmaurice and dissenting opinions by Judge Padilla Nervo.

The pendency of this litigation unfortunately did not prevent the 1972/1973 "cod war" involving incidents between Icelandic fishery patrol vessels and British naval units assigned to protect U.K. fishing trawlers.

As the proceedings on the merits were still in progress the Court, on 12 July 1973, re-examined the provisional measures. By eleven votes to three it confirmed the orders of 1972 with the necessary adjustments, these orders to remain in force until final judgment in each case. Judge Ignacio-Pinto appended a declaration, and Judges Gros and Petrén dissenting opinions.

In judgments delivered on 25 July 1974, the Court found by ten votes to four that the 1972 Regulations of Iceland extending the zone of its exclusive fishing rights were not "opposable" to the United Kingdom or the Federal Republic, that Iceland had no right to unilaterally exclude British or West German fishing vessels from areas between the 12-mile and 50-mile limits or unilaterally to impose restrictions on their activities in such areas. The judgments also indicated various factors which were to be taken into account in future negotiations to reach an equitable solution of the disputes. Those factors included preferential rights of Iceland, the established rights of the United Kingdom and of the Federal Republic, conservation of the fishery resources and joint examination of the measures required for this. President Lachs and Judges Nagendra Singh and Ignacio-Pinto appended declarations, Judges Forster, Bengzon, Jiménez de Aréchaga, Nagendra Singh and Ruda a joint separate opinion, Judges Dillard, de Castro and Sir Humphrey Waldock separate opinions, and Judges Gros, Petrén and Onyeama dissenting opinions.[39]

These judgments were published in the middle of the second session (1974) of the Third United Nations Conference on the Law of the Sea. Here one of the major issues for decision was the extent and nature of coastal State jurisdiction over the natural resources of the sea and the sea-bed adjacent to but beyond the outer limits of the territorial sea. The Court carefully avoided pronouncing on the validity of the Icelandic fishery regulations in general. To have done so would undoubtedly have prejudiced those negotiations, which ultimately led to agreement on the breadth of the territorial sea of 12 nautical miles and acceptance of the concept of the exclusive economic zone formulated principally in articles 55 to 75 of the 1982 Convention on the Law of the Sea. The Court also ruled that all parties concerned were under a duty to enter into meaningful negotiations to reach agreement on the reconciliation of Iceland's preferential rights and the legitimate interests of Britain and the Federal Republic.

Although all the orders and judgments in these cases are in virtually identical terms, the two cases were not joined but "paired". Therefore they proceeded independently but simultaneously. In Article 47 of the 1978 Rules, the Court formalized this by permitting the Court "without effecting any formal joinder" to direct "common action" in the written or oral proceedings.

To some extent the law stated by the Court in these cases, even though the Court refused to decide *sub specie legis ferendae* (in its own words), has been overtaken and completed by the Third United Nations Conference on the Law of the Sea. The cautious and tentative pronouncement by the Court was a useful clarification to that Conference and to the political process which led to recognition of the right of the coastal State to exercise preferential or exclusive jurisdiction over natural resources in the maritime areas adjacent to its coasts (the exclusive economic zone). In the evolution of the law of the sea these judgments occupy an important place.

FRENCH NUCLEAR TESTS IN THE PACIFIC OCEAN

On 9 May 1973 Australia and New Zealand both filed applications instituting independent proceedings against France contesting the legality of atmospheric nuclear weapons tests by France in the South Pacific Ocean. On 16 and 18 May respectively Fiji made application to intervene in each of these cases, on the basis of Article 62 of the Statute and its particular concern in the proceedings. France, for its part, informed the

Court of its view that the Court lacked jurisdiction; it asked for the cases to be removed from the list and refused to take any part in the proceedings. Both Australia and New Zealand also requested the Court to indicate interim measures calling upon France to desist from any further tests pending the judgment of the Court. After hearings at which France was not represented the Court, on 22 June 1973, issued two orders, by eight votes to six, calling upon the Governments concerned to ensure that no action was taken which might aggravate or extend the disputes submitted to it or prejudice the rights of the other party in respect of the carrying out of whatever decision might finally be rendered by the Court. More particularly the Court called upon France to avoid nuclear tests causing the deposit of radioactive fall-out on Australian territory or on the territory of New Zealand, the Cook Islands, Niue or the Tokelau Islands. At that stage the Court could not accede to the French request to remove the case from the list, but it ordered that the questions of its jurisdiction to entertain the disputes and the admissibility of the applications should be pleaded first. Judges Jiménez de Aréchaga, Sir Humphrey Waldock, Nagendra Singh and Judge *ad hoc* Sir Garfield Barwick each appended a declaration, and Judges Forster, Gros, Petrén and Ignacio-Pinto dissenting opinions.

Both Australia and New Zealand had based the Court's jurisdiction upon Article 17 of the 1928 General Act for the Pacific Settlement of International Disputes as well as on the compulsory jurisdiction. As a matter of law the status of the 1928 General Act for the Pacific Settlement of Disputes, which at the time was part of the League of Nations system, is controversial. A revised version was adopted by the General Assembly in 1949, but few States have accepted it. The Court has exhibited the greatest caution in pronouncing itself on this question, since any statement in one case could have an impact extending beyond the relations of the parties litigating a case before it. France maintained its refusal to take any formal part in the proceedings. However, in 1973 France sent a document to the Court explaining why it considered that the Court was "manifestly not competent" in the case. Later, while the cases were in progress, it issued a number of public statements, including statements made by the President of the French Republic and the Ministers of Defence and of Foreign Affairs, in which the French Government announced that it would discontinue its nuclear tests in the atmosphere, after the series of tests planned for the summer of 1974 had been completed. The atmospheric tests would be replaced by underground tests at France's nuclear testing station on Mururoa atoll in French Polynesia, approximately 6000 kilometres east of Australia.

Referring to these latter statements, the Court found by nine votes to six, in two separate judgments of 20 December 1974, that inasmuch as the applicants' real objective in instituting proceedings had been to obtain a cessation of any further atmospheric nuclear tests in the Pacific Ocean, the claims no longer had any object and that the Court was not called upon to give a decision on them. President Lachs appended a declaration, together with a joint declaration by Judges Bengzon, Onyeama, Dillard, Jiménez de Aréchaga, and Sir Humphrey Waldock; separate opinions were filed by Judges Forster, Gros, Petrén and Ignacio-Pinto, and Judges Onyeama, Dillard, Jiménez de Aréchaga and Sir Humphrey Waldock a joint dissenting opinion, and Judge de Castro and Judge *ad hoc* Sir Garfield Barwick dissenting opinions. With the delivery of these judgments the provisional measures lapsed.[40] This judgment enabled the Court to avoid pronouncing itself on the controversial issue of the status of the General Act for the Pacific Settlement of Disputes.

Subsequent to the Court's judgments, France continued its underground nuclear tests in French Polynesia in the face of opposition from a number of States in the region. In 1995 New Zealand attempted to reopen the case in response to a final series of underground tests without success (see p. 217 below).

As for the attempted intervention by Fiji, the Court at first decided to hold up its decision on that until after it had decided the issues of jurisdiction and admissibility. After the judgments of 1974, the applications for permission to intervene became "moot".

As in the two *Fisheries Jurisdiction* cases, these two cases were not formally joined but "paired". They proceeded independently and simultaneously. The French member of the Court continued to sit in the case, and both Australia and New Zealand appointed the same person as judge *ad hoc*.

During the proceedings, what looks like an unexplained "leak" from the Court's deliberations occurred in Australia. The judgment in the Australia case contains some important observations on the need to maintain the secrecy of the internal deliberations of the Court.

AEGEAN SEA CONTINENTAL SHELF DELIMITATION

The background of the dispute between Greece and Turkey over the delimitation of maritime spaces in the Aegean Sea is closely linked with the pattern of conflict and mutual animosity which characterize the relations of the two nations since Greece's independence in the 19th century and the clashes that followed the First World War. Here it is sufficient to note that on the basis of the 1958 Geneva Convention on the Continental Shelf, Greece contended that the Aegean Islands which form part of its national territory were entitled to their own portion of the continental shelf to be delimited according to the equidistance method established in that Convention. Turkey denied that the equidistance method was applicable to that delimitation, and while it fully acknowledged Greece's territorial sovereignty over the islands, it further denied that these islands had any influence over the Aegean continental shelf which, in Turkey's view, was an extension of the Asia Minor land mass. The two States entered into negotiations on the matter in 1973 after Turkey had granted permission for petroleum exploration in the area to several Turkish vessels, action which had led to protests by Greece.

Relations between the two countries worsened because of developments in Cyprus. Notwithstanding some progress during the negotiations, the two States were unable to find an acceptable solution. Greece was prepared for joint submission of the dispute to the Court, while Turkey preferred a negotiated settlement which would take account of extralegal considerations, although it was not averse to the joint submission of strictly defined issues to the Court should this prove necessary. The broader Greek approach would have enabled the Court to base itself on the rules for delimitation of the 1958 Convention, while Turkey preferred to keep the dispute in the diplomatic sphere and reach a negotiated settlement. Turkey was not a party to that instrument and was only willing to go to Court if the dispute had been narrowly defined in a process which would allow the Court to depart from those provisions. This led to an impasse in mid-1976. Turkey then recommenced seismic exploration in the Aegean, including the area claimed by Greece.

Greece's initial response was a partial mobilization of its armed forces and Turkey acted likewise. On 10 August 1976, Greece simultaneously referred the matter to the Security Council and commenced proceedings in the Court. At the same time Greece requested the indication of interim measures. Greece based the jurisdiction of the Court on Article 17 of the General Act for the Peaceful Settlement of Disputes of 1928 to which both States had been parties since the 1930s. Greece also based jurisdiction upon a joint press communiqué of 31 May 1975, issued by the Prime Ministers of the two States in Brussels. In that communiqué the Prime Ministers had expressed their desire to resolve the differences between the two countries peacefully by means of negotiations and as regards the continental shelf of the Aegean by the International Court. In that connection, they had decided to accelerate the negotiations regarding the question of the continental shelf which were being conducted by the experts of the two countries.

Turkey denied that the Court had jurisdiction over this case in the absence of a special agreement and refused to appear. As other countries had done, it made its views clear to the Court by means of communications sent from its Embassy in The Hague. Briefly, these communications denied the need for the indication of provisional measures, because the conduct of seismic exploration in the areas of the continental shelf claimed by Greece could not prejudice any rights that Greece might possess, and if any such rights were infringed, that could be compensated subsequently. Additionally, Turkey claimed that the Court had no jurisdiction to hear the case because the General Act of 1928 was no longer in force; and further that even if the Court were to determine otherwise, a reservation in Greece's accession to the Act pertaining to "the territorial status of Greece including its rights of sovereignty over its ports and lines of communications" excluded this dispute. Turkey also denied that the joint press communiqué of 31 May 1975 constituted a special agreement on which the Court's jurisdiction could be based.

In its order of 11 September 1976 the Court, by twelve votes to one, found that the circumstances, as the Court then saw them, were not such as to require an indication of provisional measures. This avoided the issue of its *prima facie* jurisdiction to indicate provisional measures. At the same time it decided that the written pleadings should first be addressed to the question of the Court's jurisdiction to entertain the dispute. President Jiménez de Aréchega and Judges Lachs, Morozov, Ruda, Mosler, Elias and Tarazi appended separate opinions, and Judge *ad hoc* Stassinopoulos a dissenting opinion.

In its judgment of 19 December 1978, the Court, by twelve votes to two, decided that it had no jurisdiction. Separate opinions were filed by Vice-President Nagendra Singh and Judges Gros, Lachs, Morozov and Tarazi, and dissenting opinions by Judge de Castro and Judge *ad hoc* Stassinopoulos.[41]

Reading this case, it is difficult to avoid the impression that both in the Security Council and in the Court there was embarrassment at the fact that each principal organ of the United Nations had been simultaneously seised of the case, the first, and so far only, occasion when the two organs have had a single dispute brought before them by the same party on one and the same day. But neither organ went so far as to disseise itself of the case on that ground. The Court again avoided the issue of the continued validity of the General Act through reliance on the Greek reservation. Neither organ put itself in a posture of controversy with the other. The dispute between the two States has continued to fester and complicate their relations. In April 1987, it flared up again leading to renewed tension and renewed desire by Greece to submit the dispute to the Court. The possibility of some future role for the Court in helping to decide the issue cannot be discounted, although it is clear as a result of the 1978 judgment that this will have to be on the basis of a joint submission by both States.

DECOLONIZATION IN THE WESTERN SAHARA

The Western Sahara is a sparsely populated desert area situated on the northwestern coast of Africa between Morocco and Mauritania. Algeria also has a short common border with the area. In 1884, Spain proclaimed a protectorate over the southern portion of this area (formerly known as the Rio de Oro) and gradually extended its control over the northern portion of this region (the Sakiet El Hamra). Spain later governed the territory as an overseas portion of Spain itself. However, following the adoption of the Declaration on the Granting of Independence to Colonial Countries and Peoples by the General Assembly (resolution 1514 (XV), 14 December 1960) and the increasing pressure of the decolonization movement, in 1961 Spain began submitting the customary information on local conditions to the General Assembly. International pressure for decolonization of the area increased from 1966 onwards.

Morocco in the meantime, after regaining its independence in 1956, laid claim to the entire territory and maintained that self-determination should take the form of its "reintegration" into Morocco. Mauritania adopted a similar position following its independence in 1960. It claimed that the territory had formed part of the pre-colonial Mauritanian entity.

Under this pressure, Spain declared that it was in favour of the decolonization of the territory emphasizing the population's right of self-determination. Both Morocco and Mauritania recognized the right of self-determination but maintained their respective claims. In 1974 when Spain proposed to conduct a referendum in the territory, Morocco countered by proposing that the dispute be submitted to the Court to determine whether the territory was *res nullius* before its colonization by Spain, or whether it possessed ties of allegiance to the then Sultan of Morocco. Spain rejected this proposal.

However, the General Assembly, by resolution 3292 (XXIX) of 13 December 1974 (on which Spain abstained), decided to request an advisory opinion on the following questions:

I. Was Western Sahara (Rio de Oro and Sakiet EI Hamra) at the time of the colonization by Spain a territory belonging to no one *(terra nullius)*? If the answer to the first question is in the negative:

II. What were the legal ties between this territory and the Kingdom of Morocco and the Mauritanian entity?

As soon as the proceedings commenced Mauritania and Morocco requested the appointment of judges *ad hoc.* They contended that the questions submitted to the Court concerned a legal question actually pending between Spain and each of them (the Court included a Member of Spanish nationality). On 22 May 1975, the Court determined by ten votes to five that the dispute between Morocco and Spain was closely connected to the request for an advisory opinion and that consequently Morocco should be allowed to appoint a judge *ad hoc.* However by a close vote of eight to seven, it decided that at the time of the submission of the request for an advisory opinion, there was no concrete dispute between Spain and Mauritania and Mauritania's request to appoint a judge *ad hoc* was denied. In his capacity of President Judge Lachs declared that further comment on this issue could be made in the advisory opinion itself, and Judge Morozov added a dissenting opinion.

Spain submitted a series of objections to the Court's answering the request. These included that the Court was not competent to deliver an advisory opinion, because the questions were not of a legal character; that they did not relate to existing legal rights but were wholly of an academic or historical nature. Spain's other basic objection was that the subject of the request was closely linked to its dispute with Morocco concerning how to effect the decolonization which it had not consented to submit to the Court in contentious proceedings and that the Court lacked competence to decide the same issue in advisory proceedings. Spain also argued in the alternative, that the Court should exercise its discretion and refrain from giving its opinion as requested.

The Court rejected these objections. By thirteen votes to three with regard to Question 1, and by fourteen votes to two with regard to Question 2, it decided to comply with the request.

The Court was unanimous in holding that Western Sahara (Rio de Oro and Sakiet El Hamra) at the time of colonization by Spain was not a territory belonging to no one *(res nullius)*. By fourteen votes to two it held that there were legal ties between the territory and the Kingdom of Morocco of the kind indicated in paragraph 162 of the Opinion, and by fifteen votes to one that there were legal ties between the territory and the Mauritanian entity of the same kind. There were declarations by Judges Gros, Ignacio-Pinto and Nagendra Singh, separate opinions by Vice-President Ammoun and Judges Forster, Petrén, Dillard, de Castro and Judge *ad hoc* Boni, and a dissenting opinion by Judge Ruda. Paragraph 162 read:

> The materials and information presented to the Court show the existence, at the time of Spanish colonization, of legal ties of allegiance between the Sultan of Morocco and some of the tribes living in the territory of Western Sahara: They equally show the existence of rights, including some rights relating to the land, which constituted legal ties between the Mauritanian entity, as understood by the Court, and the territory of Western Sahara. On the other hand, the Court's conclusion is that the materials and information presented to it do not establish any tie of territorial sovereignty between the territory of Western Sahara and the Kingdom of Morocco or the Mauritanian entity. Thus the Court has not found legal ties of such a nature as might affect the application of resolution 1514 (XV) in the decolonization of Western Sahara and, in particular, of the principle of self-determination through the free and genuine expression of the will of the peoples of the territory.[42]

Morocco refused to accept this conclusion and invaded the territory after Spanish withdrawal from the area. The territory was plunged into a guerilla conflict which is still not resolved. That conflict has both economic causes (the Western Sahara is the source of important phosphate deposits) and reasons of national prestige. Tensions also developed between Morocco and Algeria which claimed a stake in the area. This advisory opinion did not lead to a peaceful solution of the conflict.

DIPLOMATIC HOSTAGES IN TEHRAN

This was the second case to reach the Court as a result of revolutionary events in Iran. In the first Iranian revolution being *Anglo-Iranian Oil Co* case and the nationalistic government of Dr. Mossadegh and the Court proceedings which have been described above (see p. 145 above). It was also the first of a series of cases involving the United States, this time as applicant.

After the Shah's return to power in 1953, the country began a programme of Western-oriented industrialization. The transformation led to the emergence of opposition which culminated in the Islamic revolution of 1978/1979. The Government was overthrown and the Shah left the country. An unstable revolutionary Government was installed, led by the Ayatollah Khomeini, an influential and long-standing opponent of the Shah.

The pro-Shah orientation of the United States and its identification with the Shah's policies made the United States Embassy in Tehran a focal point of hostility for the revolutionary elements, especially after the ex-Shah was admitted to the United States for medical treatment in the early autumn of 1979. This culminated on 4 November 1979 in the seizure of the U.S. Embassy and its personnel (together with two private US citizens who had business on the premises that day) by militant revolutionaries. The diplomats were held hostage under degrading conditions, the embassy archives were ransacked, and the Iranian Government, although probably not the instigator of the seizure, subsequently gave its unqualified support to the action and even threatened to put members of the embassy staff on trial for alleged espionage and subversive activities.

The United States responded by a series of measures which included a total boycott of Iranian oil, the deportation of Iranian nationals illegally within the United States, and the blocking of substantial Iranian financial assets in American banks. The United States also undertook a diplomatic campaign for the release of the hostages, during which the situation was brought before the Security Council. On 29 November 1979 the United States commenced proceedings in the Court, and on the same day it requested provisional measures of protection. The jurisdiction was based on the Optional Protocols linked to the Vienna Conventions of 1961 and 1963 on Diplomatic and Consular Relations respectively, to which both States were parties. On 4 December 1979 the Security Council adopted resolution 457 (1979) in which it expressed its "deep concern and the dangerous level of tension" between the two countries, and called upon the Government of Iran immediately to release the embassy personnel and allow them to leave the country. It also decided to remain actively seized of the matter, and requested the Secretary-General to report to it urgently on developments, Iran rejected the jurisdiction of the Court and did not appear in the proceedings,

On 10 December the Court held a public hearing on the request for provisional measures, and on 18 December it unanimously issued its order, without any individual opinions, Iran should immediately ensure that the Embassy premises, Chancery and Consulates be restored to the possession of the United States and ensure their inviolability and effective protection in accordance with international law. It was to ensure the immediate release without any exception of all persons of United States nationality held as hostages, and afford them full protection under various treaties in force between the two countries and under general international law, including immunity from any form of criminal jurisdiction and freedom and facilities to leave Iran, Both Governments were to take no action which might aggravate the tension or render the existing dispute more difficult of solution. Iran rejected that Order, and on 31 December 1979 the Security Council adopted resolution 461 (1979), in which it reiterated its earlier calls, gave its backing to the Court's Order, and threatened to impose sanctions on Iran.

For its part, the Court gave each side one month to file its Memorial and Counter-Memorial, Iran having liberty to apply for reconsideration "if it appoints an Agent for the purpose of appearing before the Court and presenting its observations on the case", The case became ready for hearing on 18 February 1980, the date for the filing of the Counter-Memorial, The hearings began on 18 March, and Judgment was delivered on 24 May.

In its Judgment, the Court by thirteen votes to three, decided that Iran by its conduct as set out in the Judgment had violated in several respects and was still violating obligations owed by it to the United States under international conventions in force between the two countries, as well as under long-established rules of general international law. By the same vote it decided that the violations of those obligations engaged the responsibility of Iran towards the United States under international law. The Court was unanimous in deciding that the Government of Iran must immediately take all steps to redress the situation resulting from the events of 4 November 1979 and what followed, and in particular was to immediately terminate the unlawful detention of all the United States diplomatic and consular staff in Iran and other United States nationals and release each and every one and entrust them to the protecting Power (Switzerland). It was also unanimous in deciding that no member of the United States diplomatic or consular staff might be kept in Iran to be subjected to any form of judicial proceedings or to participate in them as a witness. By twelve votes to three it decided that Iran was under the obligation to make reparation to the United States, and by fourteen votes to one decided that the form and amount of such reparation, failing agreement between the Parties, was to be settled by the Court after further proceedings. There was a separate opinion by Judge Lachs, and dissenting opinions by Judges Morozov and Tarazi.

In January 1981, the United States and Iranian Governments reached an agreement through the mediation of Algeria, providing for the release of the hostages on the one hand, and the release by the United States of most of the blocked Iranian assets and the termination of further Court proceedings. The two Government also established the Iran/United States Claims Tribunal to arbitrate outstanding claims between the nationals of either State and the other Government or between the two Governments. Following this agreement the United States requested the termination of all further proceedings in the Court. After ensuring himself that the discontinuance was, as far as the Court was concerned, unconditional, the President recorded the termination of the proceedings on 12 May 1981.[43]

In the development of the law of the United Nations, this case occupies a pivotal place. It was the first real instance of the Court and the Security Council acting together in their efforts to bring a crisis to an end. The Court examined closely whether in the circumstances of this case the fact the Security Council remained seised of the matter, and was in fact taking various steps to try and end the crisis, prevented it from exercising its own jurisdiction.

THE W.H.O. MIDDLE EASTERN REGIONAL HEADQUARTERS

The Eastern Mediterranean Regional Headquarters of the World Health Organization situated in Alexandria and operated on the basis of a "Host Agreement" of 1951 between Egypt and the WHO. Following the conclusion in 1979 of the Treaty of Peace between Egypt and Israel, intense hostility towards Egypt developed in the Arab world. This led to the removal from Egypt of many Arab organizations whose headquarters had previously been in that country. In the World Health Assembly of 1980, 19 Arab States proposed removing the Eastern Mediterranean Headquarters of the WHO (which had been operating on the whole to general satisfaction). However, this proposal attracted strong opposition, partly for political reasons and partly because of the major dislocation it would have caused to the proper functioning not only of the Regional Organization but of the WHO as a whole. The United States looked for a compromise and by a vote of 53 to 43, with 20 abstentions, the World Health Assembly decided to put ask for an advisory opinion on a series of questions relating to the interpretation of the 1951 Host Agreement. This was the highest number and the highest percentage of negative votes on any resolution requesting an advisory opinion in any body to date.

In its advisory opinion of 20 December 1989 the Court dexterously reinterpreted the questions to ensure that they would be abstract questions concerning the interpretation of the Host Agreement. By twelve votes to one it decided to comply with the request. By the same vote it answered the questions about the legal principles and rules and the mutual obligations which they imply, regarding consultation, negotiation and notice applicable as between the WHO and Egypt before a final decision could be made on the transfer of the Regional Office outside Egypt, and by eleven to two it gave its opinion on the legal responsibilities of the WHO and Egypt in a transitional period, should it be decided to transfer the Office away from Egypt. There were separate opinions by Judges Gros, Lachs, Ruda, Mosler, Ago, El-Erian and Sette-Camara, and a dissenting opinion by Judge Morozov.[44]

This case is a good example of the "prophylactic" use of the advisory procedure to depoliticize an awkward political situation confronting a technical specialized agency.

DELIMITATION OF LIBYA'S CONTINENTAL SHELF

Since the *North Sea Continental Shelf* cases (p. 165 above), and with the major technological advances, questions of the delimitation of maritime spaces under the jurisdiction or control of coastal States have assumed increasing importance and there are many disputes over these matters all over the world. Some of these disputes have been submitted to different forms of arbitration or conciliation.[45] Others have been brought before the Court. Libya's delimitation disputes with its neighbour Tunisia and with its opposite State Malta were the first of a series of cases of this nature since the commencement of the Third United Nations Conference on the Law of the Sea (1973-1982). These cases constitute an important element in the reconstruction of the law of the sea accomplished by that Conference.

The special agreement between Libya and Malta was concluded in 1976 and that between Libya and Tunisia in 1977. That agreement was ratified first and the special agreement was filed on 25 November 1978. The Court was asked to indicate the principles and rules of international law to be applied for the area of the continental shelf "appertaining" to each of the two countries, and, in rendering its decision, to take account of equitable principles and the relevant circumstances which characterize the area, as well as "recent trends admitted at the Third United Nations Conference on the Law of the Sea". The special agreement went on to ask the Court to specify "precisely" the practical way in which those principles and rules apply in this particular situation, so as to enable the parties' experts to delimit the areas without any difficulties.

The proceedings were complicated when Malta requested permission to intervene on the ground that it had an interest of a legal nature might be affected by the decision. Both parties opposed this request. After formal interlocutory written and oral proceedings the Court, in its judgment of 14 April 1981, unanimously rejected the request. There were separate opinions by Judges Morozov and Schwebel. At the same time the Court made it clear that it would keep Malta's known interests in mind in its final decision.

The mainline proceedings were then resumed. By a judgment of 24 February 1984 the Court, by ten votes to four, answered the technical questions of maritime delimitation put to it. Here Judges Ago, Schwebel and Jiménez de Aréchaga added separate opinions, and Judges Gros, Oda and Evensen dissenting opinions.

The work of the experts ran into difficulties, and on 27 July 1984 Tunisia submitted to the Court a single application requesting revision of the judgment of 1982 (see p. 124 above), the interpretation of several passages in it, and the correction of an error. Judgment was given on 10 December 1985. The Court was unanimous on all points. The request for revision was inadmissible. The request for interpretation was admissible in part and the Court proceeded to make the necessary clarifications. The Court found that the request for the correction of an error was without object and that it was not required to give a decision on it. It also found that there was at that time no cause to order an expert survey to ascertain the precise coordinates of a certain point of the delimitation line. Judges Ruda, Oda and Schwebel, and Judge *ad hoc* Mme Bastid appended separate opinions. Mme Bastid was the first woman to sit on the Bench, and her vote and opinion are a rare example of a Judge *ad hoc* taking a position against that of the appointing State.

There was delay in the ratification of the special agreement between Libya and Malta, and incidents between the two countries even came before the Security Council. However the special agreement was filed on 26 July 1982, after the judgment in the Libya/Tunisia case. Here the Court was asked to decide what principles and rules of international law were applicable to the delimitation of the area of the continental shelf which appertains to Malta and which appertains to Libya, and how in practice such principles and rules could be applied by the parties in this particular case in order that they might without difficulty delimit such areas by agreement. This question, therefore, differed from that which was submitted to the Court by the Tunisian/Libyan special agreement.

After the Counter-Memorials were filed, Italy submitted a request for permission to intervene on the ground that it had an interest of a legal nature which might be affected by the decision in the case. As before, the two principal parties opposed that request. In its judgment of 21 March 1984 the Court, by eleven votes to five, rejected that request. Judges Morozov, Nagendra Singh, Mbaye and Jiménez de Aréchaga wrote separate opinions, and the Vice-President Sette-Camara together with Judges Oda, Ago, Schwebel and Sir Robert Jennings dissenting opinions.

The mainline proceedings were resumed. Judgment was delivered on 3 June 1985. By fourteen votes to three the Court stated the principles and rules of international law applicable to this delimitation and the circumstances and factors to be taken into consideration. As a result of the proceedings on the Italian request to intervene, it gave the precise co-ordinates of the meridians between which the median line was to be drawn. Judge El-Khani appended a declaration to the judgment, the Vice-President

Sette-Camara and Judge *ad hoc* Valticos appended separate opinions. Judges Ruda and Bedjaoui, together with Judge *ad hoc* (as he had now become, his term of office as a Member of the Court having come to an end earlier) Jiménez de Aréchaga appended a joint separate opinion, and Judges Mosler, Oda and Schwebel dissenting opinions.

There are two important aspects of this series of cases. In the first place, noteworthy is the fact that none of the Judges *ad hoc* was a national of the appointing State. This had been done before by individual States. The innovation is that in no less than five separate phases of two separate cases the three States concerned each acted in this way.

Secondly, there is no doubt that the two interventions have opened up new perspectives for international litigation. Although *formally* the requests for permission to intervene were rejected, the proceedings on those requests enabled the would-be interveners to indicate concretely, even if only in a preliminary and summary form, what their interests were. They gave these indications in adversarial proceedings with the principal parties. In addition, in each case this action led the Court to accept the position that its judgments had to be limited to those parts of the Central Mediterranean which were not subject to conflicting claims by the would-be interveners against one or other of the principal parties. Comparison of the maps included in the two judgments on the merits with the maps of the original claims, especially of Libya, will show that the proceedings on the requests for permission to intervene had the effect of reducing considerably the areas of the sea which the Court found to be within its jurisdiction in these two cases. That was the significance of the word "appertains" in the special agreements.

The *Libya/Malta* case was the first to come before the Court after the termination of the Third United Nations Conference on the Law of the Sea. Although the Convention had not yet entered into force (that event occurs on 16 November 1994), its impact was felt throughout the proceedings. Following these judgments, a series of delimitation agreements were concluded between some, but not all, of the States concerned in this part of the Mediterranean Sea.[46]

MARITIME DELIMITATION BETWEEN CANADA AND THE UNITED STATES IN THE GULF OF MAINE AREA

Overlapping claims by Canada and the United States concerning different rights in and over the sea in shared areas go back to colonial days. Questions relating to the Bay of Fundy and the Bay of Passamaquoddy were brought before the Commissioners under the Jay Treaty of 1794 (see p. 2 above). But, especially since the Second World War, population growth and increasing pressure on fish stocks had aggravated the disputes, especially between the fisherfolk of the areas concerned, in Nova Scotia and New Brunswick on the one hand and in Maine and Massachusetts on the other, and between the two Federal Governments of Canada and the United States. These disputes have come to relate both to the living resources of the sea, especially Georges Bank, one of the richest fishing grounds in the world, and to the mineral resources of the sea-bed. In 1979 a series of agreements was reached between the two Federal Governments. One of those agreements provided for the delimitation dispute in the Gulf of Maine are (including Georges Bank) to be submitted either to a special chamber of the International Court (the first instance of the employment of this new type of chamber introduced into the Statute in 1945 (see p. 58 above), or to arbitration. The United States

Senate withheld its advice and consent from this set of agreements, which accordingly never entered into force. After further negotiation the two Governments agreed to separate the delimitation dispute from the other issues, and refer that dispute either to a special chamber or to arbitration. The dispute itself was defined in the following terms:

> What is the course of the single maritime boundary that divides the continental shelf and fisheries zones of Canada and the United States of America from a point in latitude 44° 11' 12" N, longitude 67° 16' 46" W to a point to be determined by the Chamber within an area bounded by straight lines connecting the following sets of geographic coordinates: latitude 40° N, longitude 65° W; latitude 42° N, longitude 65° W?

Precise instructions were given to the Chamber, which was requested to describe the course of the maritime boundary in terms of geodetic lines connecting geographic co-ordinates or points, and for illustrative purposes only to depict the course of the boundary on specified Canadian and United States charts. The Chamber was empowered to appoint a technical expert nominated jointly by the parties to assist in respect of technical matters, including preparing the description of the maritime boundary and charts.

The special agreement called for the case to be determined by a chamber composed of "five persons, to be constituted after consultation with the Parties". It is understood that when the special agreement was being negotiated, it was intended to invite the President of the Court, then Sir Humphrey Waldock, to serve as President of the Chamber. In addition, since the United States member of the Court at that time, Judge Baxter, would have been disqualified from sitting in the case (he had advised one of the American states on the matter), no national judge or judge *ad hoc* would be appointed by either side. However, the deaths in 1981 of both Sir Humphrey and Judge Baxter radically changed the position. The new American judge was not disqualified, and the parties decided that he would be paired with a Canadian judge *ad hoc,* and that they together with three other Members of the Court would constitute the Chamber. The parties having been duly consulted by the Court and additional explanations furnished, the Court decided to constitute the Chamber as requested. That decision was embodied in an order of 20 January 1982 by eleven votes to two, with a declaration by Judge Oda and dissenting opinions by Judges Morozov and El-Khani. The term of office of one of the Members of the Court chosen for this Chamber was to expire on 5 February, when another Member of the Court of the same nationality would take his place on the Court itself. The individual opinions indicate dissatisfaction with the manner in which this Chamber was constituted, both as to its timing (immediately before the expiry of the term of office of one third of the Members of the Court) and because of the implied warning that if the Chamber was not constituted as the parties wished, the case would be withdrawn and submitted to arbitration. Objectively speaking, there may have been some merit in those objections, since Article 26, paragraph 2, of the Statute is open to more than one interpretation. However, in this particular case these objections disregard the fact that throughout the negotiation of the special agreement informal consultations with the President of the Court, Sir Humphrey, had taken place and his suggestions, designed to ensure consistency with the Statute and the Rules of Court, were incorporated.

Once the Chamber was duly constituted, the proceedings continued without incident.

The hearings, however, had to be interrupted for the hearings and decision of the full Court on Nicaragua's request for the indication of interim measures in its dispute with the United States (see p. 100 above). The Chamber rendered its judgment reached by four votes to one on 12 October 1984 (in the middle of the hearings on the jurisdictional phase of the *Nicaragua* case). The operative clause of the judgment is short and to the point. It simply states what the course of the single maritime boundary is, as defined by geodetic lines connecting four points indicated by their coordinates.

In point of fact the Chamber effectively divided the main bone of contention, Georges Bank, into two, the northern part going to Canada and the southern to the United States -a judgment of Solomon (as was to be expected) giving partial satisfaction (or dissatisfaction) to each side.

The pleadings in this case were extremely heavy and technical. The technical expert was appointed in March and his technical report is annexed to the judgment, together with an individual opinion by Judge Schwebel and a dissenting opinion by Judge Gros. As in the previous delimitation cases and following the special agreement, appropriate charts were prepared for illustrative purposes only.

Although possible interests of France (in Saint Pierre and Miquelon) might have been affected by the case, the Chamber was careful to specify in its judgment that the rights of third States in the area in question could not in any way be affected by the delimitation which the Chamber was requested to effect. No attempt at intervention appears in the record of the case.[47]

Apart from this being the first instance of recourse to an *ad hoc* Chamber specially chosen by the parties, this case is significant as it shows a major change in the thrust of maritime delimitation disputes. The previous disputes had concerned the delimitation of overlapping claims to areas of continental shelf. This case concerned overlapping claims both to the continental shelf and to the living resources of the area, and the Chamber was requested to indicate a single multi-purpose line of delimitation. Both countries were claiming an exclusive fishing zone, something which in that form is not regulated in the 1982 United Nations Convention on the Law of the Sea. That change of direction has come into prominence since. The *Gulf of Maine* case is a landmark decision in more senses that one.

DELIMITATION OF A FRONTIER IN WESTERN AFRICA

Burkina Faso (formerly Upper Volta) and Mali are two West African States, both of which had been under French colonial administration from the latter part of the nineteenth century until 1960, when each became independent. The two States share a common frontier extending approximately 1300 kilometres, of which roughly 1000 kilometres had been delimited by agreement. The remaining portion of the border, extending roughly from the frontier town of Lafou eastwards to the tripoint shared with another former French territory, Niger, was the subject of a long-standing dispute between the two countries.

That dispute had its roots in the colonial era, with the year 1919 as the starting point. The present territory of both countries had formed part of the French colony of Upper Senegal and Niger. In 1919, the *cercles* (administrative districts) which comprise the present territory of Burkina Faso were made into a separate colony named Upper Volta. The remainder of the Upper Senegal and Niger colony was divided a few years later into two territories, one of which became Niger, the other French Sudan. Niger became the present Niger, and the latter became independent under the name of the Republic of Mali. Between 1932 and 1946 Upper Volta was reincorporated into the French Sudan (Mali). By a law of 4 September 1947, the territory of Upper Volta was reconstituted, and comprised the area of the former colony of that name. This territory received independence in 1960 under the same name, changed in 1984 to Burkina Faso.

The area concerned is remote and thinly populated. During the colonial administration it had been imperfectly surveyed and was almost inaccessible. The dispute concerned the precise boundaries of the French administration, those boundaries becoming the international frontier between the two independent States.

The two countries began to demarcate their frontier immediately after independence. They reached agreement on most of the line, but not in this region. This led to hostilities between them. The Organization of African Unity attempted to mediate that dispute in 1974. An effort to demarcate the frontier by a technical commission failed. On 14 October 1983, the two Governments concluded a special agreement to submit the dispute to a Chamber composed of five judges. The agreement stressed the wish of both parties to reach a definitive solution based on the principle of respect for the pre-independence frontiers. This principle, which goes under the name of *uti possidetis juris,* had been adapted from Roman law and applied in a different context when the States of Latin America became independent from Spanish and Portuguese colonial rule in the early nineteenth century. Essentially, the principle means that the provincial boundaries between territories belonging to the same colonial power and the boundaries between territories belonging to different colonial powers, become the starting-point for the determination of the boundaries of the newly independent States. The Organization of African Unity in one of its earliest resolutions (AGH/Res.16 I of 17 July 1964) adopted this principle both with respect to the frontiers between different colonial powers, and with respect to the internal administrative boundaries between or within different colonies of the same colonial power. The purpose was to avoid the instability which would ensue if the pre-independence frontiers were called into question. It does not prevent agreed changes in those frontiers.

The Chamber, which was composed of three Members of the Court and two judges *ad hoc,* was constituted in 1985. During the course of the written proceedings, in December 1985 fighting broke out once again between the parties in the disputed border region. The OAS was concerned in the restoration of peace, and both sides submitted requests for the indication of provisional measures by the Chamber. On 9 January 1986 the Chamber unanimously gave appropriate indications of provisional measures. Both sides agreed to withdraw their armed forces from the disputed region.

The Chamber's judgment was delivered on 22 December 1986. The Chamber was unanimous, but each Judge *ad hoc* – Judges Luchaire and Abi-Saab – added separate opinions. The judgment provided for a precise delimitation of all of the border, leaving a small portion to be delimited by the experts of the parties themselves, these experts to be appointed by the Chamber. In an Order of 7 March 1987, the Chamber appointed the experts requested by the parties. They were not experts of the Chamber, and did not have to submit a report to it.[48]

Both parties accepted this decision, and agreed to carry out the remaining small adjustments for which it called, in separate communications which were addressed to the Chamber by their respective Heads of State. The Chamber had succeeded in resolving a potentially dangerous and debilitating dispute between two African States, by applying a combination of classic legal doctrine and a careful regard for the remaining divisions between the parties. This case is the first instance of reference to the Court at the instance of the Organization of African States in the course of its attempting to reach a pacific settlement of a dispute among two of its member States.

THE SITUATION IN CENTRAL AMERICA (I.) NICARAGUA V. THE UNITED STATES

This case is discussed in Chapter 5.

THE SITUATION IN CENTRAL AMERICA (II.) NICARAGUA V. COSTA RICA; NICARAGUA V. HONDURAS

Following the Court's judgment on the merits of the case between Nicaragua and the United States in June 1986, Nicaragua brought two new cases by unilateral application against two of its neighbours in Central America, Honduras and Costa Rica.

The two applications were filed simultaneously on 28 July 1986. They must be seen in the light of Nicaragua's overall diplomatic campaign to discredit support for the *Contras* who, with United States support, had been engaged in irregular warfare against the Nicaraguan Government since early 1982. The two cases are closely related to Nicaragua's earlier case against the United States, but differ in many respects from that case and from each other. The institution of these cases was a surprise, as it had been assumed that after the disposal of the case against the United States, Nicaragua would not bring any more cases of this nature against its neighbours.

In both cases, Nicaragua invoked the compulsory jurisdiction together with Article XXXI of the Inter-American Treaty on Pacific Settlement, the Pact of Bogotá of 30 April 1948. All three States are parties to that Pact, but not the United States. It provides for reference of legal disputes to the Court under certain circumstances and conditions. The declaration of Costa Rica accepting the compulsory jurisdiction, like that of Nicaragua, was unconditional, but not that of Honduras. No case was brought against El Salvador.

In its Application against Honduras, Nicaragua alleged that in addition to providing sanctuary to the *Contras,* the Honduran Government had itself instigated various armed border incidents between units of its own armed forces and those of Nicaragua, and had committed various incursions into Nicaragua's territory. Nicaragua also alleged that Honduras had provided various forms of direct and indirect support for the *Contras* including intelligence, logistical aid and even direct combat support on various occasions. Nicaragua maintained that these actions constituted breaches of various international conventions and of customary .law and that consequently Honduras was under a duty to make reparations.

The parties agreed that the proceedings should first be directed to questions of jurisdiction and admissibility. Unusually, they also agreed that Honduras should plead first. On 21 March 1988 Nicaragua filed a request for the indication of provisional measures, but this was withdrawn on 31 March. Political developments led to the postponement of the hearings to the summer of 1988. In its judgment of 20 December 1988, the Court unanimously upheld its jurisdiction under the Pact of Bogotá and the admissibility of the case. There was a declaration by Judge Lachs and separate opinions by Judges Oda, Schwebel and Shahabuddeen. Neither side appointed a judge *ad hoc* for this phase. There were further postponements, and in May 1992 Nicaragua discontinued the case.

The proceedings between Nicaragua and Costa Rica took a different course. Nicaragua's allegations against Costa Rica were less far-reaching than those directed towards Honduras. They were limited to a claim that Costa Rica had failed to prevent various border and cross-border attacks and incursions on the part of the *contras* operating from Costa Rican territory and as a result had incurred legal responsibility for not preventing those incidents.

Nicaragua's Memorial was due to be filed on 1 July 1987, but at Nicaragua's request this was postponed to 10 August. On that date the Memorial was filed. The next day Nicaragua transmitted to the Court an agreement which had been reached in Guatemala City, and on the 12th discontinued the proceedings against Costa Rica. This prevented Costa Rica from placing its case on the record.[49]

A noteworthy feature of this series of cases is the skilful use made by Nicaragua of the political and the legal machinery available to it under the United Nations Charter. However, Nicaragua's actions in 1986 in commencing cases against Costa Rica and Honduras tend to magnify the political aspects of the whole operation at the expense of its presentation as a genuine legal dispute. It is not to be wondered that the future of those two cases became tied into the Guatemala City Peace Plan (initiated by the President of Costa Rica, and earning for him the Nobel Peace Prize in 1987) of August 1987. There are many who think that these are factors pointing to a possible abuse of court procedures for the attainment of political objectives, and that the Court, especially (but not exclusively) in its various decisions of 1984, failed to give sufficient weight to those possibilities.

THE LAND AND MARITIME FRONTIER BETWEEN EL SALVADOR AND HONDURAS

There had been a long-smouldering dispute going back almost to their independence from Spain, with occasional outbreaks of violence, between EI Salvador and Honduras over a number of points of their land frontier and over maritime delimitation in the Gulf of Fonseca. Nicaragua is also a riparian of that Gulf, and was party to a case in 1917 with El Salvador in the now defunct Central American Court of Justice. Through the mediation of the Organization of American States, El Salvador and Honduras concluded a General Treaty of Peace in 1980 for the delimitation of the land boundary. By 1986 most of the frontier had been delimited, but there were still differences over six points, together with other differences about the juridical status of some islands and the delimitation of maritime spaces in the Gulf of Fonseca. By a special agreement of 24 May 1986 they agreed to refer to an *ad hoc* Chamber of the Court the delimitation of the outstanding boundary lines on land, and the determination of the legal situation of the islands and maritime spaces. That special agreement was filed on 11 December 1986. The special Chamber was to consist of three Members of the Court and two judges *ad hoc*. It was established on 8 May 1987 when the written proceedings commenced.

On 27 January 1989 one of the Judges *ad hoc* died. There was an exchange of views regarding his replacement, and on 13 December 1989 the Court declared the new composition of the Chamber. The term of office as a Member of the Court of the President of the Chamber came to an end on 6 February 1988, but he continued as President of the Chamber until its final judgment in 1992. The other two Members of the Court who were members of the Chamber were elected President and Vice-President of the Court respectively with terms of office commencing on 6 February 1991.

On 17 November 1989 Nicaragua filed a request for permission to intervene under Article 62 of the Statute, arguing that it had an interest of a legal nature which might be affected by the decision of the Court. Nicaragua thought that this request should be heard by the full Court. Honduras had no objection to the intervention provided that it was limited to expressing views on the legal status of the waters within the Gulf of Fonseca. El Salvador opposed the request.

By an order of 28 February 1990 the Court decided on technical grounds, by twelve votes to three, that the decision on the request for permission to intervene should be made by the Chamber. Judge Oda appended a declaration to that Order, and Judges Elias, Tarassov and Shahabuddeen dissenting opinions. In a judgment of 13 September 1990 the Chamber unanimously found that Nicaragua had shown that it had an interest of a legal nature which might be affected by part of the judgment of the Chamber on the merits of the case, namely its decision on the legal regime of the waters of the Gulf, but not as regards any decision by the Chamber concerning the delimitation of those waters, or any decision as to the legal situation of the maritime spaces outside the Gulf, or any decision as to the legal situation of the islands in the Gulf. It accordingly decided that Nicaragua would be permitted to intervene pursuant to Article 62 of the Statute, to the extent, in the manner, and for the purposes set out in that Judgment. There was a separate opinion by Judge Oda.

The nature and extent of that intervention was spelled out in the Judgment. In brief, Nicaragua was admitted as a "non-party" intervener in respect to the legal regime of the waters of the Gulf only.

The hearing commenced on 15 April 1991 and occupied the Chamber for 50 public sittings until 14 June 1991. Judgment was delivered on 11 September 1992. It occupies 271 printed pages – one of the longest judgments to have been delivered in the International Court. By a series of votes, either unanimous or four to one, six points of the land frontier were defined between El Salvador and Honduras. The decision on the islands was similar. With regard to the waters of the Gulf, by four votes to one the Chamber in effect decided that they were subject to the joint entitlement of all three States of the Gulf unless and until a delimitation of the relevant maritime area be effected. By the same vote it declared itself to be without jurisdiction to effect any delimitation of maritime spaces within or outside the Gulf. By another similar vote it went on to deal with the legal situation of the waters outside the Gulf. The Judgment expressly states that as Nicaragua was admitted as a non-party intervener, it is not binding on Nicaragua. There was a declaration and a dissenting opinion by Vice-President Oda, and separate opinions by Judges *ad hoc* Valticos and Torres Bernárdez.[50]

A CASE BETWEEN THE UNITED STATES AND ITALY

In the notice terminating its "Optional Clause" declaration of 1946 (p. 112 above), the United States indicated that it would continue to support the Court. It also announced agreement in principle with Italy to bring a longstanding dispute before the Court. On 6

February 1987 it filed an application against Italy alleging that measures taken by the Italian authorities in relation to American owned subsidiaries of United States corporations were violations of a Treaty of Friendship, Commerce and Navigation of 1948. .It was agreed that the case would be determined by a Chamber of five Members of the Court (which included Members of Italian and United States nationality). The President of the Court, Judge Nagendra Singh, would be President of the Chamber. His death on 11 December 1988, after the termination of the written pleadings, led to the reconstitution of the Chamber by the election of President Ruda to fill the vacancy. Italy had an objection based on the exhaustion of local remedies rule, and the parties agreed that this should be heard together with the merits.

The case proceeded without incident. An unusual feature of a case of this kind was that witnesses and experts were called by both parties. Another unusual feature was that the Italian delegation included an American attorney, and the United States delegation included an Italian attorney and another non-American. In its judgment of 29 July 1989, the Chamber was unanimous in rejecting the Italian objection to the admissibility. By four votes to one it found in favour of Italy and by a similar vote it rejected the United States claim to reparation. There was a separate opinion by Judge Oda and a dissenting opinion by Judge Schwebel. This judgment deals with a series of technical questions of international law.[51]

INTERPRETATION OF THE US/UN HEADQUARTERS AGREEMENT OF 1947

An Act of Congress of 22 December 1987 required the closing of all offices of the Palestine Liberation Organization (PLO) in the United States. This was interpreted by the United States authorities as requiring them to take steps to close the office of its Permanent Observer Mission to the United Nations in New York. That Observer Mission was established following General Assembly resolution 3237 (XXIX) of 22 November 1974, by which the PLO was invited to participate in the sessions and work of the General Assembly "in the capacity of observer". The Act became effective 90 days after its enactment (i.e. on 21 March 1988). The Secretary-General took the view that closure of that office would be a violation of the Headquarters Agreement between the United States and the United Nations of 26 June 1947. After an exchange of views with the United States authorities, he formally invoked article 21 of that Agreement regarding the settlement of disputes not resolved by negotiation. That envisaged an international arbitration. Although the Secretary of State and the Administration in general were opposed to that legislation in so far as it related to the Observer Mission in New York, after the law was enacted the Attorney General of the United States took the view that he had no choice but to attempt to implement the law. That led him to initiate appropriate proceedings in the competent federal court of New York to close the Mission's office.

On 2 March 1988 the General Assembly by a vote of 145 to 1 (not the United States, which did not participate in that vote) adopted resolution 42/229 B, in which, "taking into account the time constraint", it requested an advisory opinion on the question whether the United States was "under an obligation to enter into arbitration" under the Headquarters Agreement. The United States did not oppose that resolution.

The Court immediately assembled to examine the matter. In a procedural order of 9 March it decided to adopt an accelerated procedure as envisaged in Article 103 of the

1978 Rules of Court – the first instance of this. That order was unusual, however, in that it was not limited to questions of procedure. It also called upon the United States to provide assurance that no action would be taken that would impinge on the current arrangements for the official functions of the PLO Mission. That Order was adopted unanimously, with a separate opinion by Judge Schwebel. Without referring to that aspect, the United States later informed the General Assembly that no further steps would be taken to close the office until the U.S. courts had determined whether the law in question required that office to be closed.

After accelerated written and oral proceedings, on 26 April the Court was unanimous in answering the question in the affirmative. The advisory opinion was accompanied by a declaration by Judge Elias, and separate opinions by Judges Oda, Schwebel and Shahabuddeen. In that form the issue reverted to the General Assembly.

On 13 May 1988 the General Assembly adopted resolution 42/232. Here it expressed its appreciation to the Court for having accelerated its procedure. It took note of and endorsed the advisory opinion and urged the host country to act consistently with it. The General Assembly also asked the Secretary-General to continue his efforts, and to report without delay on developments in the matter.

The United States court, after proceedings in which the United Nations took part as *amicus curiae,* subsequently determined that the law did not require the closing of the offices of the PLO Observer Mission to the United Nations if that meant a breach of the Headquarters Agreement.[52]

MARITIME DELIMITATION BETWEEN JAN MAYEN AND GREENLAND

In August 1988 Denmark filed an application instituting proceedings against Norway for the delimitation of the fishing zone and the continental shelf by a single line between the Norwegian island of Jan Mayen and its western neighbor, Greenland. The jurisdiction was based on each country's declaration accepting the compulsory jurisdiction. The area of overlapping claims of the parties was some 65,000 square kilometers. Denmark claimed that the boundary should coincide with 200 nautical mile limit of Greenland and Norway maintained that the boundary was a median line. The principal resource of the area involved is capelin, a stock which straddles the 200 nautical mile zones of the parties and Iceland. In its judgment of 14 June 1993 the Court, by fourteen votes to one, effected the delimitation. There were a series of declarations by Vice-President Oda and Judges Evensen, Aguilar Mawdsley and Ranjeva, separate opinions by Vice-President Oda, and Judges Schwebel, Shahabuddeen, Weeramantry and Ajibola, and a dissenting opinion by Judge *ad hoc* Fischer.[53]

This was the first case were the Court was requested to effect a maritime delimitation by a unilateral application of one of the parties. Norway did not contest the jurisdiction of the Court, but argued that the adjudication should only result in a judgment which was declaratory as to the bases of delimitation, and which left the establishment of the actual boundary to negotiations between the parties. The Court rejected this argument, observing that to give only a broad indication of the manner in which the delimitation line should be established and to leave the matter to further agreement of the parties, would not be a complete discharge of the Court's duty to determine the dispute.

This was also the first case in which a court was required to establish separate boundaries for the continental shelf and a 200 mile fishing zone, instead of effecting the delimitation of all maritime zones by a single line. The delimitation effected by the Court results in the coincidence of the continental shelf and fishing zone boundaries. For the fishery zone, equitable access to the capelin resources by the parties was an important consideration to establish the location of the boundary. The main reason for locating the continental shelf boundary in the same position seems to have been that this was the preference of the parties and prevented the complications of diverging boundaries for the two jurisdictions. The Court considered that this approach in any case was within the measure of discretion conferred upon it by the need to arrive at an equitable result.

On 18 December 1995 Norway and Denmark signed an agreement implementing the terms of the Court's judgment. This agreement makes some minor technical adjustments to the boundary defined by the Court. Moreover, the agreement regulates the exploitation of continental shelf resources that straddle the boundary. An agreement of 11 November 1997 defines a further part of the boundary between Greenland and Jan Mayen. The Court had not addressed this delimitation because it also concerned the maritime zones of Iceland, which was not a party to the case. This agreement became possible after Denmark and Iceland had reached agreement on the delimitation of their maritime zones in this area. The three states cooperate for the management of the capelin resources which straddle their 200 nautical mile zones.

INCIDENTS IN THE ARABIAN/PERSIAN GULF

Incidents in the Gulf during the Iran/Iraq War of 1980-1988, and in particular the presence of United States naval units (together with others) to ensure safe passage of neutral ships through the Gulf, led to two major incidents which Iran referred to the Court in proceedings against the United States.

The first of these arose out of the accidental shooting down by USS *Vincennes* of an Iranian civilian airliner transiting the Gulf on 3 July 1988. Iran immediately brought this incident before both the Security Council and the Council of the International Civilian Aviation Organization, each of which adopted resolutions on the matter. Dissatisfied with the resolution of the ICAO Council, on 17 May 1989 Iran filed an application instituting an appeal against the resolution of the ICAO Council, acting in accordance with provisions of the Convention on Civil Aviation of 1944. At the same time Iran, citing other instruments, introduced other requests claiming a formal condemnation of the United States and reparation. Against this the United States filed preliminary objections.

Subsequent to the raising of preliminary objections, the two States entered into negotiations which led to a full and final settlement and the discontinuance of the case on the basis of a joint request by the Parties on 22 February 1996.

Other incidents, including the destruction of three offshore Iranian oil platforms by United States naval vessels in response to armed attacks in the form of mines and missile attacks against a US warship and an American flagged oil tanker under convoy of US warships which had allegedly been carried out by Iranian forces, occurred on 17 October 1987 and 18 April 1988.

On November 1992, Iran instituted proceedings against the United States, again claiming a formal condemnation and an award of damages, basing the Court's jurisdiction upon the compromissory clause contained in a 1955 Treaty of Friendship, Economic Relations and Consular Rights between the two States. At the end of 1993, within the time-limit fixed for the filing of written pleadings, the United States raised a number of preliminary objections.

The proceedings on the merits were accordingly suspended and written pleadings relating to the preliminary objections were submitted by the Parties within the new time limits established by the Court, with oral hearings on these objections being conducted in September 1996.

The Court upheld its jurisdiction in its judgment of 12 December 1996 on preliminary objections, albeit on significantly narrower grounds than those put forward by Iran in its Application. The Court found that the destruction of the oil platforms potentially affected the freedom of commerce provided for in one of the provisions of the 1955 Treaty of Amity. The Court noted further that there was a dispute between the Parties concerning the interpretations of that treaty which Iran invoked as the basis for jurisdiction. [54]

New time limits were set for the proceedings on the merits and within the time-limit set for the filing of its Counter Memorial, the United States filed a counter-claim against Iran, alleging that Iranian attacks and other measures directed against maritime commerce in the Gulf in the period of 1987-1988 constituted a breach of the freedom of commerce. Article 80 of the Rules of Court provides that a counter-claim must be directly connected with the subject matter of the claim of the other party, in this case Iran. Iran, objected to the submission of this counter-claim, maintaining that it did not meet the requirements of this provision. The Court, however, found otherwise and determined that the US counter-claim was admissible in so far as it related to Iran's alleged breach of the freedom of commerce, provided for in the relevant provision of the 1955 treaty which had been upheld as the basis for jurisdiction in the judgment on preliminary objections.

The Court extended the time limits no less than five times to allow the Parties to fully develop their respective cases on the claim of Iran and the US counter-claim. The last extension was made in August 2001 and the case is due for oral proceedings in the beginning of 2003.

PHOSPHATES IN NAURU

Nauru, a former German colony, came under a League of Nations Mandate in 1919. That Mandate was conferred on "His Britannic Majesty" as sovereign of the United Kingdom as well as of Australia and New Zealand. After the Second World War this was transformed into a Trusteeship, with the same three governments being denominated jointly as the Administering Authority. The principal administration was undertaken by Australia. Nauru's major natural resource was deposits of phosphates, a wasting asset, and its depreciation and over-exploitation had been a matter of dispute between the Nauruans and the administering authorities, especially Australia, even before Nauru attained independence.

Nauru became independent on 31 January 1968. It did not apply for membership in the United Nations. On 18 November 1987 Nauru became a party to the Statute of the

Court, and on 29 January 1988 deposited a declaration accepting the compulsory jurisdiction. Attempts to settle the dispute over the exploitation of the phosphate lands were unsuccessful, and on 19 May 1989 Nauru filed an application instituting proceedings against Australia, alleging various breaches of the Trusteeship Agreement and requesting reparation. Nauru based itself on the compulsory jurisdiction.

Australia raised a series of preliminary objections going both to the jurisdiction of the Court and to the admissibility of the application. In its judgment of 26 June 1992, the Court by various majorities (the lowest being nine votes to four) rejected all the objections except one, and by the same vote held that it had jurisdiction to entertain the application and that the application was admissible. There was a separate opinion by Judge Shahabuddeen, and dissenting opinions by the President, Sir Robert Jennings, the Vice-President, Judge Oda, and Judges Ago and Schwebel. There was no judge *ad hoc* in this phase.

Following that judgment, the case proceeded to the merits stage. However, negotiations between the parties continued and in August 1993 they reached agreement on the settlement of the dispute and the discontinuance of the case. By that agreement Nauru also undertook not to make any claim in the International Court or elsewhere against Australia, the United Kingdom and New Zealand arising out of or concerning the administration of Nauru during the period of the mandate or trusteeship. This was notified to the Court jointly on 9 September 1993.[55]

THE LEGAL STATUS OF A UNITED NATIONS RAPPORTEUR

During 1988, a special rapporteur of the Sub-Commission on the Prevention of Discrimination and Protection of Minorities of the Commission of Human Rights, a Romanian national named Dumitru Mazilu, was prevented by the Government of the Socialist Republic of Romania (under President Ceausescu) from exercising his functions. The Sub-Commission thereupon recommended to its parent body, the Commission on Human Rights, to request the Economic and Social Council to seek an advisory opinion on a priority basis on the legal question of the applicability of a provision in the Convention on the Privileges and Immunities of the United Nations in the case of Mazilu as a special rapporteur of the Commission. ECOSOC adopted this request on 24 May 1989 by 24 votes to 8 with 22 abstentions, after rejecting an amendment to delete the reference to "on a priority basis" by a vote of 17 to 9 with 22 abstentions. On 15 December 1989 the Court unanimously replied that the relevant provision was applicable to Mazilu. The implication of this was that the Government of the Socialist Republic of Romania had violated its obligations under the Privileges and Immunities Convention when it prevented him from carrying out his functions. Although the Court was unanimous, separate opinions were appended by Judges Oda, Evensen and Shahabuddeen.[56]

In the proceedings before the Court, the unadvised reader might think that Mazilu was an innocent victim of Communist persecution. However, after the collapse of Socialist Romania and the troubles that beset that country, it came out that Mazilu had been a prominent member of the Communist Party but had fallen out with Ceausescu and the official leadership.

The issues raised in this case were technical questions of treaty interpretation.

The Court's clarification of the legal status of Special Rapporteurs of the United

Nations, of whom there are many operating in many different circumstances, is useful.

This was the first instance of the invocation of the advisory competence of the Court by ECOSOC. The roundabout way in which the Sub-Commission on the Prevention of Discrimination and Protection of Minorities had to proceed in order to obtain this opinion has re-opened the question of whether the advisory competence ought not to be opened to a wider circle of international organs than exists at present. However, the Sub-Commission itself is not composed of States but of individual experts (hence the legal question put to the Court). Likewise, technically the members of the Commission on Human Rights, a functional commission of ECOSOC, are not necessarily representatives of States since the persons who sit on the Commission require the approval of the Secretary-General of the United Nations before they assume office.

THE "AOUZOU STRIP" DISPUTE BETWEEN CHAD AND LIBYA

This territorial dispute between two neighbouring African countries, although under discussion between the former colonial Powers, France and Italy, came into the open between independent Chad and independent Libya only in the 1970s. Eventually the dispute came before the Organization of African Unity, and under its auspices a Framework Agreement was concluded between the two countries on 31 August 1989. By this Framework Agreement the two countries agreed to try and settle the territorial dispute by all political means, and in the absence of a political settlement, to submit the dispute to the Court. The Framework Agreement also included some interim measures to be observed by the parties until the Court handed down its final judgment on the territorial dispute.

No political settlement having been reached, on 31 August 1990 Libya, and on 3 September 1990 Chad, respectively instituted proceedings against each other according to the Framework Agreement. The proceedings in the Court were without incident. In its judgment of 3 February 1994, the Court fixed the line, acceding to the claims of Chad. The decision was virtually unanimous, sixteen votes to one. There was a declaration by Judge Ago, separate opinions by Judges Shahabuddeen and Ajibola, and a dissenting opinion by Judge *ad hoc* Sette-Camara.[57]

It is believed that this was the first case in which a party (Chad) received financial assistance from the United Nations Trust Fund (see p. 39 above) to enable it to pursue this litigation. After the judgment the Security Council assisted the parties in its implementation (resolution 915, 4 May 1994). The case is significant in that it disposed of a dispute which had long poisoned the relations between the two countries and contributed to undermining stability in the region and was a major factor, leading to armed clashes between them, including outside military intervention. Following the judgment, Libya announced its intention to fully comply with its terms and proceeded to completely withdraw its military forces and administration form the contested region.

THE EAST TIMOR CASE

East Timor had been a Portuguese colony from the sixteenth century. Its closest neighbour is Indonesia, which became independent from the Netherlands in the decolonization process after the Second World War. It is separated from Australia by the Timor Sea in which significant deposits of petroleum have been known to be located under the continental shelf since the 1970s.

Following the 1974 'Carnation Revolution' in Portugal, in which the armed forces overthrew the extreme right wing government and initiated a process of painful transition towards democracy and decolonization, a complicated situation arose in East Timor, where local independence movements took root alongside other movements favouring integration with Indonesia. Fighting erupted between these movements which the small Portuguese civil and military administration was unable to control.

In December 1975 Indonesia occupied East Timor and the last remnants of the Portuguese administration, which during the fighting had withdrawn to a small offshore island forming part of the territory, were forced to leave Timor completely. Portugal, however, maintained that it was still the lawful administering power over the territory, until such time as the East Timor population was able to assert its rights to self-determination and brought the situation to the attention of the United Nations. In a series of resolutions, the Security Council up to 1976 and the General Assembly up to 1982, reaffirmed the right of the people of East Timor to self-determination and apparently accepted Portugal's status as the administering power of East Timor under the relevant provisions of the Charter dealing with non-self-governing territories. The occupation and subsequent incorporation of East Timor within Indonesia led to a bloody and protracted guerilla war inside East Timor between the Indonesian army and security services, supported by Timorese militias supportive of the union with Indonesia and the Timorese independence movement known as FRETILIN.

In the meantime, Australia, which had already reached agreement with Indonesia on the delimitation of the continental shelf with Indonesian West Timor in 1972, proceeded towards gradual recognition of Indonesian sovereignty over East Timor and entered into negotiations with Indonesia concerning the delimitation of the remainder of the continental shelf area separating East Timor and Australia. This resulted in the conclusion of the Timor Gap Treaty in 1989, which provided for a joint exploitation regime of the oil in that area pending a definite agreement. Portugal had protested vehemently against the conclusion of this treaty seeing it as an usurpation of the right of the East Timorese people to self-determination and control over their natural resources; but Australia refused to enter into any negotiations with Portugal. Accordingly, on 22 February 1991, Portugal instituted proceedings against Australia. It based the jurisdiction of the Court on the Optional Clause declarations accepting the compulsory jurisdiction of the Court of Portugal and Australia respectively. It bears pointing out that Portugal was unable to institute proceedings against Indonesia, since Indonesia has issued no acceptance of the Court's jurisdiction.

The case was conducted normally with several rounds of written proceedings, stretching over the course of 1991-1993. Oral pleadings were conducted in early 1995, with both parties exercising their right to appoint a judge *ad hoc*. The Court issued its Judgment on 30 June 1995. Australia had raised a number of objections to the Court's jurisdiction and the admissibility of the dispute during the proceedings, among which, it had contended that any judgment of the Court concerning the legality of Australia's conclusion of the Timor Gap treaty with Indonesia, would inevitably involve a decision on the lawfulness of Indonesia's entry into and continuing presence in East Timor, in the absence of any consent by Indonesia to the Court's jurisdiction.

Portugal had attempted to counter this argument which relied on the 'indispensable third party' precedent formulated by the Court in the *Monetary Gold* case (see above p. 148) by pointing to the *erga omnes* character of the right of self-determination, which in Portugal's view placed a positive legal obligation upon all States, including Australia, to respect the right of self-determination of the people of East Timor, irrespective of the conduct of any other State. In the event, the Court ruled in favour of upholding the Australian objection, by a majority of fourteen to two. The Court noted that while Portugal's position that the right of self-determination possessed an *erga omnes* character was "irreproachable", this nevertheless did not change the fact that the Court was precluded from ruling on the lawfulness of a third State's conduct, without that State's consent to the Court's jurisdiction.[58]

The wider significance of the proceedings was that notwithstanding the rejection of Portugal's case, they probably contributed to a renewal of international attention to the situation in East Timor. The awarding of the Nobel Peace Prize to two prominent East Timorese supporters of the independence movement in 1996 was an indication of this attention. This renewed attention, combined with important changes inside Indonesia, led to the conclusion of an agreement between Portugal and Indonesia in May 1999 concerning the conducting of a referendum in East Timor under UN supervision in which the population could choose between independence or continued integration with Indonesia as an autonomous province. In the event the population rejected autonomy within Indonesia and the progress towards achieving self-determination continued with United Nations support in the form of a temporary administration known as UNTAET (United Nations Transitional Administration in East Timor). The territory achieved full independence in May 2002.

THE MARITIME DELIMITATION OF GUINEA-BISSAU AND SENEGAL

Guinea-Bissau, a former Portuguese colony, is one of the few States of West Africa which attained its independence only after a bitter armed struggle. It was immediately faced with serious problems of delimitation of its maritime spaces, both with its neighbour to the south, Guinea, and with its neighbour to the north, Senegal. Both Guinea and Senegal had been French colonial possessions before they became independent, and delimitation issues had been agreed between the two colonial powers, France and Portugal, but before the modern law of the sea had become settled. The maritime delimitation dispute between Guinea-Bissau and Guinea was resolved by an arbitral award of 14 February 1985. That arbitration took place at The Hague. All the arbitrators were Members of the Court, and the Rules of Court governed the procedure of the arbitration. The arbitral award itself is structured along the same lines as a judgment of the Court, and in the hierarchy of international judicial decisions the award can rank as a judgment of an *ad hoc* Chamber of the Court.

A second arbitration was organized to deal with the dispute with Senegal. One of the arbitrators was a Member of the Court: the others were prominent international lawyers. This award was rendered on 31 July 1989, but was found unsatisfactory by Guinea-Bissau on a number of technical grounds relating to the law of international arbitration procedure. This dissatisfaction led Guinea-Bissau to accept the compulsory jurisdiction unconditionally on 7 August and to institute proceedings against Senegal in the International Court on 23 August 1989. By virtue of Article 17 of the Statute of the Court, the Member of the Court who had been one of the arbitrators recused himself from sitting in the proceedings in the Court.

Although Senegal at first hinted that it would contest the jurisdiction of the Court, it did not pursue that course, especially after Guinea-Bissau had clarified that its application to the Court related exclusively to the validity of the arbitral award, and was not directed at the delimitation issue itself.

Incidents involving each party occurred in the disputed zone. On 18 January 1990 Guinea-Bissau filed a request for provisional measures designed to prevent actions of any kind in the disputed area during the whole duration of the proceedings until the Court gave its decision. For a number of technical reasons based on the fact that the Court was not dealing directly with the delimitation dispute, but with another dispute relating to the validity of the arbitral award, the Court, by fourteen votes to one, dismissed that request, and the proceedings on the merits of that new dispute continued. To that order, Judges Evensen and Shahabuddeen added separate opinions, and Judge *ad hoc* Thierry a dissenting opinion.

On 12 March 1991 Guinea-Bissau filed another application instituting proceedings against Senegal, asking the Court what should be, on the basis of the international law of the sea and of all the relevant elements in the case, including the future decision of the Court in the arbitral award case, the line (to be drawn on a map) delimiting all the maritime territories appertaining respectively to Guinea-Bissau and Senegal. At a meeting with the President of the Court on 5 April 1991, the representatives of the Parties agreed that no measure should be taken in the case until the Court had delivered its decision in the case concerning the arbitral award of 1989.

Judgment on the arbitral award dispute was delivered on 12 November 1991. The Court was unanimous in dismissing a contention by Guinea-Bissau that the arbitral award of 1989 was "inexistent". By eleven votes to four it rejected the argument that the award was "absolutely null and void". By twelve votes to three it rejected a submission that Senegal was not justified in seeking to require Guinea-Bissau to apply the 1989 award; and on a countersubmission by Senegal found that the award "is valid and binding" for Senegal and Guinea-Bissau, "which have the obligation to apply it". Judge Tarassov and Judge *ad hoc* Mbaye (himself a former Member of the Court whose term of office had come to an end while the case was pending) appended declarations to that judgment. Vice-President Oda, and Judges Lachs, Ni and Shahabuddeen appended separate opinions, and Judges Aguilar Mawdsley and Ranjeva a joint dissenting opinion, Judge Weeramantry and Judge *ad hoc* Thierry dissenting opinions. This judgment is an important contribution to different technical aspects of the law regarding international arbitration procedure.[59]

After the judgment on the arbitral award, the parties continued negotiations to reach agreement on the pending issues of maritime delimitation. While these negotiations took place no time-limit was fixed for the initial pleadings in the case concerning maritime delimitation. On 14 October 1993 Guinea-Bissau and Senegal concluded an agreement, which provides for the joint exploitation of the maritime zone situated between the azimuths 268° and 220° drawn from the terminal point of their land boundary. Fishery resources of this zone are to be shared equally between the parties and continental shelf resources shall be shared in a proportion of 85 per cent for Senegal and 15 per cent for Guinea-Bissau. A further agreement of 12 June 1995 addresses the establishment and functioning of a bilateral agency for the management of the zone. After the parties had informed the Court of these agreements and their agreement to discontinue the proceedings in the case concerning maritime delimitation the case was removed from the General list by an order on 8 November 1995.

PASSAGE THROUGH THE GREAT BELT (STORE BÆLT)

In 1987 Denmark decided on the construction of a "fixed traffic connection" across the strait of the Great Belt and in 1989 decided that this connection would be by means of a high-level bridge. This caused concern in Finland, since the Great Belt provides the only passage to and from the Baltic for certain deep-draught rigs and drill-ships which Finnish shipyards were constructing. Attempts to meet these concerns failed, and on 17 May 1991 Finland filed an application instituting proceedings against Denmark. Jurisdiction was based on the declarations of each country accepting the compulsory jurisdiction. In addition, Finland indicated another possible basis for jurisdiction in the Optional Protocol of the First United Nations Conference on the Law of the Sea of 1958, to which both countries are parties. The Court was asked to declare that there is a right of free passage through the Great Belt and that this right applies to all ships entering and leaving Finnish ports and shipyards; that this right extended to drill ships, oil rigs and reasonably foreseeable ships; that the construction of a fixed bridge over the Great Belt as currently contemplated by Denmark would be incompatible with the right of free passage; and that the two countries should start negotiations in good faith on how the right of free passage should be guaranteed. This right of free passage was said to be based on the Treaty of Copenhagen of 1857 and on the codified law of the sea of 1958 and 1982. Clearly, this case raised a number of major questions concerning the right of passage through straits used for international navigation.

On 22 May 1991 Finland filed a request for provisional measures. It asked the Court to indicate that pending the Court's decision, Denmark should refrain from continuing its construction works in connection with the planned bridge, and should refrain from any other action that might prejudice the outcome of the proceedings. Unusually, both the written and the oral proceedings on this phase were heavy. The hearings were held early in July and lasted a week, and the Court's decision on that request was made on 29 July. The Court was unanimous in finding that "the circumstances, as they now present themselves to the Court" were not such as to require the indication of provisional measures. A declaration by Judge Tarassov was appended, together with separate opinions by Vice-President Oda, Judge Shahabuddeen and Judge *ad hoc* Broms. The proceedings on the merits then resumed their normal course, the parties agreeing that they would be limited to a single round of written pleadings.

Although the Court declined to indicate any provisional measures, its carefully measured order gave indications to each party of major legal aspects of their cases which, as mentioned, had been quite fully presented to the Court in the provisional measures phase. Those indications laid the basis for further negotiations between the parties, and a few days before the hearings on the merits were due to commence, they reached agreement on the outstanding issues, and Finland discontinued the case.[60]

A DELIMITATION DISPUTE BETWEEN QATAR AND BAHRAIN

On 8 July 1991 Qatar filed an application against Bahrain in connection with a dispute over various islands and the maritime boundary between the two states. Bahrain contested the jurisdiction of the Court, and the parties reached agreement that the question of jurisdiction should be decided first. On 1 July 1994 the Court delivered a first judgment on jurisdiction and admissibility. By a 15 to 1 majority the Court decided a number of questions, the only negative votes being cast by Judge Oda.[61] The Court found:

> that two exchanges of letters between the King of Saudi Arabia and the respective parties and a document headed 'Minutes', signed by the Ministers of Foreign Affairs of the three states in 1990 in Doha are international agreements creating rights and obligations for the parties; and that by the terms of those agreement the parties have undertaken to submit to the Court the whole of the dispute between them, as circumscribed by the text proposed by Bahrain to Qatar in 1988 and accepted by Qatar in 1990, referred to as the 'Bahraini formula'.[62]

The Court decided to afford the parties the opportunity to submit to the Court the whole of the dispute and fixed 30 November 1994 as the time-limit within which the parties were, jointly or separately, to take action to this end. There were separate opinions by Vice-President Schwebel and Judge *ad hoc* Valticos, a declaration by Judge Shahabuddeen and a dissenting opinion by Judge Oda.

The parties concurred with the Court that the exchanges of letters with the King of Saudi Arabia constituted an international agreement with binding force in their mutual relations. This is in accordance with international practice, which places weight on substance, not form, to establish whether commitments in writing constitute an international agreement in the sense of the Vienna Convention on the Law of Treaties.

The parties did not agree on whether the 1990 Minutes constituted an agreement and to what rights and obligations it and the 1987 instruments gave rise. The Minutes were signed by the Foreign Ministers of Qatar and Bahrain and provided for submission of their dispute to the Court. The Court had to decide if the Minutes formed a record of the meeting between the Foreign Ministers, or whether they contained a commitment to submit the dispute to the Court. The Court adhered to the second point of view, pointing out that the Minutes did not merely give an account of discussions and summarize points of agreement and disagreement, but enumerated the commitments to which the parties had consented. Thus, they constituted an international agreement.

The 1987 exchanges of notes and the 1990 Minutes indicated that the parties can refer certain matters in dispute between to the Court. These documents indicated the subject matter of a submission and the method of seising the Court. The Court found that the parties had agreed to submit the whole of their dispute to the Court. It observed that the application of Qatar did not contain all elements of the dispute. Bahrain had contended that under the 1990 Minutes the Court could only be seised jointly by the two parties, and not unilaterally as had been done by Qatar. The Court did not squarely face this issue but provided the parties an opportunity, if they could reach agreement, to submit the whole of the dispute as defined in the 1990 Minutes and the Bahraini formula to the Court.

A particularity of the judgment, which was called "novel - and disquieting"[63] by Vice-President Schwebel in his separate opinion, is that it did not address the final submissions of either of the parties. Qatar had requested the Court in its final submissions to hold that it had jurisdiction to entertain the dispute referred to in the application by Qatar and that it was admissible. Bahrain's final submission was that the Court did not have jurisdiction over the dispute brought before it by the application.

Judge Oda in his dissenting opinion observed in this connection that the Court had "opted for the role of conciliator instead of finding, as I believe it ought to have done, that it lacks jurisdiction."[64] This raises the question whether the Court went beyond the powers accorded to it by its Statute. It has been noted that the Statute attributes a broad discretion to the Court as to how it will deal with matters of jurisdiction. In a number of cases preceding the 1994 judgment, there had also been signs that the Court is prepared to accept delays in the judicial treatment of a dispute if this is conducive to the settlement of a dispute being reached outside the Court.[65] In the present case, the Court found with an overwhelming majority that there was an agreement between the parties to bring the whole dispute before it. The Court in its judgment indicated the parties a course for them to do this, without prejudice to the rights of either party and leaving open all questions which the submissions of the parties asked it to decide. This 'cautious' approach is also justified by the consideration that the parties in any case would have had the possibility to submit the whole dispute to the Court, even if the Court would have ruled that it could not entertain the 1991 application of Qatar because it did not cover the whole dispute.

On 30 November 1994 the Agent of Qatar filed a document in the Registry to comply with paragraphs 3 and 4 of the judgment of the Court of 1 July 1994. The document noted the absence of agreement between the parties to act jointly and that it was intended to submit the whole of the dispute between Qatar and Bahrain as circumscribed by the text of the 1990 Minutes and the Bahraini formula. This document included among the issues in dispute the status of the Zubarah region in the peninsula of Qatar. This matter had not been included in the 1991 application of Qatar. On the same day, Bahrain submitted a document to the Registry, indicating that it considered that submission of the dispute had to be consensual. Moreover, Qatar had denied Bahrain the possibility to define the dispute over Zubarah in a way it considered acceptable.

The Court found that the 1990 Minutes permitted a submission by one of the parties. This finding was not only based on an interpretation of the text in accordance with the ordinary meaning to be given to terms in their context, but also by the object and purpose of the 1990 Minutes, which was to advance settlement of the dispute by giving formal effect to the commitment of the parties to refer their dispute to the Court.

The Court also had to deal with the issue of admissibility of the submission as Bahrain had contended that Qatar had limited the scope of the dispute by the way in which it had formulated the issues to be decided by the Court. The Court considered that the terms used by Qatar accurately described the subject of the dispute and concluded that the application of Qatar was admissible. The Court decided that it had jurisdiction and that the application of Qatar as formulated on 30 November 1994 was admissible by 10 votes to 5. Vice-President Schwebel, Judges Oda, Shahabuddeen and Koroma and Judge *ad hoc* Valticos appended dissenting opinions to the judgment.

In this second judgment on jurisdiction and admissibility the Court had to address whether both parties had given their consent to submission of the dispute to it. In its first judgment on these matters of 1994 the Court had circumvented this question by offering the parties a time period to reach agreement on the definition of the dispute and its submission. These two judgments on jurisdiction and admissibility recognize the significance of framework agreements for the submission of disputes to the Court. Although in these cases there is agreement on the principle of settlement of a dispute by the Court, the parties have not been able to work out the specific terms of reference. The judgments indicate that this does not preclude the Court from adjudicating upon the dispute. At the same time, the absence of a special agreement defining the dispute and its mode of submission open up the possibility to argue, as did Bahrain, that the consent of one of the parties to bring the dispute to the Court was lacking. Moreover, the framework agreement itself was open to different interpretations on this point. These themes were also raised in a number of the dissenting opinions appended to the second judgment.[66]

Following the second judgment on jurisdiction and admissibility the merits phase of the case was initiated. One particularity of this phase was that Bahrain questioned the authenticity of 82 documents presented by Qatar. On 30 September 1998 Qatar submitted a report, in which it indicated it had decided to "disregard all the 82 challenged documents for the purposes of the present case so as to enable the Court to address the merits of the case without further procedural complications." In an order of the President of the Court of 17 February 1999 this decision was placed on record and it was decided that the Replies of the parties would not rely on these documents. This event had a significant impact on the case as these documents played an essential role in Qatar's arguments concerning sovereignty over the Hawar Islands. Once the authenticity of these documents had been successfully challenged by Bahrain, Qatar did not abandon its claim to the Hawar islands, but developed an alternative argument, which it had not employed initially.

On 16 March 2001 the Court handed down its judgment on the merits. The Court found unanimously that Qatar had sovereignty over Zubarah. By 12 votes to 5 it found that Bahrain had sovereignty over the Hawar Islands. By thirteen votes to four it found that Qatar had sovereignty over Janan Island. By twelve votes to five it found that Bahrain had sovereignty over the island of Qit'at Jaradah. By a unanimous vote, the Court decided that the low-tide elevation of Fasht ad Dibal fell under the sovereignty of Qatar. By thirteen votes to four it established the single maritime boundary dividing the various maritime zones of the parties. Judge Oda appended a separate opinion, Judges Bedjaoui, Ranjeva and Koroma appended a joint dissenting opinion, Judges Herczegh, Vereshchetin and Higgins appended declarations, Judges Parra-Aranguren, Kooijmans and Al-Khasawneh appended separate opinions, Judge *ad hoc* Torres Bernárdez appended a dissenting opinion, and Judge *ad hoc* Fortier appended a separate opinion.[67]

Probably the most contentious issue in the merits phase was the basis upon which the sovereignty over the Hawar Islands had to be decided. The majority of the Court upheld a decision by the British authorities of 1939, which had decided that these islands, which are situated very close to the coast of Qatar, formed part of Bahrain. It would certainly not be impossible to question this finding. The acceptance of the 1939 decision by the ruler of Qatar is not without a certain ambiguity. At the same time, it does not seem that other arguments advanced by the parties offered a better basis upon which to decide the issue of sovereignty over the Hawar Islands. Such a choice at the same time would have implied disregarding or diminishing the significance of the 1939 decision of the British authorities. This would have opened up the possibility to other states to question boundaries established during the colonial era and led to an additional factor of instability in sometimes already volatile transboundary relations.

The judgment does not diverge from earlier case law as far as the delimitation of the maritime boundary is concerned. It is, however, noteworthy that the Court gives a restrictive interpretation of the rules concerning the establishment of straight baselines. It is difficult to reconcile this interpretation with much of the state practice on straight baselines. More in general, the judgment illustrates that establishing the relevant baselines in complex geographical situations is fraught with difficulties. The judgment confirms that low tide elevations and small islands should be given limited weight in establishing a maritime boundary.

Qatar and Bahrain have notified the Court that they welcome its judgment. It has been suggested that the resolution of the dispute will result in a strengthening of the economic ties between the two states.

THE 'AERIAL INCIDENT' AT LOCKERBIE (SCOTLAND)

On 21 December 1988 an American civil airliner exploded in mid-air over the Scottish village of Lockerbie killing all of the passengers and crew on board, as well as a number of people on the ground below. Investigations by the British and American authorities led to the conclusion that the cause of the explosion was a bomb concealed in the aircraft by two named persons of Libyan nationality. The Lord Advocate of Scotland charged those persons with various offences connected with that incident. Similarly, a Federal Grand Jury of the United States District Court for the District of Columbia indicted those same persons. The charge and indictment were duly communicated to Libya and the extradition of the persons concerned was requested on the basis of the 1971 Montreal Convention for the Suppression of Unlawful Acts against the Safety of Civil Aviation. On Libya's refusal to extradite the persons to either the United Kingdom or the United States of America, those two countries, together with France (which was concerned with another similar incident involving a French civil airliner) brought the matter before the Security Council. On 21 January 1992 the Security Council adopted its resolution 731 in which it urged Libya immediately to provide a full and effective response to the various requests for co-operation in establishing responsibility for the terrorist acts against the American and French aircraft. The Secretary-General was also requested to seek the co-operation of the Libyan Government in this. The Security Council decided to remain "seised" of the matter, a technical expression indicating that it could reconsider the matter if future developments made this necessary. The underlying implication was that if Libya did not find a way to co-operate satisfactorily with the authorities of the three countries concerned, the Security Council would consider imposing "sanctions" on Libya.

On 3 March 1992 Libya filed two separate but identical applications instituting proceedings against the United Kingdom and against the United States of America, asking the Court to declare that it had fully complied with its obligations under the Montreal Convention, that the United Kingdom and the United States were each themselves violating the Convention and were under a legal obligation immediately to cease and desist from such breaches and from the use of any and all force or threats against Libya, including the threat of force against Libya, and from all violations of the sovereignty, territorial integrity and the political independence of Libya.

On the same day, Libya filed requests for provisional measures. The object of these requests was to obtain from the Court a ruling that would prevent the United Kingdom and the United States from proceeding further in the Security Council, and especially to seek a resolution imposing sanctions against Libya. The hearings on these two requests were held in common in accordance with Article 47 of the Rules of Court of 1978, the first instance of this. At the same time, the cases were kept separate. While Libya's case against the two respondents was identical, the two respondents pleaded their cases independently of each other. These hearings took place between 26 and 28 March 1992. On 31 March 1992 the Security Council adopted its resolution 748 in which, acting under Chapter VII of the Charter, it imposed binding sanctions on Libya.

On 14 April 1992 the Court issued its two orders. In each case, by eleven votes to five, the Court found that the circumstances were not such as to require the Court to indicate provisional measures. Vice-President Acting President Oda and Judge Ni appended declarations; Judges Evensen, Tarassov, Guillaume and Aguilar Mawdsley appended a joint declaration; Judges Lachs and Shahabuddeen appended separate opinions; and Judges Bedjaoui, Weeramantry, Ranjeva and Ajibola together with Judge *ad hoc* Kosheri appended dissenting opinions. Proceedings on the merits then took place, with Libya requesting exceptionally long time limits for the filing of its Memorials. These documents were filed only at the end of 1993.[68]

This was the first case to raise head-on a major issue involving the relationship between the Court and the Security Council. The Court's decision avoided a direct conflict between these two principal organs of the United Nations. The declarations and opinions appended to the orders indicated the discomfort felt in the Court at the issues which it faced.

However, the issue involving the relationship between the Security Council and the Court did not wholly disappear because the Court had rejected Libya's request for provisional measures. Libya maintained that the US and UK were under an obligation to rely exclusively upon the Montreal Convention in relation to the possible extradition of two Libyan nationals suspected of involvement in the destruction of the airliner and that attempts to utilize the Security Council to effect the surrender of the two Libyan suspects were a violation of Libya's rights under that Convention.

For their part, the US and UK denied the applicability of the Montreal Convention to the situation and argued that any rights Libya might have had been superseded by the relevant decisions of the Security Council under Chapter VII of the Charter, thereby rendering Libya's application moot, that is to say without object.

These positions were put by the parties to the Court in proceedings devoted in first instance to the question of the Court's jurisdiction and the admissibility of the dispute, since both the US and UK had raised preliminary objections within the time limits set for the filing of written pleadings. Following oral hearings which were held in October 1997, the Court issued its judgments on the preliminary objections on 27 February 1998. In those decisions, the Court rejected two of the preliminary objections put forward by the US and UK and determined that the question of whether Libya's Application was without object did not have an exclusively preliminary character. This meant that the Court would rule on this point in any judgment on the merits it might subsequently make.[69]

The proceedings on the merits were resumed with new time limits for the filing of Counter Memorials by the US and UK, which were extended at the request of those States until 31 March 1999. Libya subsequently requested a new round of written proceedings which resulted in the filing of a Reply by Libya in June 2000 and Rejoinders by the US and UK in August 2001.

These rather exceptionally protracted written pleadings and extensive time limits were affected by developments outside the Court and the strict confines of this case. Diplomatic initiatives of the UN Secretary General, assisted through the mediation of the Governments of Saudi Arabia and South Africa, had led to an agreement between the Netherlands and the interested States to establish a Scottish Criminal Court in the Netherlands to try the two Libyan individuals suspected of involvement in the destruction of the American airliner in September 1998. This agreement was endorsed by the Security Council in its Resolution 1192 and the two individuals were transferred to the Netherlands in conformity with this agreement and the resolution of the Security Council in April 1999.

While the criminal proceedings at the Scottish Court in the Netherlands and the dispute between Libya and the United States and United Kingdom before the International Court are in no way formally connected, the fact of the agreement and subsequent progress of the former, has inevitably affected the latter. The proceedings before the Scottish Criminal Court in the Netherlands have resulted in the acquittal of one of the accused and the conviction of the other, which was upheld in an appeal to the High Court of Scotland. It remains to be seen how the outcome of the criminal proceedings may affect the conduct of the case before the International Court.

THE COURT AND THE CONFLICT IN THE FORMER YUGOSLAVIA

I GENERAL INTRODUCTION

The breakup and ensuing armed conflict in the former Yugoslavia has involved the Court at various stages and in various ways, ever since the Court was first approached by Bosnia Herzegovina in March 1993. The Court is currently seized of three different (sets of) disputes, totalling nine separate cases, all of which possess distinct aspects and have progressed largely independently of each other; but are nevertheless at the same time related in various ways and have a number of common elements, notwithstanding the differences between them and the fact that the proceedings in the individual cases are in no way formally linked.

This is not the place to go into the overall history of the conflict, or to attempt to draw conclusions concerning the broader legal and political significance of these cases beyond what is necessary for a basic understanding of the Court's role hitherto in the treatment of the respective cases brought before it. However, some general introductory comments are called for in so far as they will help in providing some understanding of the potential impact and the limitations thereon, of the Court's involvement in the successive stages of that conflict.

Firstly, until now, the Court's impact upon the events in the former Yugoslavia has been relatively limited. This should not come as a surprise in view of the fact that the efforts of the international community as a whole; including the United Nations Security Council, various regional organizations, amongst which were the European Union and the NATO Alliance, and the diplomatic efforts of the major Powers were all unsuccessful in bringing about an end to the conflict, or preventing large scale and systematic violations of international law over most of the course of the conflict.

Secondly, one of the reasons for the Court's limited impact has been the relatively narrow jurisdictional basis on which the cases have been based, especially when compared to the generally much broader scope of the claims put forward by the various parties at different stages of the respective cases. Essentially, the only potential basis for the jurisdiction of the Court on the merits of these cases has been Article IX of the Convention on the Prevention and Punishment of the Crime of Genocide of 1948, which provides for the Court's jurisdiction in the event of a dispute relating to the interpretation and application of that convention. Attempts to broaden the basis of the Court's jurisdiction by involving other treaties and on the basis of the Optional Clause have been largely unsuccessful. Since many of the claims of the various parties to the respective cases involve issues which are not covered by the Genocide Convention; such as allegations of unlawful use of force, violations of humanitarian law, territorial changes by force and interpretation of Security Council resolutions, they have not been able to be addressed by the Court.

Finally it seems virtually certain that the potential influence of the proceedings and possible judgments on the merits has been significantly lessened due to the very changed circumstances since these cases were brought before the Court. When the first of the three cases, that between Bosnia-Herzegovina and the Federal Republic of Yugoslavia (Serbia and Montenegro) was initiated in March 1993, the war in that country was in full swing, direct outside intervention was confined to the presence of an almost impotent and beleaguered UN peacekeeping force and Mr. Slobodan Milošević was in firm control of the Yugoslav Government, to name but several important differences with the present situation.

In addition, the International Criminal Tribunal for the Former Yugoslavia had not yet been established, much less begun to function and Bosnia-Herzegovina, along with the rest of the former Yugoslavia, was subject to an arms embargo imposed by the UN Security Council under a resolution adopted in 1991 at the outset of the armed conflict. The effect of this arms embargo upon the Bosnian war effort was arguably the chief reason for this case being brought in the first place.

None of these circumstances are still present at this time. Another factor of importance which has changed the scene significantly is the change of government in Yugoslavia, which has greatly altered the situation in the region and lessened that country's isolation. This in turn has led to the admission of Yugoslavia as a new member of the United Nations in November 2000. This calls into question the matter of Yugoslavia's standing before the Court to an even greater extent than the ambiguous situation which surrounded Yugoslavia's status at the time all of these cases were initiated. While this by no means automatically signifies that the cases will be ultimately discontinued or dismissed, it does potentially raise its possibility.

Nevertheless, regardless of the outcome of these cases, and notwithstanding the relatively limited impact of the Court upon the conflict in the former Yugoslavia, they are not without interest, nor are they devoid of significance. The claims of State responsibility for acts of alleged genocide are in themselves of importance and are unprecedented. Moreover, any decision on the part of the States which are parties to these cases to discontinue proceedings, or any decision of the Court which either dismisses the cases, or (partially) upholds the claims of the parties, will inevitably have an impact on an overall diplomatic solution.

II THE CONFLICT IN BOSNIA-HERZEGOVINA

On 20 March 1993 Bosnia and Herzegovina filed an application against Yugoslavia (Serbia and Montenegro) alleging a series of violations of the Convention on the Prevention and Punishment of the Crime of Genocide of 1948, basing jurisdiction on the appropriate provision of that Convention. The application also alleged violations of a number of other instruments, including the Charter of the United Nations, the Four Geneva Conventions of 1949 and the Additional Protocol Number I of 1977 on the Protection of Victims of International Armed Conflict, the Hague Regulations of 1907 on Land Warfare, the Universal Declaration of Human Rights and general and customary international law. Simultaneously Bosnia-Herzegovina filed a request for provisional measures, which included a cease and desist order against Yugoslavia from all acts of genocide against the people and State of Bosnia and Herzegovina, cease and desist from support for the Bosnian Serbs, and a declaration that under current circumstances Bosnia has the right to request the immediate assistance of any State in its defence and that any State has the right to come to the immediate defence of Bosnia and Herzegovina. The underlying object of that request was to obtain from the Court a statement to the effect that the arms embargo which the Security Council had imposed on the whole of Yugoslavia in its resolution 713 of 25 September 1991, and which it had reaffirmed many times since, including in resolutions adopted after Bosnia-Herzegovina had been admitted to the United Nations on 22 May 1992, was not applicable to Bosnia-Herzegovina.

The Court rejected Yugoslavia's request for adequate time to prepare for the hearings, which were scheduled for 1 and 2 April. In its written observations on that request, Yugoslavia recommended to the Court to indicate certain provisional measures which it considered should be taken by the Government of Bosnia. On 8 April the Court issued its order. On the question of jurisdiction, it was emphatic in stating that its jurisdiction was limited to the alleged violations of the Genocide Convention. Unanimously it indicated that Yugoslavia should immediately take all measures in its power to prevent the commission of the crime of genocide. By thirteen votes to one it indicated that Yugoslavia should in particular ensure that any military, paramilitary or irregular armed units which may be directed or supported by it, as well as any organization and persons which may be subject to its control, direction or influence, do not commit any acts of genocide, of conspiracy to commit genocide, or of complicity in genocide, whether directed against the Muslim population of Bosnia and Herzegovina or against any other national, ethnical, racial or religious group. The Court unanimously indicated to both Governments that they should not take any action and should ensure that no action was taken which might aggravate or extend the existing dispute over the prevention and punishment of the crime of genocide, or render it more difficult of solution. There were no judges *ad hoc* at this stage, and Judge Tarassov appended a declaration.

That decision of the Court gave little satisfaction to Bosnia, since it left the arms embargo ordered by the Security Council untouched. On 27 July 1993 Bosnia filed a second request for provisional measures. The measures requested were substantially similar to those requested in March, and again the underlying objective was to obtain from the Court a pronouncement against the application of the arms embargo to Bosnia. This time the Court fixed 25 August for the opening of the hearing, and rejected all requests by Bosnia to set an earlier date. The President also refused a request by Bosnia to act on the request without any hearing. On the other hand the President, in exercise of his special powers, sent a personal appeal to each party to act in accordance with the provisional measures ordered in April, which were still in force.

On this occasion, Yugoslavia filed both a series of observations on the second request, and a formal request of its own for an indication of provisional measures to be observed by Bosnia. For its part, Bosnia again attempted to broaden the basis of the jurisdiction of the Court, amongst other things invoking the Treaty of Saint Germain-en-Laye of 10 September 1919 between the Principal Allied and Associated Powers of that epoch and what was then called the Kingdom of the Serbs, Croats and Slovenes, a contention which could bring out a sensitive question of whether the so-called *Minorities Treaties* of 1919 were in force in 1993. Each side appointed a judge *ad hoc* on this occasion.

In its order of 13 September 1993, the Court reaffirmed that its jurisdiction was limited to the allegations of breach of the Genocide Convention. By thirteen votes to two, the Court reaffirmed its first provisional measure of April of that year; by the same vote it reaffirmed the second of those measures; and by fourteen votes to one it reaffirmed the third. In each case the measure indicated "should be immediately and effectively implemented". Vice-President Oda appended a declaration, Judges Shahabuddeen, Weeramantry, Ajibola and Judge *ad hoc* E. Lauterpacht separate opinions, and Judge Tarassov with Judge *ad hoc* Kreća dissenting opinions.

This case too had the potential for a head-on clash between the Court and the Security Council. In a difficult political situation which had so far defied the efforts of the Security Council and the competent European organizations to find a solution, this attempt to implicate the Court failed.

At Bosnia's request long time limits were fixed for the first round of written proceedings. Within those limits, Yugoslavia raised a number of preliminary objections relating to both the Court's jurisdiction and the admissibility of the dispute.

Between 29 April and 3 May the Court heard oral argument on the question of Yugoslavia's preliminary objections. On 11 July 1996, the Court handed down its Judgment on the Preliminary Objections, rejecting all of them by large majorities ranging from fourteen to one to eleven to four. The Court also rejected the additional basis of jurisdiction put forward by Bosnia-Herzegovina by a vote of fourteen to one, which meant that the case would go forward to the merits stage of written proceedings, but solely on the basis of the alleged violation of the Genocide Convention.[70]

Following that judgment, time limits were fixed, with 23 July 1997 being set as the time limit for the submission of Yugoslavia's counter-memorial. Within that time limit, Yugoslavia requested the Court to rule on the admissibility of the submission of counter-claims. In its counter-claims, Yugoslavia requested the Court to adjudge that "Bosnia and Herzegovina is responsible for the acts of genocide committed against the Serbs in Bosnia and Herzegovina" and that it has the responsibility to ensure the punishment of the responsible persons and prevent recurrence of further acts.

The Court ruled that these counter-claims were admissible and fell within the scope of Article 80 of the Rules of Court, reaching its decision on 17 December 1997 on the basis of written observations submitted by both parties, without hearing the parties in Court.[71] This was the first time that the Court had ruled on the admissibility of counter-claims at a preliminary stage of the proceedings. New time limits were set and further extended at the request of Bosnia to 23 April 1998 for the reply of Bosnia and 22

January 1999 for Yugoslavia's Rejoinder. The last limit was extended by another month to 22 February 1999 at Yugoslavia's request.

Subsequent to the filing of this round of written pleadings, Yugoslavia filed on 24 April 2001 an application for Revision of the Judgment of 11 July 1996 on Preliminary Objections, on the basis of Article 61 of the Court's Statute. This provision provides in relevant part that an application for revision of a previous judgment can only be made when it is due to a new fact that was unknown, both to the Court and to the party claiming revision, on the condition that such ignorance was not due to negligence.

Yugoslavia's basis for making this claim was its admission as a new member of the United Nations in November 2000. Yugoslavia's position is that if it only became a Member of the United Nations on that date, there could be no basis for the Court assuming jurisdiction in 1996 based on the presumption that it remained a party to the Court's Statute following the break-up of the former Yugoslavia. The logic of this position also led Yugoslavia to withdraw its counter-claim on 10 September 2001.

This step will now lead to the next stage of the proceedings being directed at the question of the possible revision of the judgment on preliminary objections. It remains to be seen what effect this new development might have, both upon this case and the other cases brought before the Court on the basis of the Genocide Convention, in which Yugoslavia is a party. The Court is expected to decide on this issue in the course of early 2003.

III CROATIA BRINGS A CLAIM AGAINST YUGOSLAVIA

On 2 July 1999, the Republic of Croatia instituted proceedings against the Federal Republic of Yugoslavia alleging a number of violations of the Genocide Convention in the period between 1991 and 1995, including in particular the 'ethnic cleansing' of ethnic Croatians from Serb held areas in Croatia in 1991-2 and directing ethnic Serbs of Croatian nationality to evacuate the Knin region in 1995. Croatia additionally maintained that ethnic Serb militias under the direct control and with the support of the federal Yugoslav armed forces were responsible for the death of numerous Croatian citizens and for widespread material damage.

As in the case between Bosnia-Herzegovina and Yugoslavia, this claim concerned allegations of State Responsibility in the traditional sense for acts of proxy Serb militias (allegedly) under the control of Yugoslavia on the territory of a neighbouring republic which had formed part of the former Yugoslavia and was not concerned with the criminal responsibility of individuals who were involved in the perpetration of those acts. One major difference between the two cases was that while the claims of Bosnia-Herzegovina, at least in early stages of the litigation, were primarily directed at the lifting of the UN arms embargo in force against the entire territory of the former Yugoslavia and had been made while hostilities were still ongoing; those of Croatia were primarily directed at proving Yugoslav complicity in the acts perpetrated in Croatia and obtaining financial compensation long after the fighting on Croatian territory had ceased.

Time limits were initially set by the Court at 14 March 2000 for the submission of the Croatian Memorial and 14 September 2000 for the submission of the Yugoslav Counter Memorial. These were later extended by the Court to 14 September 2000 and 14 September 2001 respectively. These time limits were extended yet again, at the request of Croatia, which wanted an additional six months for the preparation and submission of its Memorial. Yugoslavia had no objection to this extension provided it was granted an equal additional period to submit its Counter Memorial.

Accordingly, the Court fixed the new time limits for Croatia's Memorial at 14 March 2001 and 11 September 2002 for Yugoslavia's Counter Memorial.[72]

It remains to be seen how this case will subsequently develop in light of the possible developments in the case between Bosnia-Herzegovina and Yugoslavia.

IV YUGOSLAVIA V. NATO: ALLIED INTERVENTION IN KOSOVO

Following the conclusion of the Dayton Peace Agreement in 1995 and the termination of hostilities in the rest of the former Yugoslavia, the conflict shifted to the longstanding tensions between the Albanian majority population and the Yugoslav Government in Kosovo. Those tensions are considered by some observers to have contributed in no small measure to the breakup of the Yugoslav federation in 1990-1991; although Kosovo, which until 1989 had been an autonomous republic inside Serbia, and since the revocation of its autonomy had been ruled directly by Belgrade, had escaped the fighting in neighbouring Bosnia-Herzegovina in the period 1991-5.

Those tensions increased dramatically throughout 1997-1998, culminating in the outbreak of fighting between the Kosovar Liberation Army (KLA) and the Yugoslav security forces in early 1998 and the re-imposition of an arms embargo by the UN Security Council in March 1998. It should be pointed out that the position of the Western Powers in relation to the situation in Kosovo differed from the outset significantly from the policy they had pursued during most of the fighting in the rest of the former Yugoslavia, which had been largely characterized by a policy of limited intervention and humanitarian assistance coupled with diplomatic mediation. This policy had proved largely unsuccessful, and especially since the fall of the Muslim enclave of Srebrenica in 1995, which saw the massacre of a large number of the male population of the enclave despite its status as a UN 'protected area', this policy was replaced by much greater pressure upon the Yugoslav Government and the Serbian militias under its influence to come to terms. This change in policy had gone so far as to include direct military intervention by the NATO Powers in the closing stages of the Bosnian conflict which was one factor in the ending of the conflict.

As a result, the Western Powers were much more ready to confront the Yugoslav Government directly with very heavy diplomatic and economic pressure and even with the possibility of direct military intervention, than they had been at comparable stages in the earlier conflicts in the former Yugoslavia. At the same time, since the conflict was now on the territory of the Federal Republic of Yugoslavia and the target was clearly a sovereign State and not a rebellious faction such as the Bosnian Serb entity within Bosnia-Herzegovina; this meant that intervention would bring about a direct confrontation between the international community and Yugoslavia in a way which had not been seen earlier. This possibility of a direct military intervention, enjoying a significant measure of support within the NATO member States and to a lesser extent elsewhere, was nevertheless not greeted with universal approval. In particular, it became clear in the course of 1998- early 1999 that NATO was unlikely to receive UN Security Council authorization if it chose to intervene militarily, due to the attitudes of the Russian Federation and China, both of which were opposed to NATO military intervention against Yugoslavia and both of which as Permanent Members of the Security Council were in a position to block Council authorization for the use of force.

When it became clear to the Western Powers that further measures under Chapter VII of the Charter were impossible to be agreed upon within the Security Council, they decided that unilateral military intervention was the only means which could prevent further violence against civilians or further escalation of the conflict and restore the situation.

In March 1999, NATO military aircraft commenced 'Operation Allied Force' which involved bombardments of targets inside Kosovo and the rest of Yugoslavia by military aircraft from ten NATO Member States, with the aim of compelling the Yugoslav Government to accept the terms of a diplomatic settlement proposed at the conference held in Rambouillet, France immediately prior to the outbreak of hostilities; the terms of which had been rejected by the Yugoslav Government.

On 29 April 1999, the Federal Republic of Yugoslavia instituted proceedings against ten NATO Member States: Belgium, Canada, France, Germany, Italy, Netherlands, Portugal, Spain, the United Kingdom and the United States. Yugoslavia based the jurisdiction of the Court upon a declaration under Article 36(2) of the Statute (the 'Optional Clause') deposited on 26 April 1999, three days prior to the institution of proceedings, in which Yugoslavia accepted the Court's compulsory jurisdiction; and additionally upon Article IX of the 1948 Genocide Convention. Simultaneously with the submission of its Application, Yugoslavia entered a Request for the Indication of Provisional Measures aimed at halting the bombing of Yugoslav territory by NATO military aircraft.

In its Application, Yugoslavia alleged the unlawful use of force, unlawful intervention, violation of the humanitarian law of armed conflict, violation of the fundamental human rights of the Yugoslav population, breach of the obligation to respect Yugoslavia's right of free navigation of navigable rivers, and violation of the Genocide Convention through the use of weapons containing depleted uranium, on the part of the Respondent States.

The Court determined in parallel decisions issued on 2 June 1999, that it lacked the *prima facie* jurisdiction necessary to indicate provisional measures in any of these cases. Although the submissions of Yugoslavia were identical in all of these cases and they are all closely linked, it is nevertheless important to bear in mind that the cases against each of the Respondent parties are separate and that the jurisdictional relationship between Yugoslavia and the Respondents differs in certain important respects, notwithstanding the identical bases of jurisdiction put forward by Yugoslavia in all of them.[73]

These differences led to two of the cases; *Yugoslavia v. Spain* and *Yugoslavia v. The United States* being dismissed in the provisional measures phase of proceedings on the basis of "manifest lack of jurisdiction". In the other eight cases, the Court, while rejecting the Request of Yugoslavia for the Indication of Provisional Measures for the reason indicated above (lack of prima facie jurisdiction), determined that it remained seised (a technical term indicating that those cases remained upon the Court's docket) of those cases pending further proceedings. The reason why the cases against Spain and the United States were dismissed at this early stage is to be found in the terms of their respective accessions to the Genocide Convention, which included reservations to the Court's jurisdiction under Article IX of that convention.

The Court's determination that it lacked *prima facie* jurisdiction, particularly in relation to Yugoslavia's invocation of jurisdiction under the 'Optional Clause' and its dismissal of the cases against two of the Respondents, including the United States, greatly weakened Yugoslavia's position and deprived the remaining eight cases of much of their potential legal and political significance. The Court's exclusion of Yugoslavia's 'Optional Clause' declaration as a potential basis for jurisdiction, due to the fact that the dispute arose prior to the date of Yugoslavia's effective acceptance of the Court's compulsory jurisdiction, not only resulted in the rejection of Yugoslavia's request for provisional measures, but made it clear that the only likely basis for the presentation of Yugoslavia's subsequent case would be within the scope of Article IX of the Genocide Convention. A decision of the Court on the question of *prima facie* jurisdiction for the purposes of deciding whether provisional measures can and should be indicated is not generally determinative of either the merits or the question of the Court's mainline jurisdiction. However, the categorical terms in which the Court determined that the dispute arose prior to the date of Yugoslavia's acceptance of the compulsory jurisdiction; coupled with the dismissal of the cases against two of the Respondents, one of which, Spain, had made a declaration accepting the Court's jurisdiction under the 'Optional Clause', made it clear that there was virtually no chance that the Court would reverse its position on this question at a later stage in the proceedings against the remaining eight Respondents. This in turn had the effect of excluding all of Yugoslavia's claims which were not linked to an alleged violation of the Genocide Convention, including the most sensitive and potentially tenable claims relating to the alleged illegal use of force, alleged illegal intervention and alleged violations of humanitarian law. As a result, it is unlikely that the Court will be in a position to make any clear pronouncements on the controversial question of 'humanitarian intervention', even if any of the cases should ultimately reach the stage of a judgment on the merits. This is perhaps regrettable, but nevertheless very understandable and is a practical illustration of the Court's functions and limitations as a court of law.

Following these decisions on provisional measures, the Court fixed time limits on the subsequent presentation of written memorials, determining that Yugoslavia's Memorials in each of the eight cases were to be submitted by 5 January 2000 and the Counter Memorials of the Respondents by 5 July 2000. On 5 July 2000, within the time limits, the eight Respondent States brought forward preliminary objections relating to the jurisdiction of the Court and the admissibility of the dispute. Consequently, the proceedings on the merits were suspended under Article 79, paragraph 3 of the Rules of Court and time limits were subsequently set at 5 April 2001 for the submission of written observations on the preliminary objections. Subsequently, Yugoslavia requested the Court on 18 January 2001 to grant a stay of the proceedings or to extend the time limits for Yugoslavia's observations on the preliminary objections by a further twelve months in view of recent diplomatic initiatives. The Court granted this request in view of the agreement between the parties, with new time limits being set at 5 April 2002.

It remains to be seen what the subsequent developments in these cases will be in view of the far-reaching changes in the political situation and subsequent legal developments which have occurred since the cases were first brought before the Court.

THE COURT AND NUCLEAR WEAPONS

The question of the legality of the threat or use of nuclear weapons was put before the Court in two separate requests for an advisory opinion, the first from the World Health

Organization (WHO) in a request adopted by the World Health Assembly on 14 May 1993, and the second in a request from the UN General Assembly adopted by that body on 15 December 1994. The terms and scope of the requests differed notably in certain respects. The request by the WHO was the narrower of the two, posing the question whether the use of nuclear weapons in war or other armed conflict would breach obligations under international law, including the WHO Constitution. The request by the General Assembly was broader in scope and requested the Court to pronounce on the question whether the threat or use of nuclear weapons is permitted in any circumstances under international law.

The proceedings on the two requests were conducted separately and the Opinions were issued separately by the Court, albeit on the same day. As pointed out in Chapter 4 (see above pp. 86), the procedure in relation to advisory cases differs somewhat from that in contentious cases, since there is no "dispute" and consequently no parties to a dispute in a procedural sense. Instead, the Court will concern itself only with the question whether the requesting organ or agency has the competence to request an advisory opinion and whether the request falls within the scope of that competence. Additionally, the Court might be called upon to examine whether there are overriding reasons why the Court should decline to accede to a request, even if it is an authorized one in terms of competence to pose a request to the Court.

The procedure essentially consists of the Court providing the interested States and organizations the opportunity to put forward their views relating to the question before the Court in written and oral statements. These can relate both to the substantive aspects of the question, or the propriety of the Court rendering an opinion or the competence of the organ or agency requesting an opinion to issue such a request. However, such observations do not constitute claims or submissions, nor if they are directed to procedural aspects of the request do they constitute preliminary objections in the sense these terms are used within the context of contentious proceedings.

In both requests for an advisory opinion, the Court made use of the procedure referred to above and a large number of statements were presented to the Court in both written and oral form between February and October 1995.

On July 8 1996, the Court issued its decision in relation to both requests.[74] The WHO request was dismissed on the grounds that it fell outside the competence of the WHO as a specialized agency concerned with improving measures and coordinating activities in the realm of public health to request an advisory opinion on the question of the legality of the use of nuclear weapons. Article 96, paragraph 2 of the UN Charter provides specialized agencies with the competence to request advisory opinions on legal questions arising within the scope of their activities. The Court reasoned that the activities of the WHO aimed at dealing with the effects on public health of a possible use of nuclear weapons would be the same, irrespective of whether they were used legally or illegally. This, however, was different with respect to the request from the General Assembly. The General Assembly, as one of the two primary political organs within the United Nations, has in common with the Security Council the power to request an advisory opinion on any legal question, as provided under Article 96, paragraph 1 of the UN Charter. Moreover, the question of the legality of nuclear weapons has been the subject of numerous resolutions adopted in the General Assembly, as has been the related question of nuclear disarmament.

Consequently, there could be little doubt regarding the competence of the General Assembly to request an advisory opinion on this matter. This, however, does not automatically signify that the Court must accede to such a request. Article 65 of the Statute provides that the Court may give an advisory opinion at the request of any body authorized to make such a request. The Court has interpreted this to mean that it will accede to a duly authorized request, unless there are compelling reasons why it should refuse to deliver an advisory opinion. In this case the Court found no compelling reason why it should refuse to deliver an advisory opinion, notwithstanding the obvious political, military and moral implications of the question of the threat or use of nuclear weapons. The Court pointed out that the existence of extra legal considerations had never been a bar to reaching a decision, so long as there was a legal question involved which it was called upon to answer.

With respect to the substantive aspects of the request, the Court divided evenly, with the 'casting vote' of the President necessary for the Court to reach a majority. Although this division did not exactly correspond to a simple vote in favour or against the legality of nuclear weapons, it did reflect the extreme difficulty in reaching a decision upon such a delicate and controversial question, and the profound division in international opinion on this question.

The bulk of the Court's opinion was understandably devoted to analyzing the legality of nuclear weapons within the context of the humanitarian law of armed conflict. The Court identified a number of the basic principles of that body of law and pointed out the unique character of nuclear weapons in terms of their destructive power and the duration of the effects of their use. On the basis of this, the Court determined that the use of nuclear weapons seemed to be "scarcely reconcilable" with respect for the requirements of humanitarian law which it had identified.

However, it determined that it did not have sufficient facts at its disposal to definitively conclude that any use of nuclear weapons would violate the rules and principles of the law of armed conflict. The Court also pointed to the "fundamental right of a State to survivial" and the policy of deterrence practiced by the nuclear weapons States and their allies over a long period and concluded that with regard to the present state of international law and the available facts, it was unable to reach "a definitive conclusion as to the legality or illegality of the use of nuclear weapons in an extreme circumstance of self-defence, in which the survival of a State would be at stake".

This was in effect a *non-liquet*, a term referring to a refusal by a Court to answer a question on the grounds that the law was not clear, the first in the Court's history. This, together with various conclusions by the Court, generated a considerable amount of controversy, although since both sides on the question of the legality of nuclear weapons could point to elements in the opinion which supported their position, it probably did little long term damage to the Court. However, whether this is also true in relation to the Court's rendition of the law of armed conflict is another matter, but one which goes beyond the scope of this book.

THE LAND AND MARITIME BOUNDARY BETWEEN CAMEROON AND NIGERIA

In March 1994, Cameroon instituted proceedings against its neighbour Nigeria concerning sovereignty over the Bakassi Peninsula which lies at the southern end of the long frontier between the two States on the Gulf of Guinea. Cameroon also requested the Court to determine the maritime boundary between the two States, in so far as it had not been previously established in an agreement dating from 1975. Cameroon filed an Additional Application in June 1994 relating to sovereignty over areas in the vicinity of Lake Chad and further requested the Court to definitively specify the frontier between Lake Chad and the sea. Cameroon based the Court's jurisdiction upon the respective Optional Clause declarations of the two countries.

The Cameroonian-Nigerian boundary, in common with most African States, is based essentially on the pre-independence boundary established by the former colonial powers and the principle of *uti possidetis juris* which had been adopted by the Organization of African Unity and applied by the Court in previous disputes relating to African boundaries, most notably that between Burkina Faso and Mali (see above p. 181). Cameroon referred in fact to the principle of *uti possidetis juris* in its Application and alleged that Nigeria, by calling into question the validity of those treaties and understandings, had breached the principle of *uti possidetis juris*. Cameroon further alleged a number of military incursions on the part of Nigerian forces and the illegal presence of large numbers of Nigerian civilians on Cameroonian territory with the support of the Nigerian authorities, which it claimed had engaged the responsibility of Nigeria. The Court determined in the absence of any objection by Nigeria, that the Additional Application would be treated as an amendment to the original Application and fixed time limits (16 March 1995 for Cameroon and 18 December 1995) for the filing of Memorial and Counter-Memorial respectively.

Following armed incidents between the two States' armed forces in the Bakassi Peninsula, which triggered a request for the indication of Provisional Measures by Cameroon, the Court issued an Order on 15 March 1996, indicating provisional measures directed at both parties aimed at preventing further incidents. After Nigeria raised a number of preliminary objections within the allotted time limits, the proceedings on the merits were suspended in accordance with Article 79, paragraph 3 of the Rules of Court and the Court directed Cameroon to submit written observations and submissions relating to Nigeria's contestation of jurisdiction by 15 May 1996. Subsequently, both parties submitted additional documents relating to the preliminary objections and procedural aspects of the case during the course of the remainder of 1996 and 1997. This resulted in the oral proceedings on the question of preliminary objections being delayed until March 1998, four years after the original Application was filed.

The Court, after hearing argument, issued its Judgment on Preliminary Objections on 11 June 1998. Since neither party was represented by a judge of its nationality, both had exercised their prerogative of appointing a Judge *ad hoc* to the Bench. The Court dismissed seven of Nigeria's eight preliminary objections and determined that the eighth preliminary objection did not possess an exclusively preliminary character, in so far as an extension of the maritime boundary beyond the point agreed in 1975, could potentially impact upon the rights and interests of third States. In this context, the Court made the interesting observation that "[w]hether such third States would choose to exercise their rights to intervene in these proceedings pursuant to the Statute remains to be seen". This was a somewhat novel approach for the Court to take in relation to the possibility of third party intervention and seems to indicate a somewhat more liberal attitude on this question.

In the event, one of those third States, Equatorial Guinea, chose to intervene in order to safeguard its rights and interests in relation to the prolongation of the maritime boundary between Nigeria and Cameroon. It did so as a non-party intervener on the basis of Article 62 of the Statute and strictly limited its intervention to the question of the maritime areas in question, without wishing to have the Court indicate the maritime boundaries between itself and Cameroon or Nigeria.

Neither of the parties objected to the intervention, which was correspondingly unanimously granted by the Court in an Order dated 21 October 1999.

Nigeria proceeded subsequent to this Order to present counter-claims in relation to Cameroon's amended Application. The Court ruled on 30 June 1999 that Nigeria's counter-claims were admissible which resulted in new rounds of written pleadings enabling Cameroon and Nigeria respectively to present their arguments in relation to Nigeria's counter-claims.

The Court set 4 July 2001 as the time limit for the submission of those additional pleadings. The oral hearings on the merits were held over most of February 2002.

On 10 October 2002 the Court handed down its judgment on the merits. The Court determined the boundary in the area of Lake Chad by fourteen votes to two. The decision on which instruments had delimited the boundary between the area of Lake Chad and the Bakassi peninsula was taken by fifteen votes to one. The decisions concerning the precise course of the boundary in seventeen areas covered by these instruments were taken unanimously. The decisions concerning the Bakassi peninsula and the first part of the maritime boundary were taken by a majority of 13 to 3. The Court decided unanimously on the delimitation of the second part of the maritime boundary and the question of state responsibility. There were declarations appended to the Judgment by Judges Oda, Herczegh and Rezek and separate opinions by Judges Ranjeva, Parra-Aranguren, Al-Khasawneh and Judge *ad hoc* Mbaye. Judge Koroma and Judge *ad hoc* Ajibola appended dissenting opinions.

The Court decided that the delimitation in the Lake Chad region had been established by two declarations of 1919 and 1929-1930 between France and the United Kingdom, the administrative powers of Cameroon and Nigeria. Nigeria argued that the existence of a number of *effectivités* gave it title to the area concerned. The Court considered that, as the boundary had been delimited by the two above mentioned declarations, it necessarily followed that any Nigerian *effectivités* had to be evaluated for their legal consequences as acts *contra legem*. The relevant facts led the Court to conclude that there was no acquiescence by Cameroon in the abandonment of its title in the Lake Chad area in favour of Nigeria.

The second issue the Court addressed concerned the land boundary between the Lake Chad area and the Bakassi peninsula. This part of the boundary had been delimited by four instruments. Both parties recognized the relevance of these instruments, but differed on the precise task of the Court in their respect. Cameroon considered that the uncertainties and ambiguities these documents displayed had to be addressed by the parties in a demarcation of the boundary. Nigeria held that there were a number of difficulties concerning the delimitation which had to be resolved before any eventual demarcation. The Court noted that there was a dispute between the parties concerning the interpretation or application of the four instruments delimiting this part of the land boundary. In addressing these issues of interpretation and application, the Court dealt with 17 separate areas of this part of the land boundary. This concerned areas of limited size if compared to the Bakassi peninsula. In a number of instances the Court accepted the position of one of the parties and in other instances adopted a position diverging from those of the parties.

The sovereignty over the Bakassi peninsula probably raised most controversy. This issue was not only of importance for the land boundary, but depending on the outcome of this part of the case, the maritime boundary between both states would start respectively on the eastern or western side of the Bakassi peninsula. The population of the Bakassi peninsula is Nigerian. Both the Bakassi peninsula and the adjacent sea areas are important for hydrocarbon resources.

Cameroon considered to have title on the basis of a treaty of 1913 between the former colonial powers, the United Kingdom and Germany. Nigeria contended that the United Kingdom at that time did not have a title to the Bakassi peninsula. The United Kingdom had concluded a treaty with the Kings and Chiefs of Old Calabar establishing a protectorate over an area including Bakassi in 1884. According to Nigeria, the title to Bakassi had remained with the Kings and Chiefs of Old Calabar and the United Kingdom could not transfer this title. Upon independence of Nigeria, this title had been transferred to it. The Court rejected the position of Nigeria. In this connection, it noted that certain treaties concerning protectorates had been concluded with entities which as a result retained a previously existing sovereignty under international law. However, in other instances, such treaties where concluded with local rulers, not States. In these cases, sovereignty over the territory concerned passed to the colonial power. This implied the United Kingdom was entitled to cede the Bakassi peninsula to Germany. The Court indicated that developments after 1913, both before and after independence of Cameroon and Nigeria confirmed that the parties had accepted this state of affairs. The Court reached the same conclusions concerning Nigerian *effectivités* as it did for the Lake Chad area.

In the maritime delimitation, the Court first of all took into account the rights of third states. This concerned Equatorial Guinea and Sao Tome and Principe. The former state had been granted permission to intervene in the case to protect its legal rights in the Gulf of Guinea. Sao Tome and Principe had refrained from intervening in the case. The Court in its Judgment found that in establishing the maritime boundary between Cameroon and Nigeria, it had to ensure not to adopt a position which might affect the rights of third states. This case reconfirms the caution with which the Court addresses this issue.

In the delimitation of the maritime boundary, two sectors were distinguished. In respect of the first part of this boundary, there existed a number of bilateral declarations. Nigeria contended that one of these declarations did not constitute a binding instrument and that another declaration lacked legal validity, since it had only been signed by the Nigerian Head of State and not been ratified in accordance with the Nigerian constitution. The Court found in respect of this latter declaration that it provided for immediate entry into force upon signature. Under international law, this is an accepted procedure for the entry into force of treaties. The Court then turned to the significance of the fact that the internal treaty ratification process of Nigeria had not been followed. It considered that this did not concern a manifest violation of a rule of internal law of fundamental importance, in which case the consent of Nigeria would have been invalidated.

The last part of the maritime boundary was established by the Court. This part of the Judgment does not diverge from earlier case law as far as the applicable law is concerned. The Judgment might suggest a somewhat increased importance of equidistance and a more limited role for relevant circumstances in establishing maritime boundaries.

Following the Judgment, a controversy arose over Court's decision, especially as regards the Bakassi peninsula. Nigeria asserted that the Judgment did not consider "fundamental facts" about the Nigerian inhabitants of the Bakassi peninsula. During a meeting with Secretary-General Kofi Annan of the United Nations in November 2002, the presidents of Cameroon and Nigeria agreed to establish a mixed commission, to be chaired by a Special Envoy of the Secretary-General, to consider ways of following up Judgment of the ICJ. The mixed commission is to consider all the implications of the Judgment, including the need to protect the rights of the affected populations in both states. The commission has also been entrusted with the task of demarcating the land boundary between the two states. In view of the complexity of the procedure and the comprehensiveness of the dispute, this is without doubt one of the most important border disputes the Court has had to deal with.[75]

THE *ESTAI* CASE (SPAIN/CANADA)

On 9 March 1995, Canadian authorities boarded and arrested the Spanish-flagged fishing vessel *Estai*, despite the fact that the vessel was engaged in fishing on the high seas, just outside the 200 nautical miles (nm) Canadian exclusive economic zone (EEZ). The legality of the Canadian action was highly controversial as the 1982 United Nations Convention on the Law of the Sea (LOS Convention) stipulates that the high seas is governed by the primacy of flag State jurisdiction (Spain in this case). The recognized exceptions to this primacy-rule were not relevant here. Moreover, while Canada was at that time not a party to the LOS Convention (but Spain was), a rule as fundamental as this primacy-rule would almost certainly be binding upon Canada as customary international law.

The exceptional Canadian action followed the dramatic decline of the fisheries on the Grand Banks off Newfoundland; one of the oldest and most productive in the world. As part of the Grand Banks lie beyond the Canadian EEZ, and most fish stocks move back and forth between (straddle) EEZ and high seas, fishing activity on either side has transboundary effects. In order to deal with these effects, most States fishing in the area cooperate within the Northwest Atlantic Fisheries Organization (NAFO). During the late 1980s and early 1990s, the status of the straddling fish stocks within NAFO's competence continued to worsen despite NAFO measures, including moratoria. The eventual collapse of commercial fisheries led to massive unemployment in Newfoundland and Nova Scotia. Whereas the impact of Canadian fishing activity in the Canadian EEZ was acknowledged as having been one of the contributing factors, foreign fishing in the NAFO Regulatory Area (high seas) was also regarded as responsible, especially by the general public.

On 12 May 1994, the Canadian Coastal Fisheries Protection Act was amended to allow that foreign fishing in the NAFO Regulatory Area be brought under its regulatory scope, specifically including enforcement powers at sea. Attention was at first mainly focused on stateless vessels and vessels flying the flag of non-parties to NAFO. However, in January 1995 the European Community (EC), to which Portugal and Spain as EC Member States had transferred most of their competence in fisheries, formally objected to the Greenland halibut quota adopted by NAFO and set its own (autonomous) quota. Subsequently, Canada amended the implementing Regulations of its Coastal Fisheries Protection Act to ensure that Spanish and Portuguese vessels would fall under its regulatory scope. The seizure of the *Estai* and the arrest of its master on 9 March 1995 were based on this Act and its implementing regulations. The Canadian authorities claimed that the inspection revealed that the *Estai* had been fishing contrary to several NAFO measures.

These events took place during the final stages of the negotiations of the United Nations Conference on Straddling Fish Stocks and Highly Migratory Fish Stocks, which eventually culminated in the signature of the UN Fish Stocks Agreement on 4 December 1995. This Conference was established to resolve exactly the types of conflicts in interests between coastal States and flag States that were also at the heart of the *Estai* dispute. As the Canadian unilateral action took place less than three weeks before the fifth Conference session, it seems very likely that it was also intended to exert pressure on the negotiation-process. Views differ as to whether the Canadian action actually strengthened or weakened the coastal State position in the process or in fact threatened the success of the process itself.

Both Spain and the EC issued formal and strongly-worded protests upon the seizure of the *Estai*. On 12 March 1995 Canada released the master on bail and, three days later, the vessel was released on bond. Shortly thereafter the EC and Canada started consultations which eventually led to the signature of an 'Agreed Minute' on 20 April 1995. The parties thereby *inter alia* agreed on provisional control and enforcement measures, to be replaced later by NAFO measures; on their quotas for Greenland halibut for 1995; and that Canada would de-list Portugal and Spain under the Canadian fisheries regulations. Notwithstanding these consultations, on 28 March 1995 Spain instituted proceedings against Canada before the Court based on their declarations under the optional clause. As only States have standing before the Court, this option was not open to the EC, even if it had wanted to. Also, the LOS Convention offered no alternative, as Canada was not a party thereto.

The signature of the Agreed Minute on 20 April 1995 did not cause Spain to withdraw the case (see also further below). Both Canada and Spain appointed Judges *ad hoc*. Spain asked the Court to declare that the Canadian legislation, in so far as it claimed to exercise jurisdiction over foreign ships on the high seas, was not opposable to Spain; that the boarding of the *Estai* was a breach of international law; and that it was entitled to reparation in the form of an indemnity. In view of the Canadian reservations to its optional clause declaration, the Court decided there needed to be a jurisdictional phase. The relevant reservation excluded from the jurisdiction of the Court: "disputes arising out of or concerning conservation and management measures taken by Canada with respect to vessels fishing in the NAFO Regulatory Area [...] and the enforcement of such measures". On 10 May 1994, two days prior to the amendment of its Coastal Fisheries Protection Act, Canada withdrew its 1985 optional clause declaration and replaced it with an identical one, but added the reservation just cited. This approach is uncommon but not unique in the history of the Court. One of three previous occasions also involved Canada, that time in relation to its controversial 1970 Arctic Waters Pollution Prevention Act. No case was brought to the Court then.

On the issue of jurisdiction, Canada stated that the Court manifestly lacked jurisdiction due to the cited reservation. Spain disagreed, essentially by characterizing the dispute in a different and broader manner than Canada, which meant it would not be covered by the reservation. According to Spain, the dispute was not primarily about fishing but about Canada's right to exercise jurisdiction over foreign vessels on the high seas and to enforce this right by use of force. On 4 December 1998, the Court ruled by twelve votes to five that it had no jurisdiction. President Schwebel and Judges Oda, Koroma and Kooijmans added separate opinions and Vice-President Weeramantry, Judges Bedjaoui, Ranjeva and Vereshchetin, and Judge *ad hoc* Torres Bernárdez (for Spain) appended dissenting opinions.

The Judgment begins by observing that where parties disagree on the characterization of a dispute, the Court is obliged to characterize the dispute itself and thereby determine if it has jurisdiction. According to the Court, the essence of the dispute was whether the Canadian enactments and regulations as well as its enforcement action in relation to the *Estai*, violated Spain's rights under international law. Subsequently, the Court went on to determine for itself if the dispute, so characterized, fell under the scope of the Canadian reservation. The crux of this exercise concerned the rules of international law on the interpretation of optional clause declarations. By ruling that reservations under the optional clause must be interpreted in "a natural and reasonable way, having due regard to the intention of the State", the Court follows previous case law.

All of Spain's arguments were rejected, in particular the contention that the Canadian reservation should be so interpreted that it would be compatible with international law. Here the Court correctly emphasized that this would confuse the issue of consent to the Court's jurisdiction with the legality of conduct under international law. The Court essentially took the same view in the *East Timor* case (see p. 193 above), where it found it had no jurisdiction even though it accepted the *erga omnes* character of the right of self-determination. In the present case, various Judges nevertheless objected that in cases like these where the conduct was so clearly in conflict with norms of international law, the Court should have accepted jurisdiction. In his separate opinion, President Schwebel argued that finding the reservation effectively invalid would thereby invalidate the entire optional clause declaration and remove consent to the jurisdiction of the Court.

After having thus established the appropriate rules of interpretation, the Court proceeded to apply these to the Canadian reservation. Accordingly, it interpreted the various elements of the reservation in light of Canada's intention as evidenced by public statements made during the amendment of the Canadian enactments and regulations as well as the timing of the replacement of the optional clause declaration. This made the Court conclude that the Canadian acts fell within the scope of the reservation and, consequently, that the Court had no jurisdiction to deal with the case.

Judge Oda, in his separate opinion, also observed that in addition to the signature of the 1995 Agreed Minute, Canada shortly thereafter discontinued proceedings against the *Estai* and its master, discharged the bond and repaid the bail, returned the confiscated portion of the catch, and de-listed Spain from the Canadian fisheries regulations. In light of these events Judge Oda argued that it was questionable whether Spain's Application was even admissible as prior diplomatic negotiations had not been exhausted. States like Spain, whose fishing activities extend to every part of the globe, would indeed have a clear interest in upholding flag State primacy on the high seas. Worth noting is that while the Canadian Coastal Fisheries Protection Act and its implementing regulations were, at the time of writing, no longer applicable to Spanish and Portuguese vessels on the high seas, a number of other States were still listed and the optional clause reservation was still in force. The issue as to whether the Canadian enactments (and pending amendments thereto) are consistent with international law therefore still remains.

The broader relevance of the Judgment lies in the crucial role accorded to the intention of States in the interpretation of optional clause reservations. The Court thereby sent States a strong signal that reservations will be respected and consent to the Court's jurisdiction not easily assumed. Arguably, this cautious approach supports rather than undermines the optional clause system and thereby the Court's role in dispute settlement. The various dissenting and separate opinions reflected disagreement on this point. [76]

FURTHER FRENCH NUCLEAR TESTS IN THE SOUTH PACIFIC

On 21 August 1995, New Zealand filed a Request for an Examination of the Situation in accordance with Paragraph 63 of the Court's Judgment of 20 December 1974 in the *Nuclear Tests* Case (New Zealand v. France).

This request was triggered by a decision of the French Government, which it had made public on 13 June 1995, to conduct a final series of nuclear tests, starting in September 1995, at its underground testing facility at Mururoa Atoll in French Polynesia. According to New Zealand, the 1974 decision in the *Nuclear Tests* case (see p. 169 above) contained a provision (paragraph 63 of that judgment) which gave it the right to reopen the case in the light of the new circumstances. Paragraph 63 of the Court's Judgment of 20 December 1974 reads in relevant part:

> "Once the Court has found that a State has entered into a commitment concerning its future conduct it is not the Court's function to contemplate that it will not comply with it. However, the Court observes that if the basis of this Judgment were to be affected, the Applicant could request an examination of the situation in accordance with the provisions of the Statute"

Simultaneous with its request to reopen the case, New Zealand filed a "Further Request for the Indication of Provisional Measures" aimed at preventing France from conducting further nuclear tests pending the Court's decision. Shortly thereafter, a number of States in the region which were equally opposed to further French nuclear tests applied for permission to intervene in the proceedings.

Hearings were conducted on 11 and 12 September, in which New Zealand was represented on the Bench by a judge *ad hoc* to examine the question whether New Zealand's request to reopen the case fell within the provisions of paragraph 63 of the Court's 1974 judgment.

The Court saw the request as containing two elements. The first related to the procedural options opened in paragraph 63 of its 1974 Judgment. In that respect, the Court determined that the phrase of that provision stating that "the Applicant could request an examination of the situation in accordance with the provisions of the Statute" opened the possibility of a special procedure for reopening the case which was distinct from the options provided for in the Statute, such as the filing of a new application, or requesting an interpretation or revision of the Judgment, all of which would have been open to New Zealand in any case.

However, the Court determined that this procedural option would only come into play in the event circumstances were to arise which affected the basis of the 1974 Judgment. This crucial second element was missing in the Court's view, since the basis of that judgment was the publicly stated commitment by the French President and the French Minister of Defence, to refrain from further atmospheric nuclear testing. The tests planned for 1995 concerned underground nuclear tests and consequently fell outside the scope of the 1974 judgment. As a result, the Court rejected New Zealand's requests to reopen the case and for the indication of provisional measures and dismissed the applications of Australia, Samoa, the Solomon Islands, the Marshall Islands and the Federated States of Micronesia to intervene in the proceedings in its Order of 22 September 1995.[77]

KASIKILI/SEDUDU ISLAND (BOTSWANA/NAMIBIA)

Kasikili/Sedudu Island lies in the Chobe River, which forms the local boundary between Namibia (to the north) and Botswana (to the south). The island is located just west from where the Chobe joins the Zambezi River, which forms the boundary between Botswana and Zambia eastward from there. The north bank of the Chobe is part of the 'Caprivi Strip'; a corridor that gives Namibia access to the Zambezi. The island, known as 'Kasikili' in Namibia and as 'Sedudu' in Botswana, is about 3,5 square kilometers and when it is not flooded, the Chobe River surrounds it by means of a northern and a southern channel. This bifurcation has led to a dispute between Namibia and Botswana on the exact location of the boundary and sovereignty over the island. For decades the Caprivi Strip has been a problematic area due to armed conflicts in Angola and, more recently, military activities by the separatist 'Caprivi Liberation Army'.

The origin of the dispute lies in the colonial era when Germany exercised control over South West Africa (now Namibia) and Great Britain over its Protectorate of Bechuanaland (now Botswana). In 1890 the two colonial powers concluded a treaty which, among other things, sought to delimit their spheres of influence in southwestern Africa. Article III(2) of the 1890 Treaty determines that the sphere of influence in the most easterly section of the Caprivi Strip was bounded to the south by the "centre of the main channel (*Thalweg des Hauptlaufes*)" of the Chobe River. The choice for this general formula was motivated by a lack of site-specific information. Not long after the conclusion of the 1890 Treaty, however, authorities became aware of the bifurcation of the Chobe River around Kasikili/Sedudu Island and the consequential boundary difficulties. The authorities of South Africa became involved after the First World War, when it administered South West Africa under a mandate of the League of Nations and, later on, of the United Nations. South Africa's mandate was terminated by a 1966 resolution of the United Nations General Assembly. The Court, in its 1971 Advisory Opinion, determined South Africa's continued presence in Namibia as illegal (see p. 141 above). South Africa nevertheless remained in *de facto* control until Namibia's independence in 1990. Botswana became independent in 1966.

Between Botswana and Namibia the island-dispute surfaced soon after the latter's independence in 1990. After a Joint Team of Technical Experts was unable to resolve the matter, the two states decided to refer the matter to the Court by means of a Special Agreement. This Agreement was adopted on 15 February 1996, entered into force on 15 May 1996 and the proceedings commenced by notifying the Court on 29 May 1996. Pursuant to Article I of the Special Agreement, the Court was asked to determine "on the basis of the Anglo-German Treaty of 1 July 1890 and the rules and principles of international law, the boundary between Namibia and Botswana around Kasikili/Sedudu

Island and the legal status of the island." The dispute therefore consisted of two distinct but strongly related parts: (1) the land boundary and (2) the legal status of the island. The chosen formula allowed the Court to grant the island in such a way as to create an enclave or to place the island under an international regime.

Botswana argued that the main channel referred to in Article III(2) of the 1890 Treaty was the northern channel and that, consequently, the island belonged to Botswana. The arguments by Namibia were less straightforward and did not explicitly link the issue of the main channel with the legal status of the island. Its primary argument was that the southern channel was the main channel, either on the basis of the terms of the 1890 Treaty or by subsequent practice. Alternatively, Namibia argued that the island was at any rate under Namibia's sovereignty by means of effective possession that was not protested by Botswana.

By its Judgment of 13 December 1999, the Court decided by eleven votes to four that (1) the boundary between Namibia and Botswana follows the centre of the northern channel around the island and (2) the island belongs to Botswana. Moreover, the Court added unanimously that nationals and ships flying the flag of both States shall enjoy equal national treatment in both channels. Vice-President Weeramantry, Judges Fleischhauer, Parra-Aranguren and Rezek appended dissenting opinions, Judges Oda and Kooijmans appended separate opinions, Judges Ranjeva, Koroma and Higgins added declarations.[78]

The Judgment first deals with the determination of the main channel and subsequently with the legal status of the island. Arguably, this sequence indicates that the channel-issue would be decisive and that the status of the island would be decided implicitly. An enclave would have been an unlikely choice as complicated solutions only heighten the risk of conflict in this already troublesome region. In his dissenting opinion, Judge Parra-Aranguren deals first with the status of the island, which he decides is part of Namibia, but then also avoids an enclave by treating the channel-issue as consequential.

As the two States disagreed on which criteria should be applied to determine the main channel of the Chobe, the Court examined which criteria were most commonly used in international law and practice. In her declaration, Judge Higgins questioned whether such commonly used criteria in fact exist and suggested it would have been better to ascertain what Germany and Great Britain had in mind when they concluded the 1890 Treaty. The Court nevertheless determined that the criteria depth, width and navigability all clearly pointed to the northern channel as the main channel. Other relevant criteria such as flow and visibility were not conclusive of one channel above the other. As the subsequent practice of the States involved did not reveal an agreement on the channel-issue, it was not necessary to deviate from this finding.

The Court accepted the Namibian view that the phrase "and the rules and principles of international law" in Article I of the Special Agreement enabled the Court to investigate a claim to the doctrine of prescription, which is essentially based on effective possession. While the Court also accepted that Namibia may in principle be able to prove this claim, it failed to produce sufficient supporting evidence. In his separate opinion, Judge Kooijmans disagreed that the phrase in the Special Agreement should be thus interpreted and also contended that the doctrine of prescription cannot be resorted to where boundaries are as precisely formulated as in the 1890 Treaty. Dissenting Judge Fleischhauer observed that the Court should have pointed out that as regards acquisitive prescription the practice between South Africa and Botswana between 1966 and 1990 would at any rate have been irrelevant due to the illegality of South Africa's presence in Namibia.

After selecting the northern channel as the main channel and rejecting the Namibian claim to the island based on prescription, the Court concluded that this means that the island forms part of Botswana. Vice-President Weeramantry, in his dissenting opinion, argued that the two States should be obliged to develop a Joint Regulatory Regime as the island forms part of a larger ecological unit. The remainder of the Judgment was devoted to softening the ruling somewhat by granting nationals and ships of both States equal national treatment in both channels of the Chobe, even though they will be subject to the applicable national conditions on navigation and environmental protection. This is another liberal interpretation of the Court's mandate under the Special Agreement, but one that both States presumably welcomed.

CONSULAR ASSISTANCE IN THE UNITED STATES

1

Angel Francisco Breard, a Paraguayan national, was arrested, tried and convicted for a capital offence in the State of Virginia in 1992. The criminal court in Virginia sentenced Mr. Breard to death in 1993. Paraguay and the United States, in common with a large number of other States, are both parties to the Vienna Convention on Consular Relations of 24 April 1963. Article 36 of that convention provides for the right of a detained foreign national to request assistance from the consular authorities of the State of which he is a national, if he so wishes. It further provides for the duty of the arresting State to notify the consular authorities of a State, whose national has been charged with a criminal (felony) offence at the request of the detained foreign national.

During the course of the protracted appeals procedure, which is customary in relation to death sentences in the United States, the Paraguayan Government became aware in 1996 that Mr. Breard was a Paraguayan national and of the fact that the authorities of Virginia had not informed him of his rights under the Vienna Convention, nor advised the Paraguayan Consular authorities of the fact of his arrest, trial and conviction, neither of which were subsequently disputed by the United States. However, appeals at the federal court level were unsuccessful, due to the rule of 'procedural default', which governs the relationship between the federal and state court systems in the United States, and in essence says, that a defendant may not raise an issue in an appeal before a federal court which has not been raised in proceedings within the state court system. Consequently, an appeal based on alleged violation of the Vienna Convention cannot be raised in appeals before a federal court, unless it has been previously brought forward during proceedings in the state court system. This effectively ruled out any possibility of a federal court overturning the conviction, notwithstanding the fact that Mr. Breard was unaware of his rights under the Vienna Convention until after the state courts in Virginia had completed their handling of his case. Moreover, Paraguay likewise only became aware of the failure of the Virginian authorities to inform it of his conviction after the state court proceedings had been completed.

With the failure of its attempt to overturn the conviction of Mr. Breard in the federal court system, Paraguay instituted proceedings at the International Court of Justice on 3 April 1998 for alleged violations of the Vienna Convention by the United States, basing the Court's jurisdiction on Article 36, paragraph 1, of the Court's Statute and Article I of the Optional Protocol to the Vienna Convention, which provides for the Court's jurisdiction in the event of a dispute relating to the Vienna Convention.

Since Mr. Breard's execution had been set to be carried out on 14 April 1998, Paraguay simultaneously requested the indication of provisional measures aimed at preventing the carrying out of the execution before the Court could render judgment on the merits. On 9 April, the Court unanimously issued an Order calling upon the United States to take all possible measures to prevent the sentence being executed until the Court had reached a decision on Paraguay's claims on the merits. Despite this order and an appeal by the US Secretary of State, Madeleine Albright, to the Governor of Virginia to issue a stay of execution until the International Court had reached its decision on the merits, the sentence was carried out as set on 19 April 1998. The US Government formally apologized to Paraguay for failing to carry out its duties under the Vienna Convention and undertook to take measures aimed at preventing further recurrence of breaches of the Vienna Convention. This led to Paraguay deciding to discontinue further proceedings and following a request to the Court to this effect, the Court removed the case from the List on 10 November 1998.[79]

*****

2

Karl and Walter La Grand were both German nationals who had lived in the United States since they moved there with their mother as young children in 1967. In January 1982 they were arrested on suspicion of carrying out a bank robbery in the State of Arizona, whereby one of the bank employees had been killed and another seriously injured. They were charged and tried for serious offences, including murder, which potentially carries a death penalty and subsequently convicted in the District Court of the State of Arizona in February 1984.

Several aspects of the circumstances relating to the La Grand brothers resembled those relating to Angel Breard (see immediately above). Like Breard, the La Grand brothers were convicted in a state criminal court for serious criminal offences which carried the clear possibility of a death penalty. Likewise, the La Grand brothers were not informed of their rights as foreign nationals to seek consular assistance under the Vienna Convention on Consular Relations, due to the negligence of the relevant state (in this case Arizona) authorities. In the case of the La Grand brothers, the police and justice authorities were apparently initially unaware of the foreign nationality of the two defendants; however, even after the Arizona authorities became aware of the foreign nationality of the La Grand brothers, no effort was made to inform them of their right to seek consular assistance, nor was the German consulate made aware of their arrest and conviction until 1992, when the La Grand brothers sought contact with German consular officials on the basis of information they had obtained from a third party.

By this time, the criminal proceedings before the state courts of Arizona had been completed. Although appeals within the federal courts were undertaken with the assistance of the German consular authorities, the rule of 'procedural default', which had prevented the question of non-compliance with the Vienna Convention on the part of the state authorities in the case of Breard, likewise prevented the overturning of the death sentences against the La Grand brothers for virtually identical reasons. This was because the question of non-compliance with the Vienna Convention had not been brought up during proceedings before the state courts and the narrow exceptions to this rule were not considered pertinent in either of these cases. Consequently, there were similar backgrounds to the respective disputes.

At a late stage, Germany instituted proceedings against the United States before the International Court on 2 March 1999 only one day before the scheduled execution of Walter La Grand (Karl La Grand had already been executed a week earlier on 24 February 1999) on the basis of violation of Article 36 of the Vienna Convention, and simultaneously requested the indication of Provisional Measures aimed at staying the execution until the Court had reached a decision on the merits.

The Court acting *proprio motu* issued an Order hearing the parties on 3 March 1999, which called on the United States to take all possible measures to prevent the execution of Walter La Grand while the case was still pending. Following a rejection by the US Supreme Court of an appeal to stay the execution, the Governor of Arizona allowed the sentence to be carried out on 4 March 1999.

Although the US Government had admitted its non-compliance with the Vienna Convention and issued a formal apology to the German Government, the case proceeded to the merits and reached judgment on 27 June 2001. The German case rested on essentially four points. Firstly, that the United States had violated both the rights of Karl and Walter La Grand and Germany's own rights under the Vienna Convention. Secondly, that the rule of 'procedural default' as applied by the American federal courts stood in the way of compliance with the duty under the Vienna Convention to give 'full effect' to its provisions. Thirdly, that the US had violated a binding order of the International Court under Article 41 of the Court's Statute. It should be pointed out that this was the first time in the Court's history (including the Permanent Court of International Justice) that it had been squarely confronted with the question of the binding nature of its orders on Provisional Measures. Fourthly, Germany requested the Court to order the United States to provide Germany with an assurance of non-repetition of future violations of the Vienna Convention, and in particular in cases involving the death penalty to require "the United States to provide effective review of and remedies for criminal convictions impaired by a violation of the rights under Article 36" [of the Vienna Convention]. The United States, while admitting to violation of Article 36 of the Vienna Convention, called upon the Court to reject the other German submissions.

The Court ruled in Germany's favour by large majorities on all four points. It took note of the fact that the US Government had undertaken a large scale programme of education and training of law enforcement and prosecutorial authorities at both the federal and state levels aimed at ensuing compliance, and thereby had met Germany's request for the general assurance of non-repetition.

These cases, in particular the *La Grand* case, are of importance on two major points. Despite the relatively large amount of attention the *La Grand* case received in the media, the case had nothing to do with the legality of the death penalty *in abstracto* or with the way it is administered in the United States, a point which the Court emphasized in both cases. However, the Court's decision in the *La Grand* case makes clear that the right of consular assistance is both an individual right, as well as a right of the assisting State. Furthermore the Court's decision in *La Grand* has cleared up a longstanding controversy in favour of the binding nature of Provisional Measures under Article 41 of the Statute. This last point has implications well beyond the issues of consular protection.

SOVEREIGNTY OVER PULAU LIGITAN AND PULAU SIPADAN (INDONESIA V. MALAYSIA)

Indonesia and Malaysia have disagreed on the question of sovereignty over the islands Pulau Ligitan and Pulau Sipadan since 1969. On 31 May 1997, after a period of almost three decades during which the dispute was often dormant, the two States signed a Special Agreement to allow the ICJ to settle the dispute. After the Agreement entered into force on 14 May 1998, the States jointly notified the Court on 2 November 1998 to set the proceedings in motion. This joint action is exceptional as States in that region of the world rarely resort to third party binding dispute settlement. The Court was asked to determine whether Pulau Ligitan and Pulau Sipadan belong to Indonesia or to Malaysia. The Court would thereby not be precluded from allocating one island to each State. Both States appointed Judges *ad hoc*.

The two tiny islands are located in the Celebes Sea, close to the northeast coast of Borneo and near the land boundary between the Indonesian province of East Kalimantan and the Malaysian state of Sabah. The two States have not delimited their maritime zones in that area and the Court was also not asked to rule on this. Noteworthy, however, is the concave shape of the coastline and the fact that both islands are much closer to the Malaysian coast and situated only a few miles south of undisputed Malaysian islands and reefs. During the colonial era, Indonesia was governed by the Netherlands and Malaysia by Great Britain. While the Indonesian claim to the islands is mainly based on a 1891 Boundary Treaty between Great Britain and the Netherlands, the Malaysians rely on a 1878 Grant of the Sultan of Sulu as well as evidence of effective occupation.

In conformity with the time limits, the parties to the dispute had both filed Memorials, Counter-Memorials (time limits extended twice), and Replies and it was agreed that there was no need for a Rejoinder. The Replies were filed on 2 March 2001 and the oral hearings took place in June 2002. On 13 March 2001, notwithstanding the very advanced stage of the proceedings, the Philippines filed an application to intervene. This application was not based on a claim of sovereignty over the islands. However, the Philippines argued it should be allowed to intervene as a 'non-party', since the proceedings affected, at least potentially, the Philippine claim to sovereignty over North Borneo (Sabah). According to the Philippines, the heirs to the Sultan of Sulu ceded their rights over North Borneo to the Philippines in 1962. In 1963, however, the people in the territory chose to become part of Malaysia by means of a plebiscite organized by the United Nations. The crucial question for this application to intervene was whether the Philippines had a sufficiently strong legal interest. Requests for non-party intervention have rarely occurred in the Court's history and have been accepted only twice: in the El Salvador/Honduras case and the Cameroon/Nigeria case. Both Indonesia and Malaysia opposed the Philippine attempt at intervention on the grounds that it did not relate to the subject matter of the case.

After oral hearings in June 2001, the Court's Judgment of 23 October 2001 dismissed the Philippine request to intervene by fourteen votes to one. Judge Oda voted against and added a dissenting opinion. Judge Koroma and Judges *ad hoc* Weeramantry and Franck gave separate opinions and Judges Parra-Aranguren and Kooijmans added a declaration. The Court held *inter alia* that the application to intervene was not untimely as the Special Agreement had envisaged the possibility of the submission of Rejoinders after the Replies. On the main issue of the legal interest of the Philippines, the Court ruled that this interest did not need to be limited to the Court's Judgment alone, but could also relate to the Court's reasoning or interpretation of relevant treaties. Under such circumstances, however, the intervening State is charged with the burden of proving with a particular clarity and by means of documentary evidence, that such a related interest exists. The many instruments put forward by the Philippines were unable to meet this test. Nevertheless, the Philippines will not be bound by the Judgment on the merits. Judge *ad hoc* Franck, in his separate opinion, argued that the Court should have rejected the Philippine intervention as the historic title of Philippine cannot prevail in light of the overriding right of self-determination that was consumed by means of the abovementioned plebiscite in 1963.

The wider significance of this ruling lies in the Court's qualified confirmation of a right for non-party intervention. This represents a modest progressive development in relation to previous case law, such as the Court's treatment of Malta's intervention in the Libya/Tunisia case (see p. 178 above). However, the scope of this right is seriously curtailed by charging intervening States with a very considerable burden of proof. In his dissenting opinion, Judge Oda objected to the Court's approach, which he perceived as particularly unfair in cases like these where the intervener did not have access to the written pleadings and only a vague idea of the parties' legal arguments.

Following the oral hearings in mid 2002, the Court reached its Judgment on the Merits on 17 December 2002. The Court found by a near unanimous majority that neither Indonesia, nor Malaysia could prove a title on the basis of the treaties concluded during the colonial era. However, the Court determined that Malaysia had the more convincing title based upon the so-called *effectivités* (activities of the [former] Sovereign Powers on the disputed territory), over a long period of time.

GUINEA BRINGS A CASE TO THE COURT

On 28 September 1998, Guinea instituted proceedings against the Democratic Republic of the Congo (formerly known as Zaire) "with a view to diplomatic protection" of one of its nationals, Mr. Ahamadou Sadio Diallo. Guinea brought its case on the basis of a unilateral application in which it referred to the Optional Clause declarations under Article 36(2) of the Statute as the basis of the Court's jurisdiction.

In its Application, Guinea alleged that Mr. Sadio Diallo, a Guinean businessman who had been a resident of the Congo for over thirty years, had been unlawfully imprisoned for two and a half months, divested of important financial assets and subsequently expelled from the Congo in February 1996, when he had tried to recover sums allegedly owed to him by the Congolese Government and by a number of mining and oil companies operating in the Congo.

The Court fixed time limits for the filing of written pleadings in an Order dated 25 November 1999. These were subsequently extended at the request of Guinea, in an Order dated 8 September 2000, to 23 March 2001 for the filing of the Guinean Memorial and 4 October 2002 for the filing of the Counter Memorial of the Democratic Republic of the Congo.[82]

The Case is not expected to proceed to oral hearings before well into 2003.

PROBLEMS OF THE RIVER DANUBE

In 1977 Hungary and Czechoslovakia signed a treaty for the construction and joint operation of the Gabčíkovo-Nagymaros System of Locks (1977 Treaty). The project was designed to result in a large, integrated complex of structures and installations on a stretch of approximately 200 kilometers of the Danube river located between the two countries. The joint investment was aimed at the production of hydroelectricity, the improvement of navigation in this part of the Danube and flood control. The two States would contribute on an equal basis in respect of financing, construction and operation of the works. Work on the project started in 1978 and continued at a varying pace in subsequent years. Following growing awareness of the potential environmental consequences of the project, Hungary decided in 1988 on a re-evaluation of the matter, leading to the suspension of works on the Hungarian side of the frontier in 1989. After protests and failed negotiations, Czechoslovakia decided to develop an alternative solution to dam the river unilaterally. Hungary responded by claiming that this alternative solution would adversely affect its access to the water of the Danube and terminated the 1977 Treaty in May 1992. In October 1992 Czechoslovakia proceeded with the diversion of the Danube on its territory.

On 23 October 1992 Hungary filed a unilateral application against what was then known as the Czech and Slovak Federal Republic. Hungary recognized that there was no jurisdiction in this case, and invited the respondent to accept the jurisdiction, on the basis of Article 38, paragraph 5, of the Rules, a provision which was introduced in 1978 (see p. 74 above). In accordance with that Rule of Court, this application was transmitted to the respondent, which did not consent to the jurisdiction. No further action was therefore taken on that application, and the case was not entered in the Court's General List.

Negotiations were then conducted between the Parties through the mediation of the Commission of the European Communities, which lead to an agreement to submit the dispute to the Court. On 7 April 1993 Hungary and Slovakia, which by then had become an independent State, signed a special agreement that was filed in Court on 2 July 1993. The special agreement recorded that the Slovak Republic is the sole successor State of the Czech and Slovak Federal Republic in respect of rights and obligations relating to the Gabčíkovo-Nagymaros project. The Parties put three specific questions to the Court regarding the lawfulness of each State's conduct and also asked it to determine the legal consequences of its conclusions. The Court was requested to decide whether Hungary was entitled to suspend and subsequently abandon the works on the project; whether Slovakia was entitled to proceed with its alternative provisional solution and to put this system into operation; and what the legal consequences were of the notification of the termination of the 1977 Treaty by Hungary (see for the questions submitted to the Court pp. 94-95 above). The special agreement went on to deal with provisional measures pending the final judgment of the Court, and excluded the right of either party to apply to the Court itself for an indication of provisional measures.

In the written proceedings each of the Parties filed a Memorial, a Counter-Memorial and a Reply accompanied by a large number of annexes. Shortly before the beginning of the hearings Slovakia requested to produce additional documents, which the Court allowed in accordance with Article 56, paragraph 2 of the Rules. Both Parties were allowed to comment on these documents. The hearings were held between 3 March and 15 April 1997. Between those dates the members of the Court paid a visit to the

Gabčíkovo-Nagymaros project site, as well as Bratislava and Budapest in accordance with Article 66 of the Rules.

The Court delivered its judgment on 25 September 1997. It found by various majorities that both Hungary and Slovakia were in breach of their legal obligations. The Court ruled (by fourteen votes to one) that Hungary was not entitled to suspend and subsequently abandon the works on the project, rejecting Hungary's claim to "a state of ecological necessity". By a large majority (eleven votes to four) it also rejected the arguments put forward by Hungary in support of the lawfulness and effectiveness of its unilateral termination of the 1977 Treaty, finding that the treaty continued to be in force between the Parties. Hungary had relied on five defenses to support the lawfulness and effectiveness of its notification of termination of the treaty: the existence of a state of necessity; the impossibility of performance of the 1977 Treaty; the occurrence of a fundamental change of circumstances; the material breach of the 1977 Treaty by Czechoslovakia; and the development of new norms of international environmental law. The Court rejected all of these arguments, noting that the 1977 Treaty could have been terminated only on the basis of the limited grounds contained in the 1969 Vienna Convention on the Law of Treaties and that Hungary could not rely on any of these grounds in this particular case. The Court also ruled (by nine votes to six) that Czechoslovakia was within its rights to proceed with its alternative solution in November 1991, but found (by ten votes to five) that it was not entitled to put it unilaterally into operation.

In the second part of the decision the Court determined the future conduct of the Parties. It first held (by twelve votes to three) that Slovakia, as successor to Czechoslovakia, had become party to the 1977 Treaty on 1 January 1993. It then called on both States (by thirteen votes to two) to negotiate in good faith in order to ensure the achievement of the objectives of the 1977 Treaty, which it declared was still in force, while taking into account the factual situation that had developed since 1989. The Court also found (by thirteen votes to two) that a joint operational regime was to be established in accordance with the 1977 Treaty and indicated (by twelve votes to three) that each Party should compensate the other for damage incurred by the wrongful conduct of the other. President Schwebel and Judge Rezek appended declarations; Vice-President Weeramantry and Judges Bedjaoui and Koroma appended separate opinions; Judge Oda, Ranjeva, Hecxegh, Fleishhauer, Vereshchetin and Parra-Aranguren and Judge *ad hoc* Skubiszewski appended dissenting opinions.

The judgment is a good example of how the Court attempts to resolve a dispute in a manner that is acceptable to all Parties. By finding both Parties in breach of their legal obligations and by requiring them to negotiate a solution that will allow the project to continue within the bounds of the 1977 Treaty, provided present realities and new and evolving norms of international environmental law are taken into account, the Court has attempted to accommodate the interests of both Parties. This approach was not without success, as the judgment was welcomed in both countries. However, the dispute still remained to be resolved, as the Court had only provided the basic parameters for the Parties to resolve it themselves.

Following the judgment, the two governments conducted a series of negotiations. A framework agreement was drafted, which was approved by the Slovakian government on 10 March 1998. The Hungarian government did not, however, approve it and indicated that it did not provide an adequate basis for the execution of the Court's judgment. On 3 September 1998 Slovakia filed a request for an additional judgment in view of the unwillingness of Hungary to implement the judgment delivered by the Court. Slovakia invoked Article 5, paragraph 3 of the 1993 special agreement that allows either of the States to request an additional judgment to determine the modalities for executing the judgment of the Court in case they are not able to reach agreement within six months after the rendering of the judgment. On 7 October 1998 the Court requested Hungary to file by 7 December 1998 a written statement of its position on the request for an additional judgment. Hungary complied with this request and the Parties met with the Court's President shortly thereafter. The Court has taken no further action in this case since then. The Parties have continued to work towards a solution through direct negotiations.[83]

The case concerning *Gabčíkovo-Nagymaros Project* is significant in several respects. The judgment delivered by the Court contains some important pronouncements on State responsibility and provides a textbook example of the law relating to the termination of treaties. It will be remembered most, however, as the first case in which the Court has considered the concept of sustainable development and the relationship between international environmental law, the law of treaties and international watercourses law. The Court's indication that new international norms and standards have to be taken into consideration and given proper weight not only when States contemplate new activities but also when continuing activities begun in the past may have implications for many similar cases. The judgment did not, however, refer to sustainable development as a legal obligation, nor did it identify which norms and standards were precisely to be taken into consideration by the Parties. Only Vice-President Weeramantry referred explicitly in his elaborate separate opinion to the principle of sustainable development as a "principle with normative value" that is an integral part of contemporary international law. He also hinted to several procedural and substantive principles that could be considered as constituent parts of the wider principle of sustainable development, including precaution and environmental impact assessment.

ARMED ACTIVITIES IN THE CONGO I

On 23 June 1999 the Democratic Republic of the Congo (formerly known as Zaire) instituted proceedings against three neighbouring States: Uganda, Rwanda and Burundi; alleging violations of the Charters of the United Nations and the Organization of African Unity, certain other multilateral conventions including the Geneva Conventions of 1949 with their Additional Protocols of 1977, the Montreal Convention of 1971 Concerning the Safety of Civil Aviation, and the Convention against Torture of 1984, as well as other principles of customary international law. According to the Congo's Applications, which were filed simultaneously but in three separate proceedings against the respective Respondent States, these violations constituted armed aggression aimed at overthrowing the incumbent Congolese Government. Additionally, the Congo claimed that the three States were responsible for widespread violations of the humanitarian law of armed conflict, and human rights violations, as well as for the unlawful shooting down of a Congolese civil airliner in October 1998.

The jurisdictional basis relied upon by the Congo in its Application against Uganda differed significantly from that it was forced to rely upon in its Applications against Rwanda and Burundi. In the former case, there were 'Optional Clause' declarations by both Parties in force, neither of which contained any reservations other than the condition of reciprocity. This provided a clear potential basis for the wide ranging claims which the Congo had brought against Uganda. However, neither of the other two Respondent States, Rwanda and Burundi had issued a declaration accepting the Court's compulsory jurisdiction. Consequently, the Congo was forced to rely upon the compromissory clauses contained in the 1971 Montreal Convention on the Safety of Civil Aviation and the 1984 Torture Convention, whereby the jurisdictional basis for such widely ranging claims was more tenuous from the outset.

Predictably, both Rwanda and Burundi raised preliminary objections with the first round of pleadings being consequently directed exclusively to the question of the Court's jurisdiction. After the fixing of time limits in all three cases, the Congo subsequently requested the discontinuance of the proceedings against Rwanda and Burundi on 15 January 2001 and those cases were consequently removed from the Court's General List in an Order which was issued by the Court on 30 January 2001.[84]

The case between the Congo and Uganda has taken a different course, largely due to the different and less tenuous jurisdictional basis which was referred to previously. Uganda did not raise any preliminary objections and there are no apparent jurisdictional barriers which would prevent the case going forward on the merits in the absence of other developments.

Approximately a year after the initiation of proceedings, the Congo issued a request for the indication of provisional measures aimed at securing the withdrawal of Ugandan troops from Congolese territory. After written statements and hearings relating to this request had been delivered, the Court unanimously decided on 1 July 2000, to indicate provisional measures directing both Parties to abstain from any action which could prejudice the rights of the other Party or which could aggravate the dispute, in addition to calling upon the Parties to respect their obligations under international law, including compliance with a relevant Security Council resolutions and full respect for fundamental human rights and applicable provisions of humanitarian law.[85]

The case on the merits proceeded along the normal lines. Within the time limits set by the Court for the filing of written pleadings, Uganda filed its memorial containing a number of counter claims directed at the Congo under the relevant provision of the Rules of Court. Since the Congo objected that the Ugandan counter claim did not meet the requirements laid down in the Rules that counter claims be sufficiently linked to the subject matter of the primary claim, the Court directed the Parties to present written statements relating to the question of the admissibility of the counter claims. On 29 November 2001, the Court issued an Order in which it determined that two of Uganda's counter claims were admissible, while a third was deemed to be insufficiently linked to the subject matter of the claims of the Congo and was correspondingly ruled inadmissible.

The case on the merits will proceed in the light of this decision with an additional round of written proceedings, with the possibility of the Congo being given a further opportunity to present its views in writing a second time on the Ugandan counter claims. Consequently, the written phase of the proceedings will probably not be finished before sometime in 2003.

The case is without doubt a significant one in view of the wide ranging allegations of the Parties and the delicate political situation in a deeply troubled region which has seen more than its share of instability, conflict and serious breakdown of international law in recent years.

TENSIONS BETWEEN PAKISTAN AND INDIA

The relations between Pakistan and India have been tense and troubled ever since their independence in 1947. These relations have been marked by frequent border incidents; three occasions of which have erupted into armed conflict, and have resulted in two earlier cases being brought before the Court, both of which were subsequently discontinued (see above p. 166).

In August 1999 a Pakistan military aircraft was shot down in the vicinity of the border region between the two countries, with the wreckage of the plane, a naval patrol aircraft, being located some 2 km inside Pakistani territory.

On 21 September 1999, Pakistan filed an Application alleging unlawful use of armed force, and basing the Court's jurisdiction upon the Optional Clause declarations of the two countries and additionally upon the General Act for the Peaceful Settlement of Disputes of 1928. India lodged Preliminary Objections in November 1999 and the Court determined that a first round of written and oral pleadings would deal exclusively with the question of the Court's jurisdiction and fixed time limits. The parties submitted their respective memorials within these time limits and hearings were conducted in early April 2000. Since neither party had a judge of its nationality on the Court, both appointed a judge *ad hoc* for the case.

In its Judgment of 21 June 2000, the Court determined that it lacked jurisdiction on either the basis of the Optional Clause, or the General Act of 1928.[86] The Court reached its decision by a 14-2 majority, basing its decision upon the 'Commonwealth Reservation' contained in India's Optional Clause declaration, which excludes the Court's jurisdiction in disputes with any other member State of the Commonwealth of Nations, and upon an Indian notification of 1974, in which it declared that it had never considered itself bound by the acceptance of the General Act of 1928 by its predecessor State British India.

In an *obiter dictum* the Court pointed out that the absence of jurisdiction did not relieve the two States from the general obligation to resolve their disputes peaceably. Be that as it may, there is little likelihood of the Court playing a role in that process under present circumstances.

MARITIME DELIMITATION BETWEEN NICARAGUA AND HONDURAS IN THE CARIBBEAN SEA

On 8 December 1999 Nicaragua instituted proceedings against Honduras with regard to legal issues subsisting between the two States concerning maritime delimitation in the Caribbean Sea. Nicaragua and Honduras have had a long-standing dispute concerning their Caribbean maritime boundary. Nicaragua asserts that the maritime boundary between the two States has not been determined, whereas Honduras maintains that there already exists a delimitation line on the parallel of latitude that runs straight easterly from the terminal point of the land-boundary that was settled by the Court in 1960. The disagreement on the maritime boundary has led to several confrontations and mutual seizure of vessels of both nations in and around the general border area. Efforts to resolve the dispute through diplomatic channels were unsuccessful. The situation was further aggravated when Honduras concluded a maritime boundary agreement with Colombia in 1986 that applied the same parallel of latitude for the delimitation as the one claimed by Honduras as the boundary with Nicaragua. Nicaragua protested against the conclusion of this bilateral agreement, but as a third party it was unable to directly launch a legal challenge against it. After a delay of more than ten years, Honduras ratified the boundary agreement on 30 November 1999. A week later Nicaragua instituted proceedings against Honduras before the Court.

In its application Nicaragua requests the Court "to determine the course of the single maritime boundary between the areas of territorial sea, continental shelf and exclusive economic zone appertaining respectively to Nicaragua and Honduras, in accordance with equitable principles and relevant circumstances recognized by general international law as applicable to such a delimitation of a single maritime boundary." Nicaragua's application acknowledges the right of the Court to establish "different delimitations, for shelf rights and fisheries respectively" in case "this course should be necessary in order to achieve an equitable solution."

As a basis for the jurisdiction of the Court, Nicaragua has invoked Article XXXI of the American Treaty on Pacific Settlement of 30 April 1948 to which both Nicaragua and Honduras are Parties, as well as the compulsory jurisdiction under Article 36(2) of the Statute of the Court.

The case is currently in the stage of the written proceedings. On 21 March 2000 the Court issued an order fixing the time limits for the filing of the written pleadings. Nicaragua was requested to file its Memorial by 21 March 2001. Honduras was to file its Counter-Memorial by 21 March 2002. Both States complied with these requests.[87]

IMMUNITY OF A FOREIGN MINISTER

On 17 October 2000, the Democratic Republic of the Congo (formerly known as Zaire) instituted proceedings against Belgium concerning an international arrest warrant issued *in absentia* by a Belgian examining magistrate against Mr. Abdulaye Yerodia Ndombasi, the then Acting Minister for Foreign Affairs of the Congo, for alleged war crimes and crimes against humanity. The arrest warrant had been issued pursuant to a Belgian law on the prosecution and punishment of grave violations of international humanitarian law and crimes against humanity.

This law which was originally adopted in 1993 and subsequently amended in 1999 had occasioned a significant amount of interest and commentary in that it provided for criminal jurisdiction of a universal character, even in cases where there was no link between the alleged offence and Belgium, including situations when the alleged offender was not present on Belgian territory, as was the case in this instance. The warrant had been transmitted through INTERPOL to all States and sought the detention and subsequent extradition of the Congolese Foreign Minister.

Simultaneously with its Application, the Congo requested the Court to indicate provisional measures aimed at the immediate withdrawal of the arrest warrant. The Congo referred in its Application in rather general terms to Belgium's acceptance of the Court's jurisdiction and its own Application as the basis for the Court's jurisdiction. In point of fact, both Belgium and the Congo have issued 'Optional Clause' declarations accepting the Court's compulsory jurisdiction and it was on the basis of these that the Court subsequently based its jurisdiction in the course of the further proceedings.

The Court determined in an Order issued 8 December 2000, that notwithstanding the existence of a *prima facie* jurisdictional basis, there was insufficient urgency to require the indication of provisional measures, since Mr. Yerodia Ndombasi had moved from the Foreign Ministry to the position of Minister for Education as a result of a cabinet reshuffle. However, the Court also rejected a Belgian request that the case be removed from the General List on the basis of the contention that as a result of the cabinet reshuffle, whereby Mr. Yerodia Ndombasi had ceased to be Foreign Minister, the Application had become without object.

Within the time limits set by the Court for the filing of written pleadings, Belgium requested the Court to derogate from the agreed procedure in view of the fact that Mr. Yerodia Ndombasi had meanwhile ceased to be a member of the Congolese Government. This request by Belgium was likewise rejected by the Court, and new time limits were set with the agreement of the Congo on the understanding that the written pleadings would address all questions relating to preliminary objections and the merits at the same time.

In its Application, the Congo had relied on two separate legal complaints. Firstly, it claimed that Belgium's assertion of universal jurisdiction violated the principle of the sovereign equality of states and the concomitant duty to refrain from exercising State authority on the territory of another State. Secondly, the Congo claimed that Belgium's failure to recognize the immunity of an incumbent Minister for Foreign Affairs constituted a violation of the diplomatic immunity of sovereign State. However, during the course of the proceedings and in its final submissions, the Congo dropped the first of these grounds for complaint and based its cases solely on the question of Belgium's alleged violation of the immunity of an incumbent Foreign Minister under customary international law. For its part, Belgium put forward a number of preliminary objections disputing the Court's jurisdiction and the admissibility of the dispute, and in the alternative requested the Court to reject the Congo's submissions on the merits.

The Court's decision, which was handed down on 17 February 2002, rejected by near unanimous votes all of Belgium's objections relating to the Court's jurisdiction and the admissibility of the dispute. In relation to the merits, the shift in the Congo's litigation strategy with the dropping of the first of its legal complaints meant that the Court was only called upon to rule on the second of the Congo's arguments relating to the immunity of incumbent Foreign Ministers.

The Court determined by thirteen votes to three, that the issue and circulation of the arrest warrant had violated legal obligations owed by Belgium towards the Congo through failure to respect customary international law. By a smaller majority of ten votes to six, the Court directed Belgium to inform all concerned parties of this fact by means of its own choosing. The case is significant in that the Court has clarified the question of the immunity of incumbent Foreign Ministers, and by implication of incumbent Heads of State and Heads of Government from the criminal jurisdiction of the national courts of foreign States. However, the Court was unable and probably unwilling, even in the form of *obiter dicta*, to pronounce upon the question of the scope of universal jurisdiction, due to the dropping by the Congo of the first of its claims.[88]

Undoubtedly, this will remain a point of controversy in the coming period until such time that an opportunity arises to clarify what the scope of universal jurisdiction is. In view of the rapid developments in international criminal law, it was probably wise of the Court to refrain from speaking out when this was not required in order to reach a judgment.

CERTAIN PROPERTY OF LIECHTENSTEIN

On 1 June 2001, the Principality of Liechtenstein instituted proceedings against Germany concerning "decisions of Germany... to treat certain property of Liechtenstein nationals as German assets... seized for the purposes of reparation or restitution as a consequence of World War II... without ensuing any compensation".[89]

At the close of World War II, Czechoslovakia seized German property and the property of persons of German ethnicity, including the property of Liechtenstein nationals on its territory as reparations for the German occupation. In 1952 Germany signed a Convention on the "Settlement of Matters Arising Out of the War" whereby it undertook not to raise objections against measures which had been taken in relation to German external assets or property, "seized for the purpose of reparations or restitution, or as a result of the state of war'. According to Liechtenstein's Application an understanding was subsequently reached between the German and Liechtenstein Governments in which it was stipulated that this Settlement Convention did not apply to Liechtenstein assets and property, in view of Liechtenstein's separate legal personality and neutrality during the War. Additionally according to Liechtenstein, it was understood that the seizure of Liechtenstein property would be deemed to be unlawful and that German courts would not be barred from considering claims relating to such property.

In 1998, the German Federal Constitutional Court determined that a painting claimed as the property of the reigning Prince of Liechtenstein fell within the terms of the Settlement Convention. The Prince had attempted to have the painting returned while it was on loan from the Czech Republic to an exhibition in a museum in Cologne Germany. By this decision of Germany's highest court, Liechtenstein alleges that the understanding between Germany and itself concerning the non-applicability of the Settlement Convention to seized Liechtenstein property had been violated. Diplomatic protests by Liechtenstein to the German Government were unsuccessful, and in further consultations, the German position was that all Liechtenstein property fell within the regime of the Settlement Convention, according to Liechtenstein's Application.

The case has been brought on the basis of the 1957 European Convention on the Peaceful Settlement of Disputes. Germany raised preliminary objections in June 2002 and the Court will deal with that shortly.

TERRITORIAL AND MARITIME DELIMITATION DISPUTE BETWEEN NICARAGUA AND COLOMBIA

On 6 December 2001 Nicaragua filed an application instituting proceedings against Colombia concerning title to territory and maritime delimitation in the western Caribbean. The dispute revolves around several islands and keys and the surrounding maritime areas in the western Caribbean that are claimed by both States. Nicaragua asserts that the islands and keys became part of its territory in 1838 after the dissolution of the Federation of Central American States and that they have remained an integral part of Nicaraguan territory ever since. Colombia's claim is based on a treaty (the Bárcenas-Esguerra Treaty) that was concluded between Nicaragua and Colombia on 24 March 1928.

In this treaty Colombia recognized Nicaraguan sovereignty over the Mosquito Coast in exchange for recognition by Nicaragua of Colombian sovereignty over the disputed islands. Nicaragua contests the validity of this treaty, among others on the basis of the argument that it was concluded when Nicaragua was under the control of the United States. In its application Nicaragua requests the Court to declare that Nicaragua has sovereignty over the islands and keys. The case has also an important maritime delimitation dimension, because Nicaragua and Colombia have made overlapping claims to the maritime space surrounding the islands and keys. In its application Nicaragua requests the Court to determine the single maritime boundary between the areas of continental shelf and exclusive economic zone appertaining respectively to Nicaragua and Colombia.

There is a close relationship between this case and the above-mentioned maritime delimitation case that was brought to the Court by Nicaragua against Honduras in December 1999. The maritime boundary agreement that was concluded between Colombia and Honduras in 1986 implicitly recognized Colombian sovereignty over the disputed islands and keys. Nicaragua denounced this treaty as a violation of its territorial sovereignty and rights and has protested against actions to put it into effect. Colombia and Honduras ratified the maritime boundary agreement in November 1999. These actions and the failure to resolve the conflicts through direct negotiations were the main reason for Nicaragua to institute proceedings before the Court against both States.

As a basis for the jurisdiction of the Court, Nicaragua has invoked Article XXXI of the American Treaty on Pacific Settlement of 30 April 1948 to which both Nicaragua and Colombia are Parties, as well as the compulsory jurisdiction under Article 36(2) of the Statute of the Court. Colombia withdrew its declaration of acceptance of the compulsory jurisdiction of the Court under Article 36(2) shortly before Nicaragua instituted proceedings, but it has not invoked this to challenge the jurisdiction of the Court in this case.

The case is currently in the stage of the written proceedings. On 26 February 2002 the Court issued an order fixing the time limits for the filing of the written pleadings. Nicaragua was requested to file its Memorial by 28 April 2003 and Colombia its Counter-Memorial by 28 June 2004.[90]

ARMED ACTIVITIES IN THE CONGO II

On 28 May 2002, the Democratic Republic of the Congo (formerly known as Zaire) filed a new Application against Rwanda. In its Application, the Congo alleges "massive, serious and flagrant violations of human rights and of international humanitarian law" resulting "from acts of armed aggression perpetrated by Rwanda on the territory of the Democratic Republic of the Congo…"

Simultaneously with its Application, the Congo filed a Request for the Indication of Provisional Measures aimed at "preventing further irreparable harm "against its rights and to those of its population" pending the Court's final decision.

The Congo based its Application and Request for Provisional Measures on the compromissory clauses of a large number of multilateral conventions, including *inter alia,* the 1948 Genocide Convention, the 1984 Torture Convention, the 1965 Convention on the Elimination of All Forms of Discrimination, the 1979 Convention on the Elimination of All Forms of Racial Discrimination Against Women and the 1971 Montreal Convention for the Suppression of Unlawful Acts Against the Safety of Civil Aviation.

The Court held hearings on the Congo's Request for Provisional Measures on 13-14 June 2002, and reached its decision on that request on 10 July 2002, whereby it determined that it lacked *prima facie* jurisdiction to indicate provisional measures on the one hand, but rejected Rwanda's request that the case be removed from the General List on the basis of a manifest lack of jurisdiction on the other.

After meeting with the Parties, the Court fixed the time limits for the filing of written pleadings dealing with the Court's jurisdiction and the admissibility of the dispute. These time limits were set at 20 January 2003 for the Rwandan Memorial and 20 May 2003 for the Congolese Counter-Memorial.[91]

BENIN AND NIGER JOINTLY SUBMIT A BOUNDARY DISPUTE

On 11 April 2002, Benin and Niger jointly filed a Special Agreement with the Court. The Special Agreement relates to a boundary dispute between the two western African States and requests the Court to determine the course of the boundary in the sectors of the Niger and Mekrou rivers and determine the status of the islands in the Niger River, in particular Lété Island.

The Special Agreement requests the Court to refer the case to a Chamber consisting of three Members of the Court, together with two Judges *ad hoc* appointed by the respective Parties.

On 27 November 2002, the Court unanimously decided to accede to this request and formed a Special Chamber on 20 December 2002 consisting of President Guillaume, Judges Ranjeva and Kooijmans, together with Judge *ad hoc* Bedjaoui for Niger and Judge *ad hoc* Bannouna for Benin. The Court further set the time limit for the filing of a Memorial by each Party at 27 August 2003. The Parties further undertook to preserve peaceful and normal relations pending decision by the Chamber.[92]

This is a good example of two States approaching the Court in a spirit of cooperation, when they fail to reach agreement through negotiations.

7

AN ASSESSMENT

The title of the present edition of this work is "Rosenne's The World Court: What it is and how it works".

In keeping with the "spirit" of the title, I have chosen to maintain as much of the text of the previous edition as possible; adding, rewording and editing only where it seemed necessary. This applies in my view to the concluding chapter in particular, as reflecting the views of the foremost authority on the International Court of Justice. Consequently, the following assessment is largely taken from the previous edition. Starting from p. 238 below, I have added a few of my own assessments of the Court's work in recent years and made a number of observations concerning some of the challenges and opportunities facing the Court since the appearance of the last edition. Needless to say, views and assessments expressed by each of us are personal and do not necessarily represent the views of the other.

T.D. Gill

* * * *

During the first 48 years of its existence, from 1946 to the end of December 1993,94 cases have been referred to the Court. Seventy-two were contentious cases (nine cases where the Court would only have jurisdiction if the respondent accepted the invitation to litigate, contained in the application), and the remaining 22 were requests for advisory opinion. These figures, especially when compared with those of the Permanent Court, have led many observers to the view that the contribution which the present Court has been able to make to the pacific settlement of legal disputes has been less than that of the Permanent Court. But in the long run, the bare figures may be misleading as the point of departure for an evaluation of the role of the Court in the international scene today.

The figures themselves are not without interest, for they demonstrate that the real and substantial decline is in the number of requests for advisory opinion. It is quite clear that the modem political organs encounter great difficulties in mustering the majority to support a request for an advisory opinion, especially as an incident in the settlement of a political dispute of which they are seised.

On the substance, there are some striking differences between the kind of dispute brought before the Permanent Court and those coming before the present Court. As seen, the Permanent Court had much to do with marginal disputes closely connected with the major sources of international tension in the inter-War period, but it had little to do with other conflicts. Indeed, interpretation of the Peace Treaties of 1919 was one of its major preoccupations. The present Court, after a hesitant start which was not really successful, has not been required to deal with legal aspects of political disputes related even marginally to the settlement after the Second World War, and of other disputes, such as the Middle East (in the broadest sense) or the Indian Sub-Continent, it has only had to examine some peripheral incidents. This naturally has affected the amount of business brought before the Court. This is not necessarily a disadvantage, for it has freed the Court from what might have been misguided efforts to find legal solutions for conflicts which are not really legal disputes at all.

On the other hand (and leaving aside what might be termed routine legal disputes between States, of which the present Court has possibly had more than its predecessor), the Court has been invited to determine central legal issues of several other major international disputes. Some of these, in reality conflicts of interests and of national aspirations, even contained sufficient elements to give rise to concern that they might constitute a threat to international peace, if not on a universal scale then at least on a regional scale. The International Court has shown that when States are agreed that the time is ripe for a final settlement of a given dispute, it can assist them and the competent regional organizations, if they so desire, to reach that objective. That is the lesson of some of the major tension-ridden disputes that have come before the Court, the various fisheries and delimitation (maritime and terrestrial) cases, for example. On the other hand, if there is no underlying political agreement, as in *Anglo-Iranian Oil Co.* or *Right of Passage,* the Court has shown that its procedures can assist in deflecting the tension into peaceful channels so as to enable constructive diplomacy to operate.

The advisory process is dominated by *two* characteristic ambiguities. The first is the absence from the proceedings themselves of "parties" in the strict sense of the term. The second ambiguity is that the judicial pronouncement does not have the quality of *res judicata* with the obligation of compliance, whatever else it might be. (This does not prevent an agreement outside the Court proceedings from conferring a decisive or binding quality on an advisory opinion, but strictly speaking that is not a matter for the Court in the exercise of its general discretion whether to give an advisory opinion at all.) In addition, in the thesaurus of international legal norms and the manner of their creation, a resolution of a competent international organ adopting an advisory opinion, whatever language it uses to do this, has no inherent status distinguishing it from any other resolution of that organ, according to the constituent instrument of the organization in question.

Features such as these may have influenced the attitude of States towards the advisory competence. A report by the Sixth (Legal) Committee of the General Assembly in 1971 alluded to this in guarded terms when it recalled that an extension of the Court's advisory role could be prejudicial to its contentious jurisdiction proper, which under the Statute was its primary responsibility.[1]

An arresting feature of the work of the present Court is its variety, and the novelty of the objects of the litigation. The substantive work is far from being confined to issues of the interpretation or the application of treaties, which many people consider to have been the most prominent feature of the work of the Permanent Court. A great number of completely novel problems have been brought before the present Court, covering vast areas of international social and legal relationships previously untouched by the international judge. This demonstrates an undercurrent of willingness of States to agree to refer to the Court complicated issues of fact and of law, and the readiness of the Court to face up to them, given the necessary political consents.

This has a dimension in space as well as in matter.

In space, what is noticeable is the virtually complete universalization of the dispute settlement work of the Court. The Court has had to deal with disputes between States of Western Europe, North America, Latin America, Asia, Africa, Arab States, the Pacific and disputes with Socialist States of Eastern Europe. There have been transcontinental disputes embracing half the world. The cases before the present Court have related to vast areas of our planet. The Court has become truly planetary.

In matter too the Court has had to deal with cases involving the lives and the well-being of huge numbers of men and women. Much of this aspect of the Court's work has been concerned with the sea, and there is little doubt that the reconstruction of the law of the sea embodied in the United Nations Convention on the Law of the Sea of 10 December 1982 would not have been possible without the important clarifications made by the Court. Or, to move on: Who amongst my generation when we were students ever imagined having to advise –let alone argue in Court –on questions of atomic energy or nuclear power, or nuclear arms, or of the risks of radiation or the disposal of toxic or other hazardous wastes in the world's oceans, or other ecological disasters? Yet cases involving nuclear tests in the high atmosphere have been brought before the Court. Who had heard of the vast and untapped resources of the continental shelf? The list could be prolonged, and it is surely only a matter of time before the Court will be confronted with questions arising from activities in outer space. With all this, the Court as a collectivity, and its individual members, have shown that given the necessary co-operation of the parties, it can face up to new topics such as these. On the other hand, if all the parties are not willing for the Court to deal with such a case, either the Court will be unable to deal with it at all (sometimes a wise course if it thinks that a formal crystallization of the law through a judicial decision could be premature), or that its decisions will not be acceptable to those to whom they are addressed.

It is often said that the expectations generated by the decision of the San Francisco Conference to make the Court a principal organ of the United Nations, and which led to an assumption that the new Court would playa major role in the pacific settlement of international disputes, have not been fully realized. The prime cause for this is the high degree of international tension of universal spread left by the Second World War in its wake, and which is still with us even if it is diminishing. From that point of departure, there are other many and complex reasons for this state of affairs, and are only partly due to the general attitude of reserve towards the Court manifested by some of the major contemporary world Powers. There prevails in the world today a widespread questioning of the contemporary international law, and with it a reassessment of the true role of an international court. This feeling is based on the view that for the greater part international law is the inherited product of European imperialism and colonialism and does not take sufficient account of the completely changed pattern of international relationships now existing. The prolonged discussions in the United Nations and elsewhere on the codification and the progressive development of international law are the focal point for this feeling.

What is perhaps not sufficiently appreciated is that in this situation, the International Court has shown itself sympathetic towards this attitude of questioning. Careful scrutiny of its record may lead to the conclusion that it has always been alert to current trends of internationalist thought. In that respect it has performed a major service to the international community as a whole, because the need to bring international law into line with present-day requirements is real and urgent. It can be a basic assumption that in most instances of international litigation, the cases of the parties are finely balanced, and that the decision is reached by a process of choice enabling the majority of the Court to arrive at a decision which it considers just and tenable in the circumstances. Many observers feel that several of the great cases decided since 1946 would have been decided differently by the Permanent Court. The International Court does not support charges of rigid conservatism said to be a characteristic of the law. If anything, it is the

International Court, together with the International Law Commission, which has infused new dynamism into the international law of today.

* * * *

Since Shabtai Rosenne wrote his assessments of the Court's work for the previous edition, a number of the developments and trends which he commented upon have continued to evolve and new challenges and opportunities for the Court have presented themselves.

The first of these is that the Court is busier than ever. Since the work on the previous edition was completed in February 1994, some 30 contentious cases and 2 further advisory cases have been presented to the Court. Even if one takes into account the fact that the total for the contentious cases includes three requests for examination, interpretation or revision of previous judgments; and that 10 of the remaining 27 cases concern what is essentially one dispute, that between Yugoslavia and the member States of the NATO alliance relating to the Kosovo conflict, this is nevertheless an indication of the steadily increasing interest in the Court, both as instrument of diplomacy, as well as in its role in the settlement of disputes. Never before in the Court's history, even during the heyday of the Permanent Court has the Court been so active and has the Court been so involved in such a variety of different disputes, ranging over such a wide spectrum of issues and involving States from virtually all continents and regions of the globe. The universalization of the Court which Rosenne remarked upon in the previous edition has proceeded apace and shows the "World Court" probably deserves that designation more at this time, than at any other period in its history.

There are various factors which are responsible for this development including, of course, the end of the Cold War and a relaxation of, or perhaps more accurately, a more pragmatic approach towards the North-South divide, including the general perception of international law and of an institution like the International Court on the part of the newer States, which used to maintain an attitude of reserve towards international law (and judicial settlement) due to its Western origins and perceived imbalances.

More relevant to our present discussion, however, is the increased awareness of the Court's dual function; that as an instrument of diplomacy, as well as an institution for the judicial settlement of disputes. This dual function has always existed; no one has been more aware of this than Rosenne himself. However, the potentialities of utilizing the Court within the context of an overall diplomatic and litigation strategy were highlighted by Nicaragua's successful use of contentious proceedings to obtain a number of its foreign policy objectives in its dispute with the United States in the 1980's. There is no need to devote further comment to a case which has already received a considerable amount of attention in this book and elsewhere. However, one of the far-reaching effects of that case, as Rosenne pointed out, is the increased awareness of States of the potentialities of contentious proceedings as an instrument of diplomacy. Regardless whether one sees this as a positive development or one which is a cause for concern, it is without doubt a major factor in the increased recourse to the Court in recent years and one which is likely to continue to be of importance in the coming period.

There are various reasons why States can decide to institute proceedings at the Court, only one of which is necessarily the desire to depoliticize a dispute and seek a judicial settlement. This statement is in no way meant to disparage the Court's integrity or downplay its role in the settlement of disputes. However, the Court is ultimately dependent on the will of States to bring cases before it and to utilize its decisions to resolve a dispute and can only indirectly influence the reasons States may have for instituting proceedings, or their willingness to depoliticize a dispute and seek a judicial settlement on the basis of legal considerations. There is nothing inherently wrong with this, or necessarily mutually exclusive in the Court's dual function as an instrument of diplomacy and as a court of law devoted to settling disputes between States - provided the Court is careful to maintain its integrity as a judicial institution and protect itself and the system of contentious jurisdiction from abuse. One area where this is particularly true is when States attempt to utilize the Court in attempts to undermine the authority of the Security Council to deal with matters affecting international peace and security through the system of contentious jurisdiction. The Court has been rightly unresponsive to such attempts to date and will have to continue to exercise caution in order not to upset the delicate institutional structure of the United Nations, or allow itself to be manoeuvered into a role for which it is not suited.

Having said this, a clarification is called for. The role of the Security Council in the post-Cold War era has changed dramatically and is still in the process of change. There is a widely held perception that the Security Council's new activism should not result in a disregard for the fundamental legal principles and purposes underlying the Charter. It is also widely felt that the Security Council is not as representative or as sensitive to the challenges and crises facing certain regions of the world as it should be. There is consequently a real need for reform of the Security Council's membership and increased attention to the legal effects and consequences of some of its decisions. While the Court has rightly resisted attempts by States to have it intrude into areas it is neither equipped, nor designed to perform or to otherwise undermine the Security Council's authority, some Security Council decisions raise certain legal questions which the Court could make a contribution to resolving, provided the Court and the Security Council were careful to respect each others' respective functions.

The question of reform of Security Council membership and responsiveness is a political one, which will have to be resolved diplomatically at the appropriate time. However, the question of how the Court could play a constructive role in providing legal guidance to the Security Council where necessary has both a political and a legal dimension. The potential role of the Court lies through an increased use of the advisory jurisdiction in situations whereby the Security Council, or in exceptional cases the General Assembly, call upon the Court to provide legal guidance and clarification. The potential for a judicious increase in the use of the Court's advisory jurisdiction has been put forward on a number of occasions.[2] Although it is controversial and not wholly without difficulties, it seems on balance a better alternative than the partisan use of contentious proceedings as an intended mechanism by States to undercut Security Council decisions.

* * * *

Another development which calls for some comment is the relationship of the International Court of Justice to other international courts and tribunals. Closely connected to this is the potential problem of overlapping jurisdiction and potentially contradictory interpretations of the law, with correspondingly negative effects upon the delicate fabric of the international legal system.

There have already been a number of instances in which specialized or regional international courts or tribunals have been engaged in cases involving interpretation of previous decisions by the Court, or cases which are even *sub judice* at the Court. These include the *Tadiç* Appeals Decision of the International Criminal Tribunal for the Former Yugoslavia and the Advisory Opinion of the Inter-American Court of Human Rights on *The Right to Information on Consular Assistance in the Framework of the Guarantees of Due Process of Law*. In the former case, the Appeals Chamber of the ICTY determined that it had to review the Judgment of the International Court of Justice in the *Nicaragua* case; a decision which some, including the Appeal's Chamber President, Judge Shahabuddeen, found to be unnecessary and potentially counterproductive. In the latter case, the Inter-American Court issued an advisory opinion which involved an interpretation of Article 36 of the Vienna Convention on Consular Relations while the same issues were *sub judice* in a contientious case at the International Court. Rosenne has expressed a view on this elsewhere (a view I fully share that):

> "A regional court or tribunal of limited jurisdiction, both *ratione personae* and *ratione materiae*, should show the greatest restraint before embarking upon the hazardous and delicate task of interpreting the application of a universal instrument adopted under the auspices of the United Nations, and which itself provides for the jurisdiction of the International Court of Justice. The fact that the advisory opinion was requested by an interested State in the context of a pending contentious case on the same issue in the International Court of Justice is an added reason for caution."[3]

These two examples definitely highlight the need for caution and restraint. Certainly there can be no question of specialized and regional courts steering clear of a matter simply because it touches upon issues which have been before, or might come before the International Court of Justice. Neither is there any reason why another Court should blindly apply a previous decision of the International Court of Justice if it believes the decision to be inapplicable. However, this does not mean that due care, restraint and mutual respect are not essential for the maintenance of the fragile unity of international law.

With the advent of the new International Criminal Court, the potential for overlapping jurisdiction and potential conflicting interpretation will be increasingly present notwithstanding the very distinct roles and functions of the International Court of Justice and the ICC. Examples which spring to mind include interpretation of the Genocide Convention, the customary or conventional law of armed conflict, or (potentially in the future), the concept of aggression and the legality of the use of force.

A former President of the International Court of Justice, Schwebel, first put forward a suggestion that "there might be virtue in enabling other tribunals to request advisory opinions of the International Court of Justice on issues of international law that arise in cases before those tribunals that are of importance to the unity of international law."[4] This suggestion was taken over by the subsequent President of the Court, Guillaume, who in an address to the UN General Assembly on 30 October 2001 stated *inter alia* the following:

> For the purpose of maintaining the unity of the law, the various existing courts or those yet to be created could in my opinion, be empowered in certain cases - indeed encouraged - to request advisory opinions from the International Court of Justice through the intermediary of the Security Council or through the General Assembly.[5]

It is noteworthy and encouraging that this suggestion has received partial recognition through the inclusion of a provision to this effect in the Draft Relationship Agreement between the United Nations and the International Criminal Court. Under this provision it is proposed that the Assembly of State Parties to the ICC Statute may submit a request for an advisory opinion to the International Court of Justice through the UN General Assembly, which shall decide upon the request in accordance with Article 96 of the UN Charter. However, this is not enough and it is hoped that the possibility of requesting advisory opinions will be extended to other international courts and tribunals of a regional or specialized character through the appropriate regional organization or other body putting a request through the General Assembly or Security Council. This would go a long way to ensuring the unity of international law and avoiding the dangers of contradiction or conflict between different judicial bodies.

* * * *

There is one further point which deserves some comment. The increased workload of the Court and the proposals for further extending the scope of its activities through increased use of the advisory jurisdiction; both in assisting the Security Council in the discharge of its responsibilities in the maintenance of international peace and security by providing advisory opinions to the Council where appropriate, and the provision of advisory opinions to other international courts and tribunals - have a "price tag". This "price" comes in the form of ensuring that the Court's resources and procedures are adequate to cope with this increased activity and these new challenges.

In this respect, much has already been achieved. The Court is, through its new Practice Directions and other measures, making a real effort to streamline and expedite its procedures in order to ensure an orderly and effective handling of its cases. The United Nations has also moderately increased the resources available to the Court in recent years. Nevertheless, more remains to be done. In particular, notwithstanding the financial constraints on the United Nations, the necessity of increasing further the resources available deserves continuing attention. Anyone who has ever visited the Court's impressive seat in the Hague cannot fail to be struck by the fact that behind the façade of the Peace Palace, the Court is a very modest institution indeed in terms of the personnel and material resources available to it. While comparisons can always be misleading, it is worth noting that any medium sized district court in a Western nation is almost sure to have far more resources at its disposal than the principal judicial organ of the United Nations. Without losing sight of realities, this is something that can and must be remedied if the Court is to continue to play the role it has increasingly been called upon to perform.

NOTES

Chapter 1

---

[1] Isaiah ii. 4; Micah iv. 3.

[2] *De jure belli ac pacis* (1625), II, ch. xxiii, par. 8, English translation by F.W. Kelsey et al. 563 (Classics of International Law, 1925, 1964).

[3] For the position in Ancient India, see H. Chatterjee, *International Law and Inter-State Relations in Ancient India* (1958), 129; Nagendra Singh, *India and International Law* (1973); same, "The Distinguishable Characteristic of the Concept of the Law of Nations in Ancient India", *Liber Amicorum for Lord Wilberforce* 91 (M. Bos and I. Brownlie, eds., 1987); same, "The Machinery and Method for Conduct of International Relations in Ancient India", *International Law at a Time of Perplexity* 845 (Y. Dinstein and M. Tabory, eds., 1989). For a thorough treatment of Ancient and Medieval Non-European Systems of International Law see the various articles on the history of the law of nations in *Encyclopedia of Public International Law,* Instalment 7 (R. Bernhardt, ed., 1984) 126-273.

[4] A. Rechid, "L'Islam et le Droit des Gens", 60 RADI 60 (1937-11); M. Khadduri, *War and Peace in the Law of Islam* (1955). For the influence of other religious systems see: K.R.R. Sastry, "Hinduism and International Law", 117 RADI 503 (1966-I); K. Iriye, "The Principles of International Law in the Light of Confucian Doctrine", 120 ibid 1 (1967-I); K.N. Jayatilleke, "The Principles of International Law in Buddhist Doctrine", ibid. 441; H. Riedmatten, "Le catholicisme et le développement du droit international", 151 ibid. 115 (1976-111); P. Weil, "Le Judaïsme et le développement du droit international", ibid. 253; Tieya Wang, "International Law in China: Historical and Contemporary Perspectives", 221 ibid. 195 (1990-II); and my "The Influence of Judaism on the Development of International Law", *An International Law Miscellany* 509 (note 3 above).

[5] See C. Phillipson, The International Law and Custom of Ancient Greece and Rome (1911); A. Raeder, L'Arbitrage international chez les Hellènes (1912); M. Tod, International Arbitration amongst the Greeks (1913); J. Ralston, International Arbitration from Athens to Locarno (1929); M. Taube, "Les Origines de l'arbitrage international: antiquité et moyen âge", 42 RADI 1 (1932-IV); G. Tenekides, "International Law and Federal Communities in the Greece of the Cities", 90 ibid. 469 (1956-II).

[6] E. Usteri, *Bienne-Beppet* Arbitration, J.B. Moore (ed.), II *International Adjudications,* Ancient Series (1936).

[7] See J. Eppstein, *The Catholic Tradition in the Law of Nations* 113 and *passim* (1935); A.B. Bozeman, *Politics and Culture in International History* 266 (1960). Yet a warning has been issued against exaggerating the role of the Church, while emphasizing its function in creating an atmosphere in which arbitration could flourish. R. Bainton, *Christian Attitudes towards War and Peace* 116 (1960).

[8] J.B. Moore, *International Adjudications,* Modern Series, vols. 1-4 (1929-31). Vol. 5 deals with certain U.S.-Spanish and U.S.-French claims (the latter being settled, as regards individual U.S. claimants, by domestic commissions), and vol. 6 contains the proceedings of another U.S.-Great Britain Mixed Commission set up to determine the title to islands in the Passamaquoddy Bay and the Bay of Fundy, between Maine and New Brunswick.

[9] 62 *British and Foreign State Papers* 233 (1871-2); J.B. Moore, I *History and Digest of the Arbitrations to which the United States have been a party* 653 (1898); *U.S. Foreign Relations,* 1872, Pt. II, Papers relating to the Treaty of Washington of 1871, IV, 49 (42nd Cong. 3rd Sess., Ex. Doc. 1). The formal sessions of modern arbitrations taking place in Geneva are frequently held in the room in the Hôtel de Ville now known as the *Alabama Hall.*

[10] See J.B. Scott, The Reports to the Hague Conference of 1899 and 1907 (1917); same, The Proceedings of The Hague Peace Conferences: Translation of the Official Texts, 4 vols. (1920,

1921); W.I. Hull, The Two Hague Conferences and Their Contributions to International Law (1908, 1970). The Tsar's initiative was not disinterested. In the armaments race which preceded the outbreak of the First World War (1914), Russia was lagging behind, and he was in danger of losing his throne. The Conferences were convened to promote peace and disarmament and to relieve international tension. In that objective they failed, but they succeeded in codifying a great deal of international law, including the law of international arbitration. See H.A.L. Fisher, II A History of Europe, 1084 (1949); V. Potiemkine, II Histoire de la Diplomatie 161 (1946); Barbara W. Tuchman, The Proud Tower, chap. 5 (1966, paperback edition 1980). On the Permanent Court of Arbitration, see J.P.A. François, "La Cour permanente d' Arbitrage", 87 RADI 460 (1955-II); International Bureau of the Permanent Court of Arbitration, The Permanent Court of Arbitration - New Directions (1991). In General Assembly resolution 48/3, J.3 October 1993, the Permanent Court was granted observer status entitling it to participate in the work of the General Assembly of the United Nations. For the resolution of the Permanent Administrative Council of the Permanent Court of Arbitration of 3 March 1960, inviting new States to adhere to the First Hague Convention of 1907, see 54 AJIL 933 (1960). See also Succession of States to Multilateral Treaties: studies prepared by the [U.N.] Secretariat, II. Permanent Court of Arbitration and the Hague Conventions of 1899 and 1907, [1968-II] ILCYB (doc. A/CN.4/200) 26. Generally see A.M. Stuyt, Survey of International Arbitrations, 1794-1989 (1990); V. Coussirat-Coustere and P.M. Eisemann, Repertory of International Arbitral Jurisprudence (3 vols. in 4 books, 1989-1991).

[11] For analysis of the problem of fact-finding in a United Nations context, see Carl W.A. Schurmann, *A Center for International Fact-Finding: A Review and a Proposal* (1963); Report of the Secretary-General on Methods of Fact-Finding, GAOR, 20th session, annexes, agenda items 90 and 94, doc. A/5694 (1965). And see General Assembly resolutions 2104 (XX), 20 December 1965; 46/89, 9 December 1991, Declaration on Fact-finding by the United Nations in the field of the Maintenance of International Peace and Security. On international conciliation, see Jean-Pierre Cot, *International Conciliation* (1972). On Commissions of Inquiry, see M. Yasseen in 61 *Yearbook of the Institute of International Law* 313 (1983 II).

[12] In 1958 the Commission submitted a set of Model Rules on Arbitral Procedure to the General Assembly. [1958-II] ILCYB 83. By resolution 1262 (XIII) of 14 November 1958, the General Assembly brought these Model Rules to the attention of Member States for their consideration and use, in such cases and to such extent as they consider appropriate, in drawing up treaties of arbitration. An alternative method, quite common today, is to incorporate into arbitration treaties relevant rules from the practice of the International Court.

[13] M. Hudson, International Tribunals. Past and Future 7 (1944).

[14] See *Annual Digest and Reports of International Law Cases,* 16 vols. covering the period 1919-1949, and *International Law Reports* (ILR), continuous since 1950. A convenient collection of international arbitrations will be found in the U.N. series of *Reports of International Arbitral Awards* (RIAA) , vols. 9-11 covering the period 1902-1920, vols. 1-3 covering the period 1920-1940, and vols. 12 and 16 to 19 covering the period 1945-1986. The remaining volumes contain a miscellaneous collection of decisions of various mixed commissions (other than those established by the 1919 Peace Treaties).

[15] There is reason to believe that this type of constitution of an arbitration tribunal originated in Jewish private law. C.W. Jenks, *The Common Law of Mankind* 99 (1958).

[16] On international arbitration, see: A. Mérignhac, *Traité théorique et pratique de l'arbitrage international* (1895); J.H. Ralston, *The Law and Procedure of International Tribunals* (1926); I.C. Wittenberg, *L 'Organisation judiciaire, la procédure et la sentence internationales* (1937); K.S. Carlston, *The Process of International Arbitration* (1946); UN Secretariat, *Memorandum on Arbitral Procedure,* ILCYB 1950-11 (doc. *NCN.4/35)* 157; M. Bos, *Les conditions du procès en droit international public* (1957); J.L. Simpson and H. Fox, *International Arbitration, Law and Practice* (1959); UN Secretariat, *Commentary on the draft Convention on Arbitral Procedure,*

doc. *NCN.4/92* (1955). For a general overview of international arbitration in all its facets, see *The International Arbitral Process* (ed. J. Gillis Wetter, 5 vols. 1979).

[17] These obligations were completed by Article 15 giving the Council competence over disputes which were not settled by arbitration or judicial settlement. After the adoption of the Statute of the Permanent Court of International Justice, the references to arbitration in the Covenant were changed to "arbitration or judicial settlement".

[18] The leading treatise on the Permanent Court is M. Hudson, *The Permanent Court of International Justice, 1920-1942* (1943, reprinted 1972). This magisterial and definitive work – indispensable for an understanding of the Permanent Court – contains a full account of the drafting of the Covenant, the Statute and the Rules of Court, with complete references to all the documentation.

[19] For text see Appendix II. For details of these amendments, see *International Court of Justice YB* 1977-78 111. On the amendments of 1972, see Eduardo Jiménez de Aréchaga, "The Amendments to the Rules of Procedure of the International Court of Justice", 67 AJIL 1 (1973); and my "The 1972 Revision of the Rules of the International Court of Justice", 8 *Israel Law Review* 197 (1973). On the revision of 1978, see also G. Guyomar *Commentaire du reglement de la Cour Internationale de Justice, adopte le* 14 *avril* 1978: *interpretation et pratique* (1983); my *Procedure in the International Court; A Commentary on the* 1978 *Rules of the International Court of Justice* (1983).

[20] See the following cases: S.S. Wimbledon, A 1 (1923); German Settlers in Poland, B 6 (1923); Acquisition of Polish Nationality, B 7 (1923); Polish Postal Service in Danzig, B 11 (1925); Certain German Interests in Polish Upper Silesia, A 6 (1925), A 7 (1926); Factory of Chorz6w, A 9 (1927), A 12 (1927), A 13 (1927), A 17 (1928); Jurisdiction of the Courts in Danzig, B 15 (1928); Rights of Minorities in Upper Silesia (Minority Schools), A 15 (1928); Territorial Jurisdiction of the International Commission of the River Oder, A 23 (1929); Free City of Danzig and the ILO, B 18 (1930); Access to German Minority Schools in Upper Silesia, A/B 40 (1931); Access to, or Anchorage in, the Port of Danzig of Polish War Vessels, A/B 43 (1931); Treatment of Polish Nationals and Other Persons of Polish Origin or Speech in the Danzig Territory, A/B 44 (1932); Prince von Pless Administration, A/B 52 (1933), A/B 54 (1933), NB 57 (1933), A/B 59 (1933); Polish Agrarian Reform and German Minority, A/B 58 (1933), A/B 60 (1933); Consistency of Certain Danzig Legislative Decrees with the Constitution of the Free City, A/B 65 (1935).

[21] See the following cases: Railway Traffic between Lithuania and Poland, A/B 42 (1931); Interpretation of the Statute of the Memel Territory, A/B 47 (1932), A/B 49 (1932).

[22] See the following cases: Jaworzina, B 8 (1923); Monastery of Saint-Naoum, B 9 (1924); Treaty of Neuilly, Article 179, Annex, Paragraph 4 (Interpretation), A 3 (1924), A 4 (1925); Jurisdiction of the European Commission of the Danube, B 14 (1927); Interpretation of Greco-Turkish Agreement of 1 December 1926 (Final Protocol, Article IV), B 16 (1928); Greco-Bulgarian "Communities", B 17 (1930); Interpretation of the Greco-Bulgarian Agreement of 9 December 1927, A/B 45 (1932); Minority Schools in Albania, A/B 64 (1935).

[23] See the following cases: *Mavrommatis Palestine Concessions,* A 2 (1924), A 5 (1925), A 11 (1927); *Exchange of Greek and Turkish Populations,* B 10 (1925); *Interpretation of Article* 3, *Paragraph* 2, *of the Treaty of Lausanne,* B 12 (1925); *Lighthouses,* A/B 62 (1934); *Lighthouses in Crete and Samos,* A/B 71 (1937) (this dispute was finally settled only in 1956 by an arbitral award rendered through a Tribunal operating under the Hague Convention of 1907, XII RIAA 155).

[24] See the following cases: *Nationality Decrees Issued in Tunis and Morocco,* B 4 (1923); *Phosphates in Morocco,* A/B 74 (1938). For a case relating to commercial matters in the Congo, see *Oscar Chinn, A/B* 63 (1934). These cases reflected European rivalries on the African Continent and have little or no relevance following the decolonization process.

[25] The most significant instances of this are the *Lotus* and the *Borchgrave* cases. A 10 (1927) and A/B 72 and 73 (1937,1938).

[26] M. Dunne, *The United States and the World Court, 1920-1935* (1988). See also his "Isolationism of a Kind: Two Generations of World Court Historiography in the United States" in 21 *Journal of American Studies* 327 (1987).
[27] The Status of Eastern Carelia case, B 5 (1923).
[28] See note 13 above, 238.
[29] The leading study of this aspect is Sir Hersch Lauterpacht, *The Development of International Law by the International Court* (1958). See also *Encyclopedia of Public International Law* (R. Bernhardt, ed, 1981), Instalment 1, Settlement of Disputes; Instalment 2, Decisions of International Courts and Tribunals and International Arbitrations.
[30] For the work of the League of Nations in this sphere, see Rosenne's editions of Committee for the Progressive Codification of International Law [1925 1928], 2 vols. (1972); Conference for the Codification of International Law (1930), 4 vols. (1975).
[31] For instance, during the Communist period, the Socialist writers were highly critical of the law as applied by the Court. To a large degree this criticism stems from the fact that the classic Marxist-Leninist concept of the role and nature of the law is considerably different from that held by other political and social philosophies, and this of necessity leads to different scales of values for assessing the work of any Court -including the International Court. For an East European Socialist study on the Court, see C. Elian, *The International Court of Justice* (1971).

Chapter 2

[1] For the Report of the Informal Inter-Allied Committee, see British Parliamentary Paper, Cmd. 6531 (1944); republished in 39 AJIL Supplement section of documents 1 (1945). For the recommendations of the Inter-American Juridical Committee, see 38 AJIL Supplement section of documents 29 (1944).
[2] For the Dumbarton Oaks Proposals (which take their name from the estate in Washington, D.C., where the Conference at which they were finally drafted was held), see *Documents of the United Nations Conference on International Organization* (hereafter UNCIO), vol. III. For the records of the Washington Committee of Jurists, in, session between 9-20 April 1945, see XIV UNCIO. A selection of documents illustrating the work of this Committee is contained in *The International Court of Justice, Selected Documents relating to the Drafting of the Statute,* Department of State, Publication 2491, Conference Series 84 (1946). For the records of Committee IVII see XIII UNCIO. And see *The United Nations Conference on International Organization,* selected documents, Department of State, Publication 2490, Conference Series 83 (1946). For a comprehensive index to the proceedings of the San Francisco Conference, see XXI UNCIO.
[3] Judge Azevedo, Rep. 1950, 82.
[4] For judicial discussion of this interaction between Article 7 and Article 92 of the Charter, see particularly in the *Interpretation of the Peace Treaties* advisory opinion, 1950, 65 at 71-2. For application of this principle in contentious proceedings, see *Northern Cameroons* case. 1963, 15, passim.
[5] *Peace Treaties* advisory opinion, cited in previous note. Repeated in *Reservations* (1951), *Expenses* (1962), *Namibia* (1971), *Western Sahara* (1975) and *Privileges and Immunities* (1989) advisory opinions.
[6] General Assembly resolution 171 (II), 14 November 1947. The texts of this and the resolutions mentioned in the following notes can be found in Rosenne's *Documents,* pp. 558 to 599.
[7] General Assembly resolution 2625 (XXV), 24 October 1970. For the principal discussions on judicial settlement, see Report of the 1966 Special Committee on Principles of International Law concerning Friendly Relations and Co-operation among States in accordance with the Charter of the United Nations, 21 GAOR annexes, agenda item 87 (doc. A/6230, paras. 210-220) (1966); Report of the 1967 Special Committee, 22 ibid., annexes, agenda item 87 (doc. A/6799, paras. 384-393) (1967).

[8] Resolution 3232 (XXIX), 12 November 1974. For the development of this, see GAOR annexes, agenda item 96 (doc. A/8238) (1970); 26 ibid., annexes, agenda item 90 (docs. A/8382 and Add. 1-4, A/8568) (1971); 27 ibid., annexes, agenda item 90 (docs; A/8747 and A/8967) (1972); 28 ibid., annexes (doc. A/9413) (1973); 29 ibid., annexes (doc. A/9846) (1974). Further p. 28 above.

[9] Resolution 37/10, 15 November 1982, to which the Manila Declaration is annexed. This idea is not new. It was first advanced by the Institute of International Law in its resolution on the compulsory jurisdiction of international courts and tribunals of 1959. 48 *Annuaire de l'Institut de Droit International,* II, 358 (French), 380 (English). Political endorsement was first given by the General Assembly in its resolution 3232 (XXIX) of 12 November 1974, on the review of the role of the International Court of Justice.

[10] Boutros Boutros-Ghali, *An Agenda for Peace,* United Nations, DPI/1247, 1992. 47 GAOR annexes, agenda item 10 (doc. A/47/277, S/24111) (1992).

[11] 23 GAOR annexes, agenda item 14 (doc. A/7181) (1968). The report itself is included as a Supplement to the *Official Records* of the General Assembly. For trenchant criticism, see S. Engel, "Annual Reports of the International Court of Justice to the General Assembly?", 44 *British Year Book of International Law* 193 (1970).

[12] Cf. Legal Consequences for States of the Continued Presence of South Africa in Namibia notwithstanding Security Council Resolution 276 (1970) advisory opinion (1971).

[13] See discussion at the 76th meeting of the Security Council on 15 October 1946. 1 Security Council, *Official Records,* 2nd series No. 19, 466 *et seq.*

[14] GAOR, annexes, agenda item 63 (doc. A/C.6/L.454) (1959).

[15] XII RIAA 351 *et seq.*

[16] R. S. Lee (ed.) *The International Court: The Making of the Rome Statute Issues, Negotiations, Results,* pp. 2-3 (1999)

[17] Official website of the International Criminal Court: www.un.org/law/icc

[18] *id.*

[19] See C.F. Amerasinghe, "Investment Disputes, Conventions and International Centre for the Settlement of", *Encyclopedia of Public International Law,* Instalment 5, 188 (R. Bernhardt, ed. 1983)

[20] United Nations, *The Law of the Sea, Official text of the United Nations Convention on the Law of the Sea with Annexes and Index,* 1983 (separate editions exist in each of the authentic texts of the Convention); University of Virginia, Center for Oceans Law and Policy, *United Nations Convention on the Law of the Sea, 1982, A Commentary* (M. Nordquist, ed.,) vol. I (1985); and vol. V (Sh. Rosenne and L. Sohn, eds., 1988), especially articles 279-299 and Annexes V, VI, VII and VIII. The settlement of Sea-Bed disputes is also regulated in articles 186-191, to be covered in a later volume of that Commentary (in preparation).

[21] *US Diplomatic and Consular Staff in Tehran* case, 1980, 3, 20 (para. 37)

[22] On the circumstances surrounding this difficult and controversial case, see Chapter 5. The dissatisfaction of the United States at the Court's decisions in this case must not disguise the fact that the U.S. Government has traditionally been supportive of the Court's role in the settlement of disputes. Shortly after its decision in 1985 to terminate its acceptance of the compulsory jurisdiction, the U.S. Government submitted a new case on the basis of Article 36, paragraph 1 of the Statute. See the *ELSI* case, p. 185 above.

[23] *Application for Review of Judgement No.333 of the United Nations Administrative Tribunal* (Yakimetz) advisory opinion, 1987 74 (Lachs), 76 (Elias).

[24] 338th meeting, 15 July 1948.

[25] The *Tehran* case in note 21, p. 22. See also *Military and Paramilitary Activities in and against Nicaragua* (Jurisdiction and Admissibility) case (1984). These were by no means the first instances in which the Court was asked to act concurrently with another organ of the United Nations. For the difficulties which this can occasion, note the *Aegean Sea Continental Shelf* case brought by Greece against Turkey simultaneously in the Court and the Security Council (p. 172 above).

Arbitral Award Made by the King of Spain on 23 December 1906 case (1960); Arbitral Award of 31 July 1989 case (1991) (pp. 157, 193 above).
[26] Questions of Interpretation and Application of the 1971 Montreal Convention arising from the Aerial Incident at Lockerbie (Provisional Measures) cases (1992); Application of the Convention on the Prevention and Punishment of the Crime of Genocide (Provisional Measures) case (1993) (pp. 199, 203 above).
[27] *Reparation for Injuries Suffered in the Service of the United Nations* advisory opinion (1949); *Certain Expenses of the United Nations* advisory opinion (1962); *Namibia* advisory opinion; *Applicability of Obligation to Arbitrate under Section 21 of the United Nations Headquarters Agreement of 26 June 1947* advisory opinion (1988); *Privileges and Immunities* advisory opinion (pp. 131, 163, 141, 186, 190 above).
[28] Arbitral Award Made by the King of Spain on 23 December 1906 case (1960); Arbitral Award of 31 July 1989 case (1991) (pp. 194, 235 above).
[29] O, Schachter, *International Law in Theory and Practice* 40 (1991).
[30] For the text of the Relationship Agreements see *Agreements between the United Nations and the Specialized Agencies and the International Atomic Energy Agency* (doc. ST/SG/14, 1961). Later agreements are found in the relevant records of the General Assembly.
[31] This undertaking does not appear in the agreements with the international financial organizations (the World Bank complex) or with the Universal Postal Union.
[32] *Appeal relating to the Jurisdiction of the ICAO Council* case (1972, see par. 15 of the judgment and the declaration of Judge Lachs); *Aerial Incident of* 3 *July* 1988 case (discontinued in 1996, see p. 188 above).
[33] *Judgments of the Administrative Tribunal of the ILO upon Complaints made against UNESCO* advisory opinion (1955); *Constitution of the Maritime Safety Committee of IMCO* advisory opinion (1960); *Interpretation of the Agreement of* 25 *March 1951 between the WHO and Egypt* advisory opinion (1980); *Legality of the Use by a State of Nuclear Weapons in Armed Conflict* advisory opinion (pp. 149, 160, 176, 208 above).
[34] The Court awarded the United Kingdom damages totaling £843,947 in its judgment of 15 December 1949 in the *Corfu Channel* (Compensation) case. Some Albanian monetary gold recovered by the Western Allies after the Second World War was retained in the custody of the Tripartite Commission pending a final settlement of claims between the British, Albanian and other (Italian) Governments concerned. A general settlement between the Albania and United Kingdom Governments was reached on 9 May 1992. This required the restoration of the gold to Albania, and the payment of an agreed sum of money to the United Kingdom in settlement of outstanding claims, including the claims arising out of the *Corfu Channel* judgment. See G. Marston, "United Kingdom Materials on International Law", 63 *British Year Book of International Law* 781 (1992).
[35] See Rosenne's *Law and Practice* 159-161. See also Pleadings in the *Arbitral Award* case, vol. I, p. 394 *et seq.*
[36] See Keesing's *Contemporary Archives* 1959–1960, 16949A; ibid., 1961–1962, 18931B.
[37] *International Court of Justice YB* 1986–l987 166-69.
[38] See Rosenne's *Documents* 904. Note the statement of the representative of Chad in the Court on 14 July 1993.
[39] See A. Eyffinger, *The Peace Palace: Residence for Justice – Domicile of Learning (1988).*

Chapter 3

[1] Separate opinion of Judge Lachs in the *Military and Paramilitary Activities in and against Nicaragua* (Merits) case, 1986, 158.
[2] For a directive to this effect from the State Department to its Embassies abroad, see XI *Foreign Relations of the United States 1955-1957* 119.

[3] Resolution 1991 A (XVIII), 17 December 1963 (in force from 31 August 1965), fixed the regional distribution of seats on the Security Council as follows: Western (European) States 5 (including the permanent members France, United Kingdom and United States), Eastern European States 2 (including the permanent seat of the USSR, now the Russian Federation), Latin America 2, Africa 3, Asia 3 seats (including the permanent seat held by China). This change brought the necessary absolute majority in the Security Council for the election of a judge from six to eight.
[4] See Rosenne's *Documents* 823.
[5] 22 GAOR, A/PV 1456 para. 30 (Statement of Guinea) (2 November 1966).
[6] Details in Rosenne's *Documents* 843.
[7] Ibid. 814.
[8] Institut de Droit International, *Tableau général des Résolutions* (1873-1956) 157 (H. Wehberg, ed., 1957).
[9] S. Schwebel in 6 Leiden Journal of International Law 375, 378 (1993).
[10] Statute, Articles 4 to 7. Few details are available of the manner in which the nominating process is carried out. In the nature of things this is done discreetly. For the consultations of the United States National Group in 1960, see R.R. Baxter, "The Procedures employed in connection with the United States Nominations for the International Court in 1960", 55 AJIL 445 (1961). For further information on the internal practice of the United States, cf. Marjorie M. Whiteman, 12 *Digest of International Law* 1202 (1971). For particulars of the composition of the national groups of the Permanent Court of Arbitration, see the annual reports of the Permanent Administrative Committee of the Permanent Court of Arbitration.
[11] Statute, Articles 8 to 12. For the participation in the elections of the non-members of the United Nations, see General Assembly resolution 264 (III), 8 October 1948, Rosenne's *Documents* 531. And see Rules 150 and 151 of the Rules of Procedure of the General Assembly (A/520/Rev.15) and Rules 40 and 61 of the Provisional Rules of Procedure of the Security Council (S/96/Rev. 7). These Rules incorporate the current interpretation of the word "meeting", to the effect that it continues until as many candidates as are required for all the seats to be filled have obtained in one or more ballots an absolute majority of votes.
[12] See correspondence between the Prime Minister of Australia (R. Menzies) and Judge Sir Percy Spender, the *Times* (London), 12 September 1958. Also in 63 *Revue général de Droit international public* 94 (1959).
[13] In the Permanent Court Judges Viscount Finlay, Guerrero, Huber, and Deputy-Judge Beichmann. In the present Court, Members of the Court the Court participated as members of the arbitral tribunal in the following inter-State cases: *The Beagle Channel* case (Argentina/Chile) (1977), 52 ILR 93; the *Anglo-French Continental Shelf* case (1977, 1978), 54 ibid. 6; *Guinea/Guinea-Bissau Maritime Delimitation* case (1986) 77 ibid. 635; *Guinea-Bissau/Senegal Maritime Delimitation* case (1989), 83 ibid. 1. Others have participated in arbitrations in which one of the parties was not a State, and even as arbitrator sole.
[14] Statute, Article 24. The question was raised in both the *South West Africa* and *Namibia* cases: 1965,3 and 1971 at 3,6 and 9 for relevant orders, and 19 for discussion by the Court of some of the principles involved. It is also believed that the Statute permits discreet action to be taken in the same direction should one of the parties feel this to be necessary. Cf. J.D. Morley, "Relative Incompatibility of Functions in the International Court", 19 *The International and Comparative Law Quarterly* 316 (1970).
[15] The announcement of the United States of its withdrawal from further participation in the *Nicaragua* case cast doubt upon the impartially of certain judges because of their nationality and the subject-matter of the dispute. These allegations were refuted by prominent members of the American Society of International Law in a comment on the U.S. statement (see 79 AJIL 373 (1985)) and by two of the members of the Court in the Judgment on the merits. 1986, 158 (separate opinion of Judge Lachs), and 528 (dissenting opinion of Judge Sir Robert Jennings). See also M. Lachs (not in his judicial capacity), "A Few Thoughts on the Independence of Judges of

the International Court of Justice," 25 *Columbia Journal of Transnational Law* 593 (1987) and his "Some Reflections on the Nationality of Judges of the International Court of Justice", 4 *Pace Yearbook of International Law* 49 (1992). But the Court itself, through the mouth of its President, does not seem to have presented any reaction.

[16] For instances of this, see *South West Africa, North Sea Continental Shelf* and *Fisheries Jurisdiction* (Federal Republic of Germany v. Iceland) cases, 1961 at 13, 1968 at 9, and 1973 at 51.

[17] 1985 at 192.

[18] See *International Court of Justice YB* 1946-47, 55-87 for a description of the organization of the Registry, the Staff Regulations and the Instructions for the Registry.

[19] *International Court of Justice YB* 1970-1971 110.

Chapter 4

[1] *Passage through the Great Belt* case, 1991 12, 20, citing earlier cases.

[2] *Nottebohm* case (second phase), 1955 19.

[3] In the present Court see the following cases: *Ambatielos, Anglo-Iranian Oil Co., Nottebohm, Norwegian Loans, Interhandel, Guardianship Convention, Barcelona Traction,* and *ELSI, Breard, La Grand* and currently *Certain Property* and *Ahmadou Sadio Diallo.* This practice compares unfavourably with, for example, that of the European Court of Human Rights, as manifested in the *Lawless* case (1960-1). See Rosenne's "Reflections on the Position of the Individual in Inter-State Litigation in the International Court of Justice", *An International Law Miscellany* 111 (1993).

[4] UN doc. A/CONF.129/15, reproduced in 25 ILM 543 (1986). See Rosenne's *Developments in the Law of Treaties 1945–1956* 317 (1989).

[5] *Corfu Channel* (in a later stage), *Minquiers and Ecrehos,* and *Frontier Land.*

[6] *Minquiers and Ecrehos, Sovereignty over Certain Frontier Land, North Sea Continental Shelf*; *Continental Shelf* (Libya/Tunisia and Malta/Libya), *Gulf of Maine, Frontier Dispute* (Burkina Faso/Mali), *Land, Island and Maritime Frontier Dispute* (EI Salvador/Honduras); *Territorial Dispute* (Chad/Libya); *Gabčíkovo-Nagymaros Project* (Hungary/Slovakia), *Kasikili/Sedudu Island* (Botswana/Namibia). *Pulau Litigan and Pulau Sipidan* (Indonesia/Malaysia) and *Frontier Dispute* (Benin/Niger) which is currently pending.

[7] *Asylum, Arbitral Award of King of Spain* and *Territorial Dispute* (Chad/Libya) cases.

[8] Cf. the following cases: *French Nationals in Egypt, Electricité de Beyrouth, Compagnie du Port, des Quais et des Entrepôts de Beyrouth, Barcelona Traction* (two cases), *South West Africa* (two cases), *Northern Cameroons, ICAO Council, Nuclear Tests* (two cases), *Pakistani Prisoners of War, ICAO Council Appeal, Fisheries Jurisdiction* (two cases), *Aegean Sea* (partially), the *Border and Transborder Armed Actions* cases, *ELSI*, the *Aerial Incident of 3 July 1988* case, *Oil Platforms*, the two *Lockerbie* cases, the two cases concerning the *Application of the Convention on the Prevention and Punishment of the Crime of Genocide* (Bosnia-Herzegovina v. Yugoslavia), *Breard, LaGrand*, the cases (partly) between Yugoslavia and NATO Member States entitled *Legality of the Use of Force*, eight of which are still pending, *Armed Activities on the Territory of the Congo* in two cases which were subsequently discontinued and in the New Application of 28 May 2002 (Dem. Rep. Congo v. Rwanda) which is currently pending, the *Aerial Incident of 10 August 1999* (as subsequently amended as an additional basis for jurisdiction) the two *Maritime Delimitation* cases brought by Nicaragua against Honduras and Colombia respectively and *Certain Property*. The last three cases are also currently pending.

[9] Of the cases currently pending before the Court, the two Maritime Delimitation cases brought by Nicaragua against its neighbours were brought on the basis of the Inter American Convention for the Pacific Settlement of Disputes, while the *Certain Property* case between Liechtenstein en Germany was submitted on the basis of the European Convention for the Peaceful Settlement of

Disputes.

[10] The following cases: *Treatment in Hungary of Aircraft and Crews of United States of America* (two cases), *Aerial Incident* of 10 March 1953, 7 October 1952 and 4 September 1954 cases; *Antarctica* (two cases).

[11] M.O. Hudson, The Permanent Court of International Justice, 1920-1942 473 (1943).

[12] For the full texts of all declarations to date accepting the compulsory jurisdiction of the present Court and the cases in which they have been invoked, see Rosenne's *Documents* at p. 601.

[13] The United States terminated its 1946 declaration accepting the Court's compulsory jurisdiction on 7 October 1985 with effect from 7 April 1986. Since 1946 subjective reservations in one form or another have been made by the following States: France (1947), Mexico (1947), India (1956), Liberia (1952), Malawi (1966), Pakistan (1948) (1957), Philippines (1972), Senegal (1985), South Africa (1955), Sudan (1958). Many of these declarations have been withdrawn and replaced, or expired by effluxion of time. Currently only those of Mexico, Liberia, Malawi, Philippines and Sudan containing subjective reservations remain in force.

[14] Especially in their opinions in the *Norwegian Loans* and *Interhandel* cases.

[15] For the current status of the compulsory jurisdiction under Article 36, paragraphs 2 and 5, of the Statute, see the latest issue of *International Court of Justice YB*, ch. IV, section II. See also the current issue of the annual publication of the United Nations entitled *Multilateral Treaties Deposited with the Secretary-General: Status as at* 31 *December [last]*, doc. ST/LEG/SER.E–/, ch. I.4.

[16] Since 1946 the following cases have been brought on the basis of the compulsory jurisdiction: *Fisheries, Anglo-Iranian Oil Co., U.S. Nationals in Morocco, Nottebohm, Certain Norwegian Loans, Interhandel, Aerial Incident of 27 July 1955* (three cases), *Right of Passage, Temple of Preah Vihear, Nuclear Tests* (two cases), *Military and Paramilitary Activities in and against Nicaragua, Arbitral Award of 31 July 1989, Passage through the Great Belt, the Certain Phosphate Lands in Nauru, Jan Mayen, East Timor, Maritime Delimitation between Guinea Bissau and Senegal, Great Belt, Land and Maritime Boundary between Cameroon and Nigeria, Fisheries Jurisdiction* (Spain v. Canada), *Aerial Incident of 10 August 1999* (as the principal basis for jurisdiction), *Arrest Warrant, Ahmadou Sadio Diallo, Legality of the Use of Force* (in five of the ten cases as a supplementary basis for jurisdiction), *Armed Activities on the Territory of the Congo* (D.R. Congo v. Uganda). The last three (groups of) cases are currently pending.

[17] The United States is not the only State to have terminated its acceptance of the compulsory jurisdiction following litigation to which it did not consent, although it was the first to have done so while the litigation was still in progress. Iran terminated its acceptance of the compulsory jurisdiction following the proceedings in the *Anglo-Iranian Oil Co.* case, notwithstanding the Court's upholding of its preliminary objections. Thailand terminated its declaration following the Court's judgment in the *Temple of Preah Vihear* case. South Africa terminated its declaration in 1967 following a whole series of advisory opinions and judgments concerning. its administration of South West Africa (Namibia). France terminated its acceptance of the compulsory jurisdiction following the Court's decisions in the *Nuclear Tests* cases. Other States have terminated or circumscribed their acceptance of the compulsory jurisdiction when it appeared likely that proceedings would be instituted against them, or when developments in the law or the Court's practice required them to reconsider their national policy in this regard.

[18] This seems to be the combined effect of the *Aerial Incident of 27 July* 1955 and the *Temple* cases on the one hand, and the *Nicaragua* case on the other.

[19] *Barcelona Traction* (preliminary objections), 1964 26-39. Reiterated in *ICAO Council,* 1972, 53.

[20] For a thorough study of the phenomenon, see W.A. Thirlway, *Non-Appearance before the International Court of Justice* (1985). See also the resolution on *Non-appearance before the International Court of Justice* adopted by the Institute of International Law at its Basle session in 1991. Institute of International Law, 64 *Yearbook* Part II 276 (1991).

[21] In the following cases: *Anglo-Iranian Oil Co., Interhandel, Fisheries Jurisdiction* (two cases,

four orders), *Nuclear Tests* (two cases), *Pakistani Prisoners of War, Aegean Sea Continental Shelf; U.S. Diplomatic and Consular Staff in Tehran, Military and Paramilitary Activities in and against Nicaragua, Frontier Dispute, Border and Transborder Armed Actions, Arbitral Award of 31 July 1989, Passage through the Great Belt, Questions of Interpretation and Application of the 1971 Montreal Convention arising from the Aerial Incident at Lockerbie* (two cases), *Application of the Convention on the Prevention and Punishment of the Crime of Genocide,* (Bosnia-Herzegovina v. Yugoslavia) two requests, *Land and Maritime Boundary between Cameroon and Nigeria, Request for an examination of the Situation in accordance with Paragraph 63 of the Court's Judgment of 20 December 1974 in the Nuclear Tests* case (New Zealand v. France), *Breard, La Grand, Legality of the Use of Force* (10 cases and 10 requests), *Arrest Warrant,* Armed *Activities on the Territory of the Congo* (two cases, one of which is based on a new application after previously being discontinued, both of which are currently pending).

[22] This follows the principle of Roman law – *reus in excipiendo actor est* – according to which, by opposing an exception to the plaintiff's claim, the defendant assumes the role of plaintiff *et seq.*

[23] Article 79 of the 1978 Rules of Court as amended on 5 December 2000.

[24] See S. Schwebel, "Preliminary Rulings by the International Court of Justice at the Instance of National Courts", 28 *Virginia Journal of International Law* 495 (1988) and Rosenne's reply, 29 ibid. 401 (1989). And see [1976] *Digest of United States Practice* in *International Law,* 650.

[25] Cf. F. Frankfurter, "A Note on Advisory Opinions", 37 *Harvard Law Review* 1002 (1924). Generally see K.J. Keith, *The Extent of the Advisory Jurisdiction of the International Court of Justice* (1971).

[26] *Frontier between Turkey and Iraq* case, B 12 (1925). And cf. the separate opinion of Sir Hersch Lauterpacht in the *South West Africa* (voting procedure) advisory opinion, 1955, 67, 98. See on this M. Pomerance, *The Advisory Function of the International Court* in *The League and U.N. Eras* (1973).

[27] *Eastern Carelia* case, B 5 (1923). In the opinion of many, this doctrine may have been considerably weakened, if not overruled entirely, by the jurisprudence of the present Court, notably in the *Peace Treaties* and *Namibia* cases.

[28] Boutros Boutros-Ghali, *An Agenda for Peace*, United Nations, DPI/1247, 1992.47 GAOR annexes, agenda item 10 (doc. A/47/277, S/24111) (1992) at 22.

Chapter 5

[1] See *International Court of Justice YB* 1973-74 127.

[2] The principal orders and judgments in this case are as follows: Order of 10 May 1984 indicating provisional measures of protection, 1984 169; Order of 4 October 1984 dismissing the declaration of intervention by El Salvador, *ibid.* 215; Judgment of 26 November 1984 on jurisdiction and admissibility, ibid. 392; Order of 22 January 1985 fixing time-limits for the proceedings on the merits, 1985 3; Judgment of 27 June 1986 on the merits, 1986 *ibid.* 14; Order of 18 November 1987 on the compensation phase, 1987 *ibid.* 188; Order of 26 September 1991 on discontinuance of the case, 1991 *ibid.* 47.

[3] On the Agent, see Rosenne's "The Agent in Litigation in the International Court of Justice", *An International Law Miscellany* 259 (1993).

[4] See on this the dissenting opinion of Judge Schwebel in the merits phase of the case, 1986, at 320-21.

[5] See Practice Direction I, included in Appendix II.B below.

[6] See Practice Direction III, included in Appendix II.B below.

[7] See Rosenne's *Intervention* in *the International Court of Justice* (1993). Articles 81 to 86 of the Rules regulate what is termed the "incidental procedure of intervention."

[8] The Court made one such inspection in the *Gabčikovo-Nagymaros* case, but refused to do so in the *South West Africa* case and in the *Land, Island and Maritime Frontier* case.

[9] For descriptions of how deliberations were conducted under that resolution, cf. M. Hudson, *The Permanent Court of International Justice, 1920-1942,* 579 (1943).
[10] Acts and Documents concerning the Organization of the Court, No.5. *Charter of the United Nations, Statute and Rules of Court and Other Documents* 164 (1989); Rosenne's *Documents* 441.
[11] *The International Court of Justice* 58 (3rd ed., 1986, prepared by the Registry).
[12] Rules of Court, Articles 93 and 94. An analogous system of public reading and of circulation is prescribed for advisory opinions (Rules of Court, Article 107). Orders indicating provisional measures of protection are sent to the Security Council. Where orders are not read in open court, copies are sent to the parties and made available to the public. An appropriate press release is issued by the Registry regarding all activities, including judicial activities, of the Court.
[13] For the texts of these statements, see 24 ILM 246, 249, 1742 (1985).
[14] Sir Hersch Lauterpacht, *The Development of International Law by the International Court* 68 (1958). *Application for Review of Judgement No.333 of the United Nations Administrative Tribunal* (Yakimetz case), 1987 18, 45 (para. 49).
[15] Department of State, Special Report No. 132, September 1985.
[16] The literature on the *Nicaragua* case is vast. For a thorough discussion and analysis of the case see *inter alia* T.D. Gill, *Litigation Strategy of the International Court: a Case Study of the Nicaragua v. United States Dispute* 1989.
[17] In Nicaragua, the Congress enacted legislation designed to prevent the Government from settling the case, but after the change of Government this was revoked.
[18] See discussion at the 888th meeting of the Commission. ILCYB 1966, vol. I part 2, 295.
[19] See *Iran-United States Claims Tribunal Reports,* 27 volumes to date. For the basic texts, see vol. I, at 3 (1983).
[20] 1973 International Court of Justice 166, 211 (paras. 87-99).
[21] *Application for Revision and Interpretation* (Tunisia v. Libya) case, 1985 192, 216 (para. 43).
[22] See Security Council documents S/2590l, S/25929, S/26005, S/26008, S/26371 and S/26790 between 8 June and 23 November 1993, and Security Council resolutions 832 (1993) and 888 (1993), of 27 May and 30 November respectively.
[23] The so-called *Sabotage* cases before the United States/Germany Mixed Claims Commission are a well-known instance of collusive or fraudulent evidence before an international tribunal. See in particular *Lehigh Valley Railroad et al. v. Germany* (1993), VIII RIAA 160; J. G. Wetter, III *The International Arbitral Process: Public and Private* 302 (1979).

Chapter 6

[1] For the proceedings in the Security Council, see the *Official Records* of its 95th, 107th, 109th, 111th, 114th, l20th-122nd and 125th meetings, between 20 January and 3 April 1947. For the three judgments of the Court, see 1948 15; 1949 4, 244. For the orders on the appointment of the committees of experts, see 1948 124; 1949 237.
[2] For the first case, see 1948 57.
[3] 1949/174.
[4] 1951 116.
[5] [5] See the Geneva Convention of 1958 on the Territorial Sea and Contiguous Zone, and articles 3 to 13 of the 1982 Convention on the Law of the Sea. This Conference also dealt with another aspect of the law of the sea, emerging from the decision of the Permanent Court of International Justice in the *Lotus* case, A 10 (1927). There the Permanent Court held that a State could exercise criminal jurisdiction over a foreign ship on the high seas, if as a result of a collision on the high seas its nationals were injured. That decision was badly received in maritime circles, but only an international conference could change the general rule of international law which the Court found to be applicable. The 1958 Convention on the High Seas (article 11) now limits the jurisdiction, in such circumstances, to the flag State or the State of which the ship's officer concerned was a

national. This is repeated in article 97 of the 1982 Convention. In general see University of Virginia, Center for Oceans Law and Policy, II and III *The United Nations Convention on the Law of the Sea* 1982: *A Commentary* (1993, 1994, S. Nandan and Sh. Rosenne, eds.).

[6] 1950 59.

[7] 1950 266, 395; 1951 71.

[8] 1950 65, 221.

[9] For *South West Africa (Status)* case see 1950 128. For the contentious cases see 1961 13 (joinder); 1962 319 (preliminary objections); 1965 3 (Composition of the Court), 9 (Visit to the site); 1966 6 (Second phase).

[10] 1971 3, 6, 9, 12 (Composition of the Court), 16 (advisory opinion). For the change of name from South West Africa to Namibia, see General Assembly resolution 2372 (XXII), 12 June 1968.

[11] 1951 109; 1952 176. Questions relating to the Act of Algeciras also came before the Permanent Court in the *Phosphates in Morocco* case, A/B 74 (1938).

[12] 1951 15. In its opinion the Court dismissed challenges to its jurisdiction, which were similar to those put forward in the *Peace Treaties* case. Pakistan later invoked this convention as a basis for jurisdiction in the *Pakistani Prisoners of War* case and Bosnia in the case concerning the *Application of the Convention on the Prevention and Punishment of the Crime of Genocide.*

For the position in the League of Nations, see League of Nations, Committee of Experts for the Progressive Codification of International Law, *Minutes of the Third Session* (1927), Fifth Meeting, and Note by the Secretary-General, *Admissibility of Reservations to General Conventions,* docs. C.P.D.I./3rd Session/P.V. and C.357.M.130.1927.V. Reproduced in *League of Nations. The Progressive Codification of International Law* {1924-1928], vol. I lxxii, vol. II 25 (1972, ed. Sh. Rosenne). For the early position of the International Law Commission, see ILCYB 1950, II, 381; 1951, II, 125. For subsequent evolution, leading to the Vienna Convention, see ibid. 1962, II, 175; 1965, II, 161; 1966, II, 202. For the Vienna Convention, see 1155 UNTS 331. In 1993 the International Law Commission decided to undertake a re-examination of the topic of the law and practice relating to reservations to treaties in light of experience since the Vienna Convention was adopted. This was endorsed by the General Assembly in its resolution 48/31, 9 December 1993.

[14] 1952 28; 1953 10. For the award of 6 March 1956, see XII RIAA 91; 23 ILR 306 and 24 ibid. 291.

[15] (1952).

[16] 1951 89; (Provisional measures); 195293 (Preliminary objections); *International Court of Justice YB* 19525345. In the new agreement of September 1954, by which that dispute was settled, a similar power was conferred on the President of the present Court. For text, see J.C. Hurewitz, II *Diplomacy in the Near and Middle East,* 348 (1956).

[17] 1953 47.

[18] 1953 111; 1954 4.

[19] 1954 19. For the award of 20 February 1953, see XII RIAA 19; 20 ILR 441.

[20] 1954 107; 1960 186.

[21] *Awards of Compensation* case, 1954 47. By ten votes to three the Court decided to comply with the request for an advisory opinion; by nine votes to four it found that UNAT had not failed to exercise the jurisdiction vested in it; and by ten to three it held that UNAT had not committed a fundamental error in procedure which had occasioned a failure of justice. The President, Lachs, made a declaration which was the first major public statement by a Member of the Court casting doubts on the wisdom of this procedure. There was a joint declaration by Judges Forster and Nagendra Singh, separate opinions by Judges Onyeama, Dillard and Jiménez de Aréchaga. and dissenting opinions by Vice-President Ammoun and Judges Gros, de Castro and Morozov. *Application for Review of UNAT Judgement No.* 273 (Mortished), 1982 325. By nine votes to six the Court decided to comply with the request for an advisory opinion; by ten votes to five it found that UNAT did not err on a question of law relating to the Charter; and by twelve votes to three

that UNAT did not commit any excess of jurisdiction or competence. There were separate opinions by Judges Nagendra Singh, Ruda, Mosler and Oda, and dissenting opinions by Judges Lachs, Morozov, el-Khani and Schwebel. *Application for Review of UNAT Judgement No.* 333 (Yakimetz), 1987 18. Here the Court unanimously decided to comply with the' request for an advisory opinion. It was also unanimous the UNAT had not failed to exercise jurisdiction vested in it by not responding to a certain question which had been raised before it; and by eleven votes to three found that UNAT did not err on any question of law relating to the Charter. Judge Lachs made a declaration; there were separate opinions by Judges Elias, Oda and Ago, and dissenting opinions by Judges Schwebel, Sir Robert Jennings and Evensen.

[22] For these cases, see 1954 99, 103; 1956 6, 9; 1958 158; 1959 276.

[23] 1956 12, 15. There have been a series of arbitrations about the frontier between Argentina and Chile which was laid down in an obscurely worded treaty of 30 August 1855. At the end of the 19th century the British Sovereign undertook the duties of arbitrator. One award was rendered on 19 November 1902 (95 British & Foreign State Papers 162); another on 9 December 1966 (the *Palena* case) 38 ILR 10: and a third on 18 February 1977 (the *Beagle Channel* case), 52 ibid. 93. That latter did not settle the dispute which was submitted to the mediation of the Holy See, leading to the Treaty of Peace and Friendship of 29 November 1984, 24 ILM 3 (1985). The dispute between Argentina and the United Kingdom over the Falkland (Malvinas) Islands remains unsettled.

[24] 1957 9.

[25] 1957 125: 1960 6.

[26] 1958 55.

[27] 1957 105: 1959 6. For the final settlement, see Office of Alien Property, Department of Justice (Washington D.C.), *Annual Report. Fiscal Year ended June 30, 1958*, 63; *ibid. Fiscal Year ended June 30, 1965* 10.

[28] Israel v. Bulgaria, 1959 127. In the course of these proceedings, Bulgaria withdrew the other objection to the jurisdiction and agreed to defer consideration of two of the three objections to the admissibility until the proceedings on the merits. U.K. v. Bulgaria, 1959 264; U.S.A. v. Bulgaria, 1960 146.

[29] 1959 206.

[30] 1960 192; for the Award of 23 December 1906, see XI RIAA 107. For the decision of the Chairman of the Mixed Commission, see 30 ILR 76.

[31] 1961 9; 1964 6; 1970 3. For an important *layman's* account of this case, see John Brooks, "Annals of Finance, Privateer-II", *The New Yorker,* 28 May 1979,42.

[32] See Resolution A.12 (I) adopted by the Assembly of IMCO on 19 January 1959. For the Court's opinion, see 1960 150.

[33] 1961 17; 1962 6. For the statements of the Thailand government see Thailand Ministry for Foreign Affairs, *Foreign Affairs Bulletin,* vol. I, No.6, June-July 1962, 129.

[34] 1963 15.

[35] 1962 151.

[36] For the joinder, see 1968 9. For the judgment, see 1969 3. For the delimitations in the North Sea, see II *International Maritime Boundaries* 1711 (1993, J. Charney and L.M. Alexander, eds.).

[37] 1972 46.

[38] 1973 328 (Provisional measures); (Discontinuance).

[39] For the U.K. v. Iceland case, see 1972 12 (Provisional measures); 1973 3 (Jurisdiction of the Court); 302 (Continuation of provisional measures); 1974 3 (Merits). For the FRG v. Iceland case see 1972 30 (Provisional measures); 1973 49 (Jurisdiction of the Court); 313 (Continuation of provisional measures); 1974 175 (Merits).

[40] 1973 99, 135; 1974 253 (Australia), 457 (New Zealand). On the interventions by Fiji, see the orders of 12 July 1973 adopted by eight votes to five, with declarations by Judges Gros, Petrén, Onyeama and Ignacio-Pinto, 1973 320, 324; and of 20 December 1974, adopted unanimously with declarations by Judges Gros, Onyeama, a joint declaration by Judges Dillard and Sir

Humphrey Waldock, and a declaration by Judge Jiménez de Aréchaga and Judge *ad hoc* Sir Garfield Barwick, 1974 530, 535.
[41] 1976 3; 1978 3.
[42] 1975 6 (Composition of the Court); 12 (Advisory opinion).
[43] 1979 7 (Provisional measures); 1980 3 (Merits); 1981 ibid. 45 (Discontinuance).
[44] 1980 73.
[45] The major arbitrations to date on this question are the *Anglo-French Continental Shelf* case (1977,1978), 54 ILR 142; the *Jan Mayen Continental Shelf* conciliation (Iceland/Norway 1981), 62 ibid. 108; the *Guinea/Guinea Bissau Maritime Delimitation* case (1985), 77 ibid. 635; the *Guinea-Bissau/Senegal Maritime Delimitation* arbitration (1989) (and see p. 235 above); the *Delimitation of Maritime Areas between Canada and France* arbitration (1992), 31 ILM 1165; and the *Eritrea/Yemen Arbitration* (1998), 40 ILM 9000, 983. The earlier cases related to the delimitation of the continental shelf, the later to delimitation of maritime spaces more generally.
[46] *Libya/Tunisia* case, 1981 3 (Intervention of Malta); 1982 18 (Merits); 1985 192 (Revision and Interpretation). *Libya/Malta* case, 19843 (Intervention by Italy); 1985 13 (Merits). For a series of agreements for maritime delimitation in this part of the Mediterranean, see work cited in note 36 above, vol. II at 1611 (Italy/Tunisia), 1649 (Libya/Malta) 1663 (Libya/Tunisia).
[47] 1982 3 (Constitution of Chamber); 1984 165 (Appointment of Expert); 246, (Merits). For this delimitation, see the work cited in note 36 above, vol. I at 411.
[48] 1985 6 (Constitution of Chamber); 19863 (Provisional measures); 554 (Merits); 1987 ibid. 7 (Nomination of experts). For the resolution of the Organization of African Unity regarding Border Disputes among African States, see I. Brownlie (ed.), *Basic Documents on African Affairs* 360 (1971).
[49] 1987 179 (Discontinuance, Costa Rica); 1988 9 (Withdrawal of Request for provisional measures); 69 (Jurisdiction, Honduras); 1992 222 (Discontinuance).
[50] 1987 10 (Constitution of Chamber); 1989 162 {Constitution of Chamber); 1990 3 (Intervention, Order of the Court); 92 (Intervention); 1992351 (Merits). For the 1917 Judgment of the Central American Court of Justice in the case of *El Salvador v. Nicaragua,* see 11 AJIL 674 (1917).
[51] 1987 3 (Constitution of the Chamber); 1988 158 (Composition of the Chamber); 1989 15 (Merits).
[52] 1998 12. For the judgment of the United States District Court, Southern District of New York, in *United States* v. *The Palestine Liberation Organization and Others,* see 82 ILR 283.
[53] 1993 38. For earlier cases between the same parties involving Greenland, see the *Legal Status of the South-Eastern Territory of Greenland* case, A/B 48 (1932), 55 (1933, Discontinuance); *Legal Status of Eastern Greenland* case, ibid. 53 (1933). For the delimitation between Iceland and Jan Mayen through a conciliation machinery, see note 45 above.
[54] *Aerial Incident of 8 July 1988* case, 1989 132; *Oil Platforms* case, 1996 803.
[55] 1992 240; 1993 322. For the agreement of 10 August 1993 for the settlement of the case and the accompanying Joint Declaration of Principles guiding Relations between Australia and the Republic of Nauru of the same date, see 32 ILM 1471 (1993).
[56] 1989 177.
[57] 1994 6.
[58] 1995 90. For an earlier arbitration between the Netherlands and Portugal over the land frontier in the island, see the award of 25 June 1914 in the *Isle of Timor* case, XI RIM 585.
[59] 1990 64 (Provisional measures); 1991 53 (Merits). For the arbitral awards with Guinea and with Senegal, see note 45 above. On the delimitation problems in this part of Africa, see the work cited in note 36 above, vol. I 857, 867 (1993).
[60] 1991 12 (Provisional measures); 1992 348 (Discontinuance).
[61] Jurisdiction and Admissibility (Phase I) 1994 112
[62] *id.* 126-127
[63] 1994 130 (Separate Opinion Schwebel)
[64] *Id.* 135 (Dissenting Opinion Oda)

[65] S. Rosenne, "The Qatar/Bahrain Case; What is Treaty? A Framework Agreement and the Seising of the Court" in 8 (1995) *Leiden Journal of International Law* pp. 161-182, at p. 179.
[66] Jurisdiction and Admissibility (Phase II) 1995 6
[67] 2001 40 (forthcoming). The Judgement is reproduced in full in 40 ILM 847 (2001)
[68] 1992 3 (United Kingdom); 115 (United States). In the hearings, the Solicitor General of Scotland was included in the United Kingdom delegation.
[69] 1998 9 (United Kingdom); 115 (United States)
[70] 1993 3 (Provisional Measures); 1993 325 (Provisional Measures, Second Request); 1996 (Preliminary Objections).
[71] 1997 243 (Counter Claims)
[72] 1999 1015; 2000 3
[73] Provisional Measures: 1999 124 (Belgium); 1999 259 (Canada); 1999 363 (France); 1999 422 (Germany); 1999 481 (Italy); 1999 542 (Netherlands); 1999 656 (Portugal); 1999 761 (Spain); 1999 826 (United Kingdom); 1999 916 (United States).
[74] The Advisory Opinion on the request by the WHO is officially entitled *Legality of the Use by a State of Nuclear Weapons in Armed Conflict*, 1996 66; the Advisory Opinion on the request by the General Assembly is entitled *Legality of the Threat or Use of Nuclear Weapons*, 1996 226.
1998. See also the Court's communiqués 98/28 of 3 September 1998 (request for additional judgment) and 98/31 of 7 October 1998 (Hungary's written statement).
[75] 1998 275 (Preliminary Objections); 2001 9 (Intervention by Equatorial Guinea); Merits 2002 (forthcoming). The text of the unpublished decisions are available on the Court's website: www.icj-cij.org.
[76] 1998 423
[77] 1995 288
[78] 1999 248
[79] 1998 249 (Provisional Measures); 1998 426 (Discontinuance).
[82] 1999 1042; 2000 146
[83] 1997 7. For an earlier case in the Permanent Court involving the River Danube, see the advisory opinion on the *Jurisdiction of the European Commission of the River Danube*, 1314 (1927).
[84] 2001 3 (Discontinuance Burundi); 2001 6 (Discontinuance Rwanda).
[85] 2000 111
[86] 2000 12
[87] A further order was issued on 13 June 2002 fixing time limits for the filing of a Reply by Nicaragua by 12 January 2003 and for a Rejoinder by Honduras by 13 August 2003.
[88] 2002 (forthcoming). The Court's decision is reproduced in full in 41 ILM 536 (2002).
[89] Application of the Principality of Liechtenstein of 30 May 2001, para. 1. p. 1.
[90] 2002 (forthcoming). The text of these orders is available on the Court's website: www.icj-cij.org
[91] 2002 (forthcoming). The text of these orders is available on the Court's website: www.icj-cij.org
[92] See Press Release 2002/14 by the Court's information department available on the Court's website www.icj-cij.org

Chapter 7

[1] United Nations General Assembly, 21st Session, Official Records, annexes, agenda item 90, Report of the Sixth Committee, doc. A/8568, paras 45-46 (1971)
[2] See *inter alia* M. Bedjaoui, *The New World Order and the Security Council – Testing the Legality of its Acts*, T.D. Gill, "Some Legal and Political Limitations on the Power of the UN

Security Council to Exercise its Enforcement Powers under Chapter VII of the Charter, *Netherlands Yearbook of International Law* Vol. 26 (1995), pp. 22-138.

[3] Rosenne, "The Perplexities of Modern International Law", *RADI* Vol. 291, p. 129 (2002).

[4] *Id.* At p. 132 referring to a speech by the (then) President of the Court Schwebel to the UN General Assembly on 26 October 1999, A/54/PV. 39, 3. See also n. 196 *ibid.*

[5] *Id.* At 133 referring to a speech by the (then) President of the Court Guillaume to the UN General Assembly on 30 October 2001, A/56/PV. 32, p. 9.

APPENDIX I

THE CHARTER OF THE UNITED NATIONS AND THE STATUTE OF THE COURT EXTRACTS FROM THE CHARTER

CHAPTER III

Organs

Article 7

1. There are established as the principal organs of the United Nations: a General Assembly, a Security Council, an Economic and Social Council, a Trusteeship Council, an International Court of Justice, and a Secretariat.

CHAPTER VI

Pacific Settlement of Disputes

Article 33

1. The parties to any dispute, the continuance of which is likely to endanger the maintenance of international peace and security, shall, first of all, seek a solution by negotiation, enquiry, mediation, conciliation, arbitration, judicial settlement, resort to regional agencies or arrangements, or other peaceful means of their own choice.
2. The Security Council shall, when it deems necessary, call upon the parties to settle their dispute by such means.

Article 36

1. The Security Council may, at any stage of a dispute of the nature referred to in Article 33 or of a situation of like nature, recommend appropriate procedures or methods of adjustment.
2. The Security Council should take into consideration any procedures for the settlement of the dispute which have already been adopted by the parties.
3. In making recommendations under this Article, the Security Council should also take into consideration that legal disputes should as a general rule be referred by the parties to the International Court of Justice, in accordance with the provisions of the Statute of the Court.

CHAPTER XIV

The International Court of Justice

Article 92

The International Court of Justice shall be the principal judicial organ of the United Nations. It shall function in accordance with the annexed Statute, which is based upon the Statute of the Permanent Court of International Justice and forms an integral part of the present Charter.

Article 93

1. All members of the United Nations are *ipso facto* parties to the Statute of the International Court of Justice.
2. A state which is not a Member of the United Nations may become a party to the Statute of the International Court of Justice on conditions to be determined in each case by the General Assembly upon the recommendation of the Security Council.

Article 94

1. Each member of the United Nations undertakes to comply with the decision of the International Court of Justice in any case to which it is a party.
2. If any party to a case fails to perform the obligations incumbent upon it under a judgment rendered by the Court, the other party may have recourse to the Security Council, which may, if it deems necessary, make recommendations or decide upon measures to be taken to give effect to the judgment.

Article 95

Nothing in the present Charter shall prevent Members of the United Nations from entrusting the solution of their differences to other tribunals by virtue of agreements already in existence or which may be concluded In the future.

Article 96

1. The General Assembly or the Security Council may request the International Court of Justice to give an advisory opinion on any legal question.
2. Other organs of the United Nations and specialized agencies, which may at any time be so authorized by the General Assembly, may also request advisory opinions of the Court on legal questions arising within the scope of their activities.

STATUTE OF THE INTERNATIONAL COURT OF JUSTICE

Article 1

The *International Court of Justice* established by the Charter of the United Nations as the principal judicial organ of the United Nations shall be constituted and shall function in accordance with the provisions of the present Statute.

CHAPTER I

Organization of the Court

Article 2

The Court shall be composed of a body of independent judges, elected regardless of their nationality from among persons of high moral character, who possess the qualifications required in their respective countries for appointment to the highest judicial offices, or are jurisconsults of recognized competence in international law.

Article 3

1. The Court shall consist of fifteen members, no two of whom may be nationals of the same state.
2. A person who for the purposes of membership in the Court could be regarded as a national of more than one state shall be deemed to be a national of the one in which he ordinarily exercises civil and political rights.

Article 4

1. The members of the Court shall be elected by the General Assembly and by the Security Council from a list of persons nominated by the national groups in the Permanent Court of Arbitration, in accordance with the following provisions.
2. In the case of Members of the United Nations not represented in the Permanent Court of Arbitration, candidates shall be nominated by national groups appointed for this purpose by their governments under the same conditions as those prescribed for members of the Permanent Court of Arbitration by Article 44 of the Convention of The Hague of 1907 for the pacific settlement of international disputes.
3. The conditions under which a state which is a party to the present Statute but is not a member of the United Nations may participate in electing the members of the Court shall, in the absence of a special agreement, be laid down by the General Assembly upon recommendation of the Security Council.

Article 5

1. At least three months before the date of the election, the Secretary-General of the United Nations shall address a written request to the members of the Permanent Court of Arbitration belonging to the states which are parties to the present Statue, and to the members of the national groups appointed under Article 4, paragraph 2, inviting them to undertake, within a given time, by national groups, the nomination of persons in a position to accept the duties of a member of the Court.
2. No group may nominate more than four persons, not more than two of whom shall be of their own nationality. In no case may the number of candidates nominated by a group be more than double the number of seats to be filled.

Article 6

Before making these nominations, each national group is recommended to consult its highest court of justice, its legal faculties and schools of law, and its national academies and national sections of international academies devoted to the study of law.

Article 7

1. The Secretary-General shall prepare a list in alphabetical order of all the persons thus nominated. Save as provided in Article 12, paragraph 2, these shall be the only persons eligible.
2. The Secretary-General shall submit this list to the General Assembly and to the Security Council.

Article 8

The General Assembly and the Security Council shall proceed independently of one *another* to elect *the* members of the Court.

Article 9

At every election, the electors shall bear in mind not only that the persons to be elected should individually possess the qualifications required, but also that in the body as a whole the representation of the main forms of civilization and of the principal legal systems of the world should be assured.

Article 10

1. Those candidates who obtain an absolute majority of votes in the General Assembly and in the Security Council shall be considered as elected.
2. Any vote of the Security Council, whether for the election of judges or for the appointment of members of the conference envisaged in Article 12, shall be taken without any distinction between permanent and non-permanent members of the Security Council.
3. In the event of more than one national of the same state obtaining an absolute majority of the votes both of the General Assembly and of the Security Council, the eldest of these only shall be considered as elected.

Article 11

If, after the first meeting held for the purpose *of* the election, one or more seats remain to be filled, a second and, if necessary, a third meeting shall take place.

Article 12

1. If, after the third meeting, one or more seats still remain unfilled, a joint conference consisting of six members, three appointed by the General Assembly and three by the Security Council, may be formed at any time at the request of either the General Assembly or the Security Council, for the purpose of choosing by the vote of an absolute majority one name for each seat still vacant, to submit to the General Assembly and the Security Council for their respective acceptance.
2. If the joint conference is unanimously agreed upon any person who fulfils the required conditions, he may be included in its list, even though he was not included in the list of nominations referred to in Article 7.
3. If the joint conference is satisfied that It will not be successful in procuring an election, those members of the Court who have already been elected shall, within a period to be fixed by the Security Council, proceed to fill the vacant seats by selection from among those candidates who have obtained votes either in the General Assembly or in the Security Council.
4. In the event of an equality of votes among the judges, the eldest judge shall have a casting vote.

Article 13

1. The members of the Court shall be elected for nine years and may be re-elected; provided, however, that of the judges elected at the first election, the terms of five judges shall expire at the end of three years and the terms of five more judges shall expire at the end of six years.
2. The judges whose terms are to expire at the end of the above-mentioned initial periods of three and six years shall be chosen by lot to be drawn by the Secretary-General immediately after the first election has been completed.
3. The members of the Court shall continue to discharge their duties until their places

have been filled. Though replaced, they shall finish any cases which they may have begun.
4. In the case of resignation of a member of the Court, the resignation shall be addressed to the President of the Court for transmission to the Secretary-General. This last notification makes the place vacant.

Article 14

Vacancies shall be filled by the same method as that laid down for the first election, subject to the following provision: the Secretary-General shall, within one month of the occurrence of the vacancy, proceed to issue the invitations provided for in Article 5, and the date of the election shall be fixed by the Security Council.

Article 15

A member of the Court elected to replace a member whose term of office has not expired shall hold office for the remainder of his predecessor's term.

Article 16

1. No member of the Court may exercise any political or administrative function, or engage in any other occupation of a professional nature.
2. Any doubt on this point shall be settled by the decision of the Court.

Article 17

1. No member of the Court may act as an agent, counsel, or advocate in any case.
2. No member may participate in the decision of any case in which he has previously taken part as agent, counsel, or advocate for one of the parties, or as a member of a national or international court, or of a commission of enquiry, or in any other capacity.
3. Any doubt on this point shall be settled by the decision of the Court.

Article 18

1. No member of the Court can be dismissed unless, in the unanimous opinion of the other members, he has ceased to fulfill the required conditions.
2. Formal notification thereof shall be made to the Secretary-General by the Registrar.
3. This notification makes the place vacant.

Article 19

The members of the Court, when engaged on the business of the Court, shall enjoy diplomatic privileges and immunities.

Article 20

Every member of the Court shall, before taking up his duties, make a solemn declaration in open Court that he will exercise his power impartially and conscientiously.

Article 21

1. The Court shall elect its President and Vice-President for three years; they may be re-elected.
2. The Court shall appoint its Registrar and may provide for the appointment of such other officers as may be necessary.

Article 22

1. The seat of the Court shall be established at The Hague. This, however, shall not prevent the Court from sitting and exercising its functions elsewhere whenever the Court considers it desirable.
2. The President and the Registrar shall reside at the seat of the Court.

Article 23

1. The Court shall remain permanently in session, except during the judicial vacations, the dates and duration of which shall be fixed by the Court.
2. Members of the Court are entitled to periodic leave, the dates and duration of which shall be fixed by the Court, having in mind the distance between The Hague and the home of each judge.
3. Members of the Court shall be bound, unless they are on leave or prevented from attending by illness or other serious reasons duly explained to the President, to hold themselves permanently at the disposal of the Court.

Article 24

1. If, for some special reason, a member of the Court considers that he should not take part in the decision of a particular case, he shall so inform the President.
2. If the President considers that for some special reason one of the members of the Court should not sit in a particular case, he shall give him notice accordingly.
3. If in any such case the member of the Court and the President disagree, the matter shall be settled by the decision of the Court.

Article 25

1. The full Court shall sit except when it is expressly provided otherwise in the present Statute.
2. Subject to the condition that the number of judges available to constitute the Court is not thereby reduced below eleven, the Rules of the Court may provide for allowing one or more judges, according to circumstances and in rotation, to be dispensed from sitting.
3. A quorum of nine judges shall suffice to constitute the Court.

Article 26

1. The Court may from time to time form one or more chambers, composed of three or more judges as the Court may determine, for dealing with particular categories of cases; for example, labour cases and cases relating to transit and communications.
2. The Court may at any time form a chamber for dealing with a particular case. The number of judges to constitute such a chamber shall be determined by the Court with the approval of the parties.
3. Cases shall be heard and determined by the chambers provided for in this Article if the parties so request.

Article 27

A judgment given by any of the chambers provided for in Articles 26 and 29 shall be considered as rendered by the Court.

Article 28

The chambers provided for in Articles 26 and 29 may, with the consent of the parties, sit and exercise their functions elsewhere than at The Hague.

Article 29

With a view to the speedy despatch of business, the Court shall form annually a chamber composed of five judges which, at the request of the parties, may hear and determine cases by summary procedure. In addition, two judges shall be selected for the purpose of replacing judges who find it impossible to sit.

Article 30

1. The Court shall frame rules for carrying out its functions. In particular, it shall lay down rules of procedure.
2. The Rules of the Court may provide for assessors to sit with the Court or with any of its chambers, without the right to vote.

Article 31

1. Judges of the nationality of each of the parties shall retain their right to sit in the case before the Court.
2. If the Court includes upon the Bench a judge of the nationality of one of the parties, any other party may choose a person to sit as judge. Such person shall be chosen preferably from among those persons who have been nominated as candidates as provided in Articles 4 and 5.
3. If the Court includes upon the Bench no judge of the nationality of the parties, each of these parties may proceed to choose a judge as provided in paragraph 2 of this Article.
4. The provisions of this Article shall apply to the case of Articles 26 and 29. In such cases, the Present shall request one or, if necessary, two of the members of the Court forming the Chamber to give place to the members of the Court of the nationality of the parties concerned, and, failing such, or if they are unable to be present, to the judges specially chosen by the parties.
5. Should there by several parties in the same interest, they shall, for the purpose of the preceding provisions, be reckoned as one party only. Any doubt upon this point shall be settled by the decision of the Court.
6. Judges chosen as laid down in paragraphs 2, 3, and 4 of this Article shall fulfill the conditions required by Articles 2, 17 (paragraph 2), 20, and 24 of the present Statute. They shall take part in the decision on terms of complete equality with their colleagues.

Article 32

1. Each member of the Court shall receive an annual salary.
2. The President shall receive a special annual allowance.
3. The Vice-President shall receive a special allowance for every day on which he acts as President.
4. The judges chosen under Article 31, other than members of the Court, shall receive compensation for each day on which they exercise their functions.
5. These salaries, allowances, and compensation shall be fixed by the General Assembly. They may not be decreased during the term of office.
6. The salary of the Registrar shall be fixed by the General Assembly on the proposal of the Court.
7. Regulations made by the General Assembly shall fix the conditions under which

retirement pensions may be given to members of the Court and to the Registrar, and the conditions under which members of the Court and the Registrar shall have their travelling expenses refunded.
8. The above salaries, allowances, and compensation shall be free of all taxation.

Article 33

The expenses of the Court shall be borne by the United Nations in such a manner as shall be decided by the General Assembly.

CHAPTER II

Competence of the Court

Article 34

1. Only States maybe parties in cases before the Court.
2. The Court, subject to and in conformity with its Rules, may request of public international organizations information relevant to cases before it, and shall receive such information presented by such organizations on their own initiative.
3. Whenever the construction of the constituent instrument of a public international organization or of an international convention adopted thereunder is in question in a case before the Court, the Registrar shall so notify the public international organization concerned and shall communicate to it copies of all the written proceedings.

Article 35

1. The Court shall be open to the states parties to the present Statute.
2. The conditions under which the Court shall be open to other states shall, subject to the special provisions contained in treaties in force, be laid down by the Security Council, but in no case shall such conditions place the parties in a position of inequality before the Court.
3. When a state which is not a Member of the United Nations is a party to a case, the Court shall fix the amount which that party is to contribute towards the expenses of the Court. This provision shall not apply if such state is bearing a share of the expenses of the Court.

Article 36

1. The jurisdiction of the Court comprises all cases which the parties refer to it and all matters specially provided for in the Charter of the United Nations or in treaties and conventions in force.
2. The states parties to the present Statute may at any time declare that they recognize as compulsory *ipso facto* and without special agreement, in relation to any other state accepting the same obligation, the jurisdiction of the Court in all legal disputes concerning:
a. the interpretation of a treaty;
b. any question of international law;
c. the existence of any fact which, if established, would constitute a breach of an international obligation;
d. the nature or extent of the reparation to be made for the breach of an international

obligation.
3. The declarations referred to above may be made unconditionally or on condition or reciprocity on the part of several or certain states, or for a certain time.
4. Such declarations shall be deposited with the Secretary-General of the United Nations, who shall transmit copies thereof to the parties to the Statute and to the Registrar of the Court.
5. Declarations made under Article 36 of the Statute of the Permanent Court of International Justice and which are still in force shall be deemed, as between the parties to the present Statute, to be acceptances of the compulsory jurisdiction of the International Court of Justice for the period which they still have to run and in accordance with their terms.
6. In the event of a dispute as to whether the Court has jurisdiction, the matter shall be settled by the decision of the Court.

Article 37

Whenever a treaty or convention in force provides for reference of a matter to a tribunal to have been instituted by the League of Nations, or to the Permanent Court of International Justice, the matter shall, as between the parties to the present Statute, be referred to the International Court of Justice.

Article 38

1. The Court, whose function is to decide in accordance with international law such disputes as are submitted to it, shall apply:
a. international conventions, whether general or particular, establishing rules expressly recognized by the contesting states;
b. international custom, as evidence of a general practice accepted as law;
c. the general principles of law recognized by civilized nations;
d. subject to the provisions of Article 59, judicial decisions and the teachings of the most highly qualified publicists of the various nations, as subsidiary means for the determination of rules of law.
2. This provision shall not prejudice the power of the Court to decide a case *ex aequo et bono,* if the parties agree thereto.

CHAPTER III

Procedure

Article 39

1. The official languages of the Court shall be French and English. If the parties agree that the case shall be conducted in French, the judgment shall be delivered in French. If the parties agree that the case shall be conducted in English, the judgment shall be delivered in English.
2. In the absence of an agreement as to which language shall be employed, each party may, in the pleadings, use the language which it prefers; the decision of the Court shall be given in French and English. In this case the Court shall at the same time determine which of the two texts shall be considered as authoritative.
3. The Court shall, at the request of any party, authorize a language other than French or

English to be used by that party.

Article 40

1. Cases are brought before the Court, as the case may be, either by the notification of the special agreement or by a written application addressed to the Registrar. In either case the subject of the dispute and the parties shall be indicated.
2. The Registrar shall forthwith communicate the application to all concerned.
3. He shall also notify the Members of the United Nations through the Secretary-General, and also any other states entitled to appear before the Court.

Article 41

1. The Court shall have the power to indicate, if it considers that circumstances so require, any provisional measures which ought to be taken to preserve the respective rights of either party.
2. Pending the final decision, notice of the measures suggested shall f9rthwith be given to the parties and to the Security Council.

Article 42

1. The parties shall be represented by agents.
2. They may have the assistance of counselor advocates before the Court.
3. The agents, counsel, and advocates of parties before the Court shall enjoy the privileges and immunities necessary to the independent exercise of their duties.

Article 43

1. The procedure shall consist of two parts: written and oral.
2. The written proceedings shall consist of the communication to the Court and to the parties of memorials, counter-memorials and, if necessary, replies; also all papers and documents in support.
3. These communications shall be made through the Registrar, in the order and within the time fixed by the Court.
4. A certified copy of every document produced by one party shall be communicated to the other party.
5. The oral proceedings shall consist of the hearing by the Court of witnesses, experts, agents, counsel,. and advocates.

Article 44

1. For the service of all notices upon persons other than the agents, counsel, and advocates, the Court shall apply direct to the government of the state upon whose territory the notice has to be served.
2. The same provision shall apply whenever steps are to be taken to procure evidence on the spot.

Article 45

The hearing shall be under the control of the President or, if he is unable to preside, of the Vice-President; if neither is able to preside, the senior judge present shall preside.

Article 46

The hearing in Court shall be public, unless the Court shall decide otherwise, or unless the parties demand that the public be not admitted.

Article 47

1. Minutes shall be made at each hearing and signed by the Registrar and the President.
2. These minutes alone shall be authentic.

Article 48

The Court shall make orders for the conduct of the case, shall decide the form and time in which each party must conclude its arguments, and make all arrangements connected with the taking of evidence.

Article 49

The Court may, even before the hearing begins, call upon the agents to produce any document or to supply any explanations. Formal note shall be taken of any refusal.

Article 50

The Court may, at any time, entrust any individual, body, bureau, commission or other organization that it may select, with the task of carrying out an enquiry or giving an expert opinion.

Article 51

During the hearing any relevant questions are to be put to the witnesses and experts under the conditions laid down by the Court in the rules of procedure referred to in Article 30.

Article 52

After the Court has received the proofs and evidence within the time specified for the purpose, it may refuse to accept any further oral or written evidence that one party may desire to present unless the other side consents.

Article 53

1. Whenever one of the parties does not appear before the Court, or fails to defend its case, the other party may call upon the Court to decide in favour of its claim.
2. The Court must, before doing so, satisfy itself, not only that it has jurisdiction in accordance with Articles 36 and 37, but also that the claim is well founded in fact and law.

Article 54

1. When, subject to the control of the Court, the agents. counsel, and advocates have completed their presentation of the case, the President shall declare the hearing closed.
2. The Court shall withdraw to consider the judgment.
3. The deliberations of the Court shall take place in private and remain secret.

Article 55

1. All questions shall be decided by a majority of the judges present.
2. In the event of an equality of votes, the President or the judge who acts in his place shall have a casting vote.

Article 56

1. The judgment shall state the reasons on which it is based.
2. It shall contain the names of the judges who have taken part in the decision.

Article 57

If the judgment does not represent in whole or in part the unanimous opinion of the judges, any judge shall be entitled to deliver a separate opinion.

Article 58

The judgment shall be signed by the President and by the Registrar. It shall be read in open Court, due notice having been given to the agents.

Article 59

The decision of the Court has no binding force except between the parties and in respect of that particular case.

Article 60

The judgment is final and without appeal. In the event of dispute as to the meaning or scope of the judgment, the Court shall construe it upon the request of any party.

Article 61

1. An. application for revision of a judgment may be made only when it is based upon the discovery of some fact of such a nature as to be a decisive factor, which fact was, when the judgment was given, unknown to the Court and also to the party claiming revision, always provided that such ignorance was not due to negligence.
2. The proceedings for revision shall be opened by a judgment of the Court expressly recording the existence of the new fact, recognizing that it has such a character as to lay the case open to revision, and declaring the application admissible on this ground.
3. The Court may require previous compliance with the terms of the judgment before it admits proceedings in revision.
4. The application for revision must be made at latest within six months of the discovery of the new fact.
5. No application for revision may be made after the lapse of ten years from the date of the judgment.

Article 62

1. Should a state consider that it has an interest of a legal nature which may be affected by the decision in the case, it may submit a request to the Court to be permitted to intervene.
2. It shall be for the Court to decide upon this request.

Article 63

1. Whenever the construction of a convention to which states other than those concerned in the case are parties is in question, the Registrar shall notify all such states forthwith.
2. Every state so notified has the right to intervene in the proceedings; but if it uses this right, the construction given by the judgment will be equally binding upon it.

Article 64

Unless otherwise decided by the Court, each party shall bear its own costs.

CHAPTER IV

Advisory opinions

Article 65

1. The Court may give an advisory opinion on any legal question at the request of whatever body may by authorized by or in accordance with the Charter of the United Nations to make such a request.
2. Questions upon which the advisory opinion of the Court is asked shall be laid before the Court by means of a written request containing an exact statement of the question upon which an opinion is required, and accompanied by all documents likely to throw light upon the question.

Article 66

1. The Registrar shall forthwith give notice of the request for an advisory opinion to all states entitled to appear before the Court.
2. The Registrar shall also, by means of a special and direct communication, notify any state entitled to appear before the Court or international organization considered by the Court, or, should it not be sitting, by the President, as likely to be able to furnish information on the question, that the Court will be prepared to receive, within a time limit to be fixed by the President, written statements, or to hear, at a public sitting to be held for the purpose, oral statements relating to the question.
3. Should any such state entitled to appear before the Court have failed to receive the special communication referred to in paragraph 2 of this Article, such state may express a desire to submit a written statement or to be heard; and the Court will decide.
4. States and organizations having presented written or oral statements or both shall be permitted to comment on the statements made by other states or organizations in the form, to the extent, and within the time limits which the Court, or, should it not be sitting, the President, shall decide in each particular case. Accordingly, the Registrar shall in due time communicate any such written statements to states and organizations having submitted similar statements.

Article 67

The Court shall deliver its advisory opinions in open Court, notice having been given to the Secretary-General and to the representatives of Members of the United Nations, of other states and of international organizations immediately concerned.

Article 68

In the exercise of its advisory functions the Court shall further be guided by the provisions of the present Statute which apply in contentious cases to the extent to which it recognizes them to be applicable.

CHAPTER V

Amendment

Article 69

Amendments to the present Statute shall be effected by the same procedure as is provided by the Charter of the United Nations for amendments to that Charter, subject however to any provisions which the General Assembly upon recommendation of the Security Council may adopt concerning the participation of states which are parties to the present Statute but are not members of the United Nations.

Article 70

The Court shall have power to propose such amendments to the present Statute as it may deem necessary, through written communications to the Secretary-General, for consideration in conformity with the provisions of Article 69.

APPENDIX II.A

RULES OF COURT

ADOPTED ON 14 APRIL 1978
AS AMENDED ON 5 DECEMBER 2000

PREAMBLE

The Court,
Having regard to Chapter XIV of the Charter of the United Nations;
Having regard to the Statute of the Court annexed thereto;
Acting in pursuance of Article 30 of the Statute;
Adopts the amendments to Articles 79 and 80 of the Rules of Court as approved on 5 December 2000. The amended Rules shall come intor force on 1 February 2001, and shall as from that date replace the Rules adopted by the Court on 14 April 1978, save in respect of any case submitted to the Court before 1 February 2001, or any phase of such a case, which shall continue to be governed by the Rules in force before that date.

PART I

THE COURT

SECTION A. JUDGES AND ASSESSORS

Subsection 1. *The Members of the Court*

Article 1

1. The Members of the Court are the judges elected in accordance with Articles 2 to 15 of the Statute.
2. For the purposes of a particular case, the Court may also include upon the Bench one or more persons chosen under Article 31 of the Statute to sit as judges *ad hoc.*
3. In the following Rules, the term "Member of the Court" denotes any elected judge; the term "judge" denotes any Member of the Court, and any judge *ad hoc.*

Article 2

1. The term of office of Members of the Court elected at a triennial election shall begin to run from the sixth of February[1] in the year in which the vacancies to which they are elected occur.
2. The term of office of a Member of the Court elected to replace a Member whose term of office has not expired shall begin to run from the date of the election.

* Acts and Documents concerning the Organization of the Court, No.5, *Charter of the United Nations, Statute and Rules of Court and other Documents* (1989), p.93.
[1] This is the date on which the terms of office of the Members of the Court elected at the first election began in 1946.

Article 3

1. The Members of the Court, in the exercise of their functions, are of equal status, irrespective of age, priority of election or length of service.
2. The Members of the Court shall, except as provided in paragraphs 4 and 5 of this Article, take precedence according to the date on which their terms of office respectively began, as provided for by Article 2 of these Rules.
3. Members of the Court whose terms of office began on the same date shall take precedence in relation to one another according to seniority of age.
4. A Member of the Court who is re-elected to a new term of office which is continuous with his previous term shall retain his precedence.
5. The President and the Vice-President of the Court, while holding these offices, shall take precedence before all other Members of the Court.
6. The Member of the Court who, in accordance with the foregoing paragraphs, takes precedence next after the President and the Vice-President is in these Rules designated the "senior judge". If that Member is unable to act, the Member of the Court who is next after him in precedence and able to act is considered as senior judge.

Article 4

1. The declaration to be made by every Member of the Court in accordance with Article 20 of the Statute shall be as follows:

> "I solemnly declare that I will perform my duties and exercise my powers as judge honourably, faithfully, impartially and conscientiously."

2. This declaration shall be made at the first public sitting at which the Member of the Court is present. Such sitting shall be held as soon as practicable after his term of office begins and, if necessary, a special sitting shall be held for the purpose.
3. A Member of the Court who is re-elected shall make a new declaration only if his new term is not continuous with his previous one.

Article 5

1. A Member of the Court deciding to resign shall communicate his decision to the President, and the resignation shall take effect as provided in Article 13, paragraph 4, of the Statute.
2. If the Member of the Court deciding to resign from the Court is the President, he shall communicate his decision to the Court, and the resignation shall take effect as provided in Article 13, paragraph 4, of the Statute.

Article 6

In any case in which the application of Article 18 of the Statute is under consideration, the Member of the Court concerned shall be so informed by the President or, if the circumstances so require, by the Vice-President, in a written statement which shall include the grounds therefore and any relevant evidence. He shall subsequently, at a private meeting of the Court specially convened for the purpose, be afforded an opportunity of making a statement, of furnishing any information or explanations he wishes to give, and of supplying answers, orally or in writing, to any questions put to him. At a further private meeting, at which the Member of the Court concerned shall not be present, the matter shall be discussed; each Member of the Court shall state his opinion, and if requested a vote shall be taken.

Subsection 2. *Judges* ad hoc

Article 7

1. Judges *ad hoc,* chosen under Article 31 of the Statute for the purposes of particular cases, shall be admitted to sit on the Bench of the Court in the circumstances and according to the procedure indicated in Article 17, paragraph 2, Articles 35, 36, 37, Article 91, paragraph 2, and Article 102, paragraph 3, of these Rules.
2. They shall participate in the case in which they sit on terms of complete equality with the other judges on the Bench.
3. Judges *ad hoc* shall take precedence after the Members of the Court and in order of seniority of age.

Article 8

I. The solemn declaration to be made by every judge *ad hoc* in accordance with Articles 20 and 31, paragraph 6, of the Statute shall be as set out in Article 4, paragraph I, of these Rules.
2. This declaration shall be made at a public sitting in the case in which the judge *ad hoc* is participating. If the case is being dealt with by a chamber of the Court, the declaration shall be made in the same manner in that chamber.
3. Judges *ad hoc* shall make the declaration in relation to any case in which they are participating, even if they have already done so in a previous case, but shall not make a new declaration for a later phase of the same case.

Subsection 3. Assessors

Article 9

1. The Court may, either *proprio motu* or upon a request made not later than the closure of the written proceedings, decide, for the purpose of a contentious case or request for advisory opinion, to appoint assessors to sit with it without the right to vote.
2. When the Court so decides, the President shall take steps to obtain all the information relevant to the choice of the assessors.
3. The assessors shall be appointed by secret ballot and by a majority of the votes of the judges composing the Court for the case.
4. The same powers shall belong to the Chambers provided for by Articles 26 and 29 of the Statute and to the presidents thereof, and may be exercised in the same manner.
5. Before entering upon their duties, assessors shall make the following declaration at a public sitting:

> "I solemnly declare that I will perform my duties as an assessor honourably, impartially and conscientiously, and that I will faithfully observe all the provisions of the Statute and of the Rules of the Court."

SECTION B. THE PRESIDENCY

Article 10

1. The term of office of the President and that of the Vice-President shall begin to run from the date on which the terms of office of the Members of the Court elected at a triennial election begin in accordance with Article 2 of these Rules.

2. The elections to the presidency and vice-presidency shall be held on that date or shortly thereafter. The former President, if still a Member of the Court, shall continue to exercise his functions until the election to the presidency has taken place.

Article 11

1. If, on the date of the election to the presidency, the former President is still. a Member of the Court, he shall. conduct the election. If he has ceased to be a Member of the Court, or is unable to act, the election shall be conducted by the Member of the Court exercising the functions of the presidency by virtue of Article I. 3, paragraph I, of these Rules.
2. The election shall take place by secret ballot, after the presiding Member of the Court has declared the number of affirmative votes necessary for election; there shall be no nominations. The Member of the Court obtaining the votes of a majority of the Members composing it at the time of the election shall be declared elected, and shall enter forthwith upon his functions.
3. The new President shall conduct the election of the Vice-President either at the same or at the following meeting. The provisions of paragraph 2 of this Article shall apply equally to this election.

Article 12

The President shall preside at all meetings of the Court; he shall direct the work and supervise the administration of the Court.

Article 13

1. In the event of a vacancy in the presidency or of the inability of the President to exercise the functions of the presidency, these shall be exercised by the Vice-President, or failing him, by the senior judge.
2. When the President is precluded by a provision of the Statute or of these Rules either from sitting or from presiding in a particular case, he shall continue to exercise the functions of the presidency for all purposes save in respect of that case.
3. The President shall take the measures necessary in order to ensure the continuous exercise of the functions of the presidency at the seat of the Court. In the event of his absence, he may, so far as is compatible with the Statute and these Rules, arrange for these functions to be exercised by the Vice-President, or failing him, by the senior judge.
4. If the President decides to resign the presidency, he shall communicate his decision in writing to the Court through the Vice-President, or failing him, the senior judge. If the Vice-President decides to resign his office, he shall communicate his decision to the President.

Article 14

If a vacancy in the presidency or the vice-presidency occurs before the date when the current term is due to expire under Article 21, paragraph 1, of the Statute and Article 10, paragraph 1, of these Rules, the Court shall decide whether or not the vacancy shall be filled during the remainder of the term.

SECTION C. THE CHAMBERS

Article 15

1. The Chamber of Summary Procedure to be formed annually under Article 29 of the Statute shall be composed of five Members of the Court, comprising the President and Vice-President of the Court, acting ex officio, and three other members elected in accordance with Article 18, paragraph 1, of these Rules. In addition, two Members of the Court shall be elected annually to act as substitutes.
2. The election referred to in paragraph I of this Article shall beheld as soon as possible after the sixth of February in each year. The members of the Chamber shall enter upon their functions on election and continue to serve until the next election; they may be re-elected.
3. If a member of the Chamber is unable, for whatever reason, to sit in a given case, he shall be replaced for the purposes of that case by the senior in precedence of the two substitutes.
4. If a member of the Chamber resigns or otherwise ceases to be a member, his place shall be taken by the senior in precedence of the two substitutes, who shall thereupon become a full member of the Chamber and be replaced by the election of another substitute. Should vacancies exceed the number of available substitutes, elections shall be held as soon as possible in respect of the vacancies still existing after the substitutes have assumed full membership and in respect of the vacancies in the substitutes.

Article 16

1. When the Court decides to form one or more of the Chambers provided for in Article 26, paragraph I, of the Statute, it shall determine the particular category of cases for which each Chamber is formed, the number of its members, the period for which they will serve, and the date at which they will enter upon their duties.
2. The members of the Chamber shall be elected in accordance with Article 18, paragraph I, of these Rules from among the Members of the Court, having regard to any special knowledge, expertise or previous experience which any of the Members of the Court may have in relation to the category of case the Chamber is being formed to deal with.
3. The Court may decide upon the dissolution of a Chamber, but without prejudice to the duty of the Chamber concerned to finish any cases pending before it.

Article 17

1. A request for the formation of a Chamber to deal with a particular case, as provided for in Article 26, paragraph 2, of the Statute, may be filed at any time until the closure of the written proceedings. Upon receipt of a request made by one party, the President shall ascertain whether the other party assents.
2. When the parties have agreed, the President shall ascertain their views regarding the composition of the Chamber, and shall report to the Court accordingly. He shall also take such steps as may be necessary to give effect to the provisions of Article 31, paragraph 4, of the Statute.
3. When the Court has determined, with the approval of the parties, the number of its Members who are to constitute the Chamber, it shall proceed to their election, in accordance with the provisions of Article 18, paragraph 1, of these Rules. The same procedure shall be followed as regards the filling of any vacancy that may occur on the

Chamber.
4. Members of a Chamber formed under this Article who have been replaced, in accordance with Article 13 of the Statute following the expiration of their terms of office, shall continue to sit in all phases of the case, whatever the stage it has then reached.

Article 18

1. Elections to all Chambers shall take place by secret ballot. The Members of the Court obtaining the largest number of votes constituting a majority of the Members of the Court composing it at the time of the election shall be declared elected. If necessary to fill vacancies, more than one ballot shall take place, such ballot being limited to the number of vacancies that remain to be filled.
2. If a Chamber when formed includes the President or Vice-President of the Court, or both of them, the President or Vice-President, as the case may be, shall preside over that Chamber. In any other event, the Chamber shall elect its own president by secret ballot and by a majority of votes of its members. The Member of the Court who, under this paragraph, presides over the Chamber at the time of its formation shall continue to preside so long as he remains a member of that Chamber.
3. The president of a Chamber shall exercise, in relation to cases being dealt with by that Chamber, all the functions of the President of the Court in relation to cases before the Court.
4. If the president of a Chamber is prevented from sitting or from acting as president, the functions of the presidency shall be assumed by the member of the Chamber who is the senior in precedence and able to act.

SECTION D. INTERNAL FUNCTIONING OF THE COURT

Article 19

The internal judicial practice of the Court shall, subject to the provisions of the Statute and these Rules, be governed by any resolutions on the subject adopted by the Court.

Article 20

1. The quorum specified by Article 25, paragraph 3, of the Statute applies to all meetings of the Court.
2. The obligation of Members of the Court under Article 23, paragraph 3, of the Statute, to hold themselves permanently at the disposal of the Court, entails attendance at all such meetings, unless they are prevented from attending by illness or for other serious reasons duly explained to the President, who shall inform the Court.
3. Judges *ad hoc* are likewise bound to hold themselves at the disposal of the Court and to attend all meetings held in the case in which they are participating. They shall not be taken into account for the calculation of the quorum.
4. The Court shall fix the dates and duration of the judicial vacations and the periods and conditions of leave to be accorded to individual Members of the Court under Article 23, paragraph 2, of the Statute, having regard in both cases to the state of its General List and to the requirements of its current work.
5. Subject to the same considerations, the Court shall observe the public holidays customary at the place where the Court is sitting.

6. In case of urgency the President may convene the Court at any time.

Article 21

1. The deliberations of the Court shall take place in private and remain secret. The Court may however at any time decide in respect of its deliberations on other than judicial matters to publish or allow publication of any part of them.
2. Only judges, and the assessors, if any, take part in the Court's judicial deliberations. The Registrar, or his deputy, and other members of the staff of the Registry as may be required shall be present. No other person shall be present except by permission of the Court.
3. The minutes of the Court's judicial deliberations shall record only the title or nature of the subjects or matters discussed, and the results of any vote taken. They shall not record any details of the discussions nor the views expressed, provided however that any judge is entitled to require that a statement made by him be inserted in the minutes.

PART II

THE REGISTRY

Article 22

1. The Court shall elect its Registrar by secret ballot from amongst candidates proposed by Members of the Court. The Registrar shall be elected for a term of seven years. He may be re-elected.
2. The President shall give notice of a vacancy or impending vacancy to Members of the Court, either forthwith upon the vacancy arising, or, where the vacancy will arise on the expiration of the term of office of the Registrar, not less than three months prior thereto. The President shall fix a date for the closure of the list of candidates so as to enable nominations and information concerning the candidates to be received in sufficient time.
3. Nominations shall indicate the relevant information concerning the candidate, and in particular information as to his age, nationality, and present occupation, university qualifications, knowledge of languages, and any previous experience in law, diplomacy or the work of international organizations.
4. The candidate obtaining the votes of the majority of the Members of the Court composing it at the time of the election shall be declared elected.

Article 23

The Court shall eject a Deputy-Registrar: the provisions of Article 22 of these Rules shall apply to his election and term of office.

Article 24

1. Before taking up his duties, the Registrar shall make the following declaration at a meeting of the Court:

> "I solemnly declare that I will perform the duties incumbent upon me as Registrar of the International Court of Justice in all loyalty, discretion and good conscience, and that I will faithfully observe all the provisions of the Statute and of the Rules of the Court."

2. The Deputy-Registrar shall make a similar declaration at a meeting of the Court before taking up his duties.

Article 25

1. The staff-members of the Registry shall be appointed by the Court on proposals submitted by the Registrar. Appointments to such posts as the Court shall determine may however be made by the Registrar with the approval of the President.
2. Before taking up his duties, every staff-member shall make the following declaration before the President, the Registrar being present:

> "I solemnly declare that I will perform the duties incumbent upon me as an official of the International Court of Justice in all loyalty, discretion and good conscience, and that I will faithfully observe all the provisions of the Statute and of the Rules of the Court."

Article 26

1. The Registrar, in the discharge of his functions, shall:
(a) be the regular channel of communications to and from the Court, and in particular shall effect all communications, notifications and transmission of documents required by the Statute or by these Rules and ensure that the date of despatch and receipt thereof may be readily verified;
(b) keep, under the supervision of the President, and in such form as may be laid down by the Court, a General List of all cases, entered and numbered in the order in which the documents instituting proceedings or requesting an advisory opinion are received in the Registry;
(c) have the custody of the declarations accepting the jurisdiction of the Court made by States not parties to the Statute in accordance with any resolution adopted by the Security Council under Article 35, paragraph 2, of the Statute, and transmit certified copies thereof to all States parties to the Statute, to such other States as shall have deposited declarations, and to the Secretary-General of the United Nations;
(d) transmit to the parties copies of all pleadings and documents annexed upon receipt thereof in the Registry;
(e) communicate to the government of the country in which the Court or a Chamber is sitting, and any other governments which may be concerned, the necessary information as to the persons from time to time entitled, under the Statute and relevant agreements, to privileges, immunities, or facilities;
(f) be present, in person or by his deputy, at meetings of the Court, and of the Chambers, and be responsible for the preparation of minutes of such meetings;
(g) make arrangements for such provision or verification of translations and interpretations into the Court's official languages as the Court may require;
(h) sign all judgments, advisory opinions and orders of the Court, and the minutes referred to in subparagraph *(f);*
(i) be responsible for the printing and publication of the Court's judgments, advisory opinions and orders, the pleadings and statements, and minutes of public sittings in cases, and of such other documents as the Court may direct to be published;
(j) be responsible for all administrative work and in particular for the accounts and financial administration in accordance with the financial procedures of the United Nations;
(k) deal with enquiries concerning the Court and its work;
(l) assist in maintaining relations between the Court and other organs of the United Nations, the specialized agencies, and international bodies and conferences concerned with the codification and progressive development of international law;

(m) ensure that information concerning the Court and its activities is made accessible to governments, the highest national courts of justice, professional and learned societies, legal faculties and schools of law, and public information media;
(n) have custody of the seals and stamps of the Court, of the archives of the Court, and of such other archives as may be entrusted to the Court[1].

2. The Court may at any time entrust additional functions to the Registrar.
3. In the discharge of his functions the Registrar shall be responsible to the Court.

[1] The Registrar also keeps the Archives of the Permanent Court of International Justice, entrusted to the present Court by decision of the Permanent Court of October 1945 (*I.CJl. Yearbook* 1946-1947, p. 26), and the Archives of the Trial of the Major War Criminals before the International Military Tribunal at Nuremberg (1945-1946), entrusted to the Court by decision of that Tribunal of 1 October 1946; the Court authorized the Registrar to accept the latter Archives by decision of 19 November 1949.

Article 27

1. The Deputy-Registrar shall assist the Registrar, act as Registrar in the latter's absence and, in the event of the office becoming vacant, exercise the functions of Registrar until the office has been filled.
2. If both the Registrar and the Deputy-Registrar are unable to carry out the duties of Registrar, the President shall appoint an official of the Registry to discharge those duties for such time as may be necessary. If both offices are vacant at the same time, the President, after consulting the Members of the Court, shall appoint an official of the Registry to discharge the duties of Registrar pending an election to that office.

Article 28

1. The Registry shall comprise the Registrar, the Deputy-Registrar, and such other staff as the Registrar shall require for the efficient discharge of his functions.
2. The Court shall prescribe the organization of the Registry, and shall for this purpose request the Registrar to make proposals.
3. Instructions for the Registry shall be drawn up by the Registrar and approved by the Court.
4. The staff of the Registry shall be subject to Staff Regulations drawn up by the Registrar, so far as possible in conformity with the United Nations Staff Regulations and Staff Rules, and approved by the Court.

Article 29

1. The Registrar may be removed from office only if, in the opinion of two thirds of the Members of the Court, he has either become permanently incapacitated from exercising his functions, or has committed a serious breach of his duties.
2. Before a decision is taken under this Article, the Registrar shall be informed by the President of the action contemplated, in a written statement which shall include the grounds therefor and any relevant evidence. He shall subsequently, at a private meeting of the Court, be afforded an opportunity of making a statement, of furnishing any information or explanations he wishes to give, and of supplying answers, orally or in writing, to any questions put to him.
3. The Deputy-Registrar may be removed from office only on the same grounds and by

the same procedure.

PART III

PROCEEDINGS IN CONTENTIOUS CASES

SECTION A. COMMUNICATIONS TO THE COURT AND CONSULTATIONS

Article 30

All communications to the Court under these Rules shall be addressed to the Registrar unless otherwise stated. Any request made by a party shall likewise be addressed to the Registrar unless made in open court in the course of the oral proceedings.

Article 31

In every case submitted to the Court, the President shall ascertain the views of the parties with regard to questions of procedure. For this purpose he shall summon the agents of the parties to meet him as soon as possible after their appointment, and whenever necessary thereafter.

SECTION B. THE COMPOSITION OF THE COURT FOR PARTICULAR CASES

Article 32

1. If the President of the Court is a national of one of the parties in a case he shall not exercise the functions of the presidency in respect of that case. The same rule applies to the Vice-President, or to the senior Judge, when called on to act as President.
2. The Member of the Court who is presiding in a case on the date on which the Court convenes for the oral proceedings shall continue to preside in that case until 'completion of the current phase of the case, notwithstanding the election in the meantime of a new President or Vice-President. If he should become unable to act, the presidency for the case shall be determined in accordance with Article 13 of these Rules, and on the basis of the composition of the Court on the date on which it convened for the oral proceedings.

Article 33

Except as provided in Article 17 of these Rules, Members of the Court who have been replaced, in accordance with Article 13, paragraph 3, of the Statute following the expiration of their terms of office, shall discharge the duty imposed upon them by that paragraph by continuing to sit until the completion of any phase of a case in respect of which the Court convenes for the oral proceedings prior to the date of such replacement.

Article 34

1. In case of any doubt arising as to the application of Article 17, paragraph 2, of the Statute or in case of a disagreement as to the application of Article 24 of the Statute, the President shall inform the Members of the Court, with whom the decision lies.
2. If a party desires to bring to the attention of the Court facts which it considers to be of possible relevance to the application of the provisions of the Statute mentioned in the

previous paragraph, but which it believes may not be known to the Court, that party shall communicate confidentially such facts to the President in writing.

Article 35

1. If a party proposes to exercise the power conferred by Article 31 of the Statute to choose a judge *ad hoc* in a case, it shall notify the Court of its intention as soon as possible. If the name and nationality of the judge selected are not indicated at the same time, the party shall, not later than two months before the time-limit fixed for the filing of the Counter-Memorial, inform the Court of the name and nationality of the person chosen and supply brief biographical details. The judge *ad hoc* may be of a nationality other than that of the party which chooses him.
2. If a party proposes to abstain from choosing a judge *ad hoc,* on condition of a like abstention by the other party, it shall so notify the Court which shall inform the other party. If the other party thereafter gives notice of its intention to choose, or chooses, a judge *ad hoc,* the time-limit for the party which has previously abstained from choosing a judge may be extended by the President.
3. A copy of any notification relating to the choice of a judge *ad hoc* shall be communicated by the Registrar to the other party, which shall be requested to furnish, within a time-limit to be fixed by the President, such observations as it may wish to make. If within the said time-limit no objection is raised by the other party, and if none appears to the Court itself, the parties shall be so informed.
4. In the event of any objection or doubt, the matter shall be decided by the Court, if necessary after hearing the parties.
5. A judge *ad hoc* who has accepted appointment but who becomes unable to sit may be replaced.
6. If and when the reasons for the participation of a judge *ad hoc* are found no longer to exist, he shall cease to sit on the Bench.

Article 36

1. If the Court finds that two or more parties are in the same interest, and therefore are to be reckoned as one party only, and that there is no Member of the Court of the nationality of anyone of those parties upon the Bench, the Court shall fix a time-limit within which they may jointly choose a judge *ad hoc.*
2. Should any party amongst those found by the Court to be in the same interest allege the existence of a separate interest of its own, or put forward any other objection, the matter shall be decided by the Court, if necessary after hearing the parties.

Article 37

1. If a Member of the Court having the nationality of one of the parties is or becomes unable to sit in any phase of a case, that party shall there upon become entitled to choose a judge *ad hoc* within a time-limit to be fixed by the Court, or by the President if the Court is not sitting.
2. Parties in the same interest shall be deemed not to have a judge of one of their nationalities upon the Bench if the Member of the Court having one of their nationalities is or becomes unable to sit in any phase of the case.
3. If the Member of the Court having the nationality of a party becomes able to sit not later than the closure of the written proceedings in that phase of the case, that Member of the Court shall resume his seat on the Bench in the case.

SECTION C. PROCEEDINGS BEFORE THE COURT

Subsection 1. Institution of Proceedings

Article 38

1. When proceedings before the Court are instituted by means of an application addressed as specified in Article 40, paragraph I, of the Statute, the application shall indicate the party making it, the State against which the claim is brought, and the subject of the dispute.
2. The application shall specify as far as possible the .legal grounds upon which the jurisdiction of the Court is said to be based; it shall also specify the precise nature of the claim, together with a succinct statement of the facts and grounds on which the claim is based.
3. The original of the application shall be signed either by the agent of the party submitting it, or by the diplomatic representative of that party in the country in which the Court has its seat, or by some other duly authorized person. If the application bears the signature of someone other than such diplomatic representative, the signature must be authenticated by the latter or by the competent authority of the applicant'~ foreign ministry.
4. The Registrar shall forthwith transmit to the respondent a certified copy of the application.
5. When the applicant State proposes to found the jurisdiction of the Court upon a consent thereto yet to be given or manifested by the State against which such application is made, the application shall be transmitted to that State. It shall not however be entered in the General List, nor any action be taken in the proceedings, unless and until the State against which such application is made consents to the Court's jurisdiction for the purposes of the case.

Article 39

1. When proceedings are brought before the Court by the notification of a special agreement, in conformity with Article 40, paragraph 1, of the Statute, the notification may be effected by the parties jointly or by any one or more of them. I f the notification is not a joint one, a certified copy of it shall forthwith be communicated by the Registrar to the other party.
2. In each case the notification shall be accompanied by an original or certified copy of the special agreement. The notification shall also, in so far as this is not already apparent from the agreement, indicate the precise subject of the dispute and identify the parties to it.

Article 40

1. Except in the circumstances contemplated by Article 38, paragraph 5, of these Rules, all steps on behalf of the parties after proceedings have been instituted shall be taken by agents. Agents shall have an address for service at the seat of the Court to which all communications concerning the case are to be sent. Communications addressed to the agents of the parties shall be considered as having been addressed to the parties themselves.
2. When proceedings are instituted by means of an application, the name of the agent for the applicant shall be stated. The respondent, upon receipt of the certified copy of

the application, or as soon as possible thereafter, shall inform the Court of the name of its agent.
3. When proceedings are brought by notification of a special agreement, the party making the notification shall state the name of its agent. Any other party to the special agreement, upon receiving from the Registrar a certified copy of such notification, or as soon as possible thereafter, shall inform the Court of the name of its agent if it has not already done so.

Article 41

The institution of proceedings by a State which is not a party to the Statute but which, under Article 35, paragraph 2, thereof, has accepted the jurisdiction of the Court by a declaration made in accordance with any resolution adopted by the Security Council under that Article[1], shall be accompanied by a deposit of the declaration in question, unless the latter has previously been deposited with the Registrar. If any question of the validity or effect of such declaration arises, the Court shall decide.

Article 42

The Registrar shall transmit copies of any application or notification of a special agreement instituting proceedings before the Court to: *(a)* the Secretary-General of the United Nations; *(b)* the Members of the United Nations; *(c)* other States entitled to appear before the Court.

Article 43

Whenever the construction of a convention to which States other than those concerned in the case are parties may be in question within the meaning of Article 63, paragraph 1, of the Statute, the Court shall consider what directions shall be given to the Registrar in the matter.

Subsection 2. The Written Proceedings

Article 44

1. In the light of the information obtained by the President under Article 31 of these Rules, the Court shall make the necessary orders to determine, *inter alia,* the number and the order of filing of the pleadings and the time limits within which they must be filed.
2. In making an order under paragraph I of this Article, any agreement between the parties which does not cause unjustified delay shall be taken into account.
3. The Court may, at the request of the party concerned, extend any time-limit, or decide that any step taken after the expiration of the time-limit fixed therefor shall be considered as valid, if it is satisfied that there is adequate justification for the request. In either case the other party shall be given an opportunity to state its views.
4. If the Court is not sitting, its powers under this Article shall be exercised by the President, but without prejudice to any subsequent decision of the Court. If the consultation referred to in Article 31 reveals persistent disagreement between the parties as to the application of Article 45, paragraph 2, or Article 46, paragraph 2, of these Rules, the Court shall be convened to decide the matter.

Article 45

1. The pleadings in a case begun by means of an application shall consist, in the following order, of: a Memorial by the applicant; a Counter-Memorial by the respondent.
2. The Court may authorize or direct that there shall be a Reply by the applicant and a Rejoinder by the respondent if the parties are so agreed, or if the Court decides, *proprio motu* or at the request of one of the parties, that these pleadings are necessary.

Article 46

1. In a case begun by the notification of a special agreement, the number and order of the pleadings shall be governed by the provisions of the agreement, unless the Court, after ascertaining the views of the parties, decides otherwise.
2. If the special agreement contains no such provision, and if the parties have not subsequently agreed on the number and order of pleadings, they shall each file a Memorial and Counter-Memorial, within the same time limits. The Court shall not authorize the presentation of Replies unless it finds them to be necessary.

Article 47

The Court may at any time direct that the proceedings in two or more cases be joined. It may also direct that the written or oral proceedings, including the calling of witnesses, be in common; or the Court may, without effecting any formal joinder, direct common action in any of these respects.

Article 48

Time limits for the completion of steps in the proceedings may be fixed by assigning a specified period but shall always indicate definite dates. Such time limits shall be as short as the character of the case permits.

Article 49

1. A Memorial shall contain a statement of the relevant facts, a statement of law, and the submissions.
2. A Counter-Memorial shall contain: an admission or denial of the facts stated in the Memorial; any additional facts, if necessary; observations concerning the statement of law in the Memorial; a statement of law in answer thereto; and the submissions.
3. The Reply and Rejoinder, whenever authorized by the Court, shall not merely repeat the parties' contentions, but shall be directed to bringing out the issues that still divide them.
4. Every pleading shall set out the party's submissions at the relevant stage of the case, distinctly from the arguments presented, or shall confirm the submissions previously made.

Article 50

1. There shall be annexed to the original of every pleading certified copies of any relevant documents adduced in support of the contentions contained in the pleading.
2. If only parts of a document are relevant, only such extracts as are necessary for the purpose of the pleading in question need be annexed. A copy of the whole document shall be deposited in the Registry, unless it has been published and is readily available.
3. A list of all documents annexed to a pleading shall be furnished at the time the

pleading is filed.

Article 51

1. If the parties are agreed that the written proceedings shall be conducted wholly in one of the two official languages of the Court, the pleadings shall be submitted only in that language. If the parties are not so agreed, any pleading or any part of a pleading shall be submitted in one or other of the official languages.
2. If in pursuance of Article 39, paragraph 3, of the Statute a language other than French or English is used, a translation into French or English certified as accurate by the party submitting it, shall be attached to the original of each pleading.
3. When a document annexed to a pleading is not in one of the official languages of the Court, it shall be accompanied by a translation into one of these languages certified by the party submitting it as accurate. The translation may be confined to part of an annex, or to extracts therefrom, but in this case it must be accompanied by an explanatory note indicating what passages are translated. The Court may however require a more extensive or a complete translation to be furnished.

Article 52

1. The original of every pleading shall be signed by the agent and filed in the Registry. It shall be accompanied by a certified copy of the pleading, documents annexed, and any translations, for communication to the other party in accordance with Article 43, paragraph 4, of the Statute, and by the number of additional copies required by the Registry, but without prejudice to an increase in that number should the need arise later.
2. All pleadings shall be dated. When a pleading has to be filed by a certain date, it is the date of the receipt of the pleading in the Registry which will be regarded by the Court as the material date.
3. If the Registrar arranges for the printing of a pleading at the request of a party, the text must be supplied in sufficient time to enable the printed pleading to be filed in the Registry before the expiration of any time-limit which may apply to it. The printing is done under the responsibility of the party in question.
4. The correction of a slip or error in any document which has been filed may be made at any time with the consent of the other party or by leave of the President. Any correction so effected shall be notified to the other party in the same manner as the pleading to which it relates.

Article 53

1. The Court, or the President if the Court is not sitting, may at any time decide, after ascertaining the views of the parties, that copies of the pleadings and documents annexed shall be made available to a State entitled to appear before it which has asked to be furnished with such copies.
2. The Court may, after ascertaining the views of the parties, decide that copies of the pleadings and documents annexed shall be made accessible to the public on or after the opening of the oral. proceedings.

Subsection 3. The Oral Proceedings

Article 54

1. Upon the closure of the written proceedings, the case is ready for hearing. The date for the opening of the oral proceedings shall be fixed by the Court, which may also decide, if occasion should arise, that the opening or the continuance of the oral proceedings be postponed.
2. When fixing the date for, or postponing, the opening of the oral proceedings the Court shall have regard to the priority required by Article 74 of these Rules and to any other special circumstances, including the urgency of a particular case.
3. When the Court is not sitting, its powers under this Article shall be exercised by the President.

Article 55

The Court may, if it considers it desirable, decide pursuant to Article 22, paragraph 1, of the Statute that all or part of the further proceedings in a case shall be held at a place other than the seat of the Court. Before so deciding, it shall ascertain the views of the parties.

Article 56

1. After the closure of the written proceedings, no further documents may be submitted to the Court by either party except with the consent of the other party or as provided in paragraph 2 of this Article. The party desiring to produce a new document shall file the original or a certified copy thereof, together with the number of copies required by the Registry, which shall be responsible for communicating it to the other party and shall inform the Court. The other party shall be held to have given its consent if it does not lodge an objection to the production of the document.
2. In the absence of consent, the Court, after hearing the parties, may, if it considers the document necessary, authorize its production.
3. If a new document is produced under paragraph I or paragraph 2 of this Article, the other party shall have an opportunity of commenting upon it and of submitting documents in support of its comments.
4. No reference may be made during the oral proceedings to the contents of any document which has not been produced in accordance with Article 43 of the Statute or this Article, unless the document is part of a publication readily available.
5. The application of the provisions of this Article shall not in itself constitute a ground for delaying the opening or the course of the oral proceedings.

Article 57

Without prejudice to the provisions of the Rules concerning the production of documents, each party shall communicate to the Registrar, in sufficient time before the opening of the oral proceedings, information regarding any evidence which it intends to produce or which it intends to request the Court to obtain. This communication shall contain a list of the surnames, first names, nationalities, descriptions and places of residence of the witnesses and experts whom the party intends to call, with indications in general terms of the point or points to which their evidence will be directed. A copy of the communication shall also be furnished for transmission to the other party.

Article 58

1. The Court shall determine whether the parties should present their arguments before or after the production of the evidence; the parties shall. however, retain the right to comment on the evidence given.
2. The order in which the parties will be heard, the method of handling the evidence and of examining any witnesses and experts, and the number of counsel and advocates to be heard on behalf of each party, shall be settled by the Court after the views of the parties have been ascertained in accordance with Article 31 of these Rules.

Article 59

The hearing in Court shall be public, unless the Court shall decide otherwise, or unless the parties demand that the public be not admitted. Such a decision or demand may concern either the whole or part of the hearing, and may be made at any time.

Article 60

1. The oral statements made on behalf of each party shall be as succinct as possible within the limits of what is requisite for the adequate presentation of that party's contentions at the hearing. Accordingly, they shall be directed to the issues that still divide the parties, and shall not go over the whole ground covered by the pleadings, or merely repeat the facts and arguments these contain.
2. At the conclusion of the last statement made by a party at the hearing, its agent, without recapitulation of the arguments, shall read that party's final submissions. A copy of the written text of these, signed by the agent, shall be communicated to the Court and transmitted to the other party.

Article 61

1. The Court may at any time prior to or during the hearing indicate any points or issues to which it would like the parties specially to address themselves, or on which it considers that there has been sufficient argument.
2. The Court may, during the hearing, put questions to the agents, counsel and advocates, and may ask them for explanations.
3. Each judge has a similar right to put questions, but before exercising it he should make his intention known to the President, who is made responsible by Article 45 of the Statute for the control of the hearing.
4. The agents, counsel and advocates may answer either immediately or within a time-limit fixed by the President.

Article 62

1. The Court may at any time call upon the parties to produce such evidence or to give such explanations as the Court may consider to be necessary for the elucidation of any aspect of the matters in issue, or may itself seek other information for this purpose.
2. The Court may, if necessary, arrange for the attendance of a witness or expert to give evidence in the proceedings.

Article 63

1. The parties may call any witnesses or experts appearing on the list communicated to the Court pursuant to Article 57 of these Rules. If at any time during the hearing a party wishes to call a witness or expert whose name was not included in that list, it shall so

inform the Court and the other party, and shall supply the information required by Article 57. The witness or expert may be called either if the other party makes no objection or if the Court is satisfied that his evidence seems likely to prove relevant.
2. The Court, or the President if the Court is not sitting, shall, at the request of one of the parties or proprio motu, take the necessary steps for the examination of witnesses otherwise than before the Court itself.

Article 64

Unless on account of special circumstances the Court. decides on a different form of words,

(a) every witness shall make the following declaration before giving any evidence:
"I solemnly declare upon my honour and conscience that I will speak the truth, the whole truth and nothing but the truth";

(b) every expert shall make the following declaration before making any statement:
"I solemnly declare upon my honour and conscience that I will speak the truth, the whole truth and nothing but the truth, and that my statement will be in accordance with my sincere belief."

Article 65

Witnesses and experts shall be examined by the agents, counselor advocates of the parties under the control of the President. Questions may be put to them by the President and by the judges. Before testifying, witnesses shall remain out of court.

Article 66

The Court may at any time decide, either *proprio motu* or at the request of a party, to exercise its functions with regard to the obtaining of evidence at a place or locality to which the case relates, subject to such conditions as the Court may decide upon after ascertaining the views of the parties. The necessary arrangements shall be made in accordance with Article 44 of the Statute.

Article 67

1. If the Court considers it necessary to arrange for an enquiry or an expert opinion, it shall, after hearing the parties, issue an order to this effect, defining the subject of the enquiry or expert opinion, stating the number and mode of appointment of the persons to hold the enquiry or of the experts, and laying down the procedure to be followed. Where appropriate, the Court shall require persons appointed to carry out an enquiry, or to give an expert opinion, to make a solemn declaration.
2. Every report or record of an enquiry and every expert opinion shall be communicated to the parties, which shall be given the opportunity of commenting upon it.

Article 68

Witnesses and experts who appear at the instance of the Court under Article 62, paragraph 2, and persons appointed under Article 67, paragraph 1, of these Rules, to carry out an enquiry or to give an expert opinion, shall, where appropriate, be paid out of the funds of the Court.

Article 69

1. The Court may, at any time prior to the closure of the oral proceedings, either *proprio*

motu or at the request of one of the parties communicated as provided in Article 57 of these Rules, request a public international organization, pursuant to Article 34 of the Statute, to furnish information relevant to a case before it. The Court, after consulting the chief administrative officer of the organization concerned, shall decide whether such information shall be presented to it orally or in writing, and the time limits for its presentation.
2. When a public international organization sees fit to furnish, on its own initiative, information relevant to a case before the Court, it shall do so in the form of a Memorial to be filed in the Registry before the closure of the written proceedings. The Court shall retain the right to require such information to be supplemented, either orally or in writing, in the form of answers to any questions which it may see fit to formulate, and also to authorize the parties to comment, either orally or in writing, on the information thus furnished.
3. In the circumstances contemplated by Article 34, paragraph 3, of the Statute, the Registrar, on the instructions of the Court, or of the President if the Court is not sitting, shall proceed as prescribed in that paragraph. The Court, or the President if the Court is not sitting, may, as from the date on which the Registrar has communicated copies of the written proceedings and after consulting the chief administrative officer of the public international organization concerned, fix a time-limit within which the organization may submit to the Court its observations in writing. These observations shall be communicated to the parties and may be discussed by them and by the representative of the said organization during the oral proceedings.
4. In the foregoing paragraphs, the term "public international organization" denotes an international organization of States.

Article 70

1. In the absence of any decision to the contrary by the Court, all speeches and statements made and evidence given at the hearing in one of the official languages of the Court shall be interpreted into the other official language. If they are made or given in any other language, they shall be interpreted into the two official languages of the Court.
2. Whenever, in accordance with Article 39, paragraph 3, of the Statute, a language other than French or English is used, the necessary arrangements for interpretation into one of the two official languages shall be made by the party concerned; however, the Registrar shall make arrangements for the verification of the interpretation provided by a party of evidence given on the party's behalf. In the case of witnesses or experts who appear at the instance of the Court, arrangements for interpretation shall be made by the Registry.
3. A party on behalf of which speeches or statements are to be made, or evidence given, in a language which is not one of the official languages of the Court, shall so notify the Registrar in sufficient time for him to make the necessary arrangements.
4. Before first interpreting in the case, interpreters provided by a party shall make the following declaration in open court:

"I solemnly declare upon my honour and conscience that my interpretation will be faithful and complete."

Article 71

1. A verbatim record shall be made by the Registrar of every hearing, in the! official

language of the Court which has been used. When the language used is not one of the two official languages of the Court, the verbatim record shall be prepared in one of the Court's official languages.
2. When speeches or statements are made in a language which is not one of the official language of the Court, the party on behalf of which they are made shall supply to the Registry in advance a text thereof in one of the official languages, and this text shall constitute the relevant part of the verbatim record.
3. The transcript of the verbatim record shall be preceded by the names of the judges present, and those of the agents, counsel and advocates of the parties.
4. Copies of the transcript shall be circulated to the judges sitting in the case, and to the parties. The latter may, under the supervision of the Court, correct the transcripts of speeches and statements made on their behalf, but in no case may such corrections affect the sense and bearing thereof. The judges may likewise make corrections in the transcript of anything they may have said.
5. Witnesses and experts shall be shown that part of the transcript which relates to the evidence given, or the statements made by them, and may correct it in like manner as the parties.
6. One certified true copy of the eventual corrected transcript, signed by the President and the Registrar, shall constitute the authentic minutes of the sitting for the purposes of Article 47 of the Statute. The minutes of public hearings shall be printed and published by the Court.

Article 72

Any written reply by a party to a question put under Article 61, or any evidence or explanation supplied by a party under Article 62 of. these Rules, received by the Court after the closure of the oral proceedings, shall be communicated to the other party, which shall be given the opportunity of commenting upon it. If necessary the oral proceedings may be reopened for that purpose.

SECTION D. INCIDENTAL PROCEEDINGS

Subsection 1. *Interim Protection*

Article 73

1. A written request for the indication of provisional measures may be made by a party at any time during the course of the proceedings in the case in connection with which the request is made.
2. The request shall specify the reasons therefor, the possible consequences if it is not granted, and the measures requested. A certified copy shall forthwith be transmitted by the Registrar to the other party.

Article 74

1. A request for the indication of provisional measures shall have priority over all other cases.
2. The Court, if it is not sitting when the request is made, shall be convened forthwith for the purpose of proceeding to a decision on the request as a matter of urgency.
3. The Court, or the President if the Court is not sitting, shall fix a date for a hearing

which will afford the parties an opportunity of being represented at it. The Court shall receive and take into account any observations that may be presented to it before the closure of the oral proceedings.
4. Pending the meeting of the Court, the President may call upon the parties to act in such a way as will enable any order the Court may make on the request for provisional measures to have its appropriate effects.

Article 75

1. The Court may at any time decide to examine *proprio motu* whether the circumstances of the case require the indication of provisional measures which ought to be taken or complied with by any or all of the parties.
2. When a request for provisional measures has been made, the Court may indicate measures that are in whole or in part other than those requested, or that ought to be taken or complied with by the party which has itself made the request.
3. The rejection of a request for the indication of provisional measures shall not prevent the party which made it from making a fresh request in the same case based on new facts.

Article 76

1. At the request of a party the Court may, at any time before the final judgment in the case, revoke or modify any decision concerning provisional measures if, in its opinion, some change in the situation justifies such revocation or modification.
2. Any application by a party proposing such a revocation or modification shall specify the change in the situation considered to be relevant.
3. Before taking any decision under paragraph I of this Article the Court shall afford the parties an opportunity of presenting their observations on the subject.

Article 77

Any measures indicated by the Court under Articles 73 and 74 of these Rules, and any decision taken by the Court under Article 76, paragraph 1, of these Rules, shall forthwith be communicated to the Secretary-General of the United Nations for transmission to the Security Council in pursuance of Article 41, paragraph 2, of the Statute.

Article 78

The Court may request information from the parties on any matter connected with the implementation of any provisional measures it has indicated.

Subsection 2. Preliminary Objections

Article 79

1. Any objection by the respondent to the jurisdiction of the Court or to the admissibility of the application, or other objection the decision upon which is requested before any further proceedings on the merits, shall be made in writing as soon as possible, and not later than three months after the delivery of the Memorial. Any such objection made by a party other than the respondent shall be filed within the time-limit fixed for the delivery of that party's first pleading.

2. Notwithstanding paragraph 1 above, following the submission of the application and after the President has met and consulted with the parties, the Court may decide that any questions of jurisdiction and admissibility shall be determined separately.
3. Where the Court so decides, the parties shall submit any pleadings as to jurisdiction and admissibility within the time-limits fixed by the Court and in the order determined by it, notwithstanding Article 45, paragraph 1.
4. The preliminary objection shall set out the facts and the law on which the objection is based, the submissions and a list of the documents in support; it shall mention any evidence which the party may desire to produce. Copies of the supporting documents shall be attached.
5. Upon receipt by the Registry of a preliminary objection, the proceedings on the merits shall be suspended and the Court, or the President if the Court is not sitting, shall fix the time-limit within which the other party may present a written statement of its observations and submissions; documents in support shall be attached and evidence which it is proposed to produce shall be mentioned.
6. Unless otherwise decided by the Court, the further proceedings shall be oral.
7. The statements of facts and law in the pleadings referred to in paragraphs 4 and 5 of this Article, and the statements and evidence presented at the hearings contemplated by paragraph 6, shall be confined to those matters that are relevant to the objection.
8. In order to enable the Court to determine its jurisdiction at the preliminary stage of the proceedings, the Court, whenever necessary, may request the parties to argue all questions of law and fact, and to adduce all evidence, which bear on the issue.
9. After hearing the parties, the Court shall give its decision in the form of a judgment, by which it shall either uphold the objection, reject it, or declare that the objection does not possess, in the circumstances of the case, an exclusively preliminary character. If the Court rejects the objection or declares that it does not possess an exclusively preliminary character, it shall fix time-limits for the further proceedings.
10. Any agreement between the parties that an objection submitted under paragraph 1 of this Article be heard and determined within the framework of the merits shall be given effect by the Court.

Subsection 3. Counter-Claims

Article 80

1. The Court may entertain a counter-claim only if it comes within the jurisdiction of the Court and is directly connected with the subject-matter of the claim of the other party.
2. A counter-claim shall be made in the Counter-Memorial and shall appear as part of the submissions contained therein. The right of the other party to present its views in writing on the counter-claim, in an additional pleading, shall be preserved, irrespective of any decision of the Court, in accordance with Article 45, paragraph 2, of these Rules, concerning the filing of further written pleadings.
3. Where an objection is raised concerning the application of paragraph 1 or whenever the Court deems necessary, the Court shall take its decision thereon after hearing the parties.

Subsection 4. Intervention

Article 81

1. An application for permission to intervene under the terms of Article 62 of the Statute, signed in the manner provided for in Article 38, paragraph 3, of these Rules, shall be filed as soon as possible, and not later than the closure of the written proceedings. In exceptional circumstances, an application submitted at a later stage may however be admitted.
2. The application shall state the name of an agent. It shall specify the case to which it relates, and shall set out:
(a) the interest of a legal nature which the State applying to intervene considers may be affected by the decision in that case;
(b) the precise object of the intervention;
(c) any basis of jurisdiction which is claimed to exist as between the State applying to intervene and the parties to the case.
3. The application shall contain a list of the documents in support, which documents shall be attached.

Article 82

1. A State which desires to avail itself of the right of intervention conferred upon it by Article 63 of the Statute shall file a declaration to that effect, signed in the manner provided for in Article 38, paragraph 3, of these Rules. Such a declaration shall be filed as soon as possible, and not later than the date fixed for the opening of the oral proceedings. In exceptional circumstances a declaration submitted at a later stage may however be admitted.
2. The declaration shall state the name of an agent. It shall specify the case and the convention to which it relates and shall contain:
(a) particulars of the basis on which the declarant State considers itself a party to the convention;
(b) identification of the particular provisions of the convention the construction of which it considers to be in question;
(c) a statement of the construction of those provisions for which it contends;
(d) a list of the documents in support, which documents shall be attached.
3. Such a declaration may be filed by a State that considers itself a party to the convention the construction of which is in question but has not received the notification referred to in Article 63 of the Statute.

Article 83

1. Certified copies of the application for permission to intervene under Article 62 of the Statute, or of the declaration of intervention under Article 63 of the Statute, shall be communicated forthwith to the parties to the case, which shall be invited to furnish their written observations within a time-limit to be fixed by the Court or by the President if the Court is not sitting.
2. The Regjstrar shall also transmit copies to: *(a)* the Secretary-General of the United Nations; *(b)* the Members of the United Nations; *(c)* other States entitled to appear before the Court; *(d)* any other States which have been notified under Article 63 of the Statute.

Article 84

1. The Court shall decide whether an application for permission to intervene under Article 62 of the Statute should be granted, and whether an intervention under Article 63 of the Statute is admissible, as a matter of priority unless in view of the circumstances of the case the Court shall otherwise determine.
2. If, within the time-limit fixed under Article 83 of these Rules, an objection is filed to an application for permission to intervene, or to the admissibility of a declaration of intervention, the Court shall hear the State seeking to intervene and the parties before deciding.

Article 85

1. If an application for permission to intervene under Article 62 of the Statute is granted, the intervening State shall be supplied with copies of the pleadings and documents annexed and shall be entitled to submit a written statement within a time-limit to be fixed by the Court. A further time-limit shall be fixed within which the parties may, if they so desire, furnish their written observations on that statement prior to the oral proceedings. If the Court is not sitting, these time limits shall be fixed by the President.
2. The time limits fixed according to the preceding paragraph shall, so far as possible, coincide with those already fixed for the pleadings in the case.
3, The intervening State shall be entitled, in the course of the oral proceedings, to submit its observations with respect to the subject-matter of the intervention,

Article 86

1. If an intervention under Article 63 of the Statute is admitted, the intervening State shall be furnished with copies of the pleadings and documents annexed, and shall be entitled, within a time-limit to be fixed by the Court, or by the President if the Court is not sitting, to submit its written observations on the subject-matter of the intervention.
2. These observations shall be communicated to the parties and to any other State admitted to intervene. The intervening State shall be entitled, in the course of the oral proceedings, to submit its observations with respect to the subject-matter of the intervention.

Subsection 5. Special Reference to the Court

Article 87

1. When in accordance with a treaty or convention in force a contentious case is brought before the Court concerning a matter which has been the subject of proceedings before some other international body, the provisions of the Statute and of the Rules governing contentious cases shall apply.
2. The application instituting proceedings shall identify the decision or other act of the international body concerned and a copy thereof shall be annexed; it shall contain a precise statement of the questions raised in regard to that decision or act, which constitute the subject of the dispute referred to the Court.

Subsection 6. Discontinuance

Article 88

1. If at any time before the final judgment on the merits has been delivered the parties, either jointly or separately, notify the Court in writing that they have agreed to discontinue the proceedings, the Court shall make an order recording the discontinuance and directing that the case be removed from the list.
2. If the parties have agreed to discontinue the proceedings in consequence of having reached a settlement of the dispute and if they so desire, the Court may record this fact in the order for the removal of the case from the list, or indicate in, or annex to, the order, the terms of the settlement.
3. If the Court is not sitting, any order under this Article may be made by the President.

Article 89

1. If in the course of proceedings instituted by means of an application, the applicant informs the Court in writing that it is not going on with the proceedings, and if, at the date on which this communication is received by the Registry, the respondent has not yet taken any step in the proceedings, the Court shall make an order officially recording the discontinuance of the proceedings and directing the removal of the case from the list. A copy of this order shall be sent by the Registrar to the respondent.
2. If, at the time when the notice of discontinuance is received, the respondent has already taken some step in the proceedings, the Court shall fix a time-limit within which the respondent may state whether it opposes the discontinuance of the proceedings. If no objection is made to the discontinuance before the expiration of the time-limit, acquiescence will be presumed and the Court shall make an order officially recording the discontinuance of the proceedings and directing the removal of the case from the list. If objection is made, the proceedings shall continue.
3. If the Court is not sitting, its powers under this Article may be exercised by the President.

SECTION E. PROCEEDINGS BEFORE THE CHAMBERS

Article 90

Proceedings before the Chambers mentioned in Articles 26 and 29 of the Statute shall, subject to the provisions of the Statute and of these Rules relating specifically to the Chambers, be governed by the provisions of Parts I to III of these Rules applicable in contentious cases before the Court.

Article 91

1. When it is desired that a case should be dealt with by one of the Chambers which has been formed in pursuance of Article 26, paragraph 1, or Article 29 of the Statute, a request to this effect shall either be made in the document instituting the proceedings or accompany it. Effect will be given to the request if the parties are in agreement.
2. Upon receipt by the Registry of this request, the President of the Court shall communicate it to the members of the Chamber concerned. He shall take such steps as may be necessary to give effect to the provisions of Article 31, paragraph 4, of the Statute.

3. The President of the Court shall convene the Chamber at the earliest date compatible with the requirements of the procedure.

Article 92

1. Written proceedings in a case before a Chamber shall consist of a single pleading by each side. In proceedings begun by means of an application, the pleadings shall be delivered within successive time limits. In proceedings begun by the notification of a special agreement, the pleadings shall be delivered within the same time limits, unless the parties have agreed on successive delivery of their pleadings. The time limits referred to in this paragraph shall be fixed by the Court, or by the President if the Court is not sitting, in consultation with the Chamber concerned if it is already constituted.
2. The Chamber may authorize or direct that further pleadings be filed if the parties are so agreed, or if the Chamber decides, *proprio motu* or at the request of one of the parties, that such pleadings are necessary.
3. Oral proceedings shall take place unless the parties agree *to* dispense with them, and the Chamber consents. Even when no oral proceedings take place, the Chamber may call upon the parties *to* supply information or furnish explanations orally.

Article 93

Judgments given by a Chamber shall be read at a public sitting of that Chamber.

SECTION F. JUDGMENTS, INTERPRETATION AND REVISION

Subsection 1. Judgments

Article 94

1. When the Court has completed its deliberations and adopted its judgment, the parties shall be notified of the date on which it will be read.
2. The judgment shall be read at a public sitting of the Court and shall become binding on the parties on the day of the reading.

Article 95

1. The judgment, which shall state whether it is given by the Court or by a Chamber, shall contain:
the date on which it is read;
the names of the judges participating in it;
the names of the parties;
the names of the agents, counsel and advocates of the parties; a summary of the proceedings;
the submissions of the parties;
a statement of the facts;
the reasons in point of law;
the operative provisions of the judgment;
the decision, if any, in regard *to* costs;
the number and names of the judges constituting the majority;
a statement as to the text of the judgment which is authoritative.

2. Any judge may, if he *so* desires, attach his individual opinion *to* the judgment, whether he dissents from the majority or not; a judge who wishes *to* record his concurrence or dissent without stating his reasons may *do so* in the *form* of a declaration. The same shall also apply *to* orders made by the Court.
3. One copy of the judgment duly signed and sealed, shall be placed in the archives of the Court and another shall be transmitted to each of the parties. Copies shall be sent by the Registrar to: *(a)* the Secretary-General of the United Nations; *(b)* the Members of the United Nations; *(c)* other States entitled to appear before the Court.

Article 96

When by reason of an agreement reached between the parties, the written and oral proceedings have been conducted in one of the Court's two official languages, and pursuant to Article; 39, paragraph 1, of the Statute the judgment is to be delivered in that language, the text of the judgment in that language shall be the authoritative text.

Article 97

If the Court, under Article 64 of the Statute, decides that all or part of a party's costs shall be paid by the other party, it may make an order for the purpose of giving effect to that decision.

Subsection 2. Requests for the Interpretation or Revision of a Judgment

Article 98

1. In the event of dispute as to the meaning or scope of a judgment any party may make a request for its interpretation, whether the original proceedings were begun by an application or by the notification of a special agreement.
2. A request for the interpretation of a judgment may be made either by an application or by the notification of a special agreement to that effect between the parties; the precise point or points in dispute as to the meaning or scope of the judgment shall be indicated.
3. If the request for interpretation is made by an application, the requesting party's contentions shall be set out therein, and the other party shall be entitled to file written observations thereon within a time-limit fixed by the Court, or by the President if the Court is not sitting.
4. Whether the request is made by an application or by notification of a special agreement, the Court may, if necessary, afford the parties the opportunity of furnishing further written or oral explanations.

Article 99

1. A request for the revision of a judgment shall be made by an application containing the particulars necessary to show that the conditions specified in Article 61 of the Statute are fulfilled. Any documents in support of the application shall be annexed to it.
2. The other party shall be entitled to file written observations on the admissibility of the application within a time-limit fixed by the Court, or by the President if the Court is not sitting. These observations shall be communicated to the party making the application.
3. The Court, before giving its judgment on the admissibility of the application may afford the parties a further opportunity of presenting their views thereon.

4. If the Court finds that the application is admissible it shall fix time limits for such further proceedings on the merits of the application as, after ascertaining the views of the parties, it considers necessary.
5. If the Court decides to make the admission of the proceedings in revision conditional on previous compliance with the judgment, it shall make an order accordingly.

Article 100

1. If the judgment to be revised or to be interpreted was given by the Court, the request for its revision or interpretation shall be dealt with by the Court. If the judgment was given by a Chamber, the request for its revision or interpretation shall be dealt with by that Chamber.
2. The decision of the Court, or of the Chamber, on a request for interpretation or revision of a judgment shall itself be given in the form of a judgment.

SEC'TION G. MODIFICATIONS PROPOSED BY THE PARTIES

Article 101

The parties to a case may jointly propose particular modifications or additions to the rules contained in the present Part (with the exception of Articles 93 to 97 inclusive), which may be applied by the Court or by a Chamber if the Court or the Chamber considers them appropriate in the circumstances of the case.

PART IV

ADVISORY PROCEEDINGS

Article 102

1. In the exercise of its advisory functions under Article 65 of the Statute, the Court shall apply, in addition to the provisions of Article 96 of the Charter and Chapter IV of the Statute, the provisions of the present Part of the Rules.
2. The Court shall also be guided by the provisions of the Statute and of these Rules which apply in contentious cases to the extent to which it recognizes them to be applicable. For this purpose, it shall above all consider whether the request for the advisory opinion relates to a legal question actually pending between two or more States.
3. When an advisory opinion is requested upon a legal question actually pending between two or more States, Article 31 of the Statute shall apply, as also the provisions of these Rules concerning the application of that Article.

Article 103

When the body authorized by or in accordance with the Charter of the United Nations to request an advisory opinion informs the Court that its request necessitates an urgent answer, or the Court finds that an early answer would be desirable, the Court shall take all necessary steps to accelerate the procedure, and it shall convene as early as possible for the purpose of proceeding to a hearing and deliberation on the request.

Article 104

All requests for advisory opinions shall be transmitted to the Court by the Secretary-General of the United Nations or, as the case may be, the chief administrative officer of the body authorized to make the request. The documents referred to in Article 65, paragraph 2, of the Statute shall be transmitted to the Court at the same time as the request or as soon as possible thereafter, in the number of copies required by the Registry;

Article 105

1. Written statements submitted to the Court shall be communicated by the Registrar to any States and organizations which have submitted such statements.
2. The Court, or the President if the Court is not sitting, shall:
(a) determine the form in which, and the extent to which, comments permitted under Article 66, paragraph 4, of the Statute shall be received, and fix the time-limit for the submission of any such comments in writing;
(b) decide whether oral proceedings shall take place at which statements and comments may be submitted to the Court under the provisions of Article 66 of the Statute, and fix the date for the opening of such oral proceedings.

Article 106

The Court, or the President if the Court is not sitting, may decide that the written statements and annexed documents shall be made accessible to the public on or after the opening of the oral proceedings. If the request for advisory opinion relates to a legal question actually pending between two or more States, the views of those States shall first be ascertained.

Article 107

1. When the Court has completed its deliberations and adopted its advisory opinion, the opinion shall be read at a public sitting of the Court.
2. The advisory opinion shall contain:

the date on which it is delivered;
the names of the judges participating;
a summary of the proceedings;
a statement of the facts;
the reasons in point of law;
the reply to the question put to the Court;
the number and names of the judges constituting the majority;
a statement as to the text of the opinion which is authoritative.
3. Any judge may, if he so desires, attach his individual opinion to the advisory opinion of the Court, whether he dissents from the majority or not; a judge who wishes to record his concurrence or .dissent without stating his reasons may do so in the form of a declaration.

Article 108

The Registrar shall inform the Secretary-General of the United Nations, and, where appropriate, the chief administrative officer of the body which requested the advisory opinion, as to the date and the hour fixed for the public sitting to be held for the reading of the opinion. He shall also inform the representatives of the Members of the United Nations and other States, specialized agencies and public international organizations immediately concerned.

Article 109

One copy of the advisory opinion, duly signed and sealed, shall be placed in the archives of the Court, another shall be sent to the Secretary-General of the United Nations and, where appropriate, a third to the chief administrative officer of the body which requested the opinion of the Court. Copies shall be sent by the Registrar to the Members of the United Nations and to any other States, specialized agencies and public international organizations immediately concerned.

APPENDIX II.B

PRACTICE DIRECTIONS

Practice Direction I

The Court wishes to discourage the practice of simultaneous deposit of pleadings in cases brought by Special Agreement.

The Court would expect future special agreements to contain provisions as to the number and order of pleadings, in accordance with Article 46, paragraph 1, of the Rules of Court. Such provisions shall be without prejudice to any issue in the case, including the issue of burden of proof.

If the Special Agreement contains no provisions on the number and order of pleadings, the Court will expect the parties to reach agreement to that effect, in accordance with Article 46, paragraph 2, of the Rules of Court.

Practice Direction II

Each of the parties is, in drawing up its written pleadings, to bear in mind the fact that these pleadings are intended not only to reply to the submissions and arguments of the other party, but also, and above all, to present clearly the submissions and arguments of the party which is filing the proceedings.

In the light of this, at the conclusion of the written pleadings of each party, there is to appear a short summary of its reasoning.

Practice Direction III

The Court has noticed an excessive tendency towards the proliferation and protraction of annexes to written pleadings. It strongly urges parties to append to their pleadings only strictly selected documents.

Practice Direction IV

Where one of the parties has a full or partial translation of its own pleadings or of those of the other party in the other official language of the Court, these translations should as a matter of course be passed to the Registry of the Court. The same applies to the annexes.

These translations will be examined by the Registry and communicated to the other party. The latter will also be informed of the manner in which they were prepared.

Practice Direction V

With the aim of accelerating proceedings on preliminary objections made by one party under Article 79, paragraph 1, of the Rules of Court, the time-limit for the presentation by the other party of a written statement of its observations and submissions under Article 79, paragraph 5, shall generally not exceed four months.

Practice Direction VI

Article 60, paragraph 1, of the Rules provides:
"The oral statements made on behalf of each party shall be as succinct as possible within the limits of what is requisite for the adequate presentation of that party's contentions at the hearing. Accordingly, they shall be directed to the issues that still divide the parties, and shall not go over the whole ground covered by the pleadings, or merely repeat the facts and arguments these contain."
The Court requires full compliance with these provisions and observation of the requisite degree of brevity. Where objections of lack of jurisdiction or of inadmissibility are being considered, oral proceedings are to be limited to statements on the objections.

Practice Direction VII

The Court considers that it is not in the interest of the sound administration of justice that a person sit as judge *ad hoc* in one case who is also acting or has recently acted as agent, counsel or advocate in another case before the Court. Accordingly, parties, when choosing a judge *ad hoc* pursuant to Article 31 of the Statute and Article 35 of the Rules of Court, should refrain from nominating persons who are acting as agent, counsel or advocate in another case before the Court or have acted in that capacity in the three years preceding the date of the nomination. Furthermore, parties should likewise refrain from designating as agent, counsel or advocate in a case before the Court a person who sits as judge *ad hoc* in another case before the Court.

Practice Direction VIII

The Court considers that it is not in the interest of the sound administration of justice that a person who until recently was a Member of the Court, judge *ad hoc*, Registrar, Deputy-Registrar or higher official of the Court (principal legal secretary, first secretary or secretary), appear as agent, counsel or advocate in a case before the Court. Accordingly, parties should refrain from designating as agent, counsel or advocate in a case before the Court a person who in the three years preceding the date of the designation was a Member of the Court, judge *ad hoc*, Registrar, Deputy-Registrar or higher official of the Court.

Practice Direction IX

1. The parties to proceedings before the Court should refrain from submitting new documents after the closure of the written proceedings.
2. A party nevertheless desiring to submit a new document after the closure of the written proceedings shall explain why it considers it necessary to include the document in the case file and shall indicate the reasons preventing the production of the document at an earlier stage.
3. In the absence of consent of the other party, the Court will authorize the production of the new document only in exceptional circumstances, if it considers it necessary and if the production of the document at this stage of the proceedings appears justified to the

Court.
4. If a new document has been added to the case file under Article 56 of the Rules of Court, the other party, when commenting upon it, shall confine the introduction of any further documents to what is strictly necessary and relevant to its comments on what is contained in this new document.

APPENDIX III

COMPOSITION OF THE COURT 1982-2003

Thirteenth Period, 1982-1985

T.O. Elias (President)	Nigeria
K. Sette-Camara (Vice-President)	Brazil
M. Lachs	Poland
P.D. Morozov	USSR
Nagendra Singh	India
J.M. Ruda	Argentina
H. Mosler	Federal Republic of Germany
S.Oda Japan	
R. Ago	Italy
A.F. El-Khani	Syria
S.M. Schwebel	U.S.A.
Sir Robert Jennings	U.K.
G. Ladreit de Lacharrière	France
K. Mbaye	Senegal
M. Bedjaoui	Algeria

Fourteenth Period, 1985-1988

Nagendra Singh (President)	India
G. de Lacharrière (Vice-President)	France (d. 10 March 1987)
M. Lachs	Poland
P. Morozov (resigned 6 September 1985)	USSR
J.M. Ruda	Argentina
T.O. Elias	Nigeria
S. Oda Japan	
R. Ago	Italy
J. Sette Camara	Brazil
S.M. Schwebel	U.S.A.
Sir Robert Jennings	U.K.
K. Mbaye (Vice-President from 6 May 1987)	Senegal
M. Bedjaoui	Algeria
Ni Zhengyu	China (P.R.)
J. Evensen	Norway
N.K. Tarassov (from 9 December 1985)	U.S.S.R.
G. Guillaume (from 14 September 1987)	France

Fifteenth Period, 1988-1991

J.M. Ruda (President)	Argentina
Mbaye (Vice-President)	Senegal

M. Lachs	Poland
Nagendra Singh (d. 11 December 1988)	India
T.O. Elias	Nigeria
S. Oda	Japan
R. Ago	Italy
S.M. Schwebel	U.S.A.
Sir Robert Jennings	United Kingdom
M. Bedjaoui	Algeria
Ni Zhengyu	China
J. Evensen	Norway
N.K. Tarassov	USSR
G. Guillaume	France
M. Shahabuddeen	Guyana
R.S. Pathak (from 18 April 1989)	India

Sixteenth Period, 1991-1994

Sir Robert Jennings (President)	United Kingdom
S. Oda (Vice-President)	Japan
M. Lachs (d. 14 January 1993)	Poland
T.O. Elias (d. 14 August 1991)	Nigeria
R. Ago	Italy
S.M. Schwebel	U.S.A.
M. Bedjaoui	Algeria
Ni Zhengyu	China
J. Evensen	Norway
N.K. Tarassov	USSR/Russian Federation
G. Guillaume	France
M. Shahabuddeen	Guyana
A. Aguilar Mawdsey	Venezuela
C.G. Weeramantry	Sri Lanka
R. Ranjeva	Madagascar
Prince B. Ajibola (from 5 December 1991)	Nigeria
G. Herczegh (from 10 May 1993)	Hungary

Seventeenth Period, 1994-1997

M. Bedjaoui (President)	Algeria
S.M. Schwebel (Vice-President)	U.S.A.
S. Oda	Japan
R. Ago	Italy
Sir Robert Jennings	United Kingdom
N.K. Tarassov	Russian Federation
G. Guillaume	France
M. Shahabuddeen	Guyana
A. Aguilar Mawdsley	Venezuela
Ch. G. Weeramantry	Sri Lanka
R. Ranjeva	Madagascar

G. Herzegh	Hungary
Shi Jiuyong	China
C.-A. Fleischhauer	Germany
A.G. Koroma	Sierra Leone

Eighteenth Period, 1997-2000

S.M. Schwebel (President	U.S.A.
Ch.G. Weeramantry (Vice President)	Sri Lanka
S. Oda	Japan
M. Bedjaoui	Algeria
G. Guillaume	France
R. Ranjeva	Madagascar
G. Herczegh	Hungary
Shi Jiuyong	China
C.-A. Fleischhauer	Germany
A.G. Koroma	Sierra Leone
V.S. Vereshchetin	Russian Federation
R. Higgins	United Kingdom
G. Parra-Aranguen	Venezuela
P.H. Kooijmans	Netherlands
F. Rezek	Brazil

Nineteenth Period, 2000-2003

G. Guillaume (President)	France
Shi Jiuyong (Vice President)	China
S. Oda	Japan
M. Bedjaoui	Algeria (resigned 30 September 2001)
R. Ranjeva	Madagascar
G. Herczegh	Hungary
C.-A. Fleischhauer	Germany
A.G. Koroma	Sierra Leone
V.S. Vereshchetin	Russian Federation
R. Higgins	United Kingdom
G. Parra-Aranguren	Venezuela
P.H. Kooijmans	Netherlands
F. Rezek	Brazil
A.S. Al-Khasawweh	Jordan
T. Buergenthal	U.S.A. (succeeded S.M. Schwebel, who resigned 28 February 2000)
N. Elaraby	Egypt (from 12 October 2001)

APPENDIX IV

UNITED NATIONS MEMBERS STATES

Member	*Date of admission*
Afghanistan	19 November 1946
Albania	14 December 1955
Algeria	8 October 1962
Andorra	28 July 1993
Angola	1 December 1976
Antigua and Barbuda	11 November 1981
Argentina	24 October 1945
Armenia	2 March 1992
Australia	1 November 1945
Austria	14 December 1955
Azerbaijan	2 March 1992
Bahamas	18 September 1973
Bahrain	21 September 1971
Bangladesh	17 September 1974
Barbados	9 December 1966
Belarus[a]	24 October 1945
Belgium	27 December 1945
Belize	25 September 1981
Benin	20 September 1971
Bhutan	21 September 1971
Bolivia	14 November 1945
Bosnia and Herzegovina[b]	22 May 1992
Botswana	17 October 1966
Brazil	24 October 1945
Brunei Darussalam	21 September 1984
Bulgaria	14 December 1955
Burkina Faso	20 September 1960
Burundi	18 September 1962
Cambodia	14 December 1955
Cameroon	20 September 1960
Canada	9 November 1945

[a] On 19 September 1991. Byelorussia informed the United Nations that it had changed its name to Belarus.

[b] The Socialist Federal Republic of Yugoslavia was an original Member of the United Nations, the Charter having been signed on its behalf on 26 June 1945 and ratified 19 October 1945, until its dissolution following the establishment and subsequent admission as new Members of Bosnia and Herzegovina, the Republic of Croatia, the Republic of Slovenia, The former Yugoslav Republic of Macedonia, and the Federal Republic of Yugoslavia. The Republic of Bosnia and Herzegovina was admitted as a Member of the United Nations by General Assembly resolution A/RES/46/237 of 22 May 1992.

Cape Verde	16 September 1975
Central African Republic	20 September 1960
Chad	20 September 1960
Chile	24 October 1945
China	24 October 1945
Colombia	5 November 1945
Comoros	12 November 1975
Congo (Republic of the)	20 September 1960
Costa Rica	2 November 1945
Côte d'Ivoire	20 September 1960
Croatia[c]	22 May 1992
Cuba	24 October 1945
Cyprus	20 September 1960
Czech Republic[d]	19 January 1993
Democratic People's Republic of Korea	17 September 1991
Democratic Republic of the Congo[e]	20 September 1960
Denmark	24 October 1945
Djibouti	20 September 1977
Dominica	18 December 1978
Dominican Republic	24 October 1945
Ecuador	21 December 1945
Egypt[f]	24 October 1945
El Salvador	24 October 1945
Equatorial Guinea	12 November 1968
Eritrea	28 May 1993
Estonia	17 September 1991
Ethiopia	13 November 1945

[c] The Socialist Federal Republic of Yugoslavia was an original Member of the United Nations, the Charter having been signed on its behalf on 26 June 1945 and ratified 19 October 1945, until its dissolution following the establishment and subsequent admission as new Members of Bosnia and Herzegovina, the Republic of Croatia, the Republic of Slovenia, The former Yugoslav Republic of Macedonia, and the Federal Republic of Yugoslavia. The Republic of Bosnia and Herzegovina was admitted as a Member of the United Nations by General Assembly resolution A/RES/46/238 of 22 May 1992.

[d] Czechoslovakia was an original Member of the United Nations from 24 October 1945. In a letter dated 10 December 1992, its Permanent Representagtive informed the Secretary-General that the Czech and Slovak Federal Republic would cease to exist on 31 December 1992 and that the Czech Republic and the Slovak Republic, as successor States, would apply for membership in the United Nations. Following the receipt of its applictaoin, the Security Council, on 8 January 1993, recommended to the General Assembly that the Czech Republic be admitted to United Nations membership. The Czech Republic was thus admitted on 19 January of that year as a Member State.

[e] Zaire joined the United Nations on 20 September 1960. On 17 May 1997, its name was changed to the Democratic Republic of the Congo.

[f] Egypt and Syria were original Members of the United Nations from 24 October 1945. Following a plebiscite on 21 February 1958, the United Arab Republic was established by a union of Egypt and Syria and continued as a single Member. On 13 October 1961, Syria, having resumed its status as an independent State, resumed its separate membership in the United Nations. On 2 September 1971, the United Arab Republic changed its name to the Arab Republic of Egypt.

Fiji	13 October 1970
Finland	14 December 1955
France	24 October 1945
Gabon	20 September 1960
Gambia	21 September 1965
Georgia	31 July 1992
Germany [g]	18 September 1973
Ghana	8 March 1957
Greece	25 October 1945
Grenada	17 September 1974
Guatemala	21 November 1945
Guinea	12 December 1958
Guinea-Bissau	17 September 1974
Guyana	20 September 1966
Haiti	24 October 1945
Honduras	17 December 1945
Hungary	14 December 1955
Iceland	19 November 1946
India	30 October 1945
Indonesia[h]	28 September 1950
Iran (Islamic Republic of)	24 October 1945
Iraq	21 December 1945
Ireland	14 December 1955
Israel	11 May 1949
Italy	14 December 1955
Jamaica	18 September 1962
Japan	18 December 1956
Jordan	14 December 1955
Kazakhstan	2 March 1992
Kenya	16 December 1963
Kiribati	14 September 1999
Kuwait	14 May 1963
Kyrgyzstan	2 March 1992
Lao People's Democratic Republic	14 December 1955
Latvia	17 September 1991
Lebanon	24 October 1945
Lesotho	17 October 1966
Liberia	2 November 1945
Libya (Libian Arab Jamahiriya)	14 December 1955

[g] The Federal Republic of Germany and the German Democratic Republic were admitted to membership in the United Nations on 18 September 1973. Through the accession of the German Democratic Republic to the Federal Republic of Germany, effective from 3 October 1990, the two German States have united to form one sovereign State.

[h] By letter of 20 January 1965, Indonesia announced its decision to withdraw from the United Nations "at this stage and under the present circumstances". By telegram of 19 September 1966, it announced its decision "to resume full cooperation with the United Nations and to resume participation in its activities". On 28 September 1966, the General Assembly took note of this decision and the President invited representatives of Indonesia to take seats in the Assembly.

Liechtenstein	18 September 1990
Lithuania	17 September 1991
Luxembourg	24 October 1945
Madagascar	20 September 1960
Malawi	1 December 1964
Malaysia [i]	17 September 1957
Maldives	21 September 1965
Mali	28 September 1960
Malta	1 December 1964
Marshall Islands	17 September 1991
Mauritania	27 October 1961
Mauritius	24 April 1968
Mexico	7 November 1945
Micronesia (Federated States of)	17 September 1991
Moldova (Republic of)	2 March 1992
Monaco	28 May 1993
Mongolia	27 October 1961
Morocco	12 November 1956
Mozambique	16 September 1975
Myanmar	19 April 1948
Namibia	23 April 1990
Nauru	14 September 1999
Nepal	14 December 1955
Netherlands	10 December 1945
New Zealand	24 October 1945
Nicaragua	24 October 1945
Niger	20 September 1960
Nigeria	7 October 1960
Norway	27 November 1945
Oman	7 October 1971
Pakistan	30 September 1947
Palau	15 December 1994
Panama	13 November 1945
Papua New Guinea	10 October 1975
Paraguay	24 October 1945
Peru	31 October 1945
Philippines	24 October 1945
Poland	24 October 1945
Portugal	14 December 1955
Qatar	21 September 1971
Republic of Korea	17 September 1991
Romania	14 December 1955

[i] The Federation of Malaya joined the United Nations on 17 September 1957. On 16 September 1963, its name was changed to Malaysia, following the admission to the new federation of Singapore, Sabah (North Borneo) and Sarawak. Singapore became an independent State on 9 August 1965 and a Member of the United Nations on 21 September 1965.

Russian Federation[j]	24 October 1945
Rwanda	18 September 1962
Saint Kitts and Nevis	23 September 1983
Saint Lucia	18 September 1979
Saint Vincent and the Grenadines	16 September 1980
Samoa	15 December 1976
San Marino	2 March 1992
Sao Tome and Principe	16 September 1975
Saudi Arabia	24 October 1945
Senegal	28 September 1960
Serbia and Montenegro[k]	1 November 2000
Seychelles	21 September 1976
Sierra Leone	27 September 1961
Singapore	21 September 1965
Slovak Republic[l]	19 January 1993
Slovenia[m]	22 May 1992
Solomon Islands	19 September 1978
Somalia	20 September 1960
South Africa	7 November 1945
Spain	14 December 1955

---

[j] The Union of Soviet Socialist Republics was an original Member of the United Nations from 24 October 1945. In a letter dated 24 December 1991, Boris Yeltsin, the President of the Russian Federation, informed the Secretary-General that the membership of the Soviet Union in the Security Council and all other United Nations organs was being continued by the Russian Federation with the support of the 11 member countries of the Commonwealth of Independent States.

[k] The Socialist Federal Republic of Yugoslavia was an original Member of the United Nations, the Charter having been signed on its behalf on 26 June 1945 and ratified 19 October 1945, until its dissolution following the establishment and subsequent admission as new members of Bosnia and Herzegovina, the Republic of Croatia, the Republic of Slovenia, The former Yugoslav Republic of Macedonia, and the Federal Republic of Yugoslavia.
The Federal Republic was admitted as a Member of the United Nations by General Assembly resolution A/RES/55/12 of 1 November 2000.
Following the adoption and the promulgation of the Constitutional Charter of Serbia and Montenegro by the Assembly of the Federal Republic of Yugoslavia on 4 February 2003, the name of the State of the Federal Republic of Yugoslavia was changed to Serbia and Montenegro.

[l] Czechoslovakia was an original Member of the United Nations from 24 October 1945. In a letter dated 10 December 1992, its Permenent representative informed the Secretary-General that the Czech and Slovak Federal Republic would cease to exist on 31 December 1992 and that the Czech Republic and the Slovak Republic, as successor States, would apply for membership in the United Nations. Following the receipt of its application, the Security Council, on 8 January 1993, recommended to the General Assembly that the Slovak Republic be admitted to United Nations Membership. The Slovak Republic was thus admitted on 19 January of that year as a Member State.

[m] The Socialist Federal Republic of Yugoslavia was an original Member of the United Nations, the Charter having been signed on its behalf on 26 June 1945 and ratified 19 October 1945, until its dissolution following the establishment and subsequent admission as new Members of Bosnia and Herzegovina, the Republic of Croatia, The Republic of Slovenia, The former Yugoslav Republic of Macedonia, and the Federal Republic of Yugoslaiva. The Republic of Slovenia was admitted as a Member of the United Nations by General Assembly resolution A/RES/46/236 of 22 May 1992.

Sri Lanka	14 December 1955
Sudan	12 November 1956
Suriname	4 December 1975
Swaziland	24 September 1968
Sweden	19 November 1946
Switzerland	10 September 2002
Syria[n]	24 October 1945
Tajikistan	2 March 1992
Thailand	16 December 1946
The former Yugoslav Republic of Macedonia[o]	8 April 1993
Timor-Leste	27 September 2002
Togo	20 September 1960
Tonga	14 September 1999
Trinidad and Tobago	18 September 1962
Tunisia	12 November 1956
Turkey	24 October 1945
Turkmenistan	2 March 1992
Tuvalu	5 September 2000
Uganda	25 October 1962
Ukraine	24 October 1945
United Arab Emirates	9 December 1971
United Kingdom	24 October 1945
United Republic of Tanzania[p]	14 December 1961
United States	24 October 1945
Uruguay	18 December 1945
Uzbekistan	2 March 1992
Vanuatu	15 September 1981
Venezuela	15 November 1945
Vietnam	20 September 1977
Yemen [q]	30 September 1947

[n] Egypt and Syria were original Members of the United Nations from 24 October 1945, Following a plebiscite on 21 February 1958, the United Arab Republic was established by a union of Egypt and Syria and continued as a single Member, On 13 October 1961, Syria, having resumed its status as an independent State, resumed its separate membership in the United Nations.

[o] The Socialist Federal Republic of Yugoslavia was an original Member of the United Nations, the Charter having been signed on its behalf on 26 June 1945 and ratified 19 October 1945, until its dissolution following the establishment and subsequent admission as new Members of Bosnia and Herzegovina, the Republic of Croatia, The former Yugsolav Republic of Macedonia, and the Federal Republic of Yugoslavia. By resolution A/RES/47/225 of 8 April 1993, the General Assembly decided to admit as a Member of the United Nations the State being provisionally referred to for all purposes within the United Nations as "The former Yugoslav Republic of Macedonia"pending settlement of the difference that had arisen over its name.

[p] Tanganyika was a Member of the United Nations from 14 December 1961 and Zanzibar was a Member from 16 December 1963. Following the ratification on 26 April 1964 of Articles of Union between Tanganyika and Zanzibar, the United Republic of Tanganyika and Zanzibar continued as a single Member, changing its name to the United Republic of Tanzania on 1 November 1964.

Zambia	1 December 1964
Zimbabwe	25 Augustus 1980

[q] Yemen was admitted to membership in the United Nations on 30 September 1947 and Democratic Yemen on 14 December 1967, On 22 May 1990, the two countries merged and have since been represented as one Member with the name "Yemen".

APPENDIX V

JUDICIAL STATISTICS

(A) *Permanent* Court *of International Justice*

Year	New Cases Filed	Advisory Opinions	Judgments	Orders (since 1926)	Cases Dis-continued	Removed from List by Court
1922	4	3				
1923	5	5	2			
1924	5	1	2			
1925	5	3	3		1	
1926	3	1	1	2		
1927	5	1	4	4		
1928	6	2	2	17		
1929			3	8	2	
1930	2	2		7		
1931	8	4		12		
1932	7		3	19		
1933	3	3	2	17	5	
1934	1		2	2		
1935	4	2		6		
1936	3		1	14	1	
1937	2		3	11		
1938	2		1	12	1	
1939	1		3	4		
1940				2		
1941						
1942						
1943						
1944						
1945					2	
Total	66	27	32	137	12	

(B) *The International Court of Justice*

Year	New Cases Filed	Opinions	Judgments	Orders (since 1926)	Cases Discontinued	Removed from List by Court
1946						
1947	2	3				
1948	1	1	1	3		
1949	6	1	2	9		
1950	4	4	2	7	1	
1951	4	1	2	11		
1952	3			10		
1953	3	3		5		
1954	4	1	1	10	1	2
1955	8	1	1	3		
1956	2		9			4
1957	6	2		9		
1958	3	1		19		1
1959	4	3		12	1	1
1960	2	1	2	6	2	
1961	3	1		9	1	
1962	1	1	2	5		
1963	1			4		
1964	1			3		
1965	3					
1966	1			2		
1967	2	4				
1968	4					
1969	1					
1970	1	1		2		
1971	1	1	6			
1972	3	1		7		
1973	3	1	2	13	1	
1974	1	4		2		
1975	1		2			
1976	1	2				
1977	1					
1978	1	1				
1979	1	3				9
1980	1	1	1	2		
1981	2*		1	4	1	1
1982	2	1	1	5		
1983	1*			2		
1984	3	3+		7		
1985	2			4		
1986	3*			2*		

Year	New Cases Filed	Advisory Opinions	Judgments	Orders	Cases Discontinued	Removed from List by Court
1987	1*	1		10	1	1
1988	1	1	1			
1989	4	1	1+	9		
1990	1		1+	6	6	
1991	1		1	8	1	
1992	4#		2	12	2	
1993	3		1	10	1	
1994	3#		2	4		
1995	2		2	9	1	
1996	1	2	2	9	1	
1997			1	2		
1998	5		4	18		
1999	17#	1	1	33		2
2000	1		1	22		
2001	3		3	18	2	
2002	4○#		3	18		
Total	128	24	75	407**	17	10

Note: The figures for the Permanent Court are taken from M. Hudson, *The Permanent Court of International Justice, 1910-1941,* p. 779. (Corrected on the basis of the Sixteenth Report of the Permanent Court (E/16), pp. 92-197.) For the above figures, preliminary objections and requests for interim measures of protection are not included as "new cases". Requests for interpretation of judgments (two by the Permanent Court and one by the Present Court) are so listed. The General List of the Permanent Court contained 79 folios, and that of the present Court 78 folios to December 1988 (in 1948, two folios were opened for the Corfu Channel case).

Remarks:

* includes 1 case brought before a Chamber; ** includes Orders made by both the full Court and by Chambers; + includes a Judgment by the Chamber; ○ includes 2 cases brought before a Chamber, # includes an application inviting the respondent to accept the jurisdiction, on which no action was taken by the Court.

INDEX

INDEX OF THE CASES

SUBJECT INDEX

LEGAL ASPECTS OF INTERNATIONAL ORGANIZATION

1. S. Rosenne: *Procedure in the International Court.* A Commentary on the 1978 Rules of the International Court of Justice. 1983 ISBN 90-247-3045-7
2. T.O. Elias: *The International Court of Justice and Some Contemporary Problems.* Essays on International Law. 1983 ISBN 90-247-2791-X
3. I. Hussain: *Dissenting and Separate Opinions at the World Court.* 1984 ISBN 90-247-2920-3
4. J.B. Elkind: *Non-Appearance before the International Court of Justice.* Functional and Comparative Analysis. 1984 ISBN 90-247-2921-1
5. E. Osieke: *Constitutional Law and Practice in the International Labour Organisation.* 1985 ISBN 90-247-2985-8
6. O. Long: *Law and Its Limitations in the GATT Multilateral Trade System.* 1985 ISBN 90-247-3189-5; Pb: 0-86010-959-3
7. E. McWhinney: *The International Court of Justice and the Western Tradition of International Law.* The Paul Martin Lectures in International Relations and Law. 1987 ISBN 90-247-3524-6
8. R. Sonnenfeld: *Resolutions of the United Nations Security Council.* 1988 ISBN-90-247-3567-X
9. T.D. Gill: *Litigation Strategy at the International Court.* A Case Study of the Nicaragua versus United States Dispute. 1989 ISBN 0-7923-0332-6
10. S. Rosenne: *The World Court.* What It is and how It works. 4th revised ed. Prepared with the assistance of T.D. Gill. 1989 *For the 5th revised ed., see below Volume 16*
11. V. Gowlland-Debbas: *Collective Responses to Illegal Acts in International Law.* United Nations Action in the Question of Southern Rhodesia. 1990 ISBN 0-7923-0811-5
12. Y. Beigbeder: *The Role and Status of International Humanitarian Volunteers and Organizations.* The Right and Duty to Humanitarian Assistance. 1991 ISBN 0-7923-1190-6
13. A.B. Avanessian: *The Iran-United States Claims Tribunal in Action.* 1993 (also published in *International Arbitration Law Library*) ISBN 1-85333-902-4
14. R. Szafarz: *The Compulsory Jurisdiction of the International Court of Justice.* 1993 ISBN 0-7923-1989-3
15. Y.Z. Blum: *Eroding the United Nations Charter.* 1993 ISBN 0-7923-2069-7
16. S. Rosenne: *The World Court.* What It is and how It works. 5th revised ed. 1994 ISBN 0-7923-2861-2
17. P.H.F. Bekker: *The Legal Position of Intergovernmental Organizations.* AFunctional Necessity Analysis of Their Legal Status and Immunities. 1994 ISBN 0-7923-2904-X
18. S.A. Voitovich: *International Economic Organizations in the International Legal Process.* 1994 ISBN 0-7923-2766-7
19. S.A. Alexandrov: *Reservations in Unilateral Declarations Accepting the Compulsory Jurisdiction of the International Court of Justice.* 1995 ISBN 0-7923-3145-1
20. M. Hirsch: *The Responsibility of International Organizations Toward Third Parties.* Some Basic Principles. 1995 ISBN 0-7923-3286-5
21. A.S. Muller: *International Organizations and their Host States.* Aspects of their Legal Relationship. 1995 ISBN 90-411-0080-6
22. T. Kanninen: *Leadership and Reform.* The Secretary-General and the UN Financial Crisis of the late 1980s. 1995 ISBN 90-411-0102-0

LEGAL ASPECTS OF INTERNATIONAL ORGANIZATION

23. C. Tomuschat (Ed.): *The United Nations at Age Fifty.* A Legal Perspective. 1995 ISBN 90-411-0145-4
24. R. Frid: *The Relations Between the EC and International Organizations.* Legal Theory and Practice. 1995 ISBN 90-411-0155-1
25. M.M. Martin Martinez: *National Sovereignty and International Organizations.* 1996 ISBN 90-411-0200-0
26. M. Pomerance: *The United States and the World Court as a =Supreme Court of the Nations=: Dreams, Illusions and Disillusion.* 1996 ISBN 90-411-0204-3
27. E. Denters: *Law and Policy of IMF Conditionality.* 1996 ISBN 90-411-0211-6
28. P. van Dijck and G. Faber (Eds.): *Challenges to the New World Trade Organization.* 1996 ISBN 90-411-0236-1
29. C. Peck and R.S. Lee (Eds.): *Increasing the Effectiveness of the International Court of Justice.* Proceedings of the ICJ/UNITAR Colloquium to Celebrate the 50th Anniversary of the Court. 1997 ISBN 90-411-0306-6
30. B. Conforti: *The Law and Practice of the United Nations.* 1996 ISBN 90-411-0233-7
31. N.L. Wallace-Bruce: *The Settlement of International Disputes.* The Contribution of Australia and New Zealand. 1998 ISBN 90-411-0567-0
32. B. Fassbender: *UNSecurity Council Reform and the Right of Veto.* AConstitutional Perspective. 1998 ISBN 90-411-0592-1
33. R.A. Wessel: *The European Union=s Foreign and Security Policy.* A Legal Institutional Perspective. 1999 ISBN 90-411-1265-0
34. A.D. Efraim: *Sovereign (In)equality in International Organizations.* 2000 ISBN 90-411-1310-X
35. P. van Dijck and G. Faber (eds.) *The External Economic Dimension of the European Union.* 2000 ISBN 90-411-1383-5
36. B. Conforti: *The Law and Practice of the United Nations.* Second Revised Edition. 2000 ISBN 90-411-1414-9
37. N.M. Blokker and H.G. Schermers (eds.): *Proliferation of International Organizations.* Legal Issues. 2001 ISBN 90-411-1535-8
38. K.G.B¨uhler: *State Succession and Membership in International Organizations.* Legal Theories *versus* Political Pragmatism. 2001 ISBN 90-411-1553-6
39. E. Riesenhuber: *The International Monetary Fund under Constraint.* Legitimacy of its Crisis Management. 2001 ISBN 90-411-1577-3
40. Mohammed Sameh M. Amr: *Role of the International Court of Justice as the Principal Judicial Organ of the United Nations.* 2003 ISBN 90-411-2026-2
41. Terry Gill (ed.): *Rosenne's The World Court.* What It Is and How It Works. 6th revised edition. 2003 ISBN 90-04-13633-9

MARTINUS NIJHOFF PUBLISHERS – LEIDEN / BOSTON

www.ingramcontent.com/pod-product-compliance
Lightning Source LLC
Chambersburg PA
CBHW071231230926
51849CB00001B/67